W9-BWZ-323

PSYCHOLOGICAL
ISSUES

VOL. IX, No. 4   MONOGRAPH 36

PSYCHOLOGY VERSUS METAPSYCHOLOGY: PSYCHOANALYTIC ESSAYS IN MEMORY OF GEORGE S. KLEIN

Edited by

MERTON M. GILL and PHILIP S. HOLZMAN

RECEIVED

APR 1 2 1976

MANKATO STATE UNIVERSITY.
MEMORIAL LIBRARY.
MANKATO, MINN.

INTERNATIONAL UNIVERSITIES PRESS, INC.
239 Park Avenue South • New York, N.Y. 10003

BF 173
.P777

Copyright © 1976, International Universities Press, Inc.

All rights reserved. No part of this book may be reproduced by any means, nor translated into a machine language, without the written permission of the publisher.

Library of Congress Cataloging in Publication Data
Main entry under title:

Psychology versus metapsychology.

  (Psychological issues; v. 9, no. 4, monograph 36)
  Includes bibliographies.
  CONTENTS: Holzman, P. S. and Gill, M. M.   George S. Klein—
Klein, G. S.   Freud's two theories of sexuality. — Gill, M. M.   Metapsy-
chology is not psychology. [etc.]
  1. Psychoanalysis — Addresses, essays, lectures.
I. Klein, George Stuart, 1917-1971. II. Gill, Merton Max, 1914-
III. Holzman, Philip S., 1922- IV. Series. [DNLM: 1. Psychology — Essays.
2. Parapsychology — Essays. WL PS572 v. 9 no. 4/BF1031 P975]
BF173.P777   150'.19'5   75-23354
ISBN 0-8236-5586-5

Manufactured in the United States of America

PSYCHOLOGICAL ISSUES

HERBERT J. SCHLESINGER, *Editor*

Editorial Board

MARGARET BRENMAN

ERIK H. ERIKSON

SIBYLLE ESCALONA

CHARLES FISHER

MERTON M. GILL

ROBERT R. HOLT

PHILIP S. HOLZMAN

GARDNER LINDZEY

LESTER LUBORSKY

HARRY RAND

ROY SCHAFER

HERBERT J. SCHLESINGER

ROBERT S. WALLERSTEIN

SUZETTE H. ANNIN, *Editorial Assistant*

384248

CONTENTS

CONTENTS

CONTENTS

PSYCHOLOGY VERSUS METAPSYCHOLOGY: PSYCHOANALYTIC ESSAYS IN MEMORY OF GEORGE S. KLEIN

Photograph by Babette S. Whipple

EDITORS' INTRODUCTION

One central aim has guided our editing of this book of essays: to honor the memory of our friend George Klein. To that end, we have elected to present papers bearing upon his central preoccupation at the time of his death—the disentangling of the two theories of psychoanalysis, the metapsychological, or mechanistic, and the psychological, or one of meaning. At the same time, we have relaxed our goal of offering a unified volume and have sought contributions from George Klein's colleagues and friends that are addressed to other themes that were important to him.

Seven of our eleven papers directly concern the theme so lucidly set forth by Klein in his paper "Two Theories or One?," wherein he strongly endorses a psychoanalytic theory of meaning and argues against one of mechanism.

Our lead paper, "Freud's Two Theories of Sexuality," is by Klein himself. It is a brilliant application of the thesis of "Two Theories or One?" to this central concern of psychoanalysis. For Klein, this thesis is not simply a glittering abstraction, but has immediate, concrete consequences for clinical—we prefer to say "psychological," even though that assumes the thesis and might not at first be generally understood—psychoanalytic theory. This valuable paper has hitherto been available only in a relatively little-known book.

Klein's paper is followed by a group of three—by Gill, Schafer, and Holzman—which are of the same persuasion. Gill argues that Freud's metapsychology is (despite his disavowals) a natural-science theory and thus in a domain separate from that of psychology. But psychoanalysis, Gill believes, can and should be a purely psychological theory.

Schafer adds to his current series of papers in which he

1

shows how his "action language" — a language of meaning free of natural-science presuppositions — can be applied to major psychoanalytic concepts, in this instance, emotion. Schafer's action language is a radical systematic codification of what he believes to be the principles of the clinician's language, purged of any infiltration by natural-science assumptions. Its importance lies in its proposal of a constructive and consistent language of meaning to replace the language of metapsychology. Schafer is preparing a book containing an expanded version of these views.

Holt continues in the same vein as Klein by applying Klein's thesis to the psychoanalytic theory of motivation. He proposes that the metapsychological, mechanistic concept of drive be supplanted by the clinically meaningful cognitive-affective concept of wish. Holt also approvingly examines, amends, and amplifies the model of motivation that Klein described in his paper "Peremptory Ideation." He goes beyond the stated objective of his title and proposes an ambitious comprehensive model (admittedly to supplant the metapsychological) that takes into account not only subjective meanings, but bodily considerations and environmental "press" as well. We would comment that, although a comprehensive model of behavior must surely include somatic and environmental considerations, it is important to remember that psychoanalytic data and expertise lie only in the area of subjective meaning. A psychoanalytic model, in our view, is not a comprehensive model of human behavior.

Holzman's essay on schizophrenia shows one of the pernicious effects of metapsychology, the manner in which its natural-science assumptions — even though these may not be explicitly recognized — blind its adherents to the important natural-science findings on schizophrenia emerging from outside psychoanalysis. This issue has immediate and major implications for the etiology and therapy of the schizophrenias.

Wallerstein's paper on psychoanalysis as a science deals with one of the crucial implications of the meaning versus natural-science controversy: does psychoanalytic clinical theory require a natural-science, mechanistic underpinning to qualify as a science? Wallerstein attempts to clarify this issue, yet leaves unresolved an important ambiguity: whether the proponents of a psychology of meaning are necessarily committed to an atheoretical psychology. Although this may be the intent of some existentialists, we see no reason why a psychology of meaning cannot be an empirical science that is buffered by explanatory theories. The clinical theory of psychoanalysis—however encumbered and obscured by metapsychological natural-science assumptions—is just such a theory and science.

Rubinstein continues his series on the philosophical assumptions of psychoanalysis, tackling the issue of whether a strictly clinical psychoanalytic theory is possible, and concluding that, though it is possible, it is only a truncated version of what a psychoanalytic theory should be. For Rubinstein, the concept of *unconscious* meaning represents an illegitimate use of language (except perhaps in casual conversation), and therefore the existential referent of meaning must be on the natural-science plane of discourse. Although it may seem that, of our contributors, Rubinstein alone would answer "two" to the question "two theories or one?," we believe Holt's paper likewise leans in that direction and that Wallerstein may also be read this way (and possibly be misunderstood). Rubinstein himself has said that he is not opting for two theories, but that the expanded clinical theory he describes in his paper is best seen as "two interlocking levels of one theory."

Loevinger, in "Origins of Conscience," insists that the correct initial approach to data is a phenomenological one, but she is equally insistent that this does not make psychology atheoretical and that its theory is not a natural-science theory but must be one of meaning. Loevinger and Klein share similar approaches to the outlining of the basic principles of clinical psychoanalytic theory, as may be seen in Klein's recent book on these principles.

Loewald's essay seeks to develop a psychoanalytic view of memory that is more truly psychological than the mechanistic one. He writes: "Instincts remain relational phenomena, rather than being considered energies within a closed system, to be 'discharged' somewhere" (p. 303). Loewald insists that memory is an *action* in terms reminiscent of Schafer's idiom. It is noteworthy that problems relating to memory were an important concern of Klein's. His paper "The Several Grades of Memory" touches on the distinction between memory enacted and memory experienced, a distinction that Loewald conceptualizes as the difference between enacted and representational memory.

The final two papers explore the psychology of the artist, a subject that had a special, personal meaning for Klein—his wife Bessie Boris is a painter of renown. Margaret Brenman-Gibson, whose experience has been enriched by her current study of Clifford Odets, has framed an eloquent statement of the need for idiographic research that is grounded in meaning rather than on natural science.

William Gibson offers a personal statement of the travail and elation of a writer. Like the other papers in this volume, with the exception of Klein's, Gibson's is here published for the first time, although it was prepared at Klein's instigation and read at the annual meeting of the American Psychological Association in 1959.

Though the contents of this book inevitably emphasize our professional relationship with George Klein, we hope that we do not thereby obscure the fact that it is the man we here honor and mourn.

1

GEORGE S. KLEIN

PHILIP S. HOLZMAN AND MERTON M. GILL

When George S. Klein died suddenly and entirely un-expectedly on April 11, 1971, at the age of 53, he was in the midst of an ambitious project to re-examine and recast psychoanalytic theory. He was convinced that psychoanalysis is an extraordinarily powerful theory, the only one that probes deeply into motives and meanings, the whys of man's rational and irrational behavior. Having sharply distinguished be-tween the clinical and metapsychological theories of psycho-analysis (1973),[1] Klein was in the process of searching out what was basic and essential in the clinical theory. Those who were privileged to read some preliminary drafts were caught by the cogency and daring sweep of the work. It was his custom to rework his ideas and to meticulously polish their statement so that the whole would express precisely what he had in mind. It was left for others to do the final polishing as best they could and to bring out the work as a published book (Klein, 1975).

Klein's intellectual development prepared him uniquely for this project. His professional career bridged experimental and clinical pursuits, applied and theoretical studies in psychology and biological and social thought. His embrace of diverse disciplines and points of view enriched his dazzling capacity to fashion a synthesis with the ring of new truth.

George Klein was born in Brooklyn on July 15, 1919. After his undergraduate education at the College of the City of New

[1] A complete list of Klein's writings appears at the end of this book.

York, he went to Columbia University where he worked in C. J. Warden's comparative psychology laboratory. Although he co-authored with Warden and Ross a laboratory manual for experimental comparative psychology and did some animal experiments at the Bronx Zoo, it was human perception that excited him most.

Warden's emphasis on affective factors in the maze-learning behavior of rats pointed to critical individual differences in their "approach" to a task. This emphasis must have impressed Klein deeply, for he later pursued and perfected the study of individual consistencies and differences in human cognitive behavior.

His dissertation was an experimental study of motion perception and the relation between the acuity of perception of form and of motion. In this work he profited from an association with Robert S. Woodworth, Gardner Murphy, John Volkmann, and especially Selig Hecht. Characteristically for him, almost simultaneously with his dissertation in 1941 Klein published—with N. Schoenfeld—a more clinically oriented paper on the influence of ego involvement on confidence in task performance.

Shortly after receiving his doctorate, he began four years of service in the United States Army Air Force during World War II. There he supervised statistical studies in the AAF Aviation Psychology Program. He studied the value of self-appraisal of success on psychomotor tasks for predicting success in pilot training school, and he co-authored several official statistical research reports on selection, diagnostic studies, and outcome prediction in psychiatric patients.

After his discharge in 1946, he went to the Menninger Clinic where he immersed himself in diagnostic psychological testing under David Rapaport. Those few years in Topeka, he would often recall, were among the most intellectually stimulating of his life. In part because the universities were not giving adequate training to clinical psychologists, the Menninger Foundation had attracted people of unusual capacities, and it pioneered in developing psychoanalytically oriented clinical training programs for psychologists.

His clinical skills developed rapidly, and he undertook the

psychotherapy of several patients. Encouraged by Rapaport and Karl Menninger, Klein began to infuse his tradition of rigorous experimentation with the perspectives of psychoanalysis. The outcome was an enormously influential line of investigation of the consistencies of individuals in perceptual and cognitive behaviors, which can be characterized in several dimensions he at first called *perceptual attitudes* and, later, *cognitive controls.* His early facilities were primitive. With a few of his students—Herbert Schlesinger, Riley Gardner, and Philip Holzman—Klein constructed his own equipment and worked in a damp basement room. Klein's emphasis on the person doing the perceiving rather than on the act of perception sparked parallel research endeavors in a number of other laboratories, and today the terms *cognitive style, cognitive attitude,* and *cognitive control* are commonplace.

In 1949, Klein took the next step in his psychoanalytic training and began a personal psychoanalysis in Topeka. It was interrupted when, in 1950, he accepted an invitation to become a visiting professor at Harvard. While in Cambridge, he resumed his psychoanalysis and also continued his experimental program. The clinical and experimental aspects of his research moved even closer together. Although the experimental program he had begun in Topeka bridged the relationship between stimulus properties and motivational effects in perceptual and cognitive behavior, he had not yet undertaken a study of obvious extensions into the interaction of the two lines of investigation. In the late 1940's, several investigators believed they had demonstrated how needs and drives influence perception. To Klein, these studies seemed oversimplified and even to present distorted interpretations of psychoanalytic assertions about the vital role of drives and affects in human experience; in particular, it seemed to him that they overstated the degree to which drives and needs influence perception and cognition. His view was that cognitive controls serve to limit not only the environmental but also the intrapersonal influences on cognition and perception. It should be demonstrable, he felt, that the influence of a need on perception and cognition depends not only on the arousal of a need state, but also on the nature of the cognitive organization. In fact, in 1954 he did demonstrate that a group of very thirsty people showed the effects of thirst on certain perceptual tasks in idiosyncratic ways, and that how a need state influenced perception could be predicted better from a knowledge of the person's cognitive organization than from knowledge of the intensity of the need state.

At this point in his development, Klein became interested in the idea of a neurological underpinning for psychological phenomena, a methodological goal he was later to reject. Perhaps his early training with Warden and Hecht in the biological foundations of psychology made him uneasy about a purely psychological theory. While at Harvard, he and David Krech—who was also a visiting professor there—wrote a paper, published in 1952, setting forth their perspective on personality theory. The paper emphasized the organismic point of view that an adequate personality theory must account for behavior and that all theories of behavior must be personality theories. Theories of perception or cognition alone are not sufficient. The paper also endorsed the position that organismic principles of personality functioning can be treated most adequately in terms of neurological or physiological variables. But Klein's very last works on psychoanalytic theory—reflected in the major theme of this volume—are an about-face. He came to emphasize strongly a commitment to psychological explanation in *psychological* terms, arguing that psychoanalytic metapsychology with its implicit neurological assumptions did not explain clinical theory, but lay in fact in a different realm of discourse.

In 1952 Klein joined Robert R. Holt, a colleague and friend from Topeka, in founding the Research Center for Mental Health at New York University. Klein and Holt worked as a team to develop a strong graduate program that became one of the most productive psychoanalytically oriented clinical-experimental laboratories in the country. They studied dreaming, the vicissitudes of consciousness, the nature of fringe motivations, incidental perception, the effects of neuroleptic drugs such as LSD on thought and perception, and sensory isolation. Among their major collaborators were Leo Goldberger, Donald Spence, Harriet Linton, and David Wolitzky.

Klein's views on the psychoanalytic theory of consciousness, expounded in two superb papers, stemmed from the experimental work done at the Research Center, as well as from his own clinical practice, which he began in New York. His essay on consciousness and psychoanalytic theory (1959) classified the ways in which it is possible to become aware of things. He described the interaction of varying cognitive states of consciousness with motives, needs, and wishes. The waking variations in consciousness codetermine the different ways in which stimuli are organized: as percepts, ideas, images. Such awareness must be distinguished from *registration*, whether of external or internal stimuli.

"Peremptory Ideation" (1967)—discussed in Holt's contribution to this volume—was a major contribution from this middle period of Klein's career In this paper he introduced the idea that "drive" was an expendable concept in psychoanalytic theory and attempted to describe motivation or "wish" in cognitive terms. Although his proposed "feedback" model of wishing-leading-to-gratification is capable of being translated into neurological terms, Klein kept pre-eminent the *personal meaning* of the wish-gratification sequence.

Klein began to spend his summer vacations in Stockbridge, Massachusetts. He developed a deep affection for both that historic community, nestled in the lovely Berkshire Hills, and for the Austen Riggs Center which is located there. His ties to Stockbridge owed some of their strength to his lifelong friendship with William Gibson and Margaret Brenman-Gibson, who live there, and to David Rapaport, who, after he left Topeka, lived in Stockbridge until his death in 1960. When Klein began to spend increasing amounts of time in Stockbridge, Robert P. Knight, then the medical director of the Austen Riggs Center, provided him with an office and invited him to case conferences. After Knight's death, Otto Allen Will, Jr., the new medical director, continued to welcome George. Ever since he had left Topeka, Klein had not been able to attend the kind of intensive case discussions that were commonplace at the Menninger Foundation, and he was stimulated by the opportunity to discuss clinical issues again.

Perhaps this renewed tie with a clinical setting was a critical event in Klein's professional development. As we have mentioned, he became increasingly dissatisfied with the mechanistic framework that, in metapsychology, is accorded the status of explanation. The clinical theory seemed submerged in, as he put it, this "theory which 'explains' the theory." He began a major project to define the essentials of a clinical or, better, a *psychological* psychoanalytic theory of behavior, and he produced a set of papers which he had intended as chapters of a book. Some of these were published and others were in various stages of completion at the time of his death. Fortunately, the work was well enough advanced to warrant posthumous publication.

The re-examination of psychoanalytic clinical theory, while a major undertaking, did not claim all of his time. In 1959 he founded *Psychological Issues*. With the publication of the first number, Erik Erikson's *Identity and the Life Cycle*, and containing David Rapaport's introductory essay on psychoanalytic ego psychology, this series became a highly influential source of information not only for psychoanalysts, but for a broad audience of scholars in the behavioral sciences. *Psychological Issues* reflected Klein's concern with presenting experimental and clinical material from a variety of perspectives that would "confront psychological issues." His editorial statement conveys the catholicity of his grasp and of his offering:

> The Editors believe this new kind of publication outlet is needed, for in the last twenty-five years psychoanalytic interest has ranged with profit far beyond psychopathology, unconscious fantasy life, and the therapeutic process.... to develop its theoretical potentialities psychoanalysis must scrutinize data from all fields of psychological and psychiatric inquiry.... Indeed, source materials need not be explicitly psychoanalytic in point of view to make a contribution to the theory. It is only necessary that the data presented and the problems clarified amplify a schematic proposition here, fill a gap there, or suggest a productive revision of theory in another place [pp. iii-iv].

He continued his investigations of dream content, including repetitive dreams and children's dreams, the education of culturally deprived children, drug effects on cognition and perception, the psychoanalytic process, and even performed some neurophysiological studies. He began to work closely

with Merton Gill and Hartvig Dahl on the data of psychoanalytic interviews.

He resumed his psychoanalytic education in New York and
was graduated from the research-candidate program of the
New York Psychoanalytic Institute. It is noteworthy that thus
far almost all of the research candidates at the New York
Institute have been students of Klein's at the Research Center
for Mental Health. He insisted, however, that graduates of
the Institute, regardless of their academic degree, should be
accorded membership in the psychoanalytic society. In a
memorial address, the psychoanalyst and researcher Charles
Fisher, a friend and colleague, said,

> Until recently, the conditions for research membership in the
> New York Psychoanalytic Society restricted the private practice
> of psychoanalysis and denied the right to vote and to hold
> office in the Society. Among his other qualities, George was a
> man of deep convictions, willing to fight for them. He and the
> other graduates protested this situation and, by virtue of an
> articulate and impassioned defense of their position, persuaded
> the New York Psychoanalytic Society to remove these res-
> trictions. Thus, it is finally possible for nonmedical scientists
> to obtain full training with rights and status equivalent to
> those of the medical members. That this change has come about
> in New York is in large measure due to George Klein, and it
> is not the least of the legacies of this remarkable man . . .

George Klein, the scientist, left a rich legacy, too, for the
field of dynamic psychology. Only a year before his death, a
selection of his papers was published in his book *Perception,
Motives, and Personality* (1970). These papers show his bril-
liance as an experimenter, a theorist, and a critic concerned
with an unusually broad range of the spectrum of psychology.

Klein's life embraced an extraordinary diversity of interests.
He was a sports lover who avidly followed boxing, basketball,
and football, and he played tennis with ferocious intensity.
He painted occasionally, and his wife Bessie Boris, an uncommonly talented painter, highly valued his judgment,
understanding, and encouragement. He maintained a strong
interest in the theater, and in his younger years performed at
times in amateur theatricals. (He played a role in William
Gibson's *A Cry of Players* in its original amateur production in

Topeka, Kansas.) He also supported the professional theater with his typical enthusiasm. He was a member of the board of advisors of the American Place Theater in New York City and developed close friendships with many actors and directors.

The daring, the new, the innovative, all captured his attention. He was unusual in his ability to combine experimental ingenuity and clear conceptualization so that he could transform creative ideas into experimentally testable propositions. His unquenchable thirst for new ideas and his love of novelty infected his students, from whom he demanded the same dedication to the work that he insisted upon from himself. But his encouragement and support of younger people endeared him to them.

His incessant effort to integrate clinical intuition and systematic theory may be seen in this account by Margaret Brenman-Gibson:

> As I review the times when he was in a bad mood, sometimes occasioned by my bitter complaints that a first draft of a new paper of his (he always called an initial version "the garbage draft") was too hard to follow, he would lace into me for being wedded to what he called "the soft thinking," endemic among clinicians and historians. By this he meant it was simply not enough to try to see how a circumscribed clinical sequence, a case, or a history of a life seems to "hang together," and he could, with a certain crankiness, push me toward explicitly formulated, systematic theoretical statements.
>
> It was not unusual, however, that on the very next day, he would drop in, take an apple from the fruit bowl, and, with his radiant smile, say to me, "You know, the truth is you are really into the heart of the matter. There can be nothing more significant or more lively than to try to find ways to think in specific detail about the meanings of the human experience and in the successive stages of a particular life span. In *any* life, in *any* society, all the rest, and much of what *I* do," he would often add, "is just gimmicky or Talmudic hair-splitting." So extreme a comment issuing from so finely honed an intellect told me he was in a new phase of (usually) unjustified self-doubt.

George Klein, the man, was charismatic. "George's capacity to exude life was one of the characteristics that instantly grabbed you," wrote Leo Goldberger. "When he entered a room one could feel this life—in silence by his penetrating look, in light conversation by his intense warm laughter, in more formal settings by his restlessness and by his desire to cut through sham and pretense, by his wonderful openness, his intense appreciation of new ideas (and newly met people), and his delight in head-on confrontation with opposing ideas to see where it might lead him." Klein was a great raconteur and conversationalist. He was articulate, and he was incisive. No encounter with him was ever dull.

But Klein was also subject to temporary but black depressive moods. At these times he was not an easy person to be around. These moods would occur at moments—not infrequent—of self-doubt and of merciless self-criticism. He was forever short of money and rarely on time for any appointment. Absent-mindedness, procrastination, and a habit of losing things were as typical for him as for the proverbial professor. His forgetfulness, like his incisive criticism of the work of his friends and students, seemed to be without malice. But although these traits were exasperating, George rarely failed his friends or his family. Robert Holt wrote:

> I could speak of his fierce hatred of social injustice, or his deep love for his daughter Rachel [now a graduate student of history at Yale], but I want to say something to those people who occasionally felt let down by George—those who were kept waiting for appointments, or whose letters went unanswered: he had a true sense of what was important, and in really important matters his commitments could be absolutely trusted. He was a man to whom his friends turned naturally in times of serious personal trouble, one on whom many people leaned, and he never let them down.

We dedicate these essays to George S. Klein, in the spirit of his last efforts to chart new directions in psychoanalysis.

2

FREUD'S TWO THEORIES OF SEXUALITY

GEORGE S. KLEIN

*Many years I have wandered through
the land of man, and have not yet
reached the end of studying the varieties of the "erotic man". . . . There a
lover stamps around and is in love
only with his passion. There one is
wearing his differentiated feelings
like medal-ribbons. There one is en-
joying the adventures of his own fascinating effect. There one is gazing
enraptured at the spectacle of his
own supposed surrender. There one
is collecting excitement. There one is
displaying his "power." There one is
preening himself with borrowed vitality. There one is delighting to exist
simultaneously as himself and as an
idol very unlike himself. There one is
warming himself at the blaze of what
had fallen to his lot. There one is
experimenting. And so on and on—
all the manifold monologists with
their mirrors, in the apartment of the
most intimate dialogue! [Buber,
1929, pp. 29-30].*

An analyst I greatly esteem wrote to me: "Now you want to
eliminate the concept of drives. . . . Did Rapaport try it?" This
reproof made me anxious, naturally so, because I was brought

First published in *Clinical-Cognitive Psychology: Models and Integrations,* ed.
L. Breger. Englewood Cliffs, N. J.: Prentice-Hall, 1969, pp. 136-181. Reprinted
by permission.

14

up in the value system of "classical psychoanalysis," which recognizes the challenge "You are denying drives!" as an indictment, not an invitation to inquiry. A basic violation of catechism is at issue. (And in the offing, perhaps, that gentleman's pyre, intellectual isolation from the psychoanalytic community.) My testy defense was that frequent plea of the guilty, "No, no, you misunderstand!"

Here I recalled Freud's remark that conceptions of instinct are the mythology of psychoanalysis. What did he mean by this? Surely sexuality and aggression are not "mythological." It would seem, on the face of it, that holding a *theory* of sexuality and aggression which distinguishes its propositions from the *phenomena* of sexuality and aggression is an acceptable position.

This reassuring reminder revealed the have-you-stopped-beating-your-wife nature of the analyst's question. For indeed, to say "Yes" (I *do* want to eliminate the concept of drive) would imply that I am denying the importance of sexuality in neurosis and in the shaping of motivation, and surely I am not denying that. To say "No" (I do *not* want to eliminate the concept of drive) implies that I endorse the theoretical model which views sexuality as a *vis-a-tergo* force or stimulus upon the mind, one capable of building up a "demand" for "discharge" and the reduction of tension; and I do have great doubts about that theoretical model.

There is reason to believe that the psychoanalytic conception of sexuality exists in two versions. The first I will call the clinical theory because it is the one that actually guides clinical work. It centers upon the properties peculiar to sexuality, upon the values and meanings associated with sensual experiences in the motivational history of a person from birth to adulthood, upon how nonsexual motives and activities are altered when they acquire a sensual aspect, and vice versa.

The second version, which I will call the drive-discharge theory, translates this psychological conception into the quasi-physiological terms of a model of energic force that "seeks" discharge. This energic conception is connected with Freud's fundamental belief upon which his entire metapsychology was constructed: that the source of all activity in the organism, perhaps even characterizing it as "living" altogether, is its tendency to deal with the energic influxes of "stimuli," to discharge them, to reduce the tensions produced by their energic quantity. This was the all-embracing precept that included the special theory of sexuality. It was designed to serve Freud's conception of his own scientific objectives of "explanation," which have become the conventions of psychoanalytic metapsychological theorizing. Through the concepts of metapsychology, developed from this basic precept, he sought to create interfaces with other disciplines, particularly with physiology, and to relate his conceptions of human psychology to the theory of evolution.

I wish here to make the two versions explicit by contrasting them. When they are so contrasted we can see that they are on different logical planes; that they are not reducible to one another; that they require different data for confirmation; and that they are, in critical ways, inconsistent with each other. It is the clinical theory that was Freud's revolutionary contribution. The data of clinical psychoanalysis are more pertinent to investigation of the clinical theory than of the drive-discharge theory. Despite this, theoretical writings since Freud's time have put greater emphasis on the drive-discharge theory than on the clinical. It is now time to give fresh attention to the clinical theory.

Despite their differences, the two theories have become confounded in psychoanalytic discussion. (It is unlikely that Freud himself thought of the two theories as distinct from each other; there is no evidence that he did.) Indeed, the drive-discharge version of the theory of sexuality has acquired the spurious status of *the* theory of sexuality. Writers on psychoanalysis almost universally assume that the drive conception is a more abstract, more general version of the theory of infantile sexuality, an attempt to place that theory within the framework of a "pure psychology." There exists, then, the curious state of affairs in which the clinical propositions remain largely inarticulated *as theory*, even while guiding actual psychoanalytic treatment. The model that dominates theoretical reflections on clinical work is the drive-cathexis-discharge model. "Squeezed through the eyelet of the drive-discharge model" is perhaps a more appropriate expression, for I hope to show that that model is unable to encompass the propositions of the clinical theory.

So ingrained and unquestioned is the assumed identity of drive theory with the clinical theory of sexuality that, to cite a recent example, Waelder (1966) could entitle a paper "Adaptational View Ignores 'Drive,'" meaning, as we discover in the body of the paper, that the theory he is questioning ignores sexuality. I hold no brief for the adaptational theory Waelder was criticizing; I point only to the assumption of identity expressed by the title. Were sexuality and drive not identical in Waelder's mind, why should it matter that a theory ignores the concept of drive, if it does not ignore sexuality?

The drive-discharge model of sexuality has so long been a part of the climate of psychology that it retains its hold even on those who reject it; for this rejection is automatically considered a denial of the motivational primacy of sexuality. Neo-Freudians have agreed on this equation. Expressing their dissatisfaction with the drive model, they usually conclude by disputing the importance of sexuality in the structuring of personality. On the other hand, the assumption of inter-changeability is so universal that when some theorists have referred to drive *without* giving specificity to sexuality, it has gone unnoticed. For instance, Rapaport (1959) held such a notion of a generalized drive, in which sexuality loses its distinctive position among the "drives" and is relegated to a lesser status than it had for Freud.

Perhaps the failure of traditionalists to distinguish between the two theories comes from a tendency to regard the clinical propositions not as theory but as confirmed fact, and to regard its concepts simply as descriptive tools. Many analysts feel that they downgrade the conception of infantile sexuality when they regard it as a *theory*, to be investigated, tested against rival assertions, and subject to revision. As a result the propositions of the clinical theory have remained oddly static; since Freud's time there have been precious few additions from psychoanalytic sources to our systematic knowledge of sexuality. At the same time, applications of the drive model have been long on words in "explaining" clinical data, but short on actual testing with clinical data. The drive model, being constantly invoked to "explain" clinical observation, distracts from the necessary tasks of exploring, enlarging, and pruning the clinical theory, which is closer to clinical observations.

In order to appreciate Freud's revolutionary views on sexuality, we must separate the clinical propositions from the drive model. To this task I turn first.

THE SENSUAL DIMENSION OF HUMAN SEXUALITY

1. CAPACITY FOR SENSUAL EXPERIENCE

The crux of the clinical propositions is Freud's radically novel view of the essential nature of human sexuality, which enables him to see human relationships in a fresh light. The observations that led Freud to reconceptualize sexuality have been reviewed many times. Since my aim here is to highlight the principles that emerged, I shall make only sketchy reference to these observations: (a) Indications of sexual intent in hysterical symptoms. (E.g., he wrote: "According to a rule which I have found confirmed over and over again by experience, though I had not yet ventured to erect it into a general principle, a symptom signifies the representation— the realization—of a phantasy with a sexual content, that is to say, it signifies a sexual situation" [1905a, pp. 46-47].) (b) Indications that the traumatic nature of nonsexual experience was traceable to sexual encounters in early childhood. (c) Pathological and "perverse" sexuality, where sexuality has no connection with reproduction, as in people in whom sexuality is directed exclusively toward the same sex and as in other people who seek sexual satisfaction and find it without any assistance from the genital organs or their normal functioning, as, for instance, in sexual fetishism. (d) Evidence that children, a much greater number than one would imagine, show an interest at an early age in sexual matters and find pleasure in them. (e) Finally, and perhaps most important, Freud's insight into the universality of the incest taboo, a fact which made him ponder the power of impulses that would create such a universal taboo.

Some of these observations suggested that sexual conflict can occur much earlier in life than anyone had before imagined. They brought into question, too, whether sexuality is essentially dependent upon the matured capacity for reproductive behavior. They all seemed to converge upon the conclusion—strange to the mind even now—that sexuality must originate long before puberty, and *must have a bearing upon how sexuality will manifest itself in puberty.* Freud confronted a paradox that called for solution. There seemed to be common to children and adults a sexual capacity that would justify the idea of developmental continuity in sexuality, yet would be independent of *procreation.* Freud believed it was essential to identify a property of sexuality which manifests itself long before puberty but is not synonymous with an individual's particular sexual behavior. His solution was a conception of *what is common to sexuality in all its adult and infantile behavioral manifestations.* He proposed an invariant of sexual development, across different forms and manifestations of sexuality, that can be postulated to exist in children.

This invariant—the shared factor of infantile and adult sexuality—is a capacity for a *primary, distinctively poignant, enveloping experience of pleasure* that manifests itself from early infancy on (exactly *when* is an empirical issue). It is a *primary* pleasure because it can be evoked from direct stimulation of the dermal surface of the body; it has its own requirements of stimulation, its own thresholds, and its own qualities, compared with other forms of cognitive, knowledge-seeking, and sensory experiences. Sensual experience is *not simply the result of the removal of unpleasure,* or of tension as defined in the drive theory; it is directly tied to conditions of arousal specific to itself. Sensual experience is a positive aspect of a distinctive excitatory process of a body zone; it is different from the pleasurable experiences of satisfaction and reward. That is why it deserves the special designation of sensual.

It is unfortunate that, except for passing references to "sensual sucking," Freud did not refine his terminology to bring into sharper focus this critical feature of his reinterpretation of sexuality—the distinction between the sensual experience itself and the behavioral modes and regions through which it is obtained. He used the term "sexuality" to refer to both the experience of pleasure which even infants can have and the behaviors of genital sexuality which mature only in puberty. The word sexual, burdened by the older limited meaning, tended to obscure the *experiential* aspect he was pointing to. *Sensuality* might be a more natural designation for the particular pleasure component of sexuality. Moreover, reference to *sensual* pleasure distinguishes sexual pleasure from other forms of pleasurable affects, a distinction important in theory. The term "libido" as noun and adjective has been used to convey this distinction, but the absorption of the libido concept into the drive-discharge model causes difficulty in using the term for this purely classificatory purpose, so I prefer to the term *sensual pleasure.*

In Freud's proposal, the sexual pleasure experience differs in specific ways from other forms of pleasurable experience. For example, here is how Freud distinguishes the sensual aspect of sucking from sucking in eating:

> The baby's obstinate persistence in sucking gives evidence at an early age of a need for satisfaction which, though it originates from and is instigated by the taking of nourishment, nevertheless strives to obtain pleasure independently of nourishment and for that reason may and should be termed *sexual* [1940, p. 154].

Sensual sucking involves:

> . . . a complete absorption of the attention and leads either to sleep or even to a motor reaction in the nature of an orgasm. It is not infrequently combined with rubbing some sensitive part of the body such as the breast or the external genitalia. Many children proceed by this path from sucking to masturbation [1905b, p. 180].

Freud's assumption that this experience is in a category of affect unto itself seems contradicted by his later metapsychological theory which identified *all* pleasures as libidinal. This lost for the theory a certain power, for, as we shall see, that distinction between sensuality and sexuality is important for another critical proposition, namely, that sensual pleasure can serve various *functions* that are not in themselves specifically or *primarily* sexual. For instance, the search for sensual pleasure can come to be a means of eliminating unpleasure of nonsexual origin, as when sensual pleasure is used as a means of reducing the pain of an experience of failure.

The recognition of this distinction between sensuality and sexual behavior was a fundamental point separating Freud from his contemporaries, and it still separates the psychoanalytic from other conceptions of sexuality. While sensual pleasure is elicitable from infancy on, its arousal is characterized by a varying and systematic progression of behavioral manifestations; this was the justification for speaking of sexual *development*. Before Freud (and in many theories even today) sexuality was synonymous with genital behavior; it was viewed exclusively in relation to the reproductive function and the phylogenetic requirement of procreation. When Freud proposed a distinction between sensual experience and the behaviors through which it is elicited and expressed (the genital modality being but one), he presented the possibility—for the first time—of nongenital but nonetheless sexual stages of development.

Freud's defining of this distinction was revolutionary; it meant that human sensual experience is not locked in, as in lower species, to the behavior pattern of reproduction. Freud proposed something that may well be characteristic of human sexuality alone—the existence of an extended period of time in which the sensual pleasure experience is separable from reproductive sexuality. The two aspects of sexuality, the sensual pleasure experience and the modes of its evocation, eventually converge on the genital pattern. But this convergence is by no means inevitable in man; it is a *guided* process, one in which societal sanctions, values, and encouragement are vital.

From this premise—that the capacity for and means of sensual pleasure undergo systematic development—Freud evolved a conception of how this development is affected by a person's symbolized record of interpersonal encounters through which he has been sensually aroused. His theory includes assumptions about the role of their sensual significance in how relationships evolve and about how the meanings that have accrued to sensuality are also expressed in the form of symptoms. The recognition of continuity also made it possible to understand certain phenomena, such as fixation on or regression to particular modes of sensual gratification.

2. SENSUAL AROUSAL

We assume that sensual arousal results from appropriate patterned stimulation of the body's erogenous zones. With the proper stimulation, these areas are not only capable of sensation but also of producing feelings of poignant pleasure. A hard swipe on the buttocks produces pain, but it can also produce tinglings of sensual pleasure. In Freud's view, given the proper patterning of stimulation, the capabilities and possibilities of arousing sensual pleasure are multiple. In addition to the stimulation of the especially responsive dermal areas, other stimuli elicit sensual pleasure. Aerial movements, muscular exertions in play, seem capable of eliciting sensual excitement. Fathers have excited their sons by flinging them into the air and catching them, by rocking, by sitting their youngsters astride their knees, with pleasures to both not fully acknowledgeable by either.

The nature of the somatic mobilization required for the stimulation of and the experience of sensual pleasure is hardly better understood than at the time of Freud's first formulations, and is still unclear. Compared with the study of other sensations, this one has been neglected in psychophysical laboratories and still awaits investigation. The faint beginnings of a psychophysics of sensuality is suggested by Pfaffman's (1960) solitary paper on the "pleasures" of sensation. Freud offered many leads toward such a psychophysics, e.g., that different zones have different thresholds of sensual arousal. The significance of such differences for development and motivation is unknown. No one really knows, for example, how the pattern of stimulation necessary for sensual arousal in the oral region compares with requirements for the anal region. Nor have the pleasures of bowel retention and expulsion been subjected to systematic study. It also seems reasonable to assume that there are genetic differences among children in the potential of different zones for arousing sensual experiences.

3. SENSUAL AROUSAL THROUGH NONSPECIFICALLY SENSUAL MODALITIES

Although all body zones have in common the capability of eliciting sensual experience, some of these zones are not specifically sexual in function (Erikson, 1963). Moreover, the stimulation required for erotic arousal in one zone is different from the requirement of another zone. The stimulation required is quite specific to and dependent upon the form of responsiveness—i.e., the modes—of the zone, for example, the sucking and biting capabilities of the mouth. In this view, a zone is a perceptual and behavioral system, and sensual arousal is manifested in the behavioral activity of its modes. Gibson (1967), for example, writes of the mouth:

> For the infant mammal it is an apparatus for sucking, as distinguished from eating. Hence, it is originally a means of feeling the mother's nipple and causing the mother to feel the infant's mouth—a means of mutual stimulation. This is perhaps the earliest kind of social interaction in animals of our sort. In man, the mouth remains an organ of sexual-social contact throughout life, as the act of kissing demonstrates.
>
> The mouth is also an organ for haptic exploration in the infant, often with the cooperation of the hand.... It is much used for autostimulation in the sense of information-getting, and the baby appears to practice mouthing—to be interested in the regularities and possibilities of it. He drools and blows bubbles and sucks his thumb and learns how the mouth feels and what noises can be made with it [p. 135].

In short, the mouth is a versatile apparatus of information seeking and getting. It is a perceptual system.

Now the infantile conjoining of informational potential and sensual pleasure obtained through a perceptual system is important to the psychoanalytic theory of sexuality. The act of "receiving" serves for gaining both sensual pleasure and information about what is received. Presumably, the pattern of modal activity in erotic arousal is different from that of

nonsensual experience, though this is again a largely unex-
plored issue. Recent studies suggest that differently patterned
sucking movements of the mouth serve different aims; for
instance, the sucking patterns of searching and attending may
differ from those of eating (Bruner, 1968). Freud's propositions regarding sensual sucking suggest that there may exist
still another pattern which is specific to sensual experience.

This conjunction of sensual and nonsensual functions,
fulfilled through the same behavioral modes, is profoundly
important for the development of a person's motivation. The
fact that sensuality does not have its own "organs" but can be
elicited only through modalities for learning and adapting
insures the interlocking of sensual experience with nonsensual
aims in development. Not only is sensual pleasure aroused
through behavioral means that serve learning and adapting
and thus acquires meanings tied to these systems; but it also
becomes possible for the pursuit of nonsexual ends to be
complicated by sensual connotations. Thus, affects and frustrations associated with the mouth's pleasure-giving capacity
can have reverberations in its use generally as a system of
control. Erikson (1963) speaks of *social* modalities, e.g.,
general attitudes of trust or mistrust, as being rooted in the
configuration of manipulation and pleasure experiences that
evolves in a person's history of modal experiences. In short, the
negative and positive valuations associated with the control of
sensuality in a mode also become aspects of the structural
record of experiences obtained through a zonal behavioral
system. In Freud's words:

> ... we are led to the suspicion that all the connecting path-
> ways that lead from other functions to sexuality must also be
> traversable in the reverse direction. If, for instance, the common
> possession of the labial zone by the two functions is the reason
> why sexual satisfaction arises during the taking of nourishment,
> then the same factor also enables us to understand why there
> should be disorders of nutrition if the erotogenic functions of
> the common zone are disturbed.... A good portion of the
> symptomatology of the neuroses, which I have traced to dis-
> turbances of the sexual processes, is expressed in disturbances
> of other, nonsexual, somatic functions; and this circumstance,

which has hitherto been unintelligible, becomes less puzzling
if it is only the counterpart of the influences which bring
about the production of sexual excitation.

   . . . we must end with a confession that very little is as yet
known with certainty of these pathways, though they certainly
exist and can probably be traversed in both directions [1905b,
pp. 205-206].

In this assumption of the two-way traversability of connections between sensual arousal processes and nonsexual
informational functions, one may seem to recognize the
familiar version of drive-discharge theory which holds that all
motivations are circumspect forms of sexual "discharge."
Critics of Freud's sexual theories have made this a target of
particularly vigorous attack. But the clinical proposition
makes no assumption about the primacy of "discharge"; it
does not assume that the pathways of connection between
erotic sensibility and nonsexual functions are erotic "discharge
opportunities" for the former. Freud is affirming the ready ties
between sensual experience and the *instrumental* processes
serving nonsexual functions; he is proposing that the means of
pleasurable sensual manipulation are also the means of
manipulating and regulating things, and that values accruing
to the sensual potential of a mode's activity can affect the
mode's functioning generally. In the system of regulation he is
picturing, sensual experience acquires affective-cognitive
meanings from the context of actions and relationships in
which it occurs; and, conversely, the activities of a mode may
acquire erotic meanings. In theory, eating is capable of
stimulating sensual pleasure. The reverse can happen as well;
sensual arousal may evoke auxiliary desires for food. Disturbances in sensual experience may have reverberations in
the normal nonsexual uses of a mode—a factor that loomed
large in Freud's understanding of hysteria. For example,
Freud suggests this possibility: ". . . if we know that concentration of attention may give rise to sexual excitation, it seems
possible to assume that by making use of the same path, but in
a contrary direction, the condition of sexual excitation may
influence the possibility of directing the attention" (1905b, p.
206).

4. THE RECORD OF SENSUAL EXPERIENCE AS A BASIS OF
SENSUAL CRAVING

A critical proposition is that the nature of sensual pleasure is such that *once experienced it continues to be savored; the record of its occurrence is hard to relinquish.* It is proposed that sensual experience is distinctively etched in memory and concept. The occasions of sensual experience in modal activities, and the values, positive and negative, which such experiences acquire, are recorded in a cognitive structure or *schema*[1] whose activation ever after helps to shape sensual experience.

The schema includes memories of the context of past sensual arousals and also an affective record of the success or failure that attended them. The sensual pleasure of the breast is recorded in the context of the mother's responsiveness to the feeding process itself. When a mother gives signs of disapproval of the smearing of feces, her disapproval becomes associated with the sensual pleasure in the smearing. It is this cognitive matrix that carries the symbolic meaning of sexuality for each person.

The evolving cognitive record of sensual experience is thus both a product of past sensual experience and a framework which shapes the content of current sensual experience; experienced through that framework, the current sensual occurrences gather meaning beyond simply the affective sensual tone. Freud assumed that early in infancy the capacity for sensual pleasure already had some degree of internal representation. The child discovers early that sensual pleasure can be autogenically evoked; before long, he reaches down

---

[1] The concept of *schema* used here is that of Bartlett's original definition: "... an active organization of past reactions, or of past experiences which must always be supposed to be operating in any well-adapted, organic response. Whenever there is any order or regularity of behaviour, a particular response is possible only because it is related to other similar responses which have been serially organized, yet which operate not simply as individual members coming one after another, but as a unitary mass" (1932, p. 201). For an account of further developments of the concept see Wolff (1963), who relates it to Piaget's theory of the development of intelligence.

searchingly and finds the genitalia. Presumably, shortly after birth the cognitive schema of sensuality has affective and motor components, but almost no conceptual component. There is simply the zone and its mode. As development occurs, the conceptual scope of sensual experience comes to include representations of the actions and relationships through which the pleasure is won or thwarted, of restraint and controls, and of self-related meanings. Thus, the meaning *taking in* by mouth and lips becomes a conceptual aspect which colors sensual experience that is aroused by stimulation in the oral zones. "Holding back," "retaining," "expulsion," and the like, become conceptual affiliates of sensual experience through the anal zone. These developments occur in complementary response to the normal developmental shifts in the dominant zone of sensual capability. According to Freud's clinical theory, sensual experience has not only a *zone* of dominant focus but a *time* of dominant origin.

The meanings that can envelop sensual pleasure can be illustrated in regard to anal sensuality. The sensations of both a full rectum and of emptying the bowel can be primary sources of sensual pleasure, as Freud said. Associated with these can be the satisfaction of performing a function desired by the parents. But they can also acquire meanings of defying authority, of refusing to do one's job at the pot, and therefore of postponing the pleasure of emptying the bowel. In such fashion, through its embeddedness in a cognitive schema, the poignantly pleasurable sensual experience comes to acquire both high potential as an experience to be revived and sought, and connotations of an experience to be afraid of, ashamed of, held in check, or even quashed in its arousal.

The importance of the cognitive framework in structuring sensual experience is illustrated by a phenomenon to which Freud first drew attention (1898): that a zonal experience which at its occurrence had relatively little conceptual meaning as sexual (i.e., was not understood as such by the child) can retroactively acquire such a meaning at a later time when an enlarged cognitive capacity and increased sensual capability of the zone have raised the zone to prominence. Thus a recorded early genital experience may at puberty become coded with a significance it did not previously have and acquire influence in the current life situation.

The cognitive matrix of sensual arousal has much to do with what is commonly thought of as the "driving" force of sexuality. Actually, it is closer to the clinical meaning to say that the need or wish for sensual experience does not itself "drive" a person, but that he seeks sensual experience because of meanings that have become associated with it in the course of his development. Signs of "urgency," e.g., the excitement of anticipation, and fantasy, commonly regarded as the peremptory drive aspect of sexuality, are, in the clinical theory, manifestations of the cognitive schema in a state of continued or repetitive activation. We will have more to say later about the nature of "intensity" and "force" of sexual motivation.

5. DEVELOPMENT

It is as an evolving cognitive structure, not as a disembodied "blind" energic force, that sensual experience is understood in the clinical theory. Sensual pleasure elicited by sucking at one period may later be elicited by biting as well as by sucking. The anal region, particularly the junction of the skin with the anal-rectal mucous membrane, becomes a prominent locus of sensual arousal. Although zones and modes of sensual arousal are not immutable at any one period, there is a pattern of dominant and recessive zones and modes characteristic of each period, and this pattern varies from one period to another. As time passes, the cognitive aspects of the sensual experiences of one stage are subordinated to those of the next, but are nevertheless carried over to affect the next developments.

Normally, the arousal of sensual experience comes to be dominantly linked to the genital, reproductive aspects of sensuality, but these two aspects, the genital and the sensual, never do become identical. To assure this development, restraints must be internalized (i.e., learned) and connected with the arousal of the sensual experience itself. Thus the cognitive record of sensuality, of its arousal and expression, includes guiding rules and reinforcing affective associations. It is as part of this guidance that early forms of sensual experience come to be couched in terms of shame, disgust, and other affects, positive as well as negative. Early preferences for sensual pleasure are carried forward to affect later preferences. A mother's facilitation or inhibition of sensual pleasures may affect a child's subsequent sensual aims and objects. Preferred modes of early sensual pleasure may remain fixated, and in times of stress regressively emphasized. Freud describes a girl who continued thumb-sucking right into puberty, and who never achieved the sensual satisfaction from kissing that she obtained from sucking.

Conversely, the maturing of sensual potential in a newly dominant zone, the learning and internalizing of societal sanctions associated with the various zones and modes, and a person's own traumatic and other impressive experiences may retroactively organize already recorded experiences. Earlier experiences, recorded for the zone and mode that were at the time recessive, and that had little or no conceptual significance at the time, may acquire sensual significance later, when the erogenous capabilities of the zone, and the child's cognitive abilities, have matured. A memory that had a relatively benign sensual aspect may take on ominous importance through a traumatic sensual encounter that subjectively resembles the earlier occurrence. In short, continuity in sensual development, both mobilization and inhibition, is made up of changes in the zone-mode media of sensual pleasure on the one hand, and a matrix of cognitive and affective values on the other.

6. PLASTICITY

The aspects of erotic sensibility and behavior described so far indicate a general property best described as "plasticity." Sensuality is "plastic" because it can be aroused by various means; at all stages of development its stimulation can be autoerotic, heterosexual, or homoerotic. It is "plastic" in the changes in the course of development in sensual capabilities of different body zones; in the variations, within each stage of development, in what is sensually stimulating and gratifying.

MANKATO STATE UNIVERSITY
MEMORIAL LIBRARY
MANKATO, MINNESOTA

Another aspect of this plasticity is the possibility of disjunction between meanings associated with sensual experience on the one hand, and specific modal behaviors, including genital sexual behavior, on the other—for example, sexual activity unaccompanied by sensual pleasure, as in hysterical frigidity and in certain kinds of promiscuity.

But these qualities of plasticity are a source of danger in which society has a very large stake. Freud's attention to this fact makes his interpretation of sexuality a profoundly biosocial theory. This plasticity raises problems of control; the individual in our society must be guided to the goals of procreation and heterosexuality, and, within this general direction, it is mandatory that choice be guided away from societally destructive commitments. With great insight, Freud pointed to the paradox that the biologically plastic potentialities of sensuality include no built-in protection against societally destructive incest.

For a long time the most accessible, perhaps even the most satisfying, sexual objects a child are those in relation to whom society must impose unequivocally inhibiting sanctions against mature sexual behavior. The very nature of sensual pleasure—a poignantly desirable experience that is hard to relinquish and hard to forget, with a record of its first arousal a potential basis of motivational direction—requires that the means of gratification be efficiently regulated, requires that regulated choice and sanctions be internalized as operational rules, and that they become part of the developmental record, the cognitive schema, of sensuality.

As Laing (1960) has pointed out: "A good deal of effort in all societies is given to deciding which bodies may be joined with which on which occasion and at what age. Persons in all cultures are governed in their action by an intricate web of injunctions about whose bodies of what sex their own bodies should come into contact with." This is a learning experience that begins at an extremely early age, and one of the most difficult, in view of the inherent desirability of sensual experience itself and of the fact that the most natural directive principle of its satisfaction is propinquity. Very young children may respond sensually in situations that, in our moral belief, appear perverse, simply because they have not yet learned to avoid certain stimuli that are taboo, "or may never have learned to respond positively and exclusively to certain approved sexual stimuli."[2] It was this recognition of the social consequences of plasticity that opened the way to Freud's showing how many

> ... impairments of individual and group life ... stem from the meaningless management of sensuality.... he found that neurotics and perverts are not only infantile in their attitudes toward their fellow men, but also regularly impaired in their general sexuality and given to overt or covert gratifications and comforts from other than genital body zones. Moreover, their sexual impairment and their social infantility are all systematically related to their early childhood and particularly to clashes between the impulses of their infantile bodies and the inexorable training methods of their parents [Erikson, 1963, pp. 64, 60].

7. INEVITABILITY OF CONFLICT

The key element in the social regulation of sensuality and in the shaping of erotic behavior consists of the internalized values that configure sensual experiences, governing its arousal, instrumentalities, and objects. One might say that Freud's theory is not simply one of a biological appetite, but is, in the most profound sense, a "superego" theory concerned with the developmental structuring of the meanings, affects, and motives associated with this plastic organismic phenomenon.

The plasticity of sensuality creates a potential for conflict

[2] Ford and Beach (1951, pp. 258-259) make an interesting point in this connection: "Men and women who are totally lacking in any conscious homosexual leanings are as much a product of cultural conditions as are the exclusive homosexuals who find heterosexual relations distasteful and unsatisfying. Both extremes represent movement away from the original, intermediate condition which includes the capacity for both forms of sexual expression. In a restrictive society such as our own a large proportion of the population learns not to respond to or even to recognize homosexual stimuli and may eventually become in fact unable to do so." This may be regarded as an illustration of an inevitable inference from the assumption of plasticity in sensual development, in the psychoanalytic clinical theory.

that distinguishes sexuality from all other psychosomatic
cravings. Inevitable, also, are developmental crises created
between the established patterns of gratification of one stage
and the potentialities of an emerging one; success in accommodating the new hinge on making obsolete the old. The
resolutions of these conflicts and crises become part of the
internalized value structure — the cognitive meanings — of sensual experience and sexual behavior, and are carried forward
to affect sexual development. Compared to animal sexuality,
and compared to all other sensory and affective dispositions in
man, this predisposition to conflict is one of the most distinguishing characteristics of human sexuality.[3]

Since its arousal as well as the instrumentalities of its
satisfaction are subject to control and socialization, all aspects
of sensual experience and behavior are potentially subject to
conflict. Here we see an important difference between
sexuality and such "primary drives" as hunger and thirst, with
which sexuality is often compared. Most sexual rules concern
admonitions and foretastes of consequences, hence the very
arousal of sensual experience can be hedged by conflict. With
hunger and thirst the internalized rules have much more to do
with choice than with arousal. When you become hungry,
there are alternatives with respect to what you should do or
eat. When sensuality is involved, social rules govern not only
choice, but arousal itself. What you must not do, *lest* you
become sexually aroused, is also part of the rules, as well as
how to control and direct sensuality once it is aroused. There
are, of course, taboos connected with eating and drinking, but
the fantasies concerning such taboos are not a problem. On
the other hand, the nature of the taboos against sensuality
necessitate anticipatory control of its arousal, means for its

---

[3] Freud's concept of "moral masochism" is an example of a proposition
concerning one form of conflictual involvement of sensuality: "Again, masochism
creates a temptation to perform 'sinful' actions, which must then be expiated by the
reproaches of the sadistic conscience ... or by chastisement from the great
parental power of Destiny. In order to provoke punishment from his last
representative of the parents, the masochist must do what is inexpedient, must act
against his own interests, must ruin the prospects which open out to him in the real
world and must, perhaps, destroy his own real existence" (1924, pp. 169-170).

suppression and for its redirection—capabilities provided by the very plasticity which necessitates the controls!

By far the most important factor in the conflict potential of sensuality is the previously mentioned point that tabooed pleasures are so often associated with persons who are both the easiest, most convenient means of sensual gratification and sources of other important types of pleasure as well, for example, reward and the relief of distress and tensions. Heterosexual choice within the family would be the easiest and most congruent alternative for most people, because, as Lindzey (1967, p. 1056) expresses it, the organism seems to be "wired for sexual choice along dimensions of proximity and similarity." However, the child encounters a society necessarily programmed for inhibition and destruction of these tendencies. It is precisely against such choices that one of the most powerful taboos, the incest prohibition, is directed.[4] The child encounters this opposition at a time when he is poorly equipped to devise compromising patterns of response. He must learn to isolate and control the sensual pleasure mutually elicitable with mother, father, and siblings, and to internalize tacit canons of acceptable conduct.

Complicating the learning problem is the fact that the mother is a source of both sensual and of permissible nonsensual pleasures (e.g., rewards and satisfactions), and these have early to be distinguished by the child. A mother gratifies in all sorts of ways, but beyond a certain age one must not acknowledge her as a specific source of sensual experience. Other pleasures, as for instance what White (1963) calls "effectance" pleasures, are probably never subject to so severe a rule of severance. These distinctions pose an uncommonly difficult task, one that is often complicated by the mother's own conflicts, and emotional stake, in blurring these distinctions. It will happen, therefore, that the child's feelings about his relationship with his parents and about their

---

[4] The prohibition of inbreeding transcends cultures, and Lindzey gives persuasive arguments for believing that the taboo is the product of strong evolutionary reinforcement, a biological necessity for survival of a hardy human species.

attitudes toward his body and person will become deeply divided.

Preparations for the required, eventual taboo on hetero- sexual relations between parent and child long precede the actual maturing of the child's genital sexuality. This matter deserves more study than it has received, but there is good reason to suppose that a mother's handling of the infant boy is from the beginning different from her handling of a girl, guided by a subtly inbred, culture-supported premonition of the inescapable sensual estrangement that is to come.

Given, then, the plasticity of sensuality, in which a natural tendency toward erotic arousal by and culmination on ta- booed objects is ever present, "the operation of . . . negative sanctions against an almost equally strong countertendency could well constitute a psychological dilemma of enormous consequence" (Lindzey, 1967, p. 1056). Bringing this di- lemma to light for the first time was one of Freud's monu- mental achievements; it is at the center of his clinical theory of sexuality, and it is a point which separates psychoanalysis from other theories of sexuality. From this discovery emerge con- ceptions of the type of conflict that originate in this basic and ineradicable dilemma, and of the various forms of their resolution, and therefore the discovery of a range of motiva- tions unknown to other theories. The conception of the Oedipus complex, of course, and many propositions con- cerning sexual conflict in psychopathology, are linked to these assumptions.

We often hear that the importance Freud gave to sexuality was simply a reaction to the Victorian inhibitions of his time, and that in today's climate of sexual freedom his theory loses importance. But that sex is so freely discussed and its various forms openly tolerated does not minimize the profundity and relevance of the main point of Freud's theory. The dilemmas created by the plasticity of sensuality are as insistent now as in Freud's time. Although the requirement for control is differ- ently resolved by different societies, and the range and nature of tolerance vary from period to period and from society to society, the requirement for control itself remains invariant; it is secured by the universal incest taboo and by the necessity for guiding and insuring the joining of sensuality to appropriate heterosexual expression. The plasticity of sensual arousal in a context of inevitable social guidance will always make the problem of sexuality a primary one in motivational development, and, through the inevitability of Oedipal stresses, an inevitable participant in the drama of generations.

SEXUALITY IN MOTIVATION

Motive refers to the directional aspect of action, the objective for the sake of which movements and choices are made. In this view, to understand the motivational aspects of sexuality is to assess the functions of sensual pleasure, the reasons for seeking or avoiding it. The clinical theory distinguishes the appetitive aspect of sexuality from the aims involved in the seeking of sensual experience and behavior. Sensual pleasure may have multiple functions; sexual gratification per se may be an immediate but not a primary aim of sexual activity; the requirement for gratification may be the instrumental expression of a variety of motives.[5] A person may be drawn toward sensual pleasure and conditions that arouse it because they give comfort, help to blot out reality, make him feel more manly, or even, perhaps, because they have repressed incestuous meanings.

In the drive-discharge theory the issue of aim is strictly limited to the process of discharge: whatever contributes to discharge is construed as the aim of sexuality. Therefore, on the level of the economic point of view, which speaks of

[5] To my knowledge Lichtenstein (1961) was the first to raise pointedly the question of what could be the *adaptive* function of *infantile* sensual pleasure. This question seems to have escaped notice even though it is one that follows directly and uniquely from Freud's theory. For if sensual development *culminates* in a joining of the sensual pleasure capacity with the procreative function, what adaptive function is served by sensual experience in the earliest infantile stage? Lichtenstein offers the hypothesis that sensual pleasure has a critical role in the establishment of self-identity. I can give only passing mention to this intriguing idea since my objective in this section is to deal with the functional plasticity of sensuality generally.

sexuality as the vicissitudes of the libido quantity, the distinction between drive and motive is blurred. But this is not
the case in the clinical theory, which emphasizes the cognitive
matrix — the meaning — of sexuality. The clinical theory, indeed, assumes that the symbol and its appetitive-motor aspects, learned in a psychosocial process, are more important
than the purely instinctual aspect of sexual capacity. It is the
symbolization it acquires at critical periods that is crucial in
shaping sexual responsiveness and crucial even in the arousing
of sexual "need"; and it is this symbolization that accounts for
sensuality being both a source of conflict and a means of
resolving conflict.

Being a pleasure experience that is inherently desirable,
sensuality is likely to be sought. In this sense there is a point in
saying, as Koch (1956) does, that sexual activity is its own
reward, that the pleasure in sexual behavior is also the reason
for it. It would be foolish to raise the question whether the
existence of a house is separate from or identical with its
bricks and the fitting of its windows, so Koch argues in
speaking about the inherent "value properties" of sexuality as
"intrinsically motivating" and requiring no reference to "extrinsic" motivating conditions. It is true that pleasure resembles an end in being a reason for action; however, pleasure
is not an end as it does not itself terminate action since we
cannot identify it separately from the pleasurable activity.

Sexuality is therefore not only *regulative*, but *regulated*. It
is a major point of the clinical theory that sexuality is responsive to different motivations. A remarkable feature of
sensuality is that people will often go through hell for the sake
of it; but this feature cannot be set in its true light by the fact
that people *say* they are merely seeking pleasure. Although
sensual pleasure may be experienced without a sense of ul-
terior motive, the experience can be an instrument of, the
route to, other sought-for experiences, of the sort Buber
describes in the passage quoted at the beginning of this
chapter. Saying that pleasure is one's motive is confused with
being motivated by pleasure in most popular accounts. The
clinician, then, must distinguish between the motive of pleas-

ure and other motives that are to be attained through the pleasure, but are not known to the patient. People may be able to acknowledge doing things for the sake of pleasure, but, simultaneously, through the pleasure, they may reach for aims they often cannot, even must not, acknowledge; for such acknowledgment might impair the quest.

A variety of motives involving sexuality originate as resolutions of conflict. The structural consequences may appear in defensive, substitutive, and exaggerated actions, which point either to the pleasure itself or to the modes in which it is elicited. Depending upon the circumstances, conflicts may be resolved by intensifying certain avenues of sensual pleasure, by deflecting or inhibiting sensual arousal and choice (they may result in fixation in respect to modes and aims of sensual arousal), or by regression to early forms of sensual gratification.

Another class of motives emerges from the serviceability of sensuality to a person for getting rid of unpleasure and for helping to achieve essentially nonsexual aims. In these roles, one does not defend oneself against sexuality, but, when under threat, uses it as defense, as part of one's repertoire of reparative and self-renewing devices. In such cases we might more accurately define the motives as sexualized rather than as specifically sexual, as the immediate sexual action is ancillary to other aims to be achieved through it.

Because sensual pleasure is directly and even autogenously stimulable, resort to it is useful at all ages when a person seeks to rescue himself from unpleasure, pain, denigration, or humiliation. To give one example: there is accumulating evidence that in early life the reaction to separation is a powerful organizing motive centering on the unpleasurable experience induced by the absence of the familiar. In relation to this aim, sensual pleasure is a valuable option of action in two respects. It is a pleasure which counters the unpleasure of experienced isolation and separation; second, it is itself an experience of intimacy. Given the potential for sensual pleasure, one could expect its arousal and intensification to be greater when a person is experiencing isolation and separation. Segal (1963) writes that "sexually impulsive behaviour, precipitated by imagined or real object loss, is a desperate restitutional measure ... Continuing contact with such patients ... [reveals] that they manifest extreme sensitivity to imagined or actual separation or loss of a currently needed person." He describes promiscuous women whose sexual activities include bodily contact, caressing and kissing, but in whom coitus is rare and provokes disgust. This behavior serves, he says, as "a screen for a more basic desire ... the need to be closely fused with the mother in a symbiotic relationship" (p. 407).

Thus, for clinical purposes, assessing the motivational importance of sensual experience is not a matter of measuring appetitive strength; it is a matter of examining the functional significance of the sensual appetite, its cognitive values, positive and negative—how sensuality is internally represented for the person. These value aspects are the crux of its motivational importance.

This psychoanalytic clinical view should not be confused with the reductionist position of the drive-discharge theory that sees the structural consequences of sensual arousal as alternative "discharge channels" of libido energy; neither is it a version of the pansexual generalization which views all motives as "transformations of libido." Put in broad terms: the clinical theory of sexuality does not reduce motivations to a sexual history; rather, it locates sexual and nonsexual processes and their motivations in the one history they both express, which is that of the social existence of a developing self.

RELATION TO PERSONAL IDENTITY

An essential point of the clinical theory, then, is that sensual pleasure is not an autonomous experience sought after simply for its own sake. Sensual mobilization is an organismic event whose motivational importance arises from the requirements of a developing self that seeks always to perpetuate and preserve its unity, integrity, and coherence. Encounters and relationships that have linked sensual activity to self-conception and self-esteem are retained as part of the cognitive record of sensual pleasure and are thereafter very much part of the stimulation of sexual activity. Consequently, the stimulations and gratifications in every sensual experience reverberate to affect self-conception, self-identity, and self-esteem. Conversely, crises in these very respects affect the search for, the choices of, and the circumstances of sensual pleasure. In such instances, anxiety is not necessarily associated with erotic wishes per se, but rather, the erotic wishes are responses to the state of anxiety. The responsiveness of sensuality to experiences of danger and of profound loss (not specifically sexual deprivation) is well known to clinical observation. Sensual pleasure can be comforting; it helps temper the pain of social failure and deprivation. In such a case it can itself become a special kind of need to a developing selfhood, one aroused not necessarily by a specific requirement for sexual release but by an interpersonal deprivation to which an erotic value has become attached.

It is, of course, a biological fact that in pubertal development there is an accentuated association of sensual experience with the genitals. But the meanings of this association are entwined with the nature of one's self-identity at that point of development. The boy's sexual orientation is focused on the phallus, and a feeling of genital inferiority can affect his feeling of pride and growth and locomotion. Erikson describes the modality that is specific to the phallic stage as "making," in the sense of enjoyment of competition, insistence on goals, and pleasures of conquest. The boy attaches his first genital affection on the mother and develops his first sexual rivalry with her possessor, so that the rival with whom he is competing is usually his father. Sensual and aggressive fantasies about the parents may contribute to a disproportionate sense of guilt which affects the meanings that accompany sensual arousal.

Sensuality is, thus, never released from the claims and crises of self-identity, and has different meanings in different contexts of self-conception.

It is this relation to selfhood and to attitudes toward other people as objects that distinguishes sexuality in man from that

of animals. Indeed, the more human sexuality is divorced
from this centeredness in self-development, the more it resembles the mechanical, nonsymbolic character of animal sexuality. As Merleau-Ponty (1945) expressed the matter:

> ... the significance of psychoanalysis is less to make psychology
> biological than to discover a dialectical process in functions
> of thought as "purely bodily," and to reintegrate sexuality
> into the human being.... Insofar as a man's sexual history
> provides a key to his life, it is because in his sexuality is
> projected his manner of being toward the world, that is, toward
> time and other men. There are sexual symptoms at the root of
> all neuroses, but these symptoms, correctly interpreted, must
> symbolize a whole attitude, whether, for example, one of
> conquest or of flight [p. 158].

THE FORCE OF SEXUALITY

The main justification for viewing sexual behavior in the
language of "drive" and for explaining it in terms of drive
discharge has been the compelling hold that sexual craving
can have on thinking and behavior. Man's sexual desires,
active not only periodically, as in animals, can engross a great
part of his activity, frequently at the expense of constructive
activity, with which it can be in conflict. Such cravings
certainly make one feel implacably steered toward objects that
are satisfying sexually, *as if* an alien pressure were developing
from within.

All theories of drive direct themselves to this experienced
peremptoriness of sexual need. The solution of the drive-
discharge model is to postulate an actual impulsion, taking
the phenomenological fact as a model of the mechanism of
sensual craving itself. It is part of the craving that one feels
helpless to the desire; it is natural then to think of it as outside
the self, because what one calls "self" are body-connected
functions and experiences under one's control.[6] The drive

---

[6] The point is vividly illustrated in the following report by Penfield: "When the
neurosurgeon applies an electrode to the motor area of the patient's cerebral
cortex, causing the opposite hand to move, and when he asks the patient why he

model redefined this state of feeling possessed to literal possession by forces independent of the ego and operating outside of consciousness. In the drive model, the force is outside in the sense of coming from the soma without control from "above" (the brain), which is the locus of the self. The drive is regarded as a stimulus upon the central nervous system, creating an affective state ("tension") that "stimulates" a "wish," the consummation of which is the reduction of the tension and pleasure. Drive motivation refers to a condition of dammed-up libido; the force of motivation is a direct function of the quantity of libido to be discharged. In this view all sexual behavior is an expression of this impulsion.

The clinical theory makes less drastic assumptions about the unobservable impulsion. The organized appearance of a sensual appetite lends itself to metaphoric description as the reflection of an implacable force; but it is misleading to take the experience of forcefulness as the process of sexual arousal per se. The clinical theory is not obliged to assume that the appetite is itself the consequence of a peripheral condition (a "drive") independent of itself. Its focus of inquiry is the motivational context. In the clinical theory, sexuality is viewed as appetitive activity within a reticulum of motivational meanings rather than the manifestation of a linear force impelling itself against a barrier. In the clinical theory, the structural nature of sensual craving is not that of a flow of something but of an activated schema—a cognitive structure in action. Fairbairn (1952, p. 150) says, " 'impulse' is not, so to speak, a kick in the pants administered out of the blue to a surprised, and perhaps somewhat pained, ego, but ... a psychical structure doing something to something or somebody." Thus, whereas the drive-discharge model invites Newtonian metaphors of the motion of particles, the clinical theory implies a system lending itself to description in value terms, for example, actions that are permissible or not in relation to self, that have meanings of must, must not, ought not, and the

moved his hand, the response is: 'I didn't do it. You made me do it.'. . . It may be said that the patient thinks of himself as having an existence separate from his body." [*Editors' note.* We have been unable to locate the source of this quotation.]

like; of comfort, of power, of self-aggrandizement, and such. Sensual experience always involves such value meaning to self.

Thus, in the terms of the clinical theory, the language of force is replaced by the language of activity and relationships. From this perspective, need has a special meaning. A need is a state of thwarted tendency. It is misleading to picture such an active but interrupted tendency as an impersonal energic concentration separated from the ego. The need is an ego-world relationship in a state of active but aborted actualization. When the tendency is lived out, so to speak, when it is unimpededly realized, we do not speak of it as a need. Only when such a directional tendency is blocked in its course do we have a need. Gratification of a need amounts to finding ways of circumventing an obstacle. Defining a need in this way, one can say that how varied and complex are a person's needs reflects the complexity of relationships he is able to entertain with the world, and whether the actualization of these relationships encounters obstacles. Since needs are personalized projects or tasks, need satisfaction ends not only in pleasure or discomfort but also in ego-involved success or failure.

When a need involves sensual experience and sexual behavior — especially when the sensual craving is pre-emptive and nagging — the clinician suspects the active presence of a pre-emptive and nagging self-world value, and he suspects that the immediate sexual aim represents some more encompassing need in which self-conception and self-status are at issue. In such instances what hurts and disturbs is not the tension of unreleased sexual energy but the failure to actualize the self-value which has come to be symbolized through sexual accomplishment. As we have seen, the plasticity of sensual capacity makes it uniquely serviceable to various motivational aims; sensual and/or sexual gratifications can become subsidiary objectives within different motivational settings. It is these rather than the specifically sexual requirement that are in the therapist's focus.

In the clinical theory, then, felt intensity is regarded as the symptomatic expression of a motive or motives to which sexual arousal and gratification have been recruited. Desire for sensual gratification—the purely appetitive aspect of sexuality —is not the whole or even the main point of motivated sexuality. According to analytic clinical experience, in even the most flagrant cases of compulsive sexuality, the seemingly quantitative aspect of intensity involves supportive stimulations of sensuality by symbolic meanings. Therapy is conducted on the premise that if such meanings are brought to light, the intensity can often be reduced. The clinician is not misled by the patient's experience of impulsion to ignore its embeddedness in issues of self-identity, controls, and values. Compulsive sexual acting out presents the therapist with the problem of identifying the motivational matrices that govern the appetitive experience. The pertinent questions are: How easily is sensuality aroused in relation to what motivations, and what are the corollaries of sensual experience? In short, the problem is that of determining the functional requirements (meanings) that are making for persistent and repetitive sensual arousal.

When we view erotic activity in its cognitive aspect, we can more easily understand that the pursuit of sensual pleasure can become especially insistent because of its relationship to an insistent issue of self-identity. Take the phenomenon of sexual craving aroused in a state of grief. Here arousal and the efforts to gratify it are by no means the whole or even the crucial story, but rather what Kubie (1952) calls an effort to "close a circuit." The sequence of meanings encompassing sexuality under conditions of grief would be explained not as the workings of a sexual drive which builds up to intolerable intensity, but rather as a cognitive configuration in which grief leads to loss of security, to impotence, and in turn to renewal via sexual gratification. A series of interlocked purposes is involved here. As long as the grief persists, so does the sexuality. Thus, the explanation of persistence would be not in the tension produced by arousal of the sexual drive, but in the cognitive structure of grief. The motive of sexual behavior is described by the clinical statement, not by the drive-discharge model; it would be inane to assert simply that the aim of a drive is to achieve its own satisfaction.

To illustrate in detail the difference in emphasis, let us take an example developed by Erikson (1963) to illustrate this point. Peter has retained his bowel movements for a whole week. Erikson writes: "He looked miserable, and when he thought nobody watched him he leaned his bloated abdomen against a wall for support." He has reveries in which " 'I wish I had a little elephant right here in my house. But then it would grow and grow and burst the house.'" And a bad dream in which monkeys are after him trying "'to get into me'" and bees are trying "'to get at the sugar in my stomach'" (pp. 53, 54). A number of other indicators converged on several themes involving erotic sensibility. "I no longer doubted," continues Erikson, "that this little boy had a fantasy that he was filled with something precious and alive; that if he kept it, it would burst him and that if he released it, it might come out hurt or dead. In other words, he was pregnant" (p. 55). Sexuality is undoubtedly involved in the above example, but not in the sense that drive-reduction theory would have us believe. The terms of this fantasy express what Alexander (1935) aptly called an "emotional syllogism" — a rule or premise, expressing the logic of affective values, which guide behavior and thought.

From the therapeutic standpoint, the conscious and unconscious accessibility of the syllogism must be taken into account. Since the eroticism involved in this example is not simply a specific sexual wish, it is not clinically helpful to refer to the tension experienced in this instance as an anonymous drive energy that is clamoring for discharge. Rather, to alleviate the erotic intensity of the fantasy the meanings of the eroticized fantasy must be unraveled, as in Erikson's interpretation: "There was no doubt, then, that once having bloated his abdomen with retained fecal matter this boy thought he might be pregnant and was afraid to let go lest he hurt himself or 'the baby'" (p. 56). Thus Erikson told the child, "'This,' I said, 'some children do not know. They think that the bowel movements and the babies come out of the same opening in animals and in women' ".(p. 55).

Of course, there was more to the unraveling of the syl-logism. Why the retention? It turned out that an abrupt separation and loss of his nurse was crucially involved. Sensual experience was doubtless part of the tie the boy felt. The relationship had included innocent sensual approaches that were dealt with playfully, perhaps enjoyed, by the nurse. That it was a conflicted tie for the boy, however, is suggested by the fact that the approaches were noticed with clear expressions of unease and even disapproval by the mother. In this context, during a period of budding, provoked, and disapproved masculinity, the nurse's leaving was disturbing. Further, the nurse subsequently wrote to the boy that she had to leave the household because it was her custom to stay only as long as the child was a baby, because "I like best to tend babies." Subsequently, he became babyish and dependent; it is better to be a baby; and in desperation, lest you lose more, you hold on. Part of the configuration of thought evolved in the effort at repairing the loss was that "the boy identifies with *both partners of a lost relationship;* he is the nurse who is now with child and he is the baby whom he likes to tend" (pp. 57, 58).

In this instance, conflicted values associated with a source of sensual contact received expression in the symptoms des-cribed. The erotic components could not easily be described as consisting only of specifically sexual wishes nor the symptoms classified simply as efforts to reduce "libidinal tension." It seems more faithful to the events described to say that sensual experiences were configured in a complex of positive and negative meanings of which the fantasy construction of a baby held on to was a symptomatic by-product.

Diverging Paths of the Two Theories

We often hear that the drive-discharge model is only a general, more parsimonious version of the clinical theory, given in terms that intersect with other fields of data, par-ticularly physiology. It is useful, therefore, to bring the two into closer juxtaposition, to see just how faithfully drive theory mirrors the clinical propositions, to see where the theories are difficult to reconcile or are even at odds with each other. I will not retrace the ground covered by others (Holt, 1965) who have convincingly described the deficiencies of the drive-discharge model as a general paradigm for motivation, but will confine myself to the problems presented by the drive model in dealing with the clinical assumptions regarding sexuality. We will want particularly to see whether the drive theory does, in fact, encompass the range of phenomena to which the clinical concepts are explicitly tailored, and in what respect therapeutic prescriptions are affected by the two ways of looking at sexuality.

Let us first review the essentials of the drive-discharge model.

Drive is conceived as energy generated from within the body. Being energy, it is in movement; being limited in its amount, and varying in respect to the locus and the amount of its accumulation, it exerts different intensities of force, which create a momentum for discharge when a threshold of tolerable intensity is exceeded. Since the discharge is controlled cortically, the energic build-up constitutes a "stimulus on the mind." In this model the essence of sexuality is not an experience but a contentless physiological event, one could say the radiated energy of a source, extrinsic to the psychical event produced by its cortical impact. The psychological aspect of this stimulus, expressing the momentum for discharge, is the *wish*. A motive is drive energy that has acquired such structure. To the degree that motives involve drive energy, they are pressures for discharge.

One aspect of the above account should be made more explicit. There is a difference between the concept of libido and this drive-discharge model. The notion of libido is not by itself a theory of sexual motivation; it was a term Freud early employed to set apart the experiences and behaviors of sexuality from other kinds of activity, and he did this by assigning special properties to the energy involved in sexual activity. "We distinguish this libido in respect of its special origin from the energy which must be supposed to underlie mental processes in general, and we thus also attribute a *qualitative* character to it" (Freud, 1905b, p. 217). In this strictly classificatory meaning the term libido refers to an unspecified physiological substrate of all sensual experiences; the fact that it is seen as an energy could have been simply an early stage of the practice of referring to physiological processes as yet undiscovered.

Freud made these other assumptions about libidinal energy: it is generated within the soma, but its action is like that of an external stimulus because its movement—its stimulus impingement—is outside the realm of voluntary thought and action. As with an external impingement, control must be brought to bear upon it; to dampen it, deflect it, reduce its impact. But being generated from within the organism, such stimulation is particularly difficult to control compared with external stimuli; for example, escape is impossible. The force of its flow requires an especially strong counterforce, which is therefore a drain on the organism's total energic supply. A good deal of structural growth emerges from this effort, and from the attempts to conserve the supply of energy available for adaptive effort. For this reason, Freud said, instinctual (libidinal) drives are the most important bases of psychological growth. (Rapaport made this proposition the foundation of his theory of learning, though it was a general drive, rather than libido, which Rapaport proposed.)

But Freud went a step beyond this, postulating a model in which this energy is converted into sexual motivation. The model of drive discharge is not specific to sexuality, but refers to a more general regulative process concerning what Freud considered to be the basic aim of the nervous system, the discharge of excessive energic accumulation. Since libido is a "*quantitatively* variable force which could serve as a measure of processes and transformations occurring in the field of sexual excitation" (Freud, 1905b, p. 217; italics added), it seemed readily adaptable to the drive model. Although sexual energy is a particular kind of stimulation to be discharged, it shares with other types of energy the properties required by the drive-discharge model; it is in fixed quantity at any given time; it presses for discharge; the vicissitudes of its deployment and discharge lead to motivation. Thus the drive-discharge model purports to explain how libido energy leads to motivation; but it describes the workings not simply of sex, but of any drive, and in this sense it is a graft on the theory of sexuality. In short, the drive model was part of a theoretical strategy of linking psychological activity to the body through the conception of a process of discharge—the return to an optimum quantity in a region where energic pressure had risen.

We must note the distinction, because just below the surface compatibility there is a serious incompatibility between the libido concept and the drive model in their construing of the central event of sexual activity. Libido gives distinction to the specifically sexual aim; it implies that the primary event is a distinctive pleasure. This is not by any means the same as a reduction of tension, the central event in the discharge model. The pursuit of sensual pleasure may, in fact, involve tolerating a high degree of tension. In the drive-discharge notion, sexual motivation is synonymous with one aim alone, that of modulating the energic level that is felt as unpleasurable. There is even an implied difference about what the essential pleasure of sexuality is. If one looks for a phenomenological principle in the drive-discharge model, it might be that pleasure experience is to be construed as the subjective correlate of the discharge of excessive stimulation, and that this pleasure is in direct proportion to the degree of unpleasure that the "excessive stimulation" had provoked. That pleasure is certainly not a directly elicitable, specifically sexual pleasure. The quantitative aspect of the libido contains no problem for the drive model, but the qualitative assumption of the libido concept of a distinctive pleasure is anomalous with the notion of a discharge origin of the pleasure experience. The drive model has no room for the idea that libidinal activation involves, in its very nature, a distinctive pleasurable experience.

Instinct and drive are quite different concepts. Instinct can simply refer to capacity, to potential activity. A drive definitely implies a quantitative force. Thus, within the clinical conception, we may speak of sexuality as an instinct, without implying the drive model.

These distinctions have become less and less evident in the psychoanalytic literature, and have merged into the by now almost automatic tendency to describe the clinical events of sexuality in the metapsychological terms of energy, tension reduction, drive, and discharge.

The conceptions of the biological substrate differ notably in the clinical and drive conceptions of sexuality. In the clinical view this substrate is a propensity for a distinctive kind of pleasure experience, directly elicitable, having different modes, loci, and developmental phases of arousal, which constitute a pleasure system. The events that affect the mobilization of this pleasure experience, or its inhibition, are its central concern—the motivational aims to which the appetitive experience lends itself, and the ways in which the experience and its modal expressions are responsive to these aims. In the drive model the substrate is the need to relieve somatically instigated pressure. Assuming this, the drive model has no easy means, or even need, of regarding the values associated with sensual pleasure as factors which affect its arousal, and color the experience.

The fundamental difference in orientation is: in the drive-discharge model sexuality, conceived as "drive," is something to be disposed of, by consummation or sublimation. In the clinical viewpoint sexuality is a pleasure experience to be elicited or pursued, with variations of aim.

1. INTENSITY INTERPRETED AS EXPERIENCE OR AS ENERGIC PRESSURE

We have already seen how the clinical theory deals with the issue of force. We shall draw upon these points in reviewing how the two theories consider the intensity of sexual motivation. In the drive model's quantitative interpretation, drive strength is viewed as the concentration of energy at a point of potential discharge. Persistent sexual preoccupation is seen as the subjective counterpart of unrelieved pressure of the quantity of drive energy upon a channel of discharge.

One perceives demands in the external environment; but it is misleading to say that the external environment *is* demanding. Murray (1938) used the term "press" to underscore this cognitive reaction to the environment—the environment perceived as pressureful. This is helpful in thinking about sexuality. Sensual wishes can be experienced as implacable, but to infer an "internal environment," external to the self, which is demanding distracts from the psychological meaning of the felt urgency. The clinician accounts for such sensual wishes in terms of the functions served by sensual arousal, in terms of the meaning of such arousal to the self's aspirations and efforts of coping and defense, since sexual experience always has such reverberations. In accordance with the conception of need previously stated, the experience of feeling impelled or driven reflects a directional tendency (motive) enacted abortively but repetitively via the sensual pleasure system.

In conceptualizing sexuality as a peripheral force, the drive-discharge model obscures the clear implication of the clinical view that sensual arousal and mobilization are as much activities of the so-called higher centers as of lower ones. From a physiological standpoint, intense arousal involves central events; arousal is not an intrusion from the gut upon higher centers. Basic to the clinical theory is the premise that the nature of the record laid down by sensual experience has much to do with sensual arousal and inhibition of the appetitive expression of sensuality. Sensual pleasure being an exceptional experience, it is to be expected that it will leave a record that will occupy an equally exceptional role in the controlled arousal and regulation of the sensual system. Why a sexual motivation becomes a not-to-be-denied impulse would then be answered by specifying the components of the cognitive schema actively associated with the sensual system.

The clinical view of motivational intensity reflects a general outlook on psychologically intense experiences of all kinds, for instance, slight versus violent anger, weak versus strong fears, a twinge of jealousy versus its obsessional extremes, etc. In the search for criteria of intensity that cover all these emotions, and also those of sexual cravings, two stand out: (a) The first criterion is the extent and violence of bodily changes — physiological arousals — of general or specific variety. This is the one which theorists implicitly use when they explain motives on the basis of the energetics of drive. (b) The second criterion is the persisting influence of an emotion on thought and action over a comparatively long time. This is the perspective which guides the clinical viewpoint. According to this criterion, the strength of an emotion depends on how much of a man's conscious, volitional behavior can be explained by reference to it.

Note, however, that these criteria are not merely different sides of the same coin, for they may yield contradictory conclusions about intensity. As Kenny (1963) points out, if we measure a man's fear of heights by the number of times he has such a feeling, we may get a result different from the result obtained by measuring the strength of the fear by the pervasiveness of its effect on his thinking and actions. By the first criterion, a repetitive sexual craving that is relegated to the background by requirements of duty and obligation and is preoccupying only when realistically achievable is not less intense than a more intermittent craving which blots out all other motives when it occurs; but by the second criterion it is less intense. The second criterion is essentially a qualitative view of intensity.

Even if precisely measurable, the bodily phenomena of the first criterion are not identical with the phenomena of intensity of the second criterion. To account for the experience of craving the clinical theory looks to the aborted motive tendencies that are sustaining arousal. The physiological vehicles of sexuality are not themselves motives of sexual arousal. The clinical theory recognizes an intervening connection to self in the links between sexual arousal and its object, whereas the quantitative physiological criterion of the drive model lacks this element of intentionality.

2. DISTINCTION BETWEEN SENSUAL EXPERIENCE AND SEXUAL BEHAVIOR

The drive-discharge model, being focused on the presumed end state of discharge alone, not only has little to say about sensual experience but assigns no importance to it. This lack renders it insensitive to many clinical phenomena. Indeed, its only link to the phenomenology of sexuality is through the proposition that discharge is felt as pleasure. But this is in conflict with the clinical theory's assertion that sensual pleasure is not an outcome of some tension-modulating process, but is directly elicitable. It does not deny that tension-modulating events can be pleasurable; but sensual pleasure is unlike other affects, even other pleasurable ones, in being directly invoked by stimulation appropriate to the receptive potentialities of a zone. It is not a derivative of other forms of experience. That relief of any tension — not just sexual — is pleasurable is certainly supported by many findings, but that sensual pleasure and tension relief always coincide, or that the pleasure is the same, is questionable.

Freud himself was troubled by the incapacity of the drive-discharge model to provide for the pleasure aspect of sexuality, and proposed a distinctive kind of energy, libido, to explain it. But accommodating the phenomenology of sensual feeling to the drive model through the conception of libidinal tension was no easy feat, and the strain did not escape Freud's notice. In one place he wonders "how it can come about that an experience of pleasure can give rise to a need for greater pleasure." "If an erotogenic zone in a person who is not sexually excited ... is stimulated by touch, the contact produces a pleasurable feeling; but it is at the same time better calculated than anything to arouse a sexual excitation that demands an increase of pleasure" (Freud, 1905b, p. 210).

These considerations call attention to a useful distinction that the clinical theory makes possible, but that the drive-discharge model obscures: the difference between the pleasure principle and the pursuit of sensual pleasure. The pleasure principle is a basic regulative principle which holds that the organism both avoids unpleasure and seeks pleasure. The clinical theory clearly implies that the pleasure motivations of the pleasure principle are *not* synonymous with the seeking of sensual pleasure. At the same time sexuality, as a systematic organization, is itself responsive to motives arising from the pleasure as well as other regulative principles. It becomes possible to interpret some sexual behaviors as in the service of the pleasure principle, as when a particular unpleasurable state, such as grief, leads to sexual appetitive behavior. At one time Freud took pains to underscore this distinction, referring to the independent sexual instinct as the weak link in the development of the pleasure principle into the reality principle (see 1911). But he obscured this distinction in his later dual instinct theory of libido and aggression; he then tended to speak of the energies in all motivations governed by the pleasure principle as themselves libidinal and aggressive (1924).

The assumption that sensual pleasure is distinct from the pleasure of tension reduction, and from other pleasurable affects, such as those accompanying experiences of rewards and satisfactions, has barely advanced beyond its first formulation by Freud. It is by no means clear how sensual pleasure differs from these other forms of pleasure, or how infantile sensual experience differs from that of adult sexuality, or how people differ in erogenous and other forms of pleasurable excitability. Our ignorance reflects one of the unfortunate effects of the libido drive-reduction theory—to deflect interest away from the experiential properties of sexuality itself.

One other aspect of the quantitative emphasis of the drive model deserves notice. The coupling of sexual hunger with food hunger and thirst under the seemingly parsimonious conception of drive obscures the differences which are vital in accounting for the prominence of sexuality in Freud's theories. A critical difference lies in this paradox. Although sexuality is a valued and poignant source of pleasure, sexual deprivation can, nevertheless, be suffered with a tolerance far exceeding anything ever demonstrated for hunger and thirst. Moreover, unlike hunger and thirst, its arousal and consummation can be accomplished autogenously. Out of these differences in plasticity emerges the most crucial difference: in neither hunger nor thirst do we see the magnitude of associated values of guilt, sin, license — the superego valuations generally — that are characteristic of sexuality. Experiences that elicit such valuations tell the clinician that he is in a realm of phenomena easily caught up in conflict. This potential for conflict, as distinguished from frustration, separates the sexual appetite from appetites serving bodily survival.

The clinical theory is helpful in preparing the analyst for possible disjunctions between sensual experience and sexual behavior. For example, sexual intent and behavior without accompanying pleasure is symptomatic of repressed ideas. Thus, sensual pleasure may be subject to repression because negative connotations of fear and anxiety stimulate its inhibition. Or again, the arousal of sensual pleasure may occasion nausea, expressing a repressed sensual involvement marked by humiliation or guilt or shame. The theory prepares the practitioner for a phenomenon such as promiscuous sexual behavior unaccompanied by sensual pleasure, as if the patient were following a syllogism of action whereby sexual indulgence is permissible provided the pleasure is not experienced. The point the clinical theory emphasizes here is that sensual experience itself is symbolized in a cognitive matrix.

The clinical propositions also provide for the expectation that the symbolic elaboration of sexual experience (for example, that of orgasm) will be different in men and women. The cognitive context of sensual encounter is framed by the presence of a penis in a boy and its absence in a girl, by the presence of a cavity in a girl (that, in Erikson's words, is destined to be filled) and its absence in a boy. The detection of these anatomical differences is a vital aspect of the different developmental tasks of each sex; the successes and failures in which they figure will color the sensual experiences closely bound up with them.

3. Phenomenology of infantile sexuality

Freud's reinterpretation of the psychological meaning of sexuality, the distinction between sensual experience and the modes of its expression, and the proposition of continuity from infancy, all contradicted the traditional view of a sexual instinct linked to procreation as the only inherent aim of the sexual "drive." The main tenet of Freud's revolutionary reinterpretations of sexuality was that the bond between sensual pleasure and genital orgasm specifies a developmental stage, but is not itself the prototype of sexuality. But in construing sexuality as a discharge phenomenon at all ages, Freud came curiously close to reverting to the traditional view, which identified sexuality with the mode of genital orgasm. He was simply pushing the matter back by speaking of earlier stages with different discharge aims.

It is evident, by now, that the drive-discharge conception is inadequate to encompass even the phenomenology of adult sexuality, not to speak of the observations of infantile sexuality.

Seeing genital sexuality in others, as well as such phenomena as sensual play, sensual handling, sensual rhythms and movements, may arouse sexual feelings. These seem more in the nature of excitatory events that evoke distinctive experience than build-ups and discharge of sexual energy. Discharge is easily imagined for the genital mode, but it is exceedingly difficult to make it fit the phenomena the clinical theory regards as prepubertal sexuality. Particularly in young children, sensual pleasure is variable in its forms, in the manner of its arousal, and in the aims for which it is sought, with the genital aim and modes least prominent at these stages. Cases of prepubertal coitus are known, but they are unlike those of full maturity. Again, these phenomena seem more in keeping with a system conception of sexuality through which sensual experience can be evoked, by body movements and contact in particular zones—indeed by appropriate manipulations of any excitatory mode of the "sensory systems," for example, touching or being touched, manipulating or being manipulated, smelling or being smelled, listening and being heard, seeing and being seen.

Although the forms of experience of childhood sexuality are not equivalent to adult sexual feelings, the two are continuous; that was Freud's main point. At all stages of development sensual experience has properties that stamp it as uniquely different from other forms of experience. This assumption of a class of experiences, sensual pleasure, which is invariant over the course of development, although with variations in the shape of sexual desire, made it possible to account for transfers forward and regressions backward in the course of sexual development.

4. CONCEPTION OF CONFLICT

In the drive model, an enforced delay in the flow of drive energy intensifies the pressure for discharge. Since the model represents only those impediments to discharge which create a condition of mounting drive tension, it does not distinguish conflict from frustration. In the clinical theory, however, it is important whether an obstacle to sensual gratification is of the nature of a frustration or is symptomatic of a conflict. A conflict involves simultaneously active but contradictory tendencies which are innervating the sensual system; identifying these tendencies is a critical therapeutic task. Thus in the clinical theory it is not the tension resulting from a conflict that is the focus of effort, but the incompatible meanings which simultaneously prescribe and proscribe sensual experience and behavior. These meanings are of key importance in the clinical theory; they tell us that the valuations attached to sensual experience, including internalized parental convictions which act as a demand structure, become extremely important in arousal itself, in shaping the aims of arousal, the choice of objects and modes of gratification, and inhibitions in all these respects. Since such values owe their origins in part to conflicts, therapy requires a probe of this history. Such considerations of value or superego components of the system of sensual arousal, and its genesis, are very difficult to capture with the purely quantitative terminology of the drive model.

Why sexuality is universally a focus of conflict is thus brought into the foreground by the clinical theory, but is virtually irrelevant to the drive-discharge model. As we saw earlier, the clinical conception tries to explain why the plasticity of the sensual pleasure system makes inevitable a societal structure which is programmed for deflecting and inhibiting tendencies of sensual arousal and choice; therefore it makes equally inevitable the conflictual confrontation which is guaranteed by the interaction of sensuality and society.

5. EQUATION OF SEXUAL ACTIVITY WITH PRIMARY MOTIVATIONAL AIM

The drive model equates discharge with motivational aim. Since erotic manifestations are viewed solely as the release of libidinal energy, the relief of sexual tensions is likely to be taken as the primary motivational objective of all instances of sexual activity.

The clinical theory proposes that much more than release is at stake, and is sought, in sexual activity; that associated value properties of sensual experience color its arousal and expression. It holds that sexual motives are based on learned expectations regarding the consequences of experienced sensuality. To bring about this experience again is a sexual motivation, but its aims, most of the time, extend beyond the relief of tension. Anticipation of sensual pleasure stimulates behavior, but this anticipatory excitement can be a "response" by-product of other aims. The motivational significance of an erotic need is revealed by the role sensuality may play in the aims of coping and mastery at the moment—an interpretive guideline which directs attention not so much to the immediate sexual arousal as to those aims which have recruited sensual experience in their behalf. As a functional system, sexual arousal is possible in situations of boredom, of emotional stress and frustration, as a means of replacing an unpleasurable experience with one more desirable and less damaging to one's sense of identity and self-coherence, where these are being threatened.

Correspondingly, the clinical theory does not have to assume that the motivations provoked by repressed ideas are necessarily primarily sexual in objective. The example of Erikson's young patient whose bowel was distended illustrates this point. There was no sexual appetite, or specific wish, clamoring for discharge. The bowel retention reflected a complex emotional syllogism originating in eroticized relationships which accounted for the specific erotization of the bowel. Effective therapeutic aid required the unraveling of this syllogism, not the satisfaction of a sexual wish or intent.

6. The Issue of Sublimation and Displacement

Both the clinical theory and the drive model provide for circumspect sexual activity through substituted aims and choices which do not have a primarily sexual intent. In the libido drive theory the sexual tendency is a potential of a certain amount of energy; this energy remains active until its release, but this release can be effected through activities of a nature utterly different from obvious sexuality. This is the essence of its notion of displaced sexuality. Sublimation is a special form of displacement which refers to the diversion of sexual energy and its discharge through higher, more socially acceptable activities that, in their adaptive aspect, are non-sexual.

The clinical conception too provides for alternative activities originating in enforced deflections of sexual aim and choice. However, an important distinction implicit in the clinical conception, but not deducible from the drive model, is the difference between substitutes *for* sensual pleasure and alternative means *of* sensual arousal.

From the assumptions of plasticity it is evident that erotic pleasure is potentially achievable in a variety of ways. The mouth, anus, genitals are in large measure interchangeable as sources of excitation, while potentially satisfying objects may range from auto- to homo- to heteroerotic, including even inanimate objects (fetishes). However, the clinical conception also recognizes that there are other sources of pleasure besides sensuality, and therefore that pleasure aims are substitutable. A deflection in aim from sensual pleasure can occur in the form of reinforcement of another pleasure aim. A critical point of difference between this and the drive model is that it is not necessary to assume that it is specifically sexual pleasure that is experienced in substitutive activity that has been generated by the thwarting of a sensual aim. It is thus within the bounds of the clinical conception that erotic sensibility may stimulate interest in subject matters in which a sensual experience is no longer an immediate objective. In the framework of the clinical theory, the nature of the pleasure aim in the substitution is an all-important consideration in analyzing substitutive behavior.

There are, indeed, activities not socially identified as sexual that do actually evoke sensual pleasure, and these may be emphasized alternatively to specifically tagged sexual outlets, for example, picking one's nose, as a masturbatory equivalent. Although not socially labeled as sexual, the sensual pleasure aroused is the main point of engaging in such activities. But it is incorrect to say that they represent what is ordinarily meant by sublimation. Actually, one finds that such permissible, available means of sensual stimulation lead to intensification of the activity, as when nose-picking becomes compulsive to the point of causing bleeding. If the substitutive activity is actually sexually stimulating, the appetite for it may increase, and the problem of control will be worsened, not alleviated. Such activities do not fall into the category of what is usually called sublimation.

But there are other activities which may indeed result from the frustration of sexuality but which in themselves are truly nonsensual, that is, they neither enhance nor relieve the sexual appetite. Thus satisfaction in another area may be great enough in a variety of ways to lessen the need for sensual gratification, not because "sexual energy" is "discharged" in an alternative channel, but simply because the role of sexuality in the motivational economy has been rendered relatively less insistent by another class of pleasurable satisfactions. Work, esthetic gratifications, and the like, may have this function. This does not rule out the possible phenomenon of erotization of work itself; we find indeed that when this occurs it generally interferes with work. I am suggesting only that the mere conjoining of reduced sexual need and heightened nonsexual activities is no evidence whatsoever that the alternative activity is a surrogate sexuality—an avenue of libidinal discharge as drive theory holds.

Here we may recall Freud's proposition regarding the two-way traversibility between the sexual and nonsexual systems, and the proposition that just as the sexual system is capable of serving nonsensual needs, other pleasure systems may be invoked in lieu of sexuality, perhaps even to participate in inhibiting its activity. We earlier discussed instances of the substitution of sexual activity for other, nonsexual aims which are frustrated. Sublimation is the other side of the coin; other pleasure systems may serve in lieu of sexual pleasure. Despite this possibility, however, there are difficulties in achieving such true sublimations; the clinical theory also tells us that the promise of sensual pleasure is not easily deflected by other aims and other forms of pleasure, is certainly not easily stilled, owing to the cognitive record of its unique poignancy, which is unmatched by other forms of pleasure.

The drive model has no room for the distinction just described. Here, the shift from the original sexual object to the secondary social object is not simply the substitution of the one by the other, but is an actual displacement of the same libidinal energy now discharged in a new direction: and this holds for all displacements, including those qualifying as sublimations. The drive model has no place for substitutions, provoked by sensuality, that are not themselves sexual in aim; it holds the substitutive activity to be a specifically sexual discharge.

7. Rapaport's Solution: Drive without Libido

Some students of Freud, Rapaport prominent among them, were caught in the dilemma created by the libido drive theory of how to attribute qualities as well as quantitative attributes to sexual energy. Rapaport resolved the problem by replacing the libido concept with a generalized conception of drive energy which is nonspecific in aim. Between the aspect of the drive theory that tried to account for sexual aim (libido) and the aspect of it that chose to deal with force (the discharge model), Rapaport chose the latter. To him the libido concept was expendable but not the drive-discharge model. Consequently, his solution was on the side of believing that the most important aspect of sexuality—its motivational aspect—would be construed in terms of the mechanics of tension alleviation and of structures resulting from the control of tension level and of discharge.

Rapaport believed the main characteristic of drive to be its peremptoriness, interpreted as tension produced by an energic pressure—a purely quantitative matter—and he felt he could save this factor within the drive-discharge model. Hence in Rapaport's model the critical terms were quantitative, such as cathexis, tension, binding, and discharge; they invoked no assumption of a qualitatively different kind of energy that was specifically sexual.

However, in speaking of mounting drive tension in the abstract, Rapaport actually ignored Freud's account of the motivational properties of erotic experience. In effect, he ignored one of the greatest of Freud's contributions, one which distinguished his theories from all other psychological theories of his time, namely, the unique conflict-inducing potential of sexual experience compared with other motivational sources. It may be that the libido theory is expendable, but surely the clinical propositions regarding sexuality that it tried to embody are not.

The net effect has been that Rapaport's version of drive theory has no clear line to clinical data; it is not intimately tied to clinical observations which in Freud's theory took on new meaning as "sexual." In his model sexual phenomena have no more uniqueness than the motivations of a nonsense-syllable learning experiment, their identifying mark as drive being only peremptoriness, like an urgent bowel movement. Eliminating considerations of the human aspects of sexuality and emphasizing a wholly quantitative concept of motivation, Rapaport's model is no longer specifically psychoanalytic.

8. DIFFERENT ASSUMPTIONS ABOUT THE PHYSIOLOGICAL SUBSTRATE

The clinical and drive theories offer differing perspectives of the physiological substrate of sexuality. In the clinical theory, sexuality is not a drive of relatively fixed quantity, small or large, but an appetite of variable quality, adjustable in different contexts. Its propositions imply a system conception of sexuality — an appetitive structure responsive to arousing and inhibiting activations, including those which emanate from cognitive structures (schemata) in which concepts and memories of sensual experiences have been organized. If at one stage of development the child reacts sensually to a stimulus in one way, and at another age in exactly the opposite way, one must realize that there is an internal structural change which decides each reaction.

A system conception seems a more congenial framework for the clinical assumptions of an evolving and changing structure than a flow model of drive. Such a sensual system would be an open system, subject to differentiation and modification in the forms in which sensual pleasure is experienced. This open system, the theory of sensuality, would encompass the person's experiencing of the world, the formation of his images of the world and his relationships. A system conception of sexuality also embraces the proposition that the modes which are capable of yielding sensual pleasure are also the means of its control and inhibition. The functioning of the system would be organized around rules of operation, subject to developmental change, regarding sensuous mobilization and inhibition — rules which specify, at each stage of development, the do's, cans, and must nots, and express the conflicts which surround sexual experience.

The cognitive activity of such a system also seems to be more congenially conveyed by the notion of a schema to which the sexual system is responsive. As we have seen, sensual pleasure is savored through activation of the record of previous arousals and reinforcement. The peremptoriness of sensual cravings has much to do with the persistent activation of this cognitive structure. It can activate the *adient* tendencies of search, moving toward, embracing, merging, and so on, which promise or afford and maintain sensual pleasure. According to the motivational context to which it is itself responsive, the schema is also capable of inducing *abient* responses of withdrawal in relation to sensual arousal. It is through the schema that memories and accumulated conceptions of sensuality thus become capable of invoking sensuality or inhibiting it.

In its early stages of development such a cognitive schema of the sensual system could scarcely extend beyond the capability of experiencing sensual pleasure (i.e., responsiveness to appropriate conditions of sensual stimulation). As sensual encounters occur, and with the emergence of capacities for anticipating (structures capable of utilizing the record of sensual encounter), there appears the potential for experiencing sensual need. It would be foolish to say that the baby from the start seeks sensual pleasure. The experience of needing, and therefore of seeking, presumes a cognitive record, not simply a contentless build-up of tension.

In the imagery of a system and schema conception, force would refer to the cognitively elaborated experience of sensual pleasure and to the extent of its pre-emption of thought and behavior. Certainly the circumspections of which sexual expression is capable, its deflections and even disavowal, are among its most remarkable features, but we need not refer these to an implacable, not-to-be denied linear force. What we actually observe—the data behind references to a sexual force or delay of drive discharge—is a pleasure that is permitted to occur or not, activities one is drawn toward for their promise of affording this experience or that are avoided for the same reason, and the capability of these tendencies of being stirred to repetitive arousal (peremptoriness) by a variety of motivational aims to which the system as a whole is responsive. If the term force is to be used at all within such a system approach, it would refer to the repetitiveness and pervasiveness of activation of the schema of sexual meanings—memories and concepts—in sensuous mobilization. It would lose its drive-model meaning of an uncoded energic quantity from the soma which moves the organism toward sexual behavior.

Obviously this is hardly an adequate account of the attributes that need to be assumed in a full-scale conception of sexuality. My purpose is to underscore the point that the drive-discharge model is essentially independent of the clinical theory, which is capable, indeed requires, another physiological interpretation. One of the importan holds of the drive model on theorists has been its seeming promise of a point of intersection between psychoanalysis and physiology, in spite of the fact that the physiological plausibility of the discharge model has been repeatedly and convincingly questioned (see, for example, Kaufman, 1960).[7]

It should be noted that in Freud's work there never was any data that directly supported the idea of a drive quantity; there was only data about the cognitive and affective matrix of erotic activity. Freud's earliest formulations of sexuality, which antedated the drive concept, included an ideational structure which he called a "wish." Even later, in his drive theory he implicitly assumed that drive always occurs in a cognitive matrix, in this fashion distinguishing wish from *Trieb* (drive). But Freud never carried his thinking about this cognitive format beyond his formulations in Chapter Seven of *The Interpretation of Dreams* (1900).

This last point is especially important. In 1900 the theory of a developing sexual structure had not yet come into being, and Freud's notion of sexuality was still tied to the conventional one referring only to genital sexuality. The cognitive aspect of sexuality was conceived solely in relation to how genital modes and aims are hemmed in by conflict, with the thwarted genital impulse being revealed in symbolic ways. Therefore, his model of the activity of the sexual wish, indeed

---

[7] Kaufman concludes (p. 324): "... it seems to me that we need no longer postulate that the panorama of sexuality as we know it in man is derived from an inborn biological urge or force pressing inexorably for discharge. Rather, we may view the manifestations of sexuality in terms of an ontogenetic development of inborn sensori-motor patterns, achieving a maturational, hierarchical, unitary structure by progressive synthesis of components through a series of transactional experiences, in the course of which the goals and thereby the drive are acquired."

the very notion of "wish," was couched in the terms of genital functions.

The concept of "wish" more easily encompasses the cognitive aspect of *genital* sexuality than that of the sexual activity of early developmental stages and the correlative phenomena of fixation and regression as proposed in the later theory. Nor can it encompass the variety of motives which include but can also take forms other than genital wishes or even forms other than wishes at all (for instance, erotization of functions).

For the later theory, the issue of immediate and remote aims of sensual gratification was crucial; it brought into the foreground the possibility that sexuality can itself serve other motivational ends. Clinicians were alerted to the possibility that wishes themselves can have extended cognitive meaning, that a craving is the visible indication of converging facilitative arousals upon the sexual system. For instance, Jacobson (1967) describes a man struggling with a crisis of threatening dissolution of self, who experienced surges of sexuality and widespread erotization of behavior. She accounts for this on the principle that sensual pleasure has various functional properties, in this instance that of serving a defensive or restitutional function.

Thus the concept of sexual wish seems a structural unit too narrow to encompass the cognitive involvements of sexuality. Indeed, it was the anachronistic persistence of the early genital wish concept as the sole means of representing cognitively elaborated erotism that contributed to the pansexual extremes to which psychoanalytic interpretations were often carried.

SUMMARY

I have tried to disentangle the psychoanalytic clinical propositions regarding sexuality from the propositions of the drive-discharge model. In the clinical view, the critical identifying mark of sexuality, at all ages, is a distinctive class of pleasure experience that differs from both sensory experience and from other pleasurable affects. The word *sensual* rather than *sexual* underscores the central importance of the experiential aspect of sexuality in the clinical theory, as an experience directly arousable through various forms of contact, principally involving human interaction, but also through self-initiated stimulation, and associated with a variety of adient behaviors. Anatomically, the equipment for its arousal is the same as the equipment for *doing*.

It is this potential for sensual experience that Freud proposed as the critical, invariant component of sexual development from infancy to adulthood. Sensual encounters and the maturing cognitive capacities form an evolving structural record of this class of experience; this record provides a schema of facilitative and inhibitive directives—canons or roles—governing all aspects of sensual sensibility. The subjective pleasure aspect of sexuality, the forms of its direct arousal, and its symbolizations encompass what is distinctive about human sexuality. For Freud they were the starting point for understanding the pervasiveness of sexuality in human motivation.

A crucial point of this radical reinterpretation of sexuality, which made it possible for Freud to conceive of stages of sexual development, was that the capability for sensual pleasure is not exclusively associated with the modes and behavior patterns of reproductive sexuality; this led to the idea that sexuality can be manifested in a wide variety of ways accompanied by sensual pleasure, and to the idea that preferences in these respects can be fixated or regressive. As an appetite of variable quality, adjustable in different contexts, it lends itself to many means of satisfaction and to many means of facilitation or inhibition. Being plastic in respect to the modes and objects of its arousal, sensuality acquires a variety of motivating functions for the person's developing self-identity, particularly for dealing with unpleasure. Through its principle of plasticity, the clinical theory offers a profound, if also complex, view of the necessity for and possibilities of control of sensuality, and of the inevitability of its provoking developmental crises and conflict.

In contrast to the clinical theory which emphasizes the meanings of sexuality, the drive-discharge theory is one of ameaning. The critical difference of emphasis between the two viewpoints may be summarized in the statement that in the drive theory pleasure is derived not from the pursuit of drive but from the getting rid of it. Condensing the issues of sensual experience, modes, and sexual motivation to a process of discharge of tension, the drive-discharge model fails to make contact with the qualitative propositions of the clinical theory, militating against even acknowledging such a subjective state as sensual experience.

The drive-discharge model served Freud as an interface concept, to fill the gap in physiological understanding created by his revolutionary clinical conceptions, which no physiological model of his time could encompass. For many analysts, this still seems to be the great virtue of the drive-discharge model. Indeed, it is usually to physiology rather than to clinical data that analysts look for confirmation of the drive model. But almost all such efforts at confirmation by physiology turn out not to involve actual tests of the model; rarely, if ever, have physiological studies been designed as tests of Freud's conception of drive. Attempts, therefore, to draw sustenance from physiological studies for the drive model amount to a tranquilizing potion, self-administered in the dosage necessary to dull sensibility to the model's clinical inadequacies.

Actually, it is questionable whether the concepts of the drive model allow direct tests against clinical data. No method has ever been devised of constructing the appropriate intermediate terms that would reduce the distance between the drive concepts and clinical observations. As Rubinstein (1968) has aptly pointed out, the drive-discharge theory has been developed on data not appropriate to its concepts; it has drawn upon the same observational domain as the clinical propositions, but by unspecified steps of inference. The data that would be specifically suited to more direct test of the drive model would have to be quite different from those available through clinical observation. It needs data that lend themselves to the specification of an energic unit according to some specific standard of quantity, chemical or physical. Such data could not be those of clinical psychoanalysis; its units are cognitive ones of meaning. In this sense, the drive model is irrelevant to clinical psychoanalysis.

The consequence of the unchallenged pre-eminence of the drive model has been a notable failure to test the implications of the clinical propositions within the context of clinical observation. That is to say, there has been a failure to regard the clinical propositions as theory, as hypotheses to guide deductive investigation, and subject to revision. Psychoanalysis can grow only by pitting its theories against rival assertions, and primarily through the use of its own clinical data. The clinical propositions of sexuality, being readily referable to clinical observation, lend themselves to such confrontation.

The situation is, then, that a theory capable of exploration through clinical data lies more or less fallow, and a theory incapable of such development is constantly used to explain these same data. As yet there has been no extensive or rigorous attempt to explore the clinical propositions. Obviously, much remains to be done, too, about specifying the theory's propositions in forms that can be tested empirically.

Guardians of Freud's heritage generally discount repudiations of the drive concept as merely an effort to repress hard-won insights about sexuality. And so the static condition of the theory is solemnized. In the light of the wide gap that exists between the drive model used for explaining sexuality and the propositions of meaning by which analysts in their consulting rooms in fact make sense of sexual phenomena, we can see that the drive-discharge model imposes a kind of stultifying scientism on the clinician's efforts to articulate his understanding and to enlarge its scope.

References

Alexander, F. (1935), The Logic of Emotions and Its Dynamic Background. *Internat. J. Psycho-Anal.*, 16:399-413.

Bartlett, F. C. (1932), *Remembering: A Study in Experimental and Social Psychology*. Cambridge: Cambridge University Press.

Bruner, J. (1968), Report at Colloquium on Affect and Cognition. Meeting of the American Psychoanalytic Association, New York, May.

Buber, M. (1929), *Dialogue Between Man and Man*, trans. R. G. Smith. London: Routledge & Kegan Paul, 1947, pp. 1-39.

Erikson, E. H. (1963), *Childhood and Society*, 2nd ed. New York: Norton.

Fairbairn, W. R. D. (1952), *Psychoanalytic Studies of the Personality*. New York: Basic Books.

Ford, C. S., & Beach, F. A. (1951), *Patterns of Sexual Behavior*. New York: Harper.

Freud, S. (1898), Sexuality in the Aetiology of the Neuroses. *Standard Edition,* 3:263-285. London: Hogarth Press, 1962.

———(1900), The Interpretation of Dreams. *Standard Edition,* 4 & 5. London: Hogarth Press, 1953.

———(1905a), Fragment of an Analysis of a Case of Hysteria. *Standard Edition,* 7:3-122. London: Hogarth Press, 1953.

———(1905b), Three Essays on the Theory of Sexuality. *Standard Edition,* 7:125-245. London: Hogarth Press, 1953.

———(1911), Formulations on the Two Principles of Mental Functioning. *Standard Edition,* 12:218-226. London: Hogarth Press, 1958.

———(1924), The Economic Problem of Masochism. *Standard Edition,* 19:159-170. London: Hogarth Press, 1961.

———(1940), An Outline of Psycho-Analysis. *Standard Edition,* 23:144-207. London: Hogarth Press, 1964.

Gibson, J. J. (1967), The Mouth as an Organ for Laying Hold on the Environment. In: *Symposium on Oral Sensation and Perception*. Springfield, Ill.: Charles C Thomas, p. 111-136.

Holt, R. R. (1965), A Review of Some of Freud's Biological Assumptions and Their Influence on His Theories. In: *Psychoanalysis and Current Biological Thought,* ed. N. S. Greenfield & W. C. Lewis. Madison: University of Wisconsin Press, pp. 93-124.

Jacobson, E. (1967), *Psychotic Conflict and Reality*. New York: International Universities Press.

Kaufman, I. C. (1960), Some Theoretical Implications from Animal Behavior Studies for the Psychoanalytic Concepts of Instinct, Energy, and Drive. *Internat. J. Psycho-Anal.,* 41:318-326.

Kenny, A. (1963), *Action, Emotion and Will*. London: Routledge & Kegan Paul.

Koch, S. (1956), Behavior as "Intrinsically" Regulated: Work Notes toward a Pretheory of Phenomena Called "Motivational." In: *Nebraska Symposium on Motivation, 1956,* ed. M. R. Jones. Lincoln: University of Nebraska Press, pp. 42-87.

Kubie, L. S. (1952), The Place of Emotions in the Feedback Concept. In: *Cybernetics: Circular, Causal and Feedback Mechanisms in Biological and Social Systems*. Transactions of the Ninth Conference, March 20-21. New York: Josiah Macy, Jr., Foundation.

Laing, R. D. (1960), *The Divided Self: An Existential Study in Sanity and Madness*. Baltimore, Md.: Penguin Books, 1965.

Lichtenstein, H. (1961), Identity and Sexuality. *J. Amer. Psychoanal. Assn.,* 9:179-260.

Lindzey, G. (1967), Some Remarks concerning Incest, the Incest Taboo, and Psychoanalytic Theory. *Amer. Psychol.,* 22:1051-1059.

Merleau-Ponty, M. (1945), *Phenomenology of Perception*. New York: Humanities Press 1962.

Murray, H. A. (1938), *Explorations in Personality*. New York: Oxford.

Pfaffman, C. (1960), The Pleasures of Sensation. *Psychol. Rev.,* 67:253-268.

Rapaport, D. (1959), The Structure of Psychoanalytic Theory: A Systematizing Attempt. *Psychol. Issues,* Monogr. No. 6. New York: International Universities Press, 1960.

Rubinstein, B. B. (1968), On the Inference and Confirmation of Clinical Interpretations. Manuscript.

Segal, M. M. (1963), Impulsive Sexuality: Some Clinical and Theoretical Observations. *Internat. J. Psycho-Anal.,* 44:407-418.

Waelder, R. (1966), Adaptational View Ignores "Drive." *Internat. J. Psychiat.,* 2:569-575.

White, R. W. (1963), Ego and Reality in Psychoanalytic Theory: A Proposal regarding Independent Ego Energies. *Psychol. Issues,* Monogr. No. 11. New York: International Universities Press.

Wolff, P. H. (1963), Developmental and Motivational Concepts in Piaget's Sensorimotor Theory of Development. *J. Amer. Acad. Child. Psychiat.,* 2:225-243.

3

METAPSYCHOLOGY IS NOT PSYCHOLOGY

MERTON M. GILL

This paper has two aims: One is to examine how the term *metapsychology* is used; the other is to propose how it should be used. These aims are important to accomplish because of the growing controversy in the analytic literature over the suggestions that we need to distinguish more sharply between the metapsychological and the clinical theories, that metapsychology is not a higher level of abstraction but rather a different type of discourse from the clinical theory, and that the confusion between the two obstructs the development of both and impedes research. I agree with these suggestions, and I will propose that the term metapsychology should be restricted to propositions about the material substrate, both neurological and biological, of psychic functioning.[1] Not much headway will be made in resolving the controversy until we can reach some agreement on what is meant by the distinction between metapsychological and clinical theory, and how these two are related to one another.

A DEFINITION OF METAPSYCHOLOGY

Many psychoanalysts seem to believe that metapsychology

[1] One could consider generalizing the definition of metapsychology to include any proposition that combines a psychoanalytic proposition and one from another discipline, whether neurology, biology, sociology, or whatever, as Kernberg (Miller, 1975) has done. In this essay, however, I use the term only for neuropsychological and biopsychological propositions.

simply means psychoanalytic theory and that therefore anyone who criticizes the general enterprise of metapsychology is rejecting psychoanalytic theory in toto. I will try to show that, by metapsychology, Freud meant a set of biological and neurological assumptions, which he applied to psychoanalytic theory – despite his frequent insistence that he remained on psychological ground. This is obviously an issue for which historical review is vital.

Freud's own published definition of metapsychology (1915b) at first blush seems to be a purely psychological one, but my position is that the metapsychological points of view are posited in a natural-science framework, which is a reductionistic attempt to convert psychological discourse to a universe alien to it — the universe of space, force, and energy. Freud wrote:

> By accepting the existence of these two (or three) psychical systems, psycho-analysis has departed a step further from the descriptive 'psychology of consciousness' and has raised new problems and acquired a new content. Up till now, it has differed from that psychology mainly by reason of its *dynamic* view of mental processes; now in addition it seems to take account of psychical *topography* as well, and to indicate in respect of any given mental act within what system or between what systems it takes place.[2] On account of this attempt, too, it has been given the name of 'depth-psychology.' We shall hear that it can be further enriched by taking yet another point of view into account [p. 173].

And later in the same paper:

> We see how we have gradually been led into adopting a third point of view in our account of psychical phenomena. Besides the dynamic and the topographical points of view, we have

[2] As I argued in an earlier work (1963), Freud's definition of topography by the general term systems rather than by the specific systems he was concerned with at the time, namely, *Ucs., Pcs.,* and *Cs.,* shows that he did not mean the term topography to be restricted to these so-called topographic systems. Instead he considered it to be a general term that also subsumes the later structural systems id, ego, and superego. To avoid confusion, the third metapsychological point of view, after dynamic and economic, should be called "systemic," rather than either topographic or structural, leaving *these two latter terms to specify the respective sets of systems.*

adopted the *economic* one. This endeavours to follow out the vicissitudes of amounts of excitation [note the neurological implications of the term] and to arrive at least at some *relative* estimate of their magnitude.

It will not be unreasonable to give a special name to this whole way of regarding our subject-matter, for it is the consummation of psycho-analytic research. I propose that when we have succeeded in describing a psychical process in its dynamic, topographical and economic aspects, we should speak of it as a *metapsychological* presentation. We must say at once that in the present state of our knowledge there are only a few points at which we shall succeed in this [p. 181].

One might think that by this definition Freud means no more than "depth" psychological theory, theory which goes beyond the psychology of consciousness. But the term has a long history in Freud, and a review of that history will show how variously he used it and thus expose the roots of its present tangled and conflicting meanings.

The letters to Fliess (Freud, 1887-1902) are invaluable in deciphering what Freud meant by metapsychology. It comes as something of a surprise to discover that Freud described the "Project" as psychology,[3] since it is generally agreed that the Project contains the first comprehensive statement of the major principles of what we now call metapsychology. Indeed, in a letter to Fliess on February 13, 1896, Freud wrote: "I am continually occupied with psychology—it is really metapsychology" (p. 157). By psychology, Freud here clearly means the Project, which he had sent to Fliess in October, 1895, and with which he was still struggling. And in an earlier letter (November 29, 1895), Freud wrote, referring to the Project, "I no longer understand the state of mind in which I concocted the psychology ..." (p. 134).

Chapter VII of *The Interpretation of Dreams* (1900), which is generally considered the first published comprehensive

[3] Kanzer (1973), having made the same observation, uses it as one of his bases for concluding that the Project is clearly psychological rather than "ostensibly neurological." I agree that much in the Project is clearly psychological, either directly so or in a neurological metaphor, but there is much else of importance in the Project—that which is specifically metapsychological, as here defined.

statement of what we now call metapsychology, is called "The Psychology of Dream Processes."

This equation of the term psychology with what we now call metapsychology would seem to justify the opinion of many that metapsychology is the highest level in the hierarchy of psychological theory. But a letter crucial for my differing conclusion is that of March 10, 1898. It includes two contrasting uses of the term metapsychology in two successive sentences. Freud was writing about his book on dreams: "It seems to me as if the wish-fulfillment theory gives only the psychological and not the biological, or rather metapsychological explanation. (Incidentally I am going to ask you seriously whether I should use the term 'metapsychology' for my psychology which leads behind consciousness)" (1887-1902, p. 246).

The first sentence connects biological with metapsychological and contrasts them with psychological. The second sentence gives a very different definition of metapsychology, since it defines it not as related to biology, but only as a psychology going beyond consciousness. Any "depth" psychological proposition, even a purely psychological one, would by this definition be called metapsychological.[4] But, as I have already indicated, despite the fact that Freud's definition of metapsychology seems at first glance to be simply a psychology beyond consciousness, it is in fact a "biological [and neurological] explanation."

---

[4] There is a third use of the term metapsychological, which I here relegate to a footnote to avoid confusion. And it is, according to Strachey, the only published use of the term metapsychology before its appearance in the paper "The Unconscious." In *The Psychopathology of Everyday Life*, Freud (1901) wrote: "...I believe that a large part of the mythological view of the world, which extends a long way into the most modern religions, *is nothing but psychology projected into the external world.* The obscure recognition (the endopsychic perception, as it were) of psychical factors and the relations in the unconscious is mirrored—it is difficult to express it in other terms, and here the analogy with paranoia must come to our aid—in the construction of a *supernatural reality,* which is destined to be changed back once more by science into the *psychology of the unconscious.* One could venture to explain in this way the myths of paradise and the fall of man, of God, of good and evil, of immortality, and so on, and to transform *metaphysics* into *metapsychology*" (pp. 258-259). According to this definition, metapsychology is the "psychology of the unconscious."

Though the term metapsychology is often used in current psychoanalytic writings as a simple equivalent to psychoanalytic theorizing, I believe it can be shown that every time Freud uses it, he does so in direct connection with neurological and biological assumptions.

Freud's Disavowal of the Material Substrate of Metapsychology

The principal reason that this connection is not recognized is that after the Project, in which these biological and neurological referents were explicit, Freud not only utilized these referents less often, but indeed explicitly denied their presence.[5] Let me cite two examples of his explicit denial.

In *The Interpretation of Dreams,* written not long after the Project, Freud (1900) wrote: "I shall entirely disregard the fact that the mental apparatus with which we are here concerned is also known to us in the form of an anatomical preparation, and I shall carefully avoid the temptation to determine psychical locality in any anatomical fashion. I shall remain on psychological ground ..." (p. 536). But the quotation most often cited to demonstrate Freud's disavowal is this statement from "The Unconscious" (1915b): "... every attempt to ... discover a localization of mental processes, every endeavour to think of ideas as stored up in nerve-cells and of excitations as travelling along nerve-fibres, has miscarried completely" (p. 174).

In his introduction to "The Unconscious," Strachey expresses the generally held view that "A few years later [after the Project], in *The Interpretation of Dreams,* a strange transformation had occurred: not only had the neurological account of psychology completely disappeared, but much of what Freud had written in the 'Project' in terms of the nervous

---

[5] Only in the sense that Kanzer (1973) fails to emphasize that the neural and biological referents of the Project became largely implicit in Freud's later theorizing do I disagree with his excellently documented argument that it is a misconception to believe that Freud abandoned the ideas stated in the Project.

system now turned out to be valid and far more intelligible when translated into mental terms" (p. 164).

The neurological account did *not* completely disappear. Some of it remained, and much of it became implicit. It is not that what was neurological in the Project later became translated into mental terms. It is rather that much of the material in the Project is stated both in mental terms and in a neurological metaphor that parallels these mental terms. What happened later is that, insofar as this aspect of the Project is concerned, much of the explicit neurological metaphor dropped away, though the neurological assumptions remained implicit.

In this sense I agree with Kanzer (1973), who argues that there was no such transformation of neurology into psychology - though this observation does not apply to all of the Project, since some of it was a psychological account in the first place. The Project also includes neurological and biological assumptions that are not simply metaphorical translations of psychological concepts. In a forthcoming book about the Project, Pribram and I (1976) argue that the Project includes many bio- and neuropsychological theses which remained part of the corpus of metapsychology, though their biological and neurological aspects became largely, though not entirely, implicit.

Holt reached the same conclusion in two persuasive and well-documented studies that appeared in 1965 and 1967. In the latter article he wrote: "Freud ... did not in fact abandon a single one of the major errors of assumption that his medical and neurological training had built into his thinking, despite his effort to give up reference to the brain. Indeed, this change had the paradoxical effect of preserving these assumptions by hiding their original nature, and by transferring the operation of the apparatus into a conceptual realm where they were insulated from correction by progress in neurophysiology and brain anatomy" (1967, p. 18).

Holt's emphasis differs from mine in that his principal point of departure is what he considers to be the erroneous nature of some of Freud's assumptions about biology and neurology and their effect on Freudian theory. I am not entirely in agreement with him in his assessment of some of these assumptions or in his analysis of their repurcussions on psychoanalytic clinical theory. But, in any case, my point is rather to emphasize that the assumptions are especially related to metapsychology rather than to clinical theory, although clinical theory may also unwittingly and unnecessarily include some of these assumptions.

I have already said that what took place for a considerable part of the Project was not a translation, but a dropping away of the neurological metaphor from the psychological concepts already clearly stated in the Project. What is more, the biological and neurological assumptions of the Project not only remain in Freud's later writings, but even remain largely explicit. How can Strachey write in one sentence that the many references in his edition of the Project to later volumes of the *Standard Edition* are "an expression of the remarkable truth that the *Project,* in spite of being ostensibly a neurological document, contains within itself the nucleus of a great part of Freud's later psychological theories," and in the next sentence: "In this respect its discovery was not only of historical interest; it actually threw light for the first time on some of the more obscure of Freud's fundamental hypotheses" (Editor's Introduction to Freud, 1895, p. 290)? If the Project is only the nucleus of Freud's *later* psychological theories, why do we need to "throw light ... on some of the more obscure of Freud's fundamental hypotheses"? Because these fundamental hypotheses are not psychological, but biological and neurological.

A major obstacle in the way of demonstrating that my view is correct — namely, that, whatever Freud's avowed intentions, the metapsychological statements are based on neurological and biological assumptions — is his inconsistency: in his general remarks directed to the question, he insists that he "remains on psychological ground," whereas other times he makes formulations on specific issues to the contrary, often in the context of the term "metapsychology." The "miscarried" quote cited above, for example, is an explicit disavowal directed to the general issue.

But let us look at what comes directly before and after the "miscarried" quote. The statement is preceded by the question whether, when a psychical act is transferred from the system *Ucs.* into the system *Cs.* (or *Pcs.*) there is a second registration in a new locality or whether the idea remains in the original locality with a change in state (1915b). Freud goes on:

> This question may appear abstruse, but it must be raised if we wish to form a more definite conception of psychical topography, of the dimension of depth in the mind. It is a difficult one because it goes beyond pure psychology and touches on the relations of the mental apparatus to anatomy. We know that in the very roughest sense such relations exist. Research has given irrefutable proof that mental activity is bound up with the function of the brain as it is with no other organ. We are taken a step further—we do not know how much—by the discovery of the unequal importance of the different parts of the brain and their special relations to particular parts of the body and to particular mental activities [p. 174].

So Freud himself acknowledges that this topographic-economic metapsychological proposition goes beyond pure psychology and impinges on neurology. And then comes the statement about how every attempt to go on from there has miscarried, followed by:

> The same fate would await any theory which attempted to recognize, let us say, the anatomical position of the system *Cs.* — conscious mental activity—as being in the cortex, and to localize the unconscious processes in the subcortical parts of the brain. There is a hiatus here which at present cannot be filled, nor is it one of the tasks of psychology to fill it. Our psychical topography has *for the present* [emphasis in the original] nothing to do with anatomy....
>
> In this respect, then, our work is untrammelled and may proceed according to its own requirements [pp. 174-175].

So it is not the task of psychology to fill this gap, and psychical topography has *for the present* nothing to do with anatomy.

But five years after these remarks on how foolish it would be to attempt to locate the system *Cs.* in the cortex of the brain, Freud (1920) wrote in "Beyond the Pleasure Principle": "Psychoanalytic speculation takes as its point of departure the impression, derived from examining unconscious processes, that consciousness may be, not the most universal attribute of mental processes, but only a particular function of them. Speaking in metapsychological terms, it asserts that consciousness is a function of a particular system which it describes as *Cs.*" (1920, p. 24). Does metapsychology here mean purely psychological or does it have a neural referent? The next sentence tells us that while the idea of a system *Cs.* need not have a neural referent, its topographic description can have such a referent.

> What consciousness yields consists essentially of perceptions of excitations coming from the external world and of feelings of pleasure and unpleasure which can only arise from within the mental apparatus; it is therefore possible to assign to the system *Pcpt.-Cs.* a position in space. It must lie on the borderline between outside and inside; it must be turned towards the external world and must envelop the other psychical systems. It will be seen that there is nothing daringly new in these assumptions; we have merely adopted the views on localization held by cerebral anatomy, which locates the 'seat' of consciousness in the cerebral cortex—the outermost, enveloping layer of the central organ. Cerebral anatomy has no need to consider why, speaking anatomically, consciousness should be lodged on the surface of the brain instead of being safely housed somewhere in its inmost interior. Perhaps *we* shall be more successful in accounting for this situation in the case of our system *Pcpt.-Cs.*" [p. 24].

We cannot argue conclusively from this that the term metapsychology was intended to include these anatomical considerations, but can there be any doubt that this "metapsychological" discussion rapidly moves to a neurological referent?

Without attempting an exhaustive review, let us look at some more of Freud's uses of the term metapsychology. I turn first to the papers that Freud himself called "Papers on Metapsychology (1915c).[6]

And what are the papers on metapsychology about? Though they include many purely psychological hypotheses as well, they deal with basic neurological and biological hypotheses much more extensively than do the essentially clinical writings of Freud. The basic assumptions of the Project and Chapter VII can readily be inferred and are sometimes even explicit, as in "Instincts and Their Vicissitudes." Freud wrote: "I am altogether doubtful whether any decisive pointers for the differentiation and classification of the instincts can be arrived at on the basis of working over the psychological material. This working-over seems rather itself to call for the application to the material of definite assumptions concerning instinctual life, and it would be a desirable thing if those assumptions could be taken from some other branch of knowledge and carried over to psychology" (1915a, p. 124).

Earlier in the same paper, Freud wrote that he would approach the basic concept of instinct from "different angles" (pp. 117-118), and these turn out to be physiology (p. 118) and biology (p. 121). Furthermore, in the same paper an equation between the mental apparatus and the nervous system seems clear. First Freud offers what he calls a biological postulate of " 'purpose' (or perhaps expediency)": "The nervous system is an apparatus which has the function of . . ." (p. 120). Soon afterward, he refers to this same proposition,

---

[6] In a footnote to the paper "A Metapsychological Supplement to the Theory of Dreams" Freud (1917) wrote: "This paper and the following one are derived from a collection which I originally intended to publish in book form under the title 'Zur Vorbereitung einer Metapsychologie' ['Preliminaries to a Metapsychology']. They follow on some papers which were printed in Volume III of the *Internationale Zeitschrift für ärztliche Psychoanalyse* ('Instincts and their Vicissitudes,' 'Repression' and 'The Unconscious'). The intention of the series is to clarify and carry deeper the theoretical assumptions on which a psychoanalytic system could be founded" (p. 222).

Strachey (Freud, 1915c, p. 105) wrote in his introduction to the papers on metapsychology that in the German edition of Freud's collected works in 1924, the paper written by Freud for the Society for Psychical Research and entitled "A Note on the Unconscious in Psycho-Analysis" (1912) is included under the rubric "Papers on Metapsychology," along with the present five papers. It did not, however, form part of the original collection.

but now substitutes "mental apparatus" for "nervous system": ". . . a necessary postulate . . . the biological purpose of the mental apparatus . . ." (p. 124).

But my concern is to show that biological and neurological assumptions do not simply play a role in psychoanalytic theory, but that they are especially and specifically related to metapsychological theory. This quotation from "The Unconscious" (1915b) draws a distinction between freely mobile and bound energy—one of the central hypotheses of the Project: "In my opinion this distinction represents the deepest insight we have gained up to the present into the nature of *nervous* energy, and I do not see how we can avoid making it. A metapsychological presentation would most urgently call for further discussion at this point, though perhaps that would be too daring an undertaking as yet" (p. 188; italics mine). Here the term metapsychology is clearly used for a proposition about nervous energy. It may well be that the distinction between mobile and bound energy is nothing but a metaphoric restatement in neurological terms of the psychological distinction between primary and secondary processes, but my point is that Freud uses the term metapsychology when he talks about "nervous energy."

Let me offer several more quotations from Freud to illustrate one or another aspect of his disavowal of neurological and biological referents of metapsychology despite their obvious presence.[7]

In Lecture 25 (on anxiety) in the *Introductory Lectures on Psycho-Analysis* (1916-1917), Freud writes:

> . . . you will certainly expect psycho-analysis to approach this subject [anxiety] too in quite a different way from academic medicine. Interest there seems mainly to be centered on tracing the anatomical paths along which the state of anxiety is brought about. We are told that the medulla oblongata is stimulated, and the patient learns that he is suffering from a neurosis of the vagus nerve. The medulla oblongata is a very serious and lovely object. I remember quite clearly how much time and trouble I

[7] Holt (1965) refers to this issue as Freud's ambivalence about the nature of his model and cites a number of additional illustrations (pp. 107-108, fn.).

devoted to its study many years ago. To-day, however, I must remark that I know nothing that could be of less interest to me for the psychological understanding of anxiety than a knowledge of the path of the nerves along which its excitations pass [p. 393].

Strachey gravely footnotes that at the age of about thirty, Freud had worked for two years on the histology of the medulla oblongata and had published three papers on the subject! This charming quotation throws anatomy out the window.

Another disavowal is to be found in Freud's (1925) "An Autobiographical Study," which is also an illustration of Freud's frequent reference to metapsychology as speculative. He wrote:

The subdivision of the unconscious [into unconscious proper and preconscious] is part of an attempt to picture the apparatus of the mind as being built up of a number of *agencies* or *systems* whose relations to one another are expressed in spatial terms, without, however, implying any connection with the actual anatomy of the brain. (I have described this as the *topographical* method of approach.) Such ideas as these are part of a speculative superstructure of psycho-analysis, any portion of which can be abandoned or changed without loss or regret the moment its inadequacy has been proved [pp. 32-33].

Later in the same paper he defined metapsychology just as he had in the metapsychological papers, in terms of the dynamic, topographic, and economic "co-ordinates" (p. 59), a definition he repeats in 1937 (pp. 226-227). In 1925 (p. 59) Freud refers to the papers he had written a decade earlier, saying,

this seemed to me to represent the furthest goal that psychology [a harking back to the early use of the term "psychology" for the later "metapsychology"] could attain. The attempt remained no more than a torso; after writing two or three papers . . . I broke off, wisely perhaps since the time for theoretical predications of this kind had not yet come. In my latest speculative works I have set about the task of dissecting our mental apparatus on the basis of the analytic view of pathological facts and have divided it into an *ego,* an *id,* and a *super-ego.*

It is noteworthy how often Freud refers to metapsychology as "speculation"; the most oft-quoted example of this is in the reference to the "witch metapsychology":

> ... the instinct is brought completely into the harmony of the ego, becomes accessible to all the influences of the other trends in the ego and no longer seeks to go its independent way to satisfaction. If we are asked by what methods and means this result is achieved, it is not easy to find an answer. We can only say: 'So muss den doch die Hexe dran!'—The Witch Metapsychology. Without metapsychological speculation and theorizing—I had almost said phantasying—we shall not get another step forward. Unfortunately, here as elsewhere, what our Witch reveals is neither very clear nor very detailed. We have only a single clue to start from—though it is a clue of the highest value—namely, the antithesis between the primary and the secondary processes; and to that antithesis I shall at this point turn [1937, p. 225].

Freud turns at this point to "taming" an instinct, implying that taming means a shift from primary to secondary process; his entire discussion is couched in "economic" terms.

I suggest that Freud so often referred to metapsychology as speculative, and seemed so much more ready to abandon or change it than most psychoanalysts, because it does not include his purely psychological hypotheses, but does include the propositions which, despite his disavowals, are based on neurological and biological assumptions.

Two Theories in Psychoanalysis

I have so far not directly asked whether Freud distinguished between the metapsychological and clinical theories, but it seems to me evident that, if he singled out certain types of propositions as specifically metapsychological, he was making such a distinction.

I noted earlier that Freud first apparently used the term psychological for what we now call metapsychological—a usage that is still to be found in our literature. I do not know who first explicitly and sharply argued that there are two theories in psychoanalysis,[8] but I note that in his comprehensive monograph on the structure of psychoanalytic theory Rapaport (1959) wrote: ". . . this essay . . . makes the distinction between what might be called the special or clinical theory and the general or psychological theory of psychoanalysis" (p. 8).

Strachey seems to feel, as do many others—for example, Adrienne Applegarth (1973) in her review of a number of books on psychoanalytic theory—that the terms "psychological," "general psychological," or even "theoretical" specify the kinds of writings Freud called metapsychology. Strachey, in his introduction to the "Papers on Metapsychology" (Freud, 1915c), wrote:

> Freud published his first extended account of his views on psychological theory in the seventh chapter of *The Interpretation of Dreams,* which incorporated, in a transmuted form, much of the substance of his earlier, unpublished "Project." Apart from occasional short discussions, such as the one in Chapter VI of his book on jokes, ten years passed before he again began to enter deeply into theoretical problems. An exploratory paper on 'Two Principles of Mental Functioning' was followed by other more or less tentative approaches—in Part III of his Schreber analysis, in his English paper on the unconscious, and in the long discussion on narcissism. Finally, in the spring and summer of 1915, he once more undertook a full-length and systematic exposition of his psychological theories [p. 105].

And at the end of the papers on metapsychology, Strachey has added an appendix that gives a "List of Writings by Freud Dealing Mainly with General Psychological Theory." But the terms psychological, general psychological, and theoretical do not resolve the issue I am stressing. And they have the additional serious disadvantage that they obscure the fact that

[8] Fenichel (1945) wrote in his preface to *The Psychoanalytic Theory of Neurosis:* "At European psychoanalytic institutes the custom was to subdivide this field [psychoanalysis] into a general part, treating the mechanisms common to all neuroses, and a special part, treating the characteristic features of the individual neuroses." Inasmuch as the "general" part of his book deals with the metapsychological points of view, shall we assume that this is what Fenichel meant by the mechanisms common to all neuroses?

there are *two* theories, a clinical and a metapsychological; it is erroneous to think in terms of clinical *data* and metapsychological *theory*—there is clinical theory, too.

George Klein sharply and explicitly insisted on this distinction by attempting to detail the differences between the metapsychological and clinical theories, first in general terms in the paper "Two Theories or One?" (1970) and then in specific terms in his paper on "Freud's Two Theories of Sexuality," which is included in this memorial volume.

The latter paper, like this one, is built upon his argument that metapsychology deals with the neurology and biology, with the physical substrate, of psychological functioning, while clinical psychoanalysis is a "pure" psychology which deals with intentionality and meaning.

It is sometimes argued that the essence of metapsychology lies in the points of view themselves, not the propositions they subsume, and that a disagreement with something postulated within one of the points of view need not have any repercussions on the schema of the points of view. Such a position would argue that one can postulate forces, energies, or structures other than those now postulated without prejudicing the points of view. That is correct and exactly the point. For the metapsychological points of view are the natural-science framework of structure, energy, and force, and it is that framework as such which is inapplicable to psychological data.

If the metapsychology is employed to *explain* clinical propositions, the effort to state psychoanalytic propositions in terms of physics and chemistry, or in terms of biological concepts like structure, function, and adaptation, becomes inevitably reductionistic.

Klein's argument is that the natural-science universe of discourse is not derivable from or testable by the specific methods of psychoanalysis. He rejects the conception that the metapsychological propositions are abstractions from the clinical propositions, arguing that they are of an entirely different order.

From his perspective, then, all concepts of structure, forces, and energy (which are the basic building blocks of, respectively, the structural, dynamic, and economic points of view) belong to a frame of reference different from that of clinical psychoanalysis. Insofar as these metapsychological concepts are alleged to be explanations of, or higher-order abstractions from, the clinical propositions, they are pseudo explanations and pseudo abstractions which, to the extent that they are related to the clinical propositions at all, are restatements of them in another, albeit systematic, language relating to a different universe of discourse. I have called such restatements "metaphorical" in the earlier parts of this essay.[9]

The Metapsychological Points of View

The economic point of view has come under attack most heavily because it lies most obviously within the natural-science framework. In fact, in many people's minds it is this point of view that has come to mean metapsychology, and in this somewhat mistaken equation the status of the other points of view has been less carefully examined.

The economic point of view encompasses at least three major propositions for psychoanalysts. In the first place, it deals with questions of quantities, how much or how little it is that one is talking about. The second major proposition of the economic point of view is a more specific one. It puts forth the constancy principle: namely, that the energy in the psychic apparatus tends to be reduced to the lowest possible amount, or at least to the maintenance of a constant amount. The third central proposition of the economic point of view postulates a so-called psychic energy. One might think that there could hardly be any question about the simple issue of quantity, even if it is measurable only in terms of "greater than" or "less

[9] Michael Basch (1973) has reached the same conclusion. Furthermore, in his thoughtful and stimulating article he tackles the difficult epistemological issue of the differences between explanation and description, an issue I sidestep in this essay.

than." But the constancy principle is criticized, among other reasons, for implying a "closed system," a drive-reduction theory, and a passive organism (Holt, 1965, 1967).

Despite the efforts of those who espouse the energy concept to deny that there is any connection between physical energy and psychological energy, it is nevertheless obvious that those who use the concept of psychological energy are employing it as a metaphor for physical energy. The laws of conservation and entropy are believed to hold for psychic as well as for physical energy.[10]

If one is clear that the objection to the economic point of view is that it is a natural-science concept, it follows that even concepts of relative quantity are regarded as inappropriate. The apparently "innocent" proposition that a person has a greater or lesser urge to do this or that is to substitute a hypothetical energic driving force for a qualitative delineation of the psychological situation (see Schafer, 1975).

The fate of the other points of view of metapsychology depends on whether or not they are tied to the energy, force,[11] and structure theory of the nervous system. I do not believe that a psychic-energy concept based solely on psychological grounds is possible, but it is more likely that a structural theory and a dynamic theory might be. A dynamic theory might be erected on the grounds of motive or intentions alone, with no reference to any bodily relationship or analogue, which of course would not exclude the psychology of sexuality, for example.

Freud (1916-1917) wrote: "We seek not merely to describe and to classify phenomena, but to understand them as signs of an interplay of forces in the mind, as a manifestation of

---

[10] Though Rapaport (1959) wrote, "These psychological energies are not equated with any known kind of biochemical energy" (p. 51), he also wrote in the same monograph, "Freud's energies and K. Lewin's tensions . . . are referents of phenomena which seem to abide by the laws of energy exchanges — conservation, entropy, least action" (p. 52).

[11] Holt writes in a personal communication: "My impression is that the concept of 'force' is used to a negligible extent in the neurosciences. Its place in Freud's metapsychology is testimony to the inappropriateness of Newtonian mechanics as a scheme to which biological phenomena can be reduced."

purposeful intentions working concurrently or in mutual opposition. We are concerned with a *dynamic view* of mental phenomena. On our view the phenomena that are perceived must yield in importance to trends which are only hypothetical" (p. 67).

One can see that the dynamic point of view can be interpreted as relating, not to some kind of hypothetical instinctual forces, but to "purposeful intentions." On the other hand, Freud's saying that "the phenomena that are perceived must yield in importance to trends which are only hypothetical" shows how, on this occasion, he seems to have elevated metapsychology above clinical psychology.

Psychoanalysts (e.g., Hartmann, 1950) generally take the position that structural theory is erected in terms of the grouping of psychological functions, with no reference to material structure. Holt (1975) finds this an empty formulation and points to these weaknesses: (1) biological functions do not define structures, since with equipotentiality many structures serve the same function (e.g., communication) while one structure serves many functions (e.g., the hand); (2) it is very difficult to set boundaries to a function; and (3) the concept is circular, since it is defined in terms of the very phenomena it is presumably designed to explain. And, of course, he is also critical of the fact that it is impossible to avoid reification. This last objection is reason enough to argue that allegedly "pure" psychological dynamic and structural theories should, in any case, be scrutinized as though they were neuropsychological constructs.

I turn to the other points of view sometimes included in the roster of metapsychology. The topographic point of view, as I argued in an earlier monograph (1963), has been superseded by the structural point of view and is now only descriptive of whether a mental process is conscious, preconscious, or unconscious. Of course there are propositions about consciousness, preconsciousness, and unconsciousness that are framed in neuropsychological terms, as, for example, the postulation of the system *Cs.* as a sense organ. But is there any valid neurological basis for such a conception? Is the hypothesis that connection to memory traces of speech is required if an unconscious process is to become preconscious valid neurologically? That a "hypercathexis" is what makes a preconscious process conscious? How can we argue that these are purely psychological hypotheses?

Rapaport and I (1959) have suggested that the genetic and adaptive be formalized as points of view in addition to the economic, dynamic, and structural triad proposed by Freud. While this suggestion has been widely accepted in the literature, there are dissenting voices, notably those of Glover and Schafer.

Glover writes:

> This last mode [genetic development or regression] is *not* however a metapsychological one. It is a description (record) of mental growth useful in clinical psychoanalysis (either normal or abnormal) and, when combined with secondary (theoretical) elaborations, can function as a *psychological* measure.
>
> Similarly in the case of adaptational standards, metapsychologically speaking, adaptation is the history of object relations and can be considered from three points of view: 1. Dynamic (instinctual) aspects, e.g., the progression of component instincts (appetitive and reactive) from earlier to later objects; 2. mechanistic aspects, e.g., the maturation of mechanisms; 3. structural aspects, e.g., modifications of the ego following object abandonment and consequent introjection. In other words, although essential to the evaluation of psychic events, developmental and adaptational measures are complex serial interpretations, not basic (irreducible) postulates [1961, p. 98 fn.].

Schafer (1970) argues that in a broad sense adaptation is a biological vantage point outside of and prior to psychology, while in a narrow sense it "leads to propositions that articulate and amplify the structural—specifically, ego-psychological— point of view" (p. 431). He regards the genetic emphasis in psychoanalysis as methodological, holding that "Explanation concerns immediate fields of force; history helps to explain the nature of these fields of force. The component factors of the field are necessarily *current* factors and these are, in the final analysis, to be explained in terms of aims (dynamics), emphases (economics), and organizations with varying degrees of independence, integration, stability and influence (structures)" (p. 432).

I believe these are persuasive arguments for the narrow adaptational perspective and for genetic considerations. They are reducible to the dynamic, economic, and structural points of view. But both Glover and Schafer agree that the examination of any mental process must include adaptational and developmental considerations. I would not be averse, then, to calling them something other than points of view on a different conceptual level from the usual triad.

Schafer's (1970) discussion of the broader adaptive perspective is another matter, however. His formulation deserves to be quoted:

> Adaptation is a natural-science—specifically, biological—point of view with the help of which one may systematically select, formulate, arrange and interrelate psychoanalytic propositions. Adaptation theory starts with the proposition that if one regards man as a biological entity, his language for discussing man's psychology should consistently reflect the fact that his psychology is one facet of his biological existence (as is his sociology . . .). Thus the language of psychology should derive from, or be consistent with, or at least make good sense with respect to, biology [p. 431].

I believe Schafer is correct. His argument leads to the conclusion that, in the broad conception of adaptation, an adaptive proposition would be a biopsychological one, and hence metapsychological, just as I have argued that many economic, structural, and dynamic propositions are neuro- and biopsychological, and hence metapsychological.

However one sees the relationship between genetic and adaptive considerations and the structural, dynamic, and economic points of view, it is clear that psychoanalytic theory includes both psychological and metapsychological genetic and adaptive propositions.

The recent series of important papers by Schafer (1972, 1973a, 1973b, 1973c, this volume, Chapter 4) has major implications for the theme of this essay. Schafer argues that the natural-science framework of forces, energies, and structures is inappropriate for a psychoanalytic psychology, and he proposes what he calls an "action language" instead. His method of taking up one major psychoanalytic conception after another and concretely demonstrating how his proposal affects our views and uses of these conceptions is especially valuable. Where his position goes beyond the view thus far stated in this paper is that he sees the natural-science framework not only in our metapsychology, but in our clinical theory as well. His primary emphasis is on the clinical theory. One might conclude that his view is that if he can demonstrate the relevance of his thesis to the clinical theory, it would apply with even greater force to the metapsychological theory, leaving little need to focus on the metapsychological theory itself.

I believe that my views are compatible with his: that the natural-science framework is inappropriate to the data of psychoanalysis, but is instead appropriate to the discipline of neuropsychology.

Schafer's views may lead to the recognition of the degree to which metapsychological thinking has imperceptibly invaded our clinical thinking and has been imported into the language we use in our talk about our work — and even in our talk to our patients. If this is true, the explicit recognition that metapsychology is neuropsychology and inappropriate to the data of the psychoanalytic situation may assist in the task of freeing our purely psychological theory from its natural-science encumbrance.

The Relationship between
Metapsychology and Psychoanalysis

I turn now to an even more difficult issue. Assuming that metapsychological and psychological propositions *are* in different universes of discourse, what is the relation between them? Is metapsychology relevant to psychoanalysis?

In earlier drafts of this paper, I argued that metapsychological propositions are neuropsychological and biopsychological and must be consonant with both psychological and neurological or biological data. I attempted to define such a combined proposition and to give illustrations of valid and invalid ones. But I gradually came to believe that if metapsychological and psychological propositions do lie in two different universes of discourse, there can be no such thing as a combined proposition. I came to believe that the idea that a metapsychological proposition had to be consonant with the data of both neurology or biology and psychology is based on the very assumption that I am disputing: that a psychological proposition makes sense in a natural-science framework. I came to the conclusion that metapsychological propositions are not psychological and are not relevant to psychoanalysis as such. The data of psychoanalysis permit and require only one theory.

Yet I found that among the very thoughtful contributors to the literature on the issues raised in this paper, there are those who, despite their agreement that metapsychological propositions lie in a different universe of discourse from psychological ones, believe that metapsychological propositions are crucial to psychoanalysis and must be consonant with neurological data. Obviously, I agree that a neurological or biological statement must be consonant with the best knowledge available in those disciplines, but I disagree that such a statement is relevant to psychoanalysis.

In the literature of psychoanalysis, I believe it is Rubinstein who has grappled with this problem the most energetically and thoughtfully. His paper in this volume testifies to that. In 1967, he wrote that a psychological proposition in terms of meaning cannot be combined with a neurological one in terms of substrate. For, as he says, these are two different languages.

Yet, in the same essay, he also wrote: "One requirement we cannot shirk: the theoretical terms, structural as well as process, in which we couch our psychological data, must be at once psychologically meaningful and acceptable protoneurophysiologically.... Protoneurophysiological terms are not neurophysiological terms. They merely in a general way *point* to neurophysiological terms and for the most part these are yet to be discovered" (p. 75). Of the clinical phenomenon of partial functional equivalence he has this to say: "According to the neurophysiological interpretation, the general clinical hypothesis of partial functional equivalence may be said to be legitimized by neurologically plausible metapsychological hypotheses" (p. 76). And finally: "According to the neurophysiological interpretation . . . explanation is not a function of the purely psychological aspect alone nor of the neurophysiological aspect alone: only the two aspects together are truly explanatory" (p. 77).

Clearly, the question is whether a purely psychological theory is possible and can be valid. Both Rubinstein and Holt explicitly say that it is not. Rubinstein (1967) states his point of view emphatically: "The principal drawback of the conception of psychoanalytic theory as a purely psychological theory is that it has never been carried through consistently. *Nor can it be!* Behavior and experience do not occur in a vacuum, without connection with other organismic events" (p. 63).

According to Holt (1967),

> Academic pure psychologies . . . have been able to maintain that their dynamic concepts were "abstract" and not to be taken as having any reference to physically measurable forces, by neglecting a detailed consideration of the powerful emotions and drives of real life, especially as seen in psychopathology. . . . For just these reasons, pure psychologies have been worthless to the clinician, who must remain true to his commitment to the physicochemical structure we call the body. Such fidelity is particularly necessary for psychoanalysis, if it is to develop in the way Freud always wanted it to: as a theory of the whole organism [p. 17].

And Freud (1914b), for all his insistence that psychoanalysis must develop untrammeled by assumptions from other disciplines, is apparently also in agreement: "we must recollect that all our provisional ideas in psychology will presumably some day be based on an organic substructure" (p. 78).

I believe it will be clarifying to consider just what kinds of

hypotheses Rubinstein thinks require neurological substantiation. We have already seen that he believes that "according
to the neurophysiological interpretation, the general clinical
hypothesis of partial functional equivalence may be said to be
legitimized by neurologically plausible metapsychological hypotheses" (1967, p. 76). He speaks of "higher-level clinical
hypotheses" and asks whether terms like "motive," "unconscious motive," "repression," and "substitute fulfillment" can
be exhaustively defined in terms of the psychological "thing-
event language" or whether they must be classified as theoretical terms. He finally concludes that

> one can speak about a nonexistential core meaning of higher-
> level hypotheses.... As far as I can see, this is the only sense in
> which psychoanalytic theory can unambiguously be said to be a
> purely psychological theory.... If the higher-level clinical hy-
> potheses are interpreted nonexistentially, then, obviously, they
> can be confirmed only clinically (or by other psychological
> methods?) [pp. 39-40].

I believe the issue turns on the word "existentially." In a
purely psychological theory, the higher-level clinical hypotheses can be confirmed only clinically or by other psychological
methods. But does this mean they are "nonexistential"? True,
their existentiality has not been demonstrated in the natural-
science framework, but does this prevent them from "existing"
in the psychological sense?

Rubinstein believes that the data of the psychoanalytic
situation are relevant to metapsychology. He seems to regard
certain concepts that I consider clinical, and verifiable on
clinical grounds alone, to be theoretical, and in need of
neurological evidence for substantiation (the double connotation of the word "substantiation" is deliberate). For example,
he considers the concept of an unconscious motive a hypothesis that requires neurological validation. I disagree, but I
believe the nature of the disagreement is clarified by stating
his further view that one must distinguish between what an
unconscious motive *is* and what it *does*. He considers the
former a neurological issue whereas the latter need not be. I
have no great difficulty in agreeing with this because I believe

a self-contained "pure" psychological theory that includes propositions about what an unconscious motive does is quite satisfactory and enables us to arrive at valid truths about reality. I assume there is a material substrate for an unconscious wish — or for a conscious wish, for that matter. Rubinstein, on the other hand, does not think that a conscious wish requires neurological substantiation because it is verified by subjective experience.

But there are two further points I must emphasize, lest these preceding remarks be misunderstood. To say that the natural-science framework is inappropriate for the clinical theory of psychoanalysis is not to say that the clinical theory cannot and need not be science. For there are sciences other than the natural sciences, sciences that have some general framework other than that of energy, force, and structure, though I make no attempt to deal with whether they show a common framework among themselves. As sciences, they conform to the general methodological canons of the scientific method. Nor shall I attempt to spell these out either. I am aware of the complex problems one runs into in attempting to spell out such principles for psychoanalytic research, whether one does so in theoretical or practical terms.

The second point of possible misunderstanding is to conclude that I deny that man is a biological organism or that I am at least espousing a "black box" approach concerned only with observable stimulus and response. I believe such a misunderstanding would arise from an equation of *intrapsychic* with *neural*. In short, I am suggesting that intrapsychic explorations can be carried out on a purely psychological level.

Both Holt and Rubinstein emphasize that a pure psychology must ignore the body. I do not believe this is true. Klein's paper in this volume bears witness to the fact that the recognition that many drive propositions are biopsychological, for example, does not mean that clinical psychoanalytic discoveries about sexuality are being discarded. Freud's important hypotheses on the sequential development of the several erotic zones were based on data derived from the psychoanalytic situation, not on any neurophysiological observations; and subsequent confirmation through the observations of infants has been based on behavioral, not neurophysiological, data. Nor should one overlook the cogent reasons for arguing that even such behavioral observations are not psychoanalytic in the psychological sense.

The recognition that a metapsychological proposition *as such* is not relevant to psychoanalysis can prevent a series of difficulties resulting from the employment of metapsychological hypotheses in psychoanalytic theory:

1. A neurological or biological proposition is considered directly applicable to psychological functioning—in direct violation of the cardinal principle of the meaning of a "stimulus" in psychoanalysis. A stimulus cannot be psychologically characterized by its external dimension, whether that stimulus arises inside or outside the skin. A stimulus is psychologically definable only in terms of its psychological significance in the psychological universe of meaning, of intentionality, or whatever other term is chosen to indicate the psychological perspective. Orality, anality, or any other bodily stimulus becomes a psychological event only as it acquires psychological significance.

2. Erroneous biological or neurological assumptions are used to develop clinical theories that do not square with the facts. Holt (1965) has made the most systematic effort so far to specify Freud's erroneous biological assumptions and their influence on his theories. He includes: (a) the tension-reduction conception of motivation and the pleasure principle; (b) issues in the theory of aggression; (c) problems of the "energy doctrine"; (d) problems in psychoanalytic psychopathology; and (e) problems in the theory of object relations. Because only the last two of these deal with clinical theory, which I regard as equivalent to the psychological (as opposed to the metapsychological) theory, and which is my concern here, I shall confine myself to these.

In the category of psychoanalytic psychopathology, Holt includes the early theory of anxiety and the related conceptions of the actual neurosis and the traumatic neurosis. But, as

he discusses these, they are all metapsychological propositions. Under problems in the theory of object relations, he discusses the idea of the primary hatred of objects, problems in accounting for *enduring* object relations, and issues in narcissism, especially the so-called U-tube theory of the fixed supply of libido according to which object libido and narcissistic libido vary reciprocally.

Considering the wealth of clinical psychoanalytic propositions, the list of erroneous clinical theories seems skimpy indeed. The difficulty is with the metapsychological rather than the psychological theory. Is this why, after an apparently devastating attack on psychoanalytic theory, Holt (1965) can nevertheless write: "... the clinical theory ... was Freud's most original and lasting contribution and for the most part it will stand unaffected by changes in the basic model" (p. 32)? While I agree with this assessment, I also think it possible that, as the metapsychology and the clinical theory are disentangled, much that is now considered clinical theory will be revealed to be metapsychology.

A somewhat different way of stating this difficulty is to say that biological assumptions, whether erroneous or not, are alleged to apply to psychological functioning when they do not. Where is the psychology in the constancy principle? Is it not strictly a neurological proposition, but one that is alleged to apply to psychological life? Are there purely psychological propositions or observations that call for the hypothesis of a constancy principle? And what about the proliferation of qualities of energy in metapsychological theory—neutral, neutralized, libidinal, aggressive, delibidinized, deaggressivized, fused, and what not?

Both constancy and qualitative-energy principles are stated solely in neurological terms. Should that not alert us to the possibility that they are not psychological propositions at all?

3. Assumptions are made which purport to be neurological but which are really only metaphoric statements of psychological propositions. Such a situation seems harmless enough, but what if the metaphors are taken seriously as explanations and thereby shut off further inquiry? Let us take, for example,

the distinction between primary- and secondary-process thought. One of the neurological hypotheses that Freud proposed as the neurophysiological substrate for the distinction between primary and secondary process is binding versus free flow. He wrote in the Project: *"Thus the process of thought* [secondary process] *would be characterized mechanically by this bound condition, which combines a high cathexis with a small flow of current.* We can think of other processes in which the current would run *parallel* to the cathexis— processes with an uninhibited discharge [primary processes]. I hope that the hypothesis of a bound condition of this kind will turn out to be tenable mechanically" (1895, pp. 368-369).

Freud continued to use the concept of binding throughout his metapsychological writings, and psychoanalysts have made extensive and varied use of it—Holt (1962) in his careful dissection, lists over a dozen different uses of the term! How often has "binding" been invoked to slough off a problem rather than to explain it? Has its use as an explanation retarded the careful clinical examination and specification of the dozen different uses to which it has been put?

Just as there are principles, like the constancy principle, that purport to be psychological but are only neurological, so are there concepts, like the various types of energy, that purport to be neurological but are only psychological.

4. Phenomena that are psychologically valid but alleged to be derived from biologically untenable assumptions are needlessly called into question. The distinction between primary and secondary processes again provides a good example. It is alleged that the distinction is necessarily based on the constancy principle, but that principle seems invalid. But that does not mean that the distinction between the primary and secondary processes is also invalid. For that distinction is based on many different varieties of clinical evidence, from dreams to symptoms.

5. Because metapsychology is regarded as explanatory of psychology, the psychological problem involved in accepting the reality of psychic reality is swept under the rug. This is a

problem, not only in the psychology of individuals, but also in the discipline of psychoanalysis as a whole.

As Klein (1970) argues, metapsychology was Freud's attempt to construct an *explanatory* theoretical model of the behaving human organism. The real rub is in determining what may be legitimately called explanatory.

I do not feel competent to tackle seriously the philosophical question of the meaning of "explanation" versus "description," but my conviction is that, in psychological terms alone, an explanation can be valid and secure knowledge even though the phenomena dealt with may have a material substrate. I believe, for example, that I do not have to consider the validity of the theory of repression provisional until its neurophysiological substrate has been identified. While I do not doubt there is one, I do not believe this neurological substrate can be meaningfully talked about by using concepts like "countercathexis" and the "withdrawal of cathexis," for these concepts are metaphors appropriate to another, albeit systematic, language. Despite the metapsychological language in which he discussed repression, Freud (1914a) was also aware of this distinction:

> If anyone sought to place the theory of repression and resistance among the *premises* instead of the *findings* of psychoanalysis, I should oppose him most emphatically. Such premises of a general psychological and biological nature do exist, and it would be useful to consider them on some other occasion; but the theory of repression is a product of psycho-analytic work, a theoretical inference legitimately drawn from innumerable observations [pp. 16-17].

It would be worthwhile to review Freud's Project in the light of some of the difficulties I have sketched, and Pribram and I have begun to do this in the monograph (1976) to which I referred earlier.[12]

Is the Project psychological, though ostensibly neurological?

[12] For an interesting and spirited discussion of the natural-science assumptions of metapsychology and an argument for maintaining metapsychology as an important part of psychoanalytic theory, see Barros (1971).

Is it manifestly psychological? Or should we call it meta-psychological? No over-all characterization will do. The Project includes a number of types of propositions, including psychological as such, psychological in neurological garb, and neurological parading as psychological.

Any opposition to the opinions I have expressed could in large measure result from two mistaken conclusions that might be drawn from them. The first is that I am advocating discarding much of clinical psychoanalysis. Such a mistaken impression is due to the complex intermixture of metapsychology and psychology in our theory and practice. If a proposition is generally considered to be metapsychological, for example, but is in fact clinical, or a complex admixture of clinical and metapsychological propositions, rather than relegating it in toto to metapsychology, it should be analyzed into its metapsychological and psychological components, and only the latter should be dealt with as psychoanalytic propositions.

That kind of analysis of propositions is an important task for psychoanalytic theory, a task to which Schafer's studies surely have much to contribute. Of course, the background was laid by the increasing discomfort, at least among a minority of analysts, with the economic point of view. Let me give just a few brief illustrations.

If we study, for example, the division of the personality into id, ego, and superego, it becomes clear that these concepts are of a very different order from the present point of view. The superego seems to be a clinical concept easily subject to observation, quite accurately reflecting the clinical data, which bespeak a group of internalized motives of an essentially "moral" character and which play a significant role in regulating human behavior. Of course, in grouping these motives together one must be careful not to elevate the alleged structure into a reified homunculus.

The id, on the other hand, is a very different concept, as is evident from the arguments that rage about how it is related to the body and how it is related to the mind. The id is sometimes described as if it were essentially a physiological concept and other times as though it were essentially a psychological one. Or, in an effort to straddle the issue, it is considered a borderline concept between the physical and the mental. As Freud wrote, it is "on the frontier between the mental and the somatic" (1915a, p. 122). The id is considered to be a repository of instincts, but then one has to make subtle distinctions between instinct and instinct representatives in order to try to make clear that one is dealing here with a mental rather than a physiological concept. The reification of the id as a homunculus is apparent throughout psychoanalytic literature.

Many major issues in psychoanalysis are discussed with intertwined metapsychological and clinical propositions. Freud's paper "On Narcissism" is, for example, regarded as a metapsychological paper. I have already referred to the "U-tube" theory he presents in that paper. Many have discarded this proposition because it seems to fit only a small segment of the clinical data on love and self-esteem. But Holt (1965) is one of the very few who has been led by this contradiction between clinical observations and metapsychological theory to an examination of the metapsychological assumptions underlying the theory. At the same time, the paper on narcissism includes many clinical propositions about narcissistic and libidinal object choice (though "libidinal" *can* have metapsychological meanings) that are not metapsychological. The abandonment of the U-tube theory does not mean the abandonment of the concept of narcissism.

I might also be mistakenly thought to mean that there are no significant connections between the brain and psychology. Of course there are, but the connection is not a direct one in the realm of meaning. An organic insult to the brain may affect memory, but that is not a psychological consequence as such, according to the meaning of psychology in this essay. The psychological result of such an insult lies in the meaning of the impairment to the individual. As I said earlier in reference to the nature of a stimulus in psychoanalysis, however profound the influence may be on psychological functioning of some alteration in the central system, the *psychologically meaningful* nature of that influence cannot be discerned from a study of the central nervous system, or even from a study of the dimensions of a psychological function like memory. It can be seen only in terms of its psychological significance to the subject.

The term "psychology" clearly can have two major meanings. As generally employed in this essay, it signifies what is meaningful to the person as a person (compare Rubinstein's essay in this volume). It may also refer to a psychological function, such as thought or memory. An insult to the brain has a direct psychological effect in the sense of an impairment of a function like memory, but only an indirect psychological effect in the sense of the personal significance of that impairment.

Even in the realm of the nonmeaningful connection between the brain and psychology, some of the precautions to be taken seem clear. A psychological concept must be erected on psychological grounds alone. Although either a psychological hypothesis or a neurological hypothesis can be a stimulus for searching for a correlate in the other discipline, the ever-present danger lurks of thinking one is on psychological grounds alone when one is using implicit neurological assumptions. For the neuropsychologist, the reverse danger doubtless exists. Yet the demonstration of feedback loops in neurology could be a major stimulus for understanding the existence of such processes in psychological life, and, conversely, the shaping of perception by unconscious fantasy could lead one to search for a neurological correlate in which central processes influence perception.

I believe the acceptance of the conclusions I advocate could have important useful repercussions on our field. The connection between metapsychology and practice has long been ambiguous and uncertain. The clinician who chooses to say he is not interested in metapsychology need not fear that he is shutting himself away from a body of knowledge with which he ought to be conversant.

The unbridled speculation that stems in part from the fact that the implicit neurological assumptions in our metapsychology do not have to run the gantlet of neurological facts might be somewhat stemmed. The sharp focus on what is neurological and what is psychological should help advance psychology and neurophysiology, too—for on the one hand it will become less easy to obscure a clinical problem by a pseudopsychological, "metapsychological" explanation, and on the other it will become less easy to obscure a neurophysiological problem by a pseudophysiological, metaphorical psychological explanation. And if what often passes for research in our field—metaphysics rather than metapsychology, to borrow Glover's (1966) phrase—is exposed for what it is, perhaps we will see more effort devoted to genuine clinical research. Metapsychological research will be left to the neuropsychologists.

I can now state my conclusions in summary form.

Conclusions

1. Metapsychological propositions are in the natural-science framework of force, energy, and structure.

2. Psychological propositions deal with intention and meaning.

3. Although Freud's metapsychology was originally explicitly neurobiological, he later denied, sometimes explicitly, the continuing implicit neurobiological assumptions of psychoanalytic metapsychology.

4. Metapsychological propositions are not an abstraction from psychological propositions, nor are they derivable from, translations of, or explanatory of such propositions. There is therefore no direct connection between metapsychology and psychology.

5. A "pure" psychology based on data like that of the psychoanalytic situation is possible and can be a science that is valid in its own right.

6. Metapsychological propositions and clinical propositions that are purely psychological must be disentangled and then examined on their appropriate grounds. For this reason, despite the argument that there is no direct connection

between metapsychology and psychology, the present state of affairs in psychoanalytic theory is such that it makes no sense to say globally that one accepts or rejects metapsychology.

REFERENCES

Applegarth, A. (1973), The Structure of Psychoanalytic Theory. *J. Amer. Psychoanal. Assn.*, 21:193-237.
Barros, C. (1971), Thermodynamic and Evolutionary Concepts in the Formal Structure of Freud's Metapsychology. In: *The World Biennial of Psychiatry and Psychotherapy*, Vol. I, ed. S. Arieti. New York: Basic Books, pp. 72-111.
Basch, M. (1973), Psychoanalysis and Theory Formation. *The Annual of Psychoanalysis*, 1:39-52. New York: Quadrangle.
Fenichel, O. (1945), *The Psychoanalytic Theory of Neurosis*. New York: Norton.
Freud, S. (1887-1902), *The Origins of Psycho-Analysis*. New York: Basic Books, 1954.
_____(1895), Project for a Scientific Psychology. *Standard Edition*, 1:283-387. London: Hogarth Press, 1966.
_____(1900), The Interpretation of Dreams. *Standard Edition*, 4 & 5. London: Hogarth Press, 1953.
_____(1901), The Psychopathology of Everyday Life. *Standard Edition*, 6. London: Hogarth Press, 1953.
_____(1912), A Note on the Unconscious in Psycho-Analysis. *Standard Edition*, 12:255-266. London: Hogarth Press, 1958.
_____(1914a), On the History of the Psycho-Analytic Movement. *Standard Edition*, 14:3-66. London: Hogarth Press, 1957.
_____(1914b), On Narcissism. *Standard Edition*, 14:67-102. London: Hogarth Press, 1957.
_____(1915a), Instincts and Their Vicissitudes. *Standard Edition*, 14:109-140. London: Hogarth Press, 1957.
_____(1915b), The Unconscious. *Standard Edition*, 14:159-215. London: Hogarth Press, 1957.
_____(1915c), Papers on Metapsychology. *Standard Edition*, 14:105-340. London: Hogarth Press, 1957.
_____(1916-1917), Introductory Lectures on Psycho-Analysis. *Standard Edition*, 15 & 16. London: Hogarth Press, 1963.
_____(1917), A Metapsychological Supplement to the Theory of Dreams. *Standard Edition*, 14:217-235. London: Hogarth Press, 1957.
_____(1920), Beyond the Pleasure Principle. *Standard Edition*, 18:3-64. London: Hogarth Press, 1955.
_____(1925), An Autobiographical Study. *Standard Edition*, 20:3-74. London: Hogarth Press, 1959.
_____(1937), Analysis Terminable and Interminable. *Standard Edition*, 23:209-253. London: Hogarth Press, 1964.
Gill, M. (1963), Topography and Systems in Psychoanalytic Theory. *Psychol. Issues*, Monogr. No. 10. New York: International Universities Press.
Glover, E. (1961), Some Recent Trends in Psychoanalytic Theory. *Psychoanal. Quart.*, 30:86-107.

————(1966), Metapsychology or Metaphysics: A Psychoanalytic Essay. *Psycho-anal. Quart.*, 35:173-190.

Hartmann, H. (1950), Comments on the Psychoanalytic Theory of the Ego. *Essays on Ego Psychology*. New York: International Universities Press, 1964, pp. 113-141.

Holt, R. R. (1962), A Critical Examination of Freud's Concept of Bound vs. Free Cathexis. *J. Amer. Psychoanal. Assn.*, 10:475-525.

————(1965), A Review of Some of Freud's Biological Assumptions and Their Influence on His Theories. In: *Psychoanalysis and Current Biological Thought*, ed. N. S. Greenfield & W. C. Lewis. Madison: University of Wisconsin Press, pp. 93-124.

————(1967), Beyond Vitalism and Mechanism: Freud's Concept of Psychic Energy. In: *Science and Psychoanalysis*, 11:1-41. New York: Grune & Stratton.

————(1975), The Past and Future of Ego Psychology. *Psychoanal. Quart.*, 44:550-576.

Kanzer, M. (1973), Two Prevalent Misconceptions about Freud's "Project" (1895). *The Annual of Psychoanalysis*, 1:83-103. New York: Quadrangle.

Klein, G. (1970), Two Theories or One? *Bull. Menninger Clin.*, 37:2,99-132, 1973.

Miller, I., rep. (1975), A Critical Assessment of the Future of Psychoanalysis: A View from Within. *J. Amer. Psychoanal. Assn.*, 23:139-153.

Pribram, K. H., & Gill, M. M. (1976), *Freud's "Project" Reassessed*. New York: Basic Books; London: Hutchinson.

Rapaport, D. (1959), The Structure of Psychoanalytic Theory: A Systematizing Attempt. *Psychol. Issues*, Monogr. No. 6. New York: International Universities Press, 1960.

———— & Gill, M. M. (1959), The Points of View and Assumptions of Metapsychology. *Internat. J. Psycho-Anal.*, 40:153-162.

Rubinstein, B. (1967), Explanation and Mere Description: A Metascientific Examination of Certain Aspects of the Psychoanalytic Theory of Motivation. In: Motives and Thought: Psychoanalytic Essays in Honor of David Rapaport, ed. R. R. Holt. *Psychol. Issues*, Monogr. No. 18/19:20-77. New York: International Universities Press.

Schafer, R. (1970), An Overview of Heinz Hartmann's Contributions to Psychoanalysis. *Internat. J. Psycho-Anal.*, 51:425-446.

————(1972), Internalization: Process or Fantasy? *The Psychoanalytic Study of the Child*, 27:411-436. New York: Quadrangle.

————(1973a), Action: Its Place in Psychoanalytic Interpretation and Theory. *The Annual of Psychoanalysis*, 1:159-196. New York: Quadrangle.

————(1973b), Concepts of Self and Identity and the Experience of Separation-Individuation in Adolescence. *Psychoanal. Quart.*, 52:42-59.

————(1973c), The Idea of Resistance. *Internat. J. Psycho-Anal.*, 54:259-285.

————(1975), Psychoanalysis without Psychodynamics. *Internat. J. Psycho-Anal.*, 56:41-55.

4

EMOTION IN THE LANGUAGE OF ACTION

ROY SCHAFER

PREFACE

In the following pages I present some of the most crucial sections of a lengthy discussion of the emotions that will constitute one chapter of my forthcoming book on the idea of action. I shall be referring repeatedly in this discussion to *action language*, which I offer as an alternative to the nineteenth-century, natural-scientific, physicochemical, and biological language that Freud used in framing his clinical and theoretical propositions, the propositions by which he constituted the new discipline of psychoanalysis. I have already published a number of papers setting forth the rationale, the rules, and some applications of this alternative language (1972, 1973a, 1973b, 1973c, 1974, 1975), and I refer the reader to these articles for a more thorough introduction to my project than I shall provide here. In one paper particularly (1974), I have set forth an approach to the emotions through action language. That paper, though more comprehensive than the present one, is also far more sketchy, having been designed for a different purpose; nevertheless, it might contain answers to questions that may arise from a study of the following argument. Also, I shall raise some important questions that I shall not attempt to deal with at this time. It ought to be possible, however, for the reader to understand this argument, so far as it is developed here, from just this exposure to it.

This work has been supported by the Foundation for Research in Psychoanalysis and the Old Dominion Fund.

I do not apologize for the fact that, in honoring the memory of George Klein, I am presenting work in progress: the truth is that all work must be work in progress, and no one would appreciate this simultaneously exciting and frustrating fact more than George, for he was always — and in the best sense of the phrase — intellectually on the go.

INTRODUCTION

There are so many links between the idea of emotion and other key ideas about human existence that the prospect of discussing the emotions seems as forbidding as the prospect of discussing life itself. This prospect becomes all the more formidable once it is realized how readily almost any reader might become emotional in reacting to what is being said about emotions, as if he or she necessarily had a large personal stake in how the topic was being handled — indeed, as if it were his or her own feelings that somehow were being endangered. And this, of course, is inevitably the case, for how one thinks of the emotions establishes what they will be, not to speak of the esteem in which they will be held. As I shall argue in the following pages, what we call our emotions are not simply "there" as entities of some sort to be thought about; they are "there" only by virtue of a certain kind of thinking that designates them entities to begin with. Moreover, few people are likely to welcome the advice to give up the infinite possibilities of literary device, both good and bad, which, in keeping with our present unsystematized approach to the emotions, continue to remain available to us, for the seemingly lifeless possibilities of systematic discourse on this topic.

Nevertheless, because it is my goal to lay out the possibility of an action language in the major areas of personal psychology, I must chance a discussion of the emotions. I shall not, however, be presenting an empirical psychology of specific emotions. Rather, I shall be working out the problems involved in using action language consistently in discussing emotions. Even for that purpose, it would be tedious to discuss in detail the action approach to every emotion of general interest. As my project is methodological, as my chief concern is with knowing *how*, it should suffice to discuss instances of emotion that are, from my standpoint of language usage, strategically significant.

Specifically, I shall be considering such questions as the following: Working within the context of action language, does it make sense to say that we express emotion or that we carry with us old or deep or pent-up emotion? When, if ever, are the words feel and feeling precise and useful in the vocabulary of emotions? Are the emotions even to be spoken of as nouns, that is, as substantives? Is it not preferable to view them as actions and ways of acting rather than as things or events we experience or as abstract designations of these? In other words, are not verbs and adverbs more suitable than nouns and adjectives for speaking of the emotions? What must we now think of other ways we have of attributing substance and spatial location to emotion, that is, when we speak of emotional withdrawal, displacement, layering, state, locus, and mixture? Further, what can it mean to speak of sincere, deep, and real emotion as opposed to artificial, shallow, and pretended emotion? What of preverbal emotions? Nonverbal empathy? And, especially, what of the vexing question of "unconscious emotion"?

Other questions we shall be considering refer to more abstract propositions. If adopting an action language entails our no longer using such mechanistic, substantializing conceptions as impulse, force, energy, threshold, and discharge, how are we to construe and use terms like activity and passivity in speaking of emotions? (See, in this regard, Rapaport, 1953.) Can we ever suffer emotions, or must we always be, in the terms of this language, making and choosing them through the actions we engage in, including self-observation and labeling? If the latter, what could it mean to say that we make and choose emotions, and what does our answer to this question entail for our ideas of situation, stimulus, reaction, and experience? Are even those emotions that are felt in extreme situations, or under compulsion, to be viewed as made and chosen rather than suffered and fully determined? If so, what place would we then give to the physiological changes that are involved in so many emotions? And what significance, if any, would be retained by "the conflict theory of emotions" and "the signal theory of emotions"? The preceding questions illustrate some of the various forms in which we shall encounter the fundamental question of activity and passivity in emotional life. But first the language itself.

The Language

1. VERBS AND ADVERBS

The logic of action language dictates the correct approach to the emotions: to forego the use of substantives in making emotion statements and to employ only verbs and adverbs for this purpose. For action language, emotions are to be rendered as actions or modes of action. Thus, one is not to speak of an emotion (or an affect or a feeling); one is to speak of doing an emotion action or doing an action emotionally. This is the correct approach because it enforces consistent regard for the principle that one is speaking of people as agents, that is, as the performers of actions. What we call emotion is one of the things people do or one of the ways in which they do things.

Verbs specify the emotion actions. These verbs include to love, to hate, to fear, to grieve, and to enjoy.

Adverbs specify the emotion modes of action. These adverbs include lovingly, hatefully, fearfully, and so on. They modify any number of verbs that are in themselves neutral, such as to walk, to talk, and to think. One speaks then of walking fearfully, talking hatefully, thinking lovingly, and so forth.

People frequently use verbs and adverbs in just these ways. Far from proposing new usage or new words, I am proposing that we limit ourselves to these ways and forego the abstract nouns or substantives, such as love, hatred, fear, grief, and joy, which people also use frequently and typically concretize and personify. In connection with love, for example, they speak of what *it* is and what *it* does, of *its* properties and *its* tendencies, of *its* source and *its* influence. In contrast, in the context of action language, one speaks of those actions a person must perform in order to love and what acting lovingly entails. Emotion is rendered as action and mode of action.

feel opposed to the idea that only verbs and adverbs may now be used as emotion words. Most people have a strong reluctance to adopting a new language and thereby committing themselves to a changed mode of thought. In making the change, even though one would still be using easily understandable and even familiar English locutions, one would have to give up using many of the familiar conventions, if not simply repeating tried-and-true phrases. One would be moving into a world of being that is different enough to be alarming. We are all used to and secure in the world in which we treat emotion as an *it*—an entity with a name of its own and properties of its own, the latter being designated by adjectives in some respects and, with regard to apparently ineffable aspects, approximated by more or less elaborate, witty, and poetic metaphors and other literary devices. In moving into the modified world of action language, emotion would become a *how* or a *thus* rather than an *it*. Emotion would be fully and necessarily designated by verbs and adverbs; there would be no residual. Within the framework of this language, to sense that there is a residual could only mean that one is dissatisfied and would like to search for additional verbs and adverbs to render one's meaning more fully or exactly. For these verbs and adverbs are not *about* emotion; they are emotion conceived. What cannot be stated with verbs and adverbs cannot be emotion, though it can become emotion once it is ultimately statable in appropriate terms; otherwise, it must remain emotion unconceived, no more than a potential idea. To accept this formulation is to allow a radical assault on the many modes of thinking by which, unconsciously, we shape our observations and our theoretical discourse.

Opposition to this thesis might, however, be grounded elsewhere than in this challenge to accustomed modes of being. It might be argued that to follow my recommendation for an action language would be to eliminate any basis for deciding on the truth value of propositions concerning emotion. In mounting such an argument, one would insist that, in any objective or true statement, there has to be some *it* to which the emotion words correspond. Certainly, to be meaningful, our empirical statements about emotions have to be falsifiable; otherwise, one could say anything concerning emotion, regardless of how empty or absurd. But this is not at all a logical consequence of my thesis. Even if they are not universally agreed upon in every respect, the rules for using the verbs and adverbs in question, or, if one prefers, the criteria for the correct application of these words, are well known and generally regarded as useful. Thus, we do know what it is to make a mistake in referring to emotion, to disagree about it, and to muster proof for our point of view. For example, what we call love or grief or hatred, using substantives, is the more or less conventional performing of certain emotion actions or of certain actions emotionally, and nothing other than that! The *it* to which the verbs and adverbs correspond is the set of actions and modes in question, and that is sufficient for practical questions of truth. This has always been the case. I shall develop this counterargument more fully as I proceed through the chapter.

Another apparent ground for criticism of my thesis is the seeming interchangeability of verb and adverb renditions of ideas concerning emotion. To hate and to act hatefully, to fear and to act fearfully, and so forth: each pair seems to consist of two ways of saying the same thing. Consequently, it could be argued that, in the interest of clarity and economy, this action language ought to settle on just one form, the verb or the adverb. But the interchangeability is not total; for example, we do not use anxiety as an active verb and so there is no direct or verb counterpart to the adverb anxiously. There is an additional consideration, having to do with the nature of the emotion verbs themselves, that should serve to mitigate dissatisfaction with this thesis. It is this: on inspection, these

emotion verbs seem to be at least moderately abstract terms
that subsume a variety of emotion actions and actions performed emotionally. For example, in saying that A fears B,
one is referring to a family of actions, including flight or
avoidance, and modes of action, including actions performed
timidly or placatingly. Ordinarily, only specific conditions
need be present before people will agree that the verb to fear
has been rightly used. That the referents of the emotion verbs
may themselves be regarded as abstractions with referents of
their own does not weaken my point about the emotion verbs.
As abstractions, these verbs facilitate flexibility and economy
of expression. Although it is true that these advantages are
gained at the expense of precision or specificity, it is also true
(a) that that expense is limited by standardized usage, which
reduces the likelihood of inconsistency or internal contradiction, and (b) that that expense is more than offset by the
important gain of flexibility and economy in communication.
It is not always to the point to spell everything out. Usage is a
good guide here. Emotion verbs are in abundant supply.

It is, however, conceivable that all the emotion adverbs are
ultimately reducible directly or indirectly to verbs, which is to
say that ultimately they refer to actions, and that a mode of
action is a set of actions with a certain kind of internal consistency. Nevertheless, for the sake of freedom of exploration
and flexibility of expression, I should like to leave this question
open at the present time. This I may do without sacrificing the
idea of the primacy of actions.

2. "HEART" AND THE BODILY REPRESENTATION OF EMOTION

It is characteristic of infantile thinking, as it is of everyday
speech, to represent emotion actions and emotion modes in
bodily terms. In ordinary language, we so take for granted the
bodily figures of speech that they seem natural, true, inevitable rather than imaginative. And yet, upon reflection, it is
not difficult to realize that we are in this way using and
suggesting common irrational, animistic fantasies about the
anatomy, physiology, life cycle, and social context of the
body. So it is that casually, even unthinkingly, we invoke the

intestines (guts), the liver (lily-livered), the spine (spineless), and the testicles (no balls), and we go on in this way about the stomach, spleen, buttocks, feces, urine, blood, senses, birth, death, contact, and, time and time again, the heart. To illustrate some of the principal consequences of these essentially archaic, though conventionalized, body-centered locutions, I shall center my remarks in this section on the idea of heart.

Obviously, the locutions in question are not drawn directly from the language of theoretical psychoanalysis. Yet it is ordinary language that is the great reservoir of the mind-formative locutions encountered by the young, language-learning child, and, as I shall try to show, we theorize with unacknowledged biases and constraints corresponding to these locutions. Far more than we have dared to realize, our psychoanalytic propositions concerning the emotions have been technical, scientific, or professional versions of this ordinary body language.

"Heart": In everyday speech we refer to the heart as the source and container of emotions. Usually, we reserve heart for positively valued emotions or emotional conduct, as when, with more or less clear meaning, we say hearty, heartfelt, big-hearted, a full heart, a broken heart, have a heart, and heavy heart. In such instances we seem to mean loving, compassionate, generous, tender, vigorous, courageous, concerned, responsible, and other such "good things." But heart is also ambiguous enough to require qualification in many instances; it does not always denote a warm, lively quality of emotions. For instance, we say chickenhearted as well as stouthearted, coldhearted as well as warmhearted, and, equally for hate and love, we say with all one's heart and from the bottom of one's heart.

The logical faults of these locutions are obvious. The heart is being put in place of the person, which is to say that the speaker is either personifying an organ or portraying a way of acting as a substance or a quantity of energy of a certain kind; moreover, this substance or energy, if it is not presented as being dispensed by a heart of a certain disposition, is at least held to emanate from the heart. In comparable synecdoches, people reduce themselves to "brain" or "mind" when they say such things as "scatterbrained" or "a logical mind" (Schafer, 1973a). Depending on the psychoanalyst's context of goals and concepts, this substitution of part for whole may be viewed as a splitting of self or ego, a projection into an organ of an attribute of self or ego or id, magical thinking, a disclaimer of responsibility, a fantasy of being invaded or controlled by some foreign agency (as by a god, e.g., Cupid), etc. But, however one views these locutions concerning heart, one must conclude from the extensive use people make of them and of comparable locutions, that the substantializing and personifying of emotion actions and emotion modes are major structural features of the way people think about themselves and others.

Here are some translations of heart locutions into the action language of verbs and adverbs. A warmhearted person is someone who deals affectionately and generously with others. A chickenhearted person is one who fearfully avoids dealing with ordinary dangers. A hearty person is one who does a variety of things vigorously, zestfully, and good-humoredly. When people have a heart-to-heart talk, they are making known to each other certain emotional ways in which they have been thinking about and dealing with each other, ways which hitherto they have kept private, indirect, vague, or even mostly unformulated or incoherently formulated.

In presenting these translations, I count on the goodhearted reader to bear in mind that translation is necessarily both approximate and transformative. In the following section I shall consider at greater length the complex action of translating ordinary emotion words into action language.

3. FIVE EXAMPLES

I now present five brief essays on specific emotions: anger, happiness, guilt, fear, and love. It is my purpose to illustrate the differences between using for our emotion words nouns on the one hand and verbs and adverbs on the other, and to show how it seems best at present to use action language with respect to the emotions. In passing, I shall have occasion to demonstrate how such theoretical ideas as aggression and libido simply repeat the modes of ordinary language.

A. *Anger and angrily.* In daily life, we have created an emotional entity that we call anger. We have done so by giving it a name in noun form. We think of this entity as being a substance or quantity of energy that behaves somehow like a person in its being insistent, devious, emphatic, destructive, and so forth. As one analysand said, "It's bad if I let it do to me what it did—overwhelm me." Speaking of a third person, another analysand said, "If his emotions of anger are aroused, they make him violent."

As a substance, the entity anger may be implicitly liquid (when it is said to spill over), solid (when it is said to crush or penetrate), gaseous (when it is said that one must keep the lid on it), or some combination of the three. Thinking unconsciously, we usually represent this entity as excrement: feces (firm or loose), urine (flooding or burning), or flatus (explosive or poisonous). Further, this excremental stuff is personified or conceived animistically so that it exhibits such properties of agency as being furtive, persecutory, or recalcitrant.

In thinking this way about anger, one necessarily thinks of oneself as having to contend with this inspirited stuff; that is to say, one thinks that, though this entity is *in* the self, it is not *of* the self, so that the self must act in relation to it or deal with it. One makes of anger (and thereby also of one's excremental substances, organs, and urges) one's demon, though sometimes one thinks of it (and them) as one's ally or valuable weapon.

Let us make a leap here (not a huge one, really) to the psychoanalytic theory of aggression. Following Freud, we have established aggression in psychoanalytic theory as an instinctual impulsion. We hold aggression to be an energy of destructive quality. It is destructive in the sense that its potential is restricted to bringing about fragmenting, oppositional, hurtful, eliminative, sullying, or alienating effects. Or, if not necessarily destructive, this energy is oppositional and divisive, perhaps useful in setting boundaries and asserting rights, privileges, and responsibilities, but in any case destined for and limited to some version of fight or attack. Further, according to our traditional Freudian theorizing, when one feels anger or expresses it, one is experiencing the increase or discharge of a quantity of aggression or aggressive energy. It should be obvious, once one has reflected on the questions of action language and of personification, that in this theory one is speaking of aggression as though it were the personified substance or quantity of everyday speech, as described above. It does not go too far, I think, to suggest that, however austerely this conceptualization may be expressed, it implies an animistic excremental model of aggression (see also Grossman and Simon, 1969).

For the purpose of developing an action language, which requires us to avoid setting up one or another kind of entity or "it," we must stop using this conception of aggression, and of such forms of it as anger. We must replace aggression with "acting aggressively" and anger with "acting angrily" (see also Hayman, 1969; Gillespie, 1971). Our criteria for using the verb and the adverb will be the same criteria we have used when invoking the term aggression, for, as before, angry is as angry does. This angry mode of acting might include certain kinds of speeded-up physiological activity, tensed muscles, striking out, thoughts of attack that may be subjectively defined as vengeance or defense or even pleasure, biting fiercely, and so on and so forth. The one who is acting angrily and the others who may be witnesses of the actions in question may not realize that he or she is acting that way, but in principle one and all could realize it; this is so because, as there is no entity emotion but only ways of acting emotionally, there can be no privileged access to anger (a point to which I shall return in several places below); there can only be more or less informed observations made by people. Among the observers may be one who is possibly, but not necessarily, an especially knowledgeable observer, the one who performs the acts in question—the agent. In his essay "Other Minds," J. L. Austin has presented a similar discussion of emotion in general and anger in particular (1946).

B. *Happiness and happily.* In daily life, we speak of one's heart as capable of filling with happiness, of people seeking and finding happiness (the pursuit of happiness), and of the destruction of happiness. In each instance we speak as though happiness were an entity. Having given it a noun name, we have apparently legitimized a concretistic way of thinking about the topic. Through similar locutions, we have made an animated "it" of joy, pleasure, hope, trust, serenity, bliss, and other such desirables.

In action language, however, the idea of happiness has to be replaced by the idea of doing actions happily. Let us accept it as a first approximation that to do actions happily is to be disposed, while doing them, to smile, laugh, sing, and dance; to embrace oneself and others; to speak favorably of oneself and one's situation and of other persons as well; and to think that one has what one wants and has it securely. When we observe others acting in some or all of these ways, we infer that they are happy, which is to say that we realize that they are doing things happily; it is not that they have or have found any entity happiness.

One of those whom one might observe doing things happily is oneself. To say this is to say that one's acting happily is something one may come to realize. In that instance, one will be making the same type of observations and drawing the same type of conclusions as one would in observing others. One would not be drawing on any privileged access to some otherwise unobservable entity called happiness. Whatever the reasons, sometimes one's readiness to sing and dance, for example, might not be visible to others—perhaps they are only minimally manifest—and in such instances one will just be better informed about oneself than others in this regard; and yet, one might also be far more biased than others in the course of observing one's own actions, as in the obvious instance of an analysand's trying in manic fashion to curb depressive actions.

One might, of course, effectively exclude doing actions one would do happily, if at all, just because of not wanting to be observed doing them in that way. Or one might be a careless or crude observer of one's own acting happily, just as one might tend to observe the actions of others faultily. Or one might not admit to oneself that one is acting happily: I have discussed this type of action in some detail in my paper on resistance (1973c). But in none of these cases is it implied that, after all these other factors have been subtracted, some residual pure emotion exists, which is in principle reachable only by the "introspecting" subject. We cannot, in this sense, ask what happiness "is." There is not even a specific physiology of happiness.

On the same grounds, we can argue the necessity, within action language, of the adverbial designations joyfully, trustfully, hopefully, pleasurably, serenely, wistfully, and so forth. In some instances, there are also available to us proper and useful verb designations, such as to hope and to trust.

In his *Ethics*, especially in Book X, Aristotle argues that we should regard pleasure as an attribute of action rather than as an entity or process: the possibility and desirability of an action language for the emotions is, I think, derivable from Aristotle's discussion, particularly with the help of Ryle's (1949) and Austin's (1946, 1956) modern contributions.

C. *Guilt and guiltily.* Guilt is another of the emotional entities we have created by giving it a name in noun form. Sometimes this entity is material, as when it is said to be a load of guilt to be cast off; sometimes it is ghostly, as when it is said to haunt or to torment. Guilt is often personified as an inner tyrant, a judge or a policeman, demanding that one be exposed and punished; it was in connection with these versions that Freud said he preferred "need for punishment" to "guilt." In any event, when we are seeking to evade guilt or to atone, we are, as it were, maneuvering in relation to this harsh authority.

In its intrapersonal rather than interpersonal aspect, one thinks that it is oneself who is doing the scolding or punishing, perhaps unconsciously. We call this aspect by the name Freud gave it, the superego. Consequently, when we speak as traditional Freudians, we no longer say that one sometimes judges one's own actions in an irrational and severely moral-istic manner, or especially that one does so even unbeknown to oneself, that is, unconsciously; now we say it is one's superego that (or who) judges one's ego (or one's self) in those ways. Thus, we set up superego as a personified entity of another sort: a so-called psychic structure that performs prohibitive, judgmental, and punitive actions.

Like the noun anger, however, the noun guilt is an unsatisfactory designation of the phenomena to which it pertains. At least, it is not acceptable within the framework of action language; in that framework, the phenomena in question are ways of acting—namely, guiltily. These ways include acting as if one expects some deserved punishment, thinks of oneself as an immoral wretch, tries to bring about a "punishing" by some agency in one's environment, or else punishes oneself through self-imposed deprivation, humiliation, pain, or injury. Both as characteristics of thinking or as features of publicly observable deeds, these ways of acting constitute the meaning of the adverb guiltily; they are its referents or what we use the word to suggest or point to.

As I mentioned, one may act guiltily without recognizing that one is doing so. In this case we might speak of unconsciously acting guiltily or unconsciously desiring punishment. Other people who are observing one's actions of this sort may not realize consciously that one is acting guiltily; this may be the result of their ignorance, their being deceived, or their behaving repressively with respect to the very idea. In principle, however, anyone, including oneself, might get to realize consciously that one is acting guiltily, for this way of acting, like acting angrily, is a knowable, even though not presently known, mode of action. It is not ineffable or privileged.

Other words with dysphoric meaning will have to be chosen and framed in the same way in the course of using action language systematically: for example, sadly rather than sadness; miserably rather than misery; depressively rather than depression; and the same for suspiciously, despairingly, and agitatedly. In some instances, suitable verb forms are directly available: for example, to suspect, to despair, to regret.

D. *Fear, to fear, and fearfully.* Along with the entities
anger, happiness, and guilt, we have created the entity fear
and endowed it with the properties of agency. We say of fear
that it grips us, strikes us, betrays us, paralyzes us, overwhelms
us. Fear may lurk, hide, creep, loom, attack. It may be a
wave, a flood, a spasm, a twinge, or a fit. As if reactively, the
self or ego may yield to it, suppress it, nip it in the bud, or use
it as a signal, as a tool of interpersonal relation, or as a mode
of erotic gratification ("libidinization of anxiety"). In contrast, we render the idea adequately through action language
in the form of the adverb fearfully and the verb to fear. In
both instances, we should be able to specify, whenever necessary, at least some of the bodily changes, public behavior, and
thought actions that are the referents, and so the occasions, of
these terms. Among other things, to fear is to engage in
fantasies of harm coming to one from some source of danger;
to develop ideas of fleeing from that danger or else attacking
its source; to make incipient movements of attack or escape,
which involve setting off physiological changes that enable the
anticipated exertions to be performed; to be restless; and
either to be hypervigilant or to avoid representing the danger
consciously (denial, repression). It is when we see people doing
these actions in these ways that we say in action language that
they fear something or that they are acting fearfully, whereas
in the substantive mode we say that they are filled with fear,
dominated by fear, stricken with fear, or something of that
sort.

It should be noted that in neither language are we implying
the necessary presence of a correct, conscious recognition of
the danger or even of *a* danger. So-called phobias and anxiety
attacks illustrate this independence of fear propositions from
consciously and correctly ascertained dangers. Freud favored
the use of fear for real, conscious dangers, and anxiety for
dangers that are irrational, unconscious, disguised, or name-
less. We may adhere to this verbal convention without under-
cutting the preceding argument concerning the uses of the
words fear, to fear, and fearfully, for the fact is that we might
just as well have considered the words anxiety and anxiously as

our key terms, and, in the same way, seen how the noun anxiety is unsuitable for action language and unnecessary in it.

E. *Love, to love, and lovingly.* In action language, to love and to act lovingly are the proper forms for rendering the idea of love. Having thereby lost its status as an entity, love can no longer make the world go round; can no longer glow, grow, or wither; and can no longer be lost or found, cherished, poisoned, or destroyed. Now we regard those kinds of concretistic and personified ideas as referring to actions we perform and ways in which we act, including thought actions and ways of thinking. It is we who regard the world as going round, in that excited sense of the image; it is we who glow, love more or love less, love at all or stop loving, or imagine wildly and perhaps unconsciously that our heart or mind has been poisoned.

We should pause to review the idea of libido in connection with this analysis of love words, for the same reasons that, earlier, we reviewed the idea of aggression in connection with anger words. In speaking of libido, we merely give the appearance of endowing discussions of sex, pleasure, and attachment with the (presumed) scientific "dignity" of mechanics or electrostatics. In fact, an impartial inspection of how we use libido makes it plain that we make this hypothetical energy serve as a poetic condensation of many concretistic, personified ideas. In our theoretical propositions, we present libido as an energy that waxes and wanes; accumulates and is discharged; attaches itself tenaciously to ideas of people and things, but may also be abruptly and totally withdrawn from them in response to the vicissitudes of existence, in which case the withdrawing agency is an ego that is itself constituted by this energy whose nature it is to bind things together. Additionally, although libido is modifiable as to its urgency, in its pure state it is imperious in its biologically based demands; in the extreme — in its uncompromising drive toward pleasure at any cost — it may even overwhelm and demolish the established ego or self and its world. With this status, libido also seems to stand as the link between body and mind; Freud presented it just this way. But barely concealed behind the physicochemical and biological words being used are, primarily, ideas of young blood coursing through one's veins, clinging lovers, rapists, unrestrained masturbators, preorgastic ecstasy, and ejaculate substance, together with warm and moist wombs, drooling mouths, and incontinent sphincters; secondarily, there are ideas about the many superficially nonsensual forms of self-satisfaction and satisfaction in others that may also be thrilling in their own way, as, for example, the forms of vanity, triumph, devotion, and awe. I suggest, therefore, that the popularity of libido rests on its serving so well as a quasi-scientific poetic metaphor for all the more or less urgent or unrestrained pleasurable actions people do or imagine doing and all the excited and pleasurable ways in which they might perform any act at all; and on its serving in the same way for the body parts, substances, and changes that may be involved in these activities and modes of activity.

As psychoanalysts generally speak of libido in connection with both love and pleasure, I did not sort out the two uses in the preceding paragraphs, even though the theme of this subsection is the idea of love. I believe that it was legitimate to proceed in this way in order further to clarify the background of my attempt to develop an action language for the emotions.

4. THE CONTROL OF EMOTION

The critical questions to be confronted by any theory of the emotions include two concerning emotional control. Just what it is that one controls when, as we say, one controls one's emotions? And just what is it that one does in controlling one's emotions? Our answers to these two questions are generally significant in that they are bound to represent essential aspects of what we mean by emotion. Let us consider the questions in order.

Three classes of referents of emotion seem implicit in the idea of control of emotion: (1) emotive actions; (2) thought actions; (3) actions to change one's situation in the environment.

(1) Emotive actions are those involved in public manifestations of acting emotionally. In controlling these, one controls the visibility of one's acting emotionally. These emotive actions include facial expressions, gestures, exclamations, tones of voice, postures, and movements toward or away from others, one's surroundings, or one's body. The nature of this class of actions is complex in that these emotive actions are not simply signals of or statements about one's acting emotionally. They are constitutive of it. Any change in the actions implies a change in the emotion; for can an emotion, understood now as acting emotionally in some way, remain unchanged once one or another of its emotive manifestations has been inhibited or disguised? In relying on the traditional psychoanalytic discharge model of emotion, which sets up emotion as a substantive, we commit ourselves to thinking that the inhibited or disguised emotion remains the same, whereas, in adopting the action model, we commit ourselves to thinking that the inhibiting or disguising person is engaging in an action which is different from, though still related to, the action of a person who is simply and unconcernedly being visibly emotional. For example, although holding back tears overlaps outright weeping in the emotional action it implies, let us say grieving, the action of holding back implies that the person in question, more than grieving at that very moment, is perhaps concerned with considerations of pride and shame before oneself and others or with the danger of being, so to say, "overwhelmed by despair." That person's relation to the grieving, a relation of representation and valuation, must be different from that of the person who simply grieves. Thus, it makes no sense to say that the emotion is the same in the two cases, even though we might still simply call it grief. Restrained grieving is *another kind* of grieving; it is a more complex emotional action. To be exact, one would have to say that the person in question is grieving restrainedly, or is refraining from grieving conspicuously, rather than saying simply that the person is grieving. In clinical psychoanalysis, one would appropriately implement the technical consideration of vigilantly taking account in one's interventions of the analysand's resisting by referring

in some useful way to the analysand's actions as grieving *restrainedly*, when that is the case. In contrast, a simple reference by the analyst to the grieving could be correctly, though concretely, characterized as an attempt to break through or circumvent the resisting instead of analyzing it.

(2) Thought actions include performances that psychoanalytic ego psychologists commonly refer to as functions and mechanisms, such as perceiving, comprehending, synthesizing, repressing, anticipating, and attending. By these thought actions, one may control one's view of one's situation, which is to control the occasion and the significance of the emotion in question, and thereby to transform one's emotional position or even eliminate the possibility of acting emotionally. For example, one may review one's impressions, gather more information, take stock of one's prospects, establish certain attitudes such as resignation or detachment, or unconsciously overlook or forget or reverse certain salient features of one's situation — all to the point where one would no longer feel the same way or feel it as strongly as before. One now has less reason or no reason to feel the same way. Like the control of emotive actions, the control of thought actions alters the emotion in question; however, of the two, its potential influence for change is much greater. Analysts presuppose this when they make interpretations.

(3) Actions to alter one's situation in the environment include leaving the scene, confronting an antagonist, offering or demanding an explanation, and finding a friend or a shelter or a weapon. Also included are the emotive actions one does or does not perform insofar as these affect the environment (e.g., the actions of others). By altering circumstances and one's relation to them in such ways, one controls one's acting emotionally by seeing to it that one no longer has grounds, or substantial grounds, for continuing to act that way. Again, it is really a *change* of emotion that is implied by the idea of control. Seeming merely to keep control of the emotion, one may even go so far as to transform it into its opposite, for better or worse. But, in this type of instance, as in the other two, it is not an entity, emotion, that is trans-

formed by one's actions; it can only be the actions and modes of actions themselves, including those that constitute one's subjective situation.

Ordinarily, the distinction between classes (2) and (3), while not absolute, is easily made both in everyday life and in clinical work. For instance, with reference to types of control, we do not confuse "I reconsidered" or "I finally understood that he was frightened" with "I got rid of that troublemaker" and "I went looking for a familiar face." And certainly, classes (1), (2), and (3) are not mutually exclusive: in grieving restrainedly, one might be concurrently (1) holding back tears, (2) looking at the bright side of things, and (3) searching for a new person to love.

The three classes of transforming (controlling) actions leave no residuals that I can identify.

The second major question I asked at the beginning of this section was this: Just what is it that one does in controlling emotions? In effect, I have already dealt with this question in the course of answering the first question: Just what is it that one controls . . .? In exercising control, we do not manipulate emotions in any sense that is analogous to manipulating objects in nature. Emotions are not entities; they are actions and modes of action. The idea of a method of control refers to how one establishes another way of engaging in emotive actions, thought actions, modifications of circumstances and relationships, or some combination of these three classes of factors. In exercising control, one behaves, thinks, and otherwise performs differently in order to be differently emotional or differently disposed emotionally.

In this discussion, the idea of control has given way completely to the idea of change! Now we are speaking of agents changing their actions in order to change their emotions, that is, their emotional actions or modes of acting emotionally.

As to its background, the idea of control is rooted in the tendency to concretize and personify mental processes in general; I have already touched on this point in several places (see also Schafer, 1972). Additionally, the idea of control seems to have considerable objective, empirical support of the following sort: repeatedly, it seems that, upon ceasing to exercise control after once having instituted it, one proceeds to act just as one initially did act or wanted to act. Aside from noting the fact that this is often a false appearance — counting to ten can make a difference! — it is important to realize that it does no harm to my argument to allow for the possibility that, following a suspension of control, one might revert to one's initial, actual, or imagined emotional actions and modes of action. Then, one's acting once again fearfully, lustfully, or furiously, for example, may be descriptively indistinguishable from one's having acted in one of those ways earlier. Allowing for this possibility does no harm to my argument, for it need not imply that some emotion entity was there, like a caged wild animal, inside and unchanged all the while it was being controlled. One might just as well — and far more rationally and systematically — say that one has again changed both one's view of one's situation and one's actions, this time repeating a view and actions that are indistinguishable from those initially established and performed or imagined; presumably matters are once again being dealt with in a less complex way.

With regard to the question how it is possible to repeat a view and perform other, related actions in this way, the following argument is the essential one: to insist that there must be some static form of the entity "there" to be reactivated or some old channels still there for the energies to flow through once more can only be a preconception. This preconception informs all of Freud's theorizing.

The use of action language offers distinct advantages in this regard: it does not require us to split off emotion from controlling person or agent; it does not commit us to substantialize and animate the emotions or the controls or defenses; it does not set up a large class of disclaimers with regard to the various aspects of emotional activity (Schafer, 1973a); and it does not impede our making further and finer observations by supporting the seductive alternative with which we are so familiar, of substituting commonplace or dramatic metaphors for thinking through our conceptual problems.

The argument of this section can be summed up simply. In

the end, although much may be changed and the consequences may be terribly disturbing or intensely gratifying, nothing is lost in a loss of control.

5. THE EXPRESSION OF EMOTION, VERBAL AND OTHERWISE

The idea of expressing emotion is based on the two interrelated presuppositions that emotion is (or may be spoken of as) a substance or quantity of energy and that self or person is (or may be spoken of as) a place, a container, or a set of channels. This is so because to speak at all of expressing emotion is to imply both that there is an entity to be "pressed" and that it is pressed from the inside to the outside. Considering the idea of expression in the light of the preceding sections of this chapter, furthermore, we can realize that its use entails rendering emotion as a noun rather than an adverb or verb. But once we reject presuppositions of substance and place, we are doubly wrong to speak of expressing emotions (Schafer, 1972, 1973a, 1973b).

In rejecting the idea of expression, we will also reject give vent to, pour out, get out, release, discharge, unpack, and other cathartic metaphors. For the same reasons, we will reject those locutions referring to *not* expressing, such as stifle, hide, store up, put the lid on, bottle up, and subdue.

There is a more subtle form of conceiving emotion as an entity rather than an action or attribute of action; we encounter it in locutions that refer in one way or another to putting feelings into words or giving voice to feelings. The idea of expressing emotion often implies putting emotions into words. This is especially so in the context of clinical psychoanalysis and other "talking treatments." Briefly, the critical argument against this usage is this: to say that one is putting an emotion into words implies both that the emotion has an independent existence and that it does not change by virtue of being verbalized; put otherwise, it implies that an emotion is what it is apart from its name and the words and gestures and other mental activities, such as self-observation, through which it appears in the world. If one makes of emotion an entity or "it," one establishes the idea that it is something one may have and about which one may do this, that, or the other thing. Thus, it seems that one may speak of an emotion in the same way one speaks of a chair, that is, as a thing that is given, whether or not one calls it by that name or by any name. (I realize, but bypass, the fact that there are even limits to the correctness of this idea about material things and their names.) A more adequate discussion of the issues raised in this section will require extended consideration of the ideas of subjective experience, naming, and interpretation; those discussions must be left for another place. Here, I have wanted to show mainly how the particular idea of expressing emotion involves us in fundamental conceptual problems.

Alternatives to the idea of expressing emotion or putting emotion into words include the following: say something emotionally and aloud; say it despite misgivings; say it more clearly and fully than before; say it demonstratively; and stop imagining it and begin to describe it, communicate it, or confess it. In each instance, one will be specifying an action or a mode of action or both, and so one will be devising locutions consistent with the rules of action language.

6. CONSCIOUS, PRECONSCIOUS, AND UNCONSCIOUS EMOTION

The ideas conscious, preconscious, and unconscious are now to be rendered as modes of action, that is, as adverbs. Accordingly, their form changes to consciously, preconsciously, and unconsciously. As I have already discussed the translation of these modes of action at some length in my paper "The Idea of Resistance" (1973c), I shall limit myself here to specifying a few propositions that bear particularly on our taken-for-granted ways of discussing the emotions in relation to consciousness.

One may be or may become consciously aware that one is engaged in an emotion action or in a certain action in an emotion mode, or one may remain more (unconsciously) or less (preconsciously) unaware that this is the case. The same may be said both of other people's witnessing one's actions and modes of action and of oneself's witnessing the actions of others. When more fixedly unaware, one is acting resistantly or defensively, not only primarily with respect to the actions and modes in question, but secondarily with respect to one's acting resistively or defensively at all in this regard (unconscious defense).

Remaining unaware may be a consequence of engaging in some other action very attentively. For example, concentrating on solving an intellectual problem, one may for a time "forget one's troubles." In this instance, it is not necessarily germane to emphasize defensive or resistant aspects of the emotional obliviousness. Whether or not it would be germane to impose that emphasis would depend on how easily and comfortably the person in question could engage attentively in the emotion actions and corresponding modes, once he or she has set the other problem aside. That one may cling to absorbing projects defensively is, of course, a familiar observation, but not one that can be made in all relevant instances.

The unawareness may pertain to the person's not yet having established a specific vantage point from which to establish the relevant actions and modes in a clearly observable and comprehensible fashion. The useful vantage points especially include knowing the right or the best designations for the prevailing emotion context. Additionally, although defensiveness or resistiveness may well have been playing a part in the person's having not yet established a good vantage point in this connection, this need not always be the case or the entire case. We see that this is so when, on occasion, analysands readily and fruitfully employ the relevant designations supplied in an analytic interpretation; in these instances, one might speak of the analysand's having been resisting merely preconsciously. But we should not automatically exclude the possibility of a person's simply learning new connections and achieving new perspectives. To take a similar case, it would be sheer and foolish psychoanalytic dogmatism to insist that the illumination and expansion of emotional life achieved through writing and reading poetry are simply matters of overcoming resistances, although at the same time it would be irrationally *anti*psychoanalytic to insist that, in principle, such illumination and expansion could never or rarely occur through involving oneself in poetry or any other art.

We must also recognize this: what we resist being attentive to may exist only in the conditional mode, that is, as some action we *would* perform or some way of acting in which we *would* engage were it not for some circumstances, consequences, or objectives we regard as being more important, such as the dangers of losing possibilities of gratification and security (Schafer, 1973c). These conditional actions and modes are the "potential affects" of which Freud (1915) spoke when he decided that the idea of unconscious affect was not correct and useful. A potential affect can only be one which *would be* experienced were it not that such and such were the case. Our using action language helps us transcend Freud's dilemma in this connection: since affect is understood to be action and mode of action, and since it is now taken as the essential content with which we deal in our psychoanalytic propositions, we need not hesitate to say that any of these actions and modes may be performed unconsciously, preconsciously, or consciously; additionally, we may readily say of the conditional action or mode that it may exist in any one of these three modes of consciousness.

What is true for present actions and conditional actions is also true for past and future actions. Thus, that one did an emotion action or could have done it may be remembered unconsciously, preconsciously, or consciously; and that one will do it or might do it in the future may be anticipated in any one of these three modes of consciousness. We recognize that this is so in everyday speech; for example, with respect to love, we make such statements as, "You don't want to think about how much you once loved her," and "You stay clear of him because you are afraid you will fall in love with him."

Often, the question of unconscious or preconscious emotion appears in another guise, that is, as the question whether experience or knowing can be other than conscious. However, we are bound to regard experience and knowing as versions of action and not as authoritative records to be consulted through some kind of introspection; these are versions of observed and remembered emotive actions, thought actions, and actions relative to environmental circumstances. Consequently, there is no reason why, unlike other actions, they can only be performed consciously.

It must be noted, however, that it would be thinking carelessly and statically to hold that performing consciously what has hitherto been performed unconsciously entails no change in the properties of the action or mode of action in question. Thinking consciously is not like turning on a light in a dark room and then seeing an object that has remained unchanged by the changes in illumination. It is true that sometimes Freud spoke as though this were the case; he did so, for instance, in his basic explanation of consciousness as being a result of one's directing attention cathexis toward an idea. And it is also true that thinking consciously often shows such features of the primary process as distortion, logical contradiction, and fluidity. But Freud also stressed that to think consciously is to expose thoughts to the secondary process, which, as we know, is to think in a very different mode from that which ordinarily characterizes thinking unconsciously (the primary process). In this way, thinking consciously transforms the unconscious idea. A similar transformation results from actually speaking emotionally to another person instead of remaining emotionally private, that is, keeping one's feelings to oneself.

Transformation or enhanced transformability of thinking and feeling is central to Freud's theory of the therapeutic effect of interpretation, or what he called making the unconscious conscious. Ordinarily, to think of something consciously is to consider it in the context of a world of factual and hypothetical relationships that are more or less orderly, rational, realistic, interactive, and, as regards infantile danger situations, safe. Actions other than this thinking are themselves transformed on this very account; this includes emotion actions. And, if it is an emotion that is in question, it can only exist in another world of experience once one is in a position to consider and perform the implied emotion actions and emotion modes consciously.

Repressing an emotion action or emotion mode is a comparable transformation of situations and performances — in the reverse direction, of course.

I need not argue here that, both experientially and therapeutically, the modes consciously, preconsciously, and unconsciously are of inestimable significance and consequence. Logically, however, they are simply attributes of action on a par with such attributes as carelessly, conscientiously, hastily, and grudgingly, which is to say that, as adverbs, they simply indicate yet other ways in which actions may be carried out.

Finally, there is the matter of my referring to consciously, preconsciously, and unconsciously as though they correspond to three altogether distinct, discontinuous modes of action. My doing so should not be construed to mean my overlooking or ruling out graduated, complex, ambiguous, and concurrent versions of any one or more of them. The variety, subtlety, and complexity of the emotions; their apparent ineffability, delicacy, and evanescence; the sense in which we claim that we may have them and know them and communicate them *wordlessly*: all these attributes and claims derive in large part from the arrangements, sequences, and transitions of modes of performing actions.

Concluding Remarks

I omitted several sections along the way. One of these sections deals with the problematic emotion verb to feel and the related idea of feelings. Another deals with the verb to be as it is used to link a subject with an emotion adjective (e.g., "I am worried") and in its relation to emotion verbs and emotion adverbs. A third contains a discussion of the idea of experience, the gist of which has been included here. In subsequent sections of my forthcoming longer treatment of this topic, I plan to take up the naming and the interpretation of the emotions and such ideas as old, accumulated, mixed, displaced, withdrawn, layered, superficial and real emotions. Then, in a section generally organized around the question of activity and passivity, I plan to consider physiological correlates of the emotions, the conflict and signal theories, the ego as the seat of the emotions, moods, empathy, and extreme situations. Finally, I intend to discuss how, within this approach, the ideas *situation, experience,* and *action* co-constitute each other or mutually imply each other, and to take up some consequences of this proposition.

The sections I have presented here contain enough of my essential argument to enable those who read them closely to anticipate much of the work that is yet to appear. But, if there truly are transformative consequences of thinking consciously and speaking publicly, then I think that no one, including myself, ought to be able to anticipate them all, and I think so happily.

REFERENCES

Austin, J. L. (1946), Other Minds. In: *Philosophical Papers,* 2nd ed. New York: Oxford University Press, 1970, pp. 76-116.

——— (1956), A Plea for Excuses. In: *Philosophical Papers,* 2nd ed. New York: Oxford University Press, 1970, pp. 175-204.

Freud, S. (1915), The Unconscious. *Standard Edition,* 14:159-215. London: Hogarth Press, 1957.

Gillespie, R. (1971), Aggression and Instinct Theory. *Internat. J. Psycho-Anal.,* 52:155-160.

Grossman, W. I., & Simon, B. (1969), Anthropomorphism: Motive, Meaning, and Causality in Psychoanalytic Theory. *The Psychoanalytic Study of the Child,* 24:78-114. New York: International Universities Press.

Hayman, A. (1969), What Do We Mean by "Id"? *J. Amer. Psychoanal. Assn.,* 17:333-352.

Rapaport, D. (1953), On the Psycho-Analytic Theory of Affects. *Internat. J. Psycho-Anal.,* 34:177-198.

Ryle, G. (1949), *The Concept of Mind.* New York: Barnes & Noble, 1965.

Schafer, R. (1972), Internalization: Process of Fantasy? *The Psychoanalytic Study of the Child,* 27:411-436. New York: Quadrangle.

——— (1973a), Action: Its Place in Psychoanalytic Interpretation and Theory. *The Annual of Psychoanalysis,* 1:159-196. New York: Quadrangle.

——— (1973b), Concepts of Self and Identity and the Experience of Separation-Individuation in Adolescence. *Psychoanal. Quart.,* 52:42-59.

——— (1973c), The Idea of Resistance. *Internat. J. Psycho-Anal.,* 54:259-286.

———(1974), A Psychoanalytic View of Emotion. *Philosoph. Stud.,* 22:157-167.

———(1975), Psychoanalysis without Psychodynamics. *Internat. J. Psycho-Anal.,* 56:41-55.

5

THEORETICAL MODELS AND THE TREATMENT OF THE SCHIZOPHRENIAS

PHILIP S. HOLZMAN

> The ultimate evil is man's ability to
> make abstract that which is concrete.
> J.-P. Sartre

Psychoanalysis developed as an interpretative discipline rather than as an observational science. Its special strengths derive from its unique access to the patient's inner experiences, including his fears and hopes, his dreams and fantasies, his prides and shames, both those that can be consciously grasped and those that conceal their influence beyond awareness. Psychoanalysis concerns itself with the patient's beliefs and with their significance and meaning within a particular life. Analysts draw inferences from the associative material and behavior of patients within the psychoanalytic interview, and particularly from within that special set of behaviors called transference. No other discipline has been able to plumb the depths of inner experiences, to explore with such sensitivity a person's most intimate feelings and behaviors, and to give to them meaning and significance. This interpretative

Parts of this paper were presented at a Panel Discussion on "The Psychotherapy of Schizophrenia," American Psychoanalytic Association, New York, December 1, 1972.

The preparation of this paper was supported by Research Grant No. MH-19477 and Research Scientist Award K05 MH-70900, U.S. Public Health Service.

134

thrust has been the source of the strength that has given psychoanalytic clinical and general theories profound influences on Western thought. The emphasis on interpretation has forced the practicing analyst to de-emphasize such other sources of information as extra-analytic reports, laboratory examinations, biochemical and physical studies, information about learning, memory, coordination, sociological data, and reports from employers and family members. But de-emphasis of these para-analytic disciplines nurtured the development of a special aspect of psychoanalysis, a concern with meaning (see Ricoeur's [1970] discussion of hermeneutics).

It has seemed to me strange, however, that so many psychoanalysts have felt some measure of discomfort, perhaps even of inferiority, about the way in which psychoanalysis has proceeded to develop its disciplined approach to the psychology of meaning. Perhaps they have continued to "live out" Freud's own self-conscious split between his physicalistic, scientistic allegiances, on the one hand, and his proclivities for introspection, romanticism, and humanism, on the other (Bernfeld, 1944; Holt, 1963; Holzman, 1970). Whatever the reason, analysts have adopted for *the* theory not the clinical theory, but the physicalistic language of energy, forces, and counterforces, and applied it to a science grounded in interpretation and meaning. Most of us within psychoanalysis use the language of mechanism and of cathexis to restate our own language of interpretation, but this language of psychoanalytic theory belongs to the lexicon of metapsychology, which, as Klein (1973) has argued, allegedly explains clinical psychoanalytic *theory*, but does not explain the clinical *phenomena* themselves.

The language of cathexis and of drives, of forces and of energies represents Freud the physicalist and not Freud the clinician and keen observer, and Klein (1970) has shown how the drive-cathexis theory of sexuality acquired the status of *the* theory of sexuality, when, indeed, it ignores the essential experiences of infantile and adult sexual life—the concrete reality of sensuality and of other pleasures. These metapsychological constructs, designed "to explain" clinical obser-

vations, actually distract us from the task of enlarging our
observations about sexuality and from constructing and re-
shaping our clinical theory to match our observations. In fact,
the concepts of drive discharge, libido, and cathexis foster a
tendency to intellectualization and therefore keep the theoretician still further away from the facts of sexual craving and
arousal, their development and their vicissitudes. Not only has
the metatheoretical language had beguiling effects on theoretical efforts, it has also diverted us to ill-conceived imitations
of the experimental and observational sciences. The physicalistic language of energy transformations and cathectic dynamics explains no more than do the statements of our clinical
theories and conveys far less meaning. Nowhere is this pseudo-
theoretical effort more hampering than in the language
psychoanalysts have adopted to explore schizophrenic pathology. Indeed, the use of physicalistic language has retarded
our understanding of the schizophrenias, for by providing us
with an apparent somatic base, the metapsychological language of forces and cathexes has diverted psychoanalysts from
an awareness of actual empirical research on the physical
bases of the schizophrenias. Metapsychology has substituted a
physical model with ties to neither actual physical phenomena
(such as genic, biochemical, and neurochemical data) nor the
genuine psychological data that emerge from a clinical base.
When speaking of the fate of libido or of the withdrawal of
cathexis in the context of exploring schizophrenic phenomena, some analysts are convinced that they are dealing with
actual somatic events or actual psychological experiences.
They lose sight of Freud's great accomplishment: the recognition of meaning and purpose in the behavior of even severely
disorganized psychotic persons. Many clinicians describe their
patients in language, not of meaning, but of hypothetical
mechanisms. Clinical description has thus suffered, and as a
result of the distance taken from description, efforts to correct
theory have been hampered, and communication between
psychoanalysts and those taking other approaches to the
understanding of psychopathology has become more difficult.

In 1951, Hartmann reminded us that progress in psychoanalysis — as in any discipline — is based on clinical discoveries. But faulty theoretical concepts lead to faulty techniques, and may even block clinical discoveries. In psychoanalysis, unfortunately, there has been a tendency to allow theory to determine what data will be examined and, indeed, even to qualify the data. The more secure methodological procedure would have theory emerging from the act of placing things known into a system. For many of us in psychoanalysis it has been apparent — to paraphrase J. J. Thomson — that theory has been a creed rather than a policy. This worshipful attitude toward theory has resulted in the elision of observation and explanation.

Speaking about the difficulties in the path of psychoanalysis, Anna Freud had this to say:

> Psychoanalytic thinking, in classical terms, implied the specific demand that every clinical fact should be approached from four aspects: *genetically*, as to its origin; *dynamically*, as to the interplay of forces of which it is the result; *economically*, with regard to its energy charge; *topographically* (later *structurally*), concerning its localization within the mental apparatus. It was the psychology based on this view of mental functioning which was singled out by the name of *metapsychology*.
>
> Nevertheless, in our times, the term metapsychology has assumed a very different meaning. What it denotes now is largely theory building, distant from the area of clinical material, an activity which demands and is reserved for a specific, speculative quality of mind. As such it has become the bugbear of the clinically oriented analyst who feels wholly divorced from it. This brings about a division which, in the long run, threatens both areas with sterility: the theoretical field due to the absence of clinical data, the clinical field due to a diminution in their theoretical evaluation and exploration. What is lost, finally, is what used to be considered as a *sine qua non* in psychoanalysis: the essential *unity* between clinical and theoretical thinking [1969, p. 153].

The crux of the matter is this: psychoanalytic theory is psychological theory in that it probes the meaning of behavioral phenomena. Some users of this metatheoretical language believe that they are talking in psychological terms when actually they are using physical terms with no coordinating definitions to either real or consistent physical events. To employ a physical, quasisomatic language to explain these behaviors makes it obscure to both those who use it and those who read it, whether what is being offered is a psychological explanation or a somatic one. But the elements of the explanatory set—for example, cathexis, aggressivized energy, neutralized energy—are disguised somatic explanations that masquerade as psychological ones. By avoiding a language that directly describes behavioral and intrapsychic events, theoreticians make it more difficult to probe into the nature of the psychological organization of the schizophrenias. To date, there is powerful evidence that there is more to schizophrenic disorganization and reorganization than is contained in the metapsychological terminology.

This is not to deny the role of theoretical infrastructures in scientific explanation. Indeed, once a cogent and consistent phenomenological pattern has been obtained, the construction of models, analogies, infrastructures are a required next step to broaden the nature of our understanding. But the language of energy and of cathexis has pre-empted this infrastructure before a cogent psychological picture of the disorder has been formulated.

I have asserted that metapsychology has distracted us from the essentials of the psychoanalytic exploration into neurotic phenomena, and it has misled us in understanding the schizophrenias. If "misled" seems too strong a term, let me remind you that a reliance on the energy-cathexis model has retarded psychoanalysts from making close clinical observations of schizophrenic phenomena. Rather, case studies are fitted into the "decathexis mold" in procrustean manner, and the extent to which the data are congruent with that mold becomes a measure of the completeness of the explanation of the data.

The psychoanalytic theory of schizophrenic psychosis has never had a stable construction. Over the years Freud continually revised his ideas about schizophrenia. His earliest attempts to study psychosis coincided with his revolutionary insight (1894) that conflicts lay at the root of neurotic suffering, that neurotic symptoms could be understood as purposive accommodations to painful conflict. He discovered purpose and meaning in paranoid symptoms, too, and he noted a rather specific defensive behavior in paranoia — disavowal of reality. These insights led him to conclude that psychopathology could be arrayed along a continuum and that a unified theory of psychopathology was possible. And so, he at first advocated that neurosis and psychosis are identical in structure, purpose, and meaning, and differ only in severity. Such formulations are, of course, subject to correction by continual evaluation of new evidence and constant testing of theory against prediction. These tests depend upon the possibility of a close linkage between concrete observation and theoretical formulation.

Freud later rejected the idea that neurosis and psychosis lie on a continuum, and in his analysis of Schreber's autobiography (Freud, 1911) he detailed several ways in which schizophrenia or psychosis differs from neurosis, including the altered use of language, disturbance in object relations, and the existence in consciousness of primitive thoughts and fantasies. His broader conceptions about the etiology of schizophrenia — couched in physicalistic terms — never satisfactorily settled for him the issue of etiology, and his focus shifted from trying to understand the nature of the internal chaotic world of the schizophrenic patient to conceptualizing the role of disturbances in the patient's relations with the real world (Freud, 1924a, 1924b). Freud's attempts to construct a unitary theory, however, led him away from a concern with concrete clinical data. He theorized about the chaos experienced by the psychotic patient in terms of the physicalism of the drive theory: withdrawal of libidinal cathexis either from drive representations or from real relationships. He saw the fate of the withdrawn libido as determining the appearance of secondary restitutional symptoms: redirection of libido onto the ego (or to oneself in the pre-1923 terminology) leads to grandiosity and paranoid overestimation of oneself; or there may be a failure to redirect the cathexis onto fantasied objects. A subtle but definite elision took place between physical and mental frames of reference. As long as Freud spoke about tension, force, or energy as *analogies* for internal psychological tensions, the theory remained one concerned with meanings. Once the terms "drive," "force," "cathexis" took on a physicalistic and physiological usage — as they did — the analogical usage shifted into causal usage. Fenichel (1945) provides us with an example of this tendency: "The experiences of estrangement and depersonalization are due to a special type of defense, namely, to a countercathexis against one's own feelings which had been altered and intensified by a preceding increase in narcissism. The results of this increase are perceived as unpleasant by the ego which therefore undertakes defensive measures against them. These defensive measures may sometimes consist in a reactive withdrawal of libido; as a rule, however, they are built up by a countercathexis" (p. 419).

In this passage, the agency causing the psychological experiences is clearly the hypothetical physical process of movement and redeployment of libido. This illustrates the dangers of losing sight of the basic language of meaning in psychoanalysis: as purpose and cause become confused, anthropomorphic explanations increase.

Psychoanalytic theory is not a hierarchical one, with precise deductions from first principles. It is, rather, a concatenated theory, organizing what is known into an orderly system and linking one empirical generalization with another, thus guiding new searches for data and suggesting new and unexpected relationships. We still require empirical generalizations prior to theory, as well as laws describing behavioral regularities that can later be brought into systematic relation with one another, but only after they have achieved the status of reliable empirical generalizations. New facts about the schizophrenias are emerging from many of the life sciences. To ignore them is inimical to a scientific attitude. Investigators of schizophrenic phenomena must be familiar with behavior genetics, biochemical findings, the psychological deficits discovered in laboratory experiments, the nature of family interactions in schizophrenia, and with the ways in which drugs affect the appearance of the psychosis. And we sorely require a consistent psychological language for describing schizophrenic phenomena, their uniqueness and differences from other psychotic phenomena. A consistent psychological language for psychoanalytic observation, it seems to me, can highlight whether there are some forms of schizophrenic psychosis that yield primarily to psychological interventions. The demonstration of a functional relationship between the symptoms of the psychosis and psychological interventions would be sufficient evidence to implicate psychological factors into the network of conditions necessary for the psychosis. It would hence not be mandatory to isolate valid psychological *etiological* factors in order for psychological factors to be involved in the systems network.

Heuristically, what is required is a systems view of the schizophrenias, a view that takes account of much of the accumulating knowledge of the schizophrenias derived from diverse vantage points. These "starting areas" for the search into the schizophrenias embrace not only the interaction between therapist and patient, but the physiological, genetic, sociological, and psychological components of a complex field organization. It is from a disruption of this "dynamic circularity" (Frank, 1951) of parts and whole, organism and surround, that schizophrenic syndromes emerge.

This systems point of view was quite congenial to Freud, who never lost sight of the multiple factors that are involved in behavior and in behavior pathology as necessary conditions. He was particularly prepared to take account of the role hereditary factors may play in neurosis and psychosis. For example, in discussing the etiology of neurosis, he wrote,

> In the pathogenesis of the major neuroses, then, heredity fulfills the role of a *precondition*, powerful in every case and even indispensable in most cases. It could not do without the collaboration of the specific causes; but the importance of hereditary disposition is proved by the fact that the same specific causes acting on a healthy individual produce no manifest pathological effect, whereas in a predisposed person their action causes the neurosis to come to light, whose development will be proportionate in intensity and extent to the degree of the hereditary precondition.

Thus the action of heredity is comparable to that of a multiplier in an electric circuit, which exaggerates the visible deviation of the needle, but which cannot determine its direction.

There is yet another thing to be noted in the relations between the hereditary precondition and the specific causes of neuroses. Experience shows—what one might have guessed in advance—that in these questions of aetiology one should not neglect the relative quantities, so to speak, of the aetiological influences. But one could not have guessed the following fact, which seems to arise from my observations: namely that heredity and the specific causes can replace each other as regards quantity, that the same pathological effect will be produced by the coincidence of a very serious specific heredity with a moderate disposition or a severely loaded nervous heredity with a slight specific influence. And we shall simply be meeting not unexpected extreme instances in this series if we come upon cases of neurosis in which we shall look in vain for any appreciable degree of hereditary disposition, provided that what is lacking is made up for by a powerful influence [1896, pp. 147-148].[1]

Psychoanalysis has derived its clinical theories—for example, those of unconscious psychological processes, of the power of sexuality and aggression, of the claims of internal conflicts, of the epigenetic development of personality, of the tendency to repeat actively that which was passively experienced—from careful and intensive studies of neurotic patients. The data base in the free associations of the neurotic patients who are the subjects of the observations has been sufficient to enable clinical psychoanalysis to unlock and unfold meanings. But in studies of the psychoses, and especially of the schizophrenias, we come upon a set of phenomena different from those presented by the free associations of nonpsychotic patients.

Psychoanalysis has been able to discern the sense in much of

---

[1] These ideas are later referred to as the "complementary series" (Freud, 1905), and show that Freud did not ignore the crucial interplay of somatic and psychological factors in etiology. Freud never wavered from these ideas. Seventeen years later, he wrote, "It would nevertheless be a serious mistake to suppose that analysis favours or aims at a *purely* psychological view of mental disorders. It cannot overlook the fact that the other half of the problems of psychiatry are concerned with the influence of organic factors (whether mechanical, toxic or infective) on the mental apparatus" (1913, p. 175).

the schizophrenic's apparent nonsense. It has, for example, been able to understand the meanings of many delusions, as well as the messages in the schizophrenic's thought slippage. In the acute schizophrenias particularly, it has contributed an understanding of patients' attempts to come to grips with disintegrating inner worlds. But the psychoanalytic theory of schizophrenia is a theory of restitution, not of etiology, although the language of the theory pretends to more. For example, Schreber reported a "profound internal change," an "internal catastrophe," as Freud interpreted this phenomenon. Basic and pervasive disturbances in reality testing in the relations of Schreber to himself and to others followed these profound internal changes. To speak of these changes as a process of "decathexis" is merely to rephrase the phenomenon in another idiom. The theory of schizophrenia promulgated by Freud was a theory of adaptation to a deficiency or dysfunction whose precise nature was beyond the scope of psychoanalytic observations. Freud, in several of his writings, protested that his experiences with schizophrenic patients were limited and that therefore he could not detail the nature of the inner catastrophe. Theoretical endeavors to deduce an etiological theory of schizophrenia from the psychoanalytic view of neurosis seem to be constructed from analogies and not from a base in observations.

The conclusions of Lidz, for example, exemplify the commitment to psychogenesis or sociogenesis made by many psychoanalysts. Consider the following statement, which describes the families of schizophrenic patients that Lidz had studied:

> As anticipated from prior studies, the mothers were, with a few exceptions, highly unstable, but the fathers were equally disturbed. The nurturant care provided the child usually had not only been faulty during the first year of life, as analytic theory predicted, but grossly disturbed through adolescence. The parents' marriages were either split by abiding conflict or distorted because one parent was ineffectual and the other had peculiar ideas of child-rearing. The family structure was distorted not only by a lack of a parental coalition but because generation boundaries were disrupted by parents acting as chil-

dren and children being used emotionally as a spouse, and parents failed to maintain their gender-linked roles. The child's socialization was impaired *because* [italics added] parents provided faulty role models and through their example made marriage and parenthood unattractive and even dangerous. Extrafamilial socialization was blocked by parental fears and idiosyncrasies and, often, by expressed distrust of outsiders. Further, one or both parents suffused a sense of the hopelessness and emptiness of life . . . The shortcomings of these families as developmental settings were so obvious and widespread that for a time my colleagues and I focused on the idea that schizophrenia was a deficiency disease—a deficiency of the essential nurturance, structuring, socialization, and enculturation requisite for a child's development into an autonomous person. But I now believe that within these flawed and deprived settings, which seriously impede the child's personality development and leave him vulnerable to disorganization, rather specific distorting schizophrenogenic influences can be isolated from the plethora of findings [1972, p. 641].

The causal model of this argument is clearly environmental and unidirectional: a hostile environment imposes its pernicious influences on an immature organism and produces vulnerability to disorganization. The crucial role of the complementary series—that is, the contribution of the organism itself to its own vulnerability—is ignored.

It is clear, however, that cross-sectional studies such as Lidz's cannot establish genetic priority. Longitudinal, prospective studies are required for such generalizations. Further, arguments such as those advanced by advocates of a purely psychogenetic theory of schizophrenia ignore the findings of Heston (1966) and of Kety et al. (1968) that a significant percentage of children of schizophrenic mothers become manifestly schizophrenic in spite of being reared in adoptive homes where familial instability is not obvious. Moreover, Lidz tends to interpret the presence of a high proportion of psychotic parents in his population as evidence for psychosocial transmission of deviance. He thus ignores the possibility of a genic transmission of some schizotaxic propensity that may unfold in a particular familial environment. Psychosocial interpretations, constructed from analogies to the psychoanalytic theory of neuroses and not from a base in observation, seem to be forced upon the data.

Psychoanalytic treatment intervention, however, has established certain observations about schizophrenic patients. These patients seem to have trouble distinguishing between their self-feelings and their feelings about others. One can infer that there has been inadequate internalization of a primary, good mothering object—of positive enough early experiences with nurturing objects—and a predominance of internalized, bad, aggressively loaded fantasied objects which the patient experiences as overwhelming, particularly when circumstances threaten to tax a vulnerable, poorly equipped organism. Wishes to fuse with another person and simultaneous fear of such fusion exist along with fear of abandonment and of isolation (see Burnham et al., 1969). Experiences of likeness and difference are bewildering, as are feelings of being fragmented. Such experiences occur predominantly during the acute psychotic phases of the illness.

While the evidence for a conflict theory as the common etiology of both schizophrenia and neurosis is flimsy—the cross-fostering studies are particularly cogent in this respect (see, e.g., Wender et al., 1974)—much can be cited to support a special psychoanalytic theory of schizophrenic restitution (e.g., London, 1973; Freeman, 1970). Even Arlow and Brenner (1969), the most articulate advocates of a unitary theory of neurosis and psychosis, disclaim any etiological significance for their formulations.

Any theory of schizophrenia must differentiate schizophrenia from other psychoses and, further, must account for non-psychotic forms of schizophrenia. The theory must not only account for the apparent "withdrawal" from personal contacts, as the idea of "decathexis" tries to, but must account for strange and awkward body movements, unusual sensitivities, thought slippage such as dereistic thinking or autistic logic, confusion and uncertainty in personal identity, body-image distortions, extraordinary dependency, pleasurelessness, characteristically poor competence, the flat or spotty modulation of affect, disproportionate rage reactions, hypochondriasis, sensory input compulsions, panic when alone, and many other behavioral symptoms not seen in neurotic conditions (Meehl, 1962; Grinker and Holzman, 1973). The psychoanalytic theory is nonspecific with regard to the factors underlying psychosis in general and the schizophrenias and paranoia in particular. Rather, it directs itself to one psychotic phenomenon, impaired reality testing, a phenomenon characteristic of all psychoses, particularly in their acute forms. Our own view coincides with those of Federn (1952), Freeman (1970), Wexler (1951), and London (1973), who regard these symptoms as having a coherence that reflects a dysfunction in internal organization and manifests itself in a sense of "some internal catastrophe." This experience of inner disaster is thus regarded as an outcome, not of conflict, as in neurosis, but of the triggering of a specific and not-yet-understood deficiency in important psychological functions necessary for growth, development, maturation, and adaptation.

Neurosis and schizophrenia are not to be conceived of as a continuum; schizophrenia and neurotic behaviors are uniquely different. The schizophrenias in their essence do not reflect compromise resolutions of conflict. They are, rather, behavioral manifestations of some organismic dysfunctions. The schizophrenias are more profitably understandable as outcomes of major internal disorganizations that may be represented psychologically as, for example, "personal" or "world destruction" experiences. Here, decathexis would refer not to defensive withdrawal, but to profound disturbances in thinking and in relating oneself to things and to people.

This formulation does not imply that the schizophrenias are primarily either functional or somatic disorders, caused by either environmental or somatic factors. It leaves room for the considerable contribution of genetic, biochemical, neurological, and other nonexperiential variables. Some behavioral manifestations of schizophrenic pathology may thus be either psychological expressions of nonpsychological factors or, as Waelder (1960) suggested, psychological consequences of organic factors. This view does insist, however, that the study of organic conditions cannot be ignored, either in etiological theory or in the treatment of schizophrenic disorders.

Schizophrenic psychosis may be the decompensation no doubt in the presence of certain environmental conditions that may either be conflict-laden or simply burdensome — of what Rado has called the "schizotype." That vastly more schizotypes remain compensated than do not is an attractive hypothesis (Meehl, 1962; Bender, 1956). It would seem likely that, just as a continuity exists between the obsessive character and obsessive neurosis or the hysterical character and hysterical neurosis, so a continuity may exist between the schizotype and the clinically overt schizophrenias. Since the psychoanalytic clinical theory is based on an intensive study of the "transference neurosis" and not the so-called narcissistic neuroses, a study of "normal" schizotypes would seem to promise valuable data concerning the character and behavior of those who may decompensate into psychosis. Such a view would suggest that, although the schizophrenias are not conflict disorders, schizophrenic people, like others, can have neurotic conflicts. But the analytic treatment of these neurotic conflicts in schizophrenic people does not affect the schizophrenic psychosis or even the schizotype characteristics. "Analysts have to admit," wrote Anna Freud, "that where quantitatively massive upheavals of the personality are concerned, such as in the psychoses, the purely psychological methods by themselves are inadequate and the organic and chemical means have the advantage over them. They do not concede the same for the neuroses" (1969, p. 131).

Psychosocial interventions in the treatment of some schizophrenic patients have been effective, particularly when combined with pharmacotherapy, despite some data that seem to relegate psychotherapy to an insignificant position when compared with the effect of the phenothiazines alone (see, for example, May, 1968). But we have also noticed that the effects of such interventions have a gentler slope than do those of relatively rapidly acting pharmacologic treatment. Moreover, psychosocial interventions affect aspects of patient functioning different from those affected by the phenothiazines. Some questions thus suggest themselves: (1) Do psychotherapeutic interventions require as intensive a schedule as does psychoanalysis with nonpsychotic patients? (2) Can the same psychotherapeutic effects be achieved by paraprofessional people or even by groups of patients themselves? (3) Does the mere stable presence of other interested persons provide the necessary support for helping to order the internal disorder and thus to help restoration? The common element in these questions is a plea to search for the essence of what is accomplished in all psychotherapies with schizophrenic patients and to find out what may be special—if anything—to some therapies. What can be dispensed with as not useful or redundant or distracting or irrelevant or as gratifying merely to the psychotherapist? And what are the elements that are absolutely necessary (Dyrud and Holzman, 1973)?

Two informative studies commend themselves to our attention. The first (Hogarty et al., 1973) examines the effects of phenothiazine treatment, combined with psychosocial, noninterpretative intervention, on the posthospital adjustment of chronic schizophrenic patients. In the early posthospital months, treatment by drugs alone showed a clear advantage over placebo treatment, whether or not psychotherapy was employed; but after about seven months the effects of psychotherapy began to show advantages in terms of job adjustment, social interactions, and the frequency of rehospitalization.

The second study (Weissman et al., 1974) compared the treatment course of 106 women who were suffering from serious depressive symptoms. These patients were chosen because they showed a response to a tricyclic antidepressant drug during the first six weeks of treatment. This group was then divided into those who did and those who did not receive psychotherapy, and each of these groups was further divided into three: those who continued to receive the antidepressant, those on placebo, and those without medication. At the end of four months, no reliable differences in social adjustment were apparent in these groups, although there was obvious symptom improvement. At the end of eight months, however, those receiving psychotherapy showed many more social improvements than those who had received no psychotherapy. Better work performance, less interpersonal friction, less anxious rumination were characteristic of those receiving psychotherapy. As with the study of chronic schizophrenic patients, psychotherapeutic effects took several months to become apparent. Both studies strongly suggest that psychotherapy and pharmacotherapy affect different aspects of functioning; drugs affect symptoms, psychotherapy improves social impairment. There is even some evidence in these studies that the effectiveness of psychotherapy depends upon the patients' remaining asymptomatic.

During the past two decades, progress in understanding and in treating the major psychoses, including the schizophrenias and manic-depressive illness, has accelerated. Progress has come from many sources, but principally from those outside of the psychoanalytic consulting room. Behavior genetics, biochemistry, psychopharmacology, family studies, epidemiology, all have made important contributions.

The schizophrenic syndrome is a process, with varied and protean pictures. It may develop in early or late childhood or in early or late adulthood; it may develop insidiously with no acute psychotic disruption or it may erupt suddenly and unexpectedly; it may never recur or it may never go on to recovery or it may recur once or many times, each time with a poorer remission. The symptoms may be mild or serious. The premorbid pictures may range widely, too. A theory that takes account of only one manifestation of schizophrenic illness — the loss of effective reality testing, for example — can only be an *ad hoc* and incomplete theory. The complexity of the phenomena make it impossible to continue to ignore the systems approach to the schizophrenias. Whether one chooses to study etiological factors (genic, biochemical, familial, demographic) or the responses to such factors (including the inner resources of the person to resist or to succumb) or the healing processes (either within the person or exogenously administered) depends upon one's proclivities and interests. But one should not mistake any of these aspects of the pathology for the complete picture of the disease or of *the* treatment. It is the imbalance among all these factors — between internal and external threats and pressures, on the one hand, and the organism's efforts to maintain itself by

thoughts, feelings, somatic shifts, and changed social relationships, on the other hand—that may be called the disease.
When one adopts a systems approach, one inevitably views an
insistence upon only one special kind of intervention as either
benignly quixotic or unconscionably unethical, depending
upon one's titer of indignation.

For example, Searles (in Gunderson, 1974, pp. 193-194) has
charged that for psychoanalysts to acknowledge and integrate
the findings about schizophrenia from such other disciplines
as genetics and psychopharmacology is to "set schizophrenic
persons apart, qualitatively and indelibly from their fellow
human beings as, in their very essence, something less than
human." He believes that attempts to show differences between schizophrenic and neurotic behaviors reflect defensive
behavior on the part of the therapist or the investigator, for
whenever the therapeutic interaction threatens to evoke "subjectively nonhuman aspects in therapists who [share the point
of view presented in this paper], they would turn relatively
quickly to the latest information from such scientific fields as
genetics and biochemistry to find reassuring evidence that the
schizophrenic patient is, after all, different from the truly
human being." Whatever differences may exist, he added, are
explained by "primitive, preindividuation, and even presymbiotic processes ... which all human beings, including those
suffering from schizophrenia share in common, as can be discovered, with reliable repetitiveness, if therapists remain
sufficiently open minded and observe the so-called counter-
transference realms of clinical phenomena."

The logic of this argument is hard to grasp, and the
counterargument—that the differences between schizophrenic
behavior and neurotic behavior are to be explained by a
primitive preindividuation and presymbiotic process—demonstrates an unfortunate retreat into abstract language from
concrete data, and exemplifies my claim that the physiological
language of metapsychology has given many analysts the conviction that they are dealing with facts, data, and concrete
events when they use terms like "presymbiotic" and "preindividuation." Such terms are too nonspecific to be of help in

solving issues of etiology. But the argument is illogical, too, in its implicit statement that if one brings genetic and bio-chemical formulations into the nomological net, then one is negating psychodynamic factors and endorsing psychothera-peutic nihilism. The recognition of the importance of bio-chemical and genetic factors surely does not in any practical or logical sense contravene the recognition of psychodynamic factors, or the ameliorative role of psychotherapy. Yet, ig-noring these factors, particularly the importance of pharma-cotherapy, would deny to masses of patients an already proven therapeutic agent—not a cure, it is true, but an effective antipsychotic medication.[2]

Treatment interventions, from the systems vantage point, would direct themselves to several parts of the system.

(1) One may focus on the form that genetic counseling could take at this stage of our knowledge, whether, indeed, such counseling would be helpful or harmful. For example, there is a risk of schizophrenic pathology's occurring among the children of schizophrenic persons, whether those children are reared by biological or adoptive parents. Can such genetic counseling be developed responsibly as an aspect of prevention?

(2) Although approximately 9 to 17 per cent of children born to one schizophrenic parent will develop schizophrenia during their lives, 83 per cent of such children will not become schizophrenic. What can we learn from those who escape the ravages of psychosis that will help in prevention? Are clues to prevention to be found in sophisticated child-care practices, and particularly from the insights of psychoanalytic studies of child development? Are there specific traumata, certain nar-cissistic injuries, separations, physical illnesses, for example,

[2] Searles's argument, of course, contains an *ad hominem* attack: all persons who make use of genetic findings, psychopharmacologic agents, and biochemical data, are simply afraid of the therapeutic relationship with schizophrenic patients; only therapists like Searles are courageous enough to endure the onslaught of the psychotic relationship, and they alone can rescue the schizophrenic patient from "the long dark night of the soul." But Searles fails to buttress his position with any data on the quality of outcome in the treatment of schizophrenia by the techniques he advocates.

that are associated with schizophrenia in vulnerable people? If so, can the dissemination of child-guidance information and work with the family prevent the development of clinical schizophrenia?

(3) What role do antischizophrenic drugs, like the phenothiazines, play in treatment? Can they be used effectively for all kinds of schizophrenias? There is some evidence, for example, that the phenothiazines may not be particularly effective with nonparanoid schizophrenic patients having a good premorbid history, and that there may be some therapeutic advantage in not administering phenothiazine medication to these patients at some phases of the illness. But does it make clinical sense to withdraw such medication uniformly from all patients in our care?

The phenothiazines, butyrophenones, and thioxanthene derivatives are effective antipsychotic agents, and, in those few studies where drug and psychotherapy have been carefully evaluated for their unique ameliorative properties, it appears that drug and psychotherapy act synergistically so that the total effect is greater than if each were administered alone. Further, the effectiveness of psychotherapeutic intervention probably depends upon the effective control of the psychosis.

(4) An acute outbreak of the schizophrenic psychosis has effects on the patient's family that differ from those resulting from an insidious and gradual onset of the illness or those that run a chronic course. What help can and should be given to the family during the phase of disorganization? Can the family be treated as a group, with a focus on support, understanding, and guidance, and perhaps thereby prevent the outbreak of a psychotic response in yet another family member?

(5) A close study of a number of successfully treated schizophrenic patients permits the therapist to divide the clinical course during treatment into four phases, which have been well described by Kayton (1973). Phase I is that of "internal disorganization," the psychotic period. During this period the patient is preoccupied with fantasies of sinister, powerful persecutory forces, with bad objects, and with powerful grandiose forces. Thought slippage, clogging, and flooding are common

at this phase. The patients are also preoccupied with fantasies of good objects and with hopes of rescue, yet extreme vulnerability to rebuffs and feelings of panic are common. During phase II, labeled "postpsychotic regression," after the resolution of the psychosis with the help of antipsychotic medication, the patient feels alone, weak, bad, empty, has many hypochondriacal concerns, and is severely impaired in concentration, attention, and reasoning. Withdrawal from other people is typical, as are silences during therapy sessions. Reversals of the sleep-waking pattern are also typical, and shifts in body image may persist. During phase III, concentration begins to improve and disorganization begins to subside. The patients begin to become concerned about their appearance and social relationships begin to reappear. During this phase, the regression can be terminated rather expeditiously by interpretation, firmness, and structure setting. Phase IV, that of the termination of the regression, is ushered in by feelings of inner strength, and by the initiation of activity. A normalized diurnal cycle appears, and there is a return of some self-confidence, although it is accomplished by lowered ambitions.

It has seemed to us that during the phase of psychosis and postpsychotic regression, working with internal conflict is less appropriate than it would be during the recovery phases. A unitary theory of neurosis and schizophrenia would dictate a standard psychoanalytic technique; our experience shows that a classical psychoanalytic approach during the psychotic and postpsychotic phase deepens the regression and delays the appearance of recovery. During the early phase of the psychotic regression, techniques of making contact with and reassuring the frightened patient, of assuring proper nutrition and other health standards should receive priority. It is a real question whether the acutely psychotic schizophrenic patient "requires" a prolonged period of regression in order to recover and to heal. Within our own group, we have discussed whether premature resolution of acute confusional periods may interfere with later phases of the treatment and whether there may be advantages to the patient in learning to live with his confusion for a while. Our treatment program tries to limit the psychotic regression. This is one area where sensitive observation can contribute to a theory of psychosis in functional terms.

Of central importance is our effort to provide stable object ties between the patient and the staff of the hospital and later to continue these ties even after the patient has been discharged. The threat of object disappearance, feelings of fragmentation, and recognition of the fragile nature of human relationships require dependable contacts with understanding persons. These, and not interpretation, in our opinion, are the nutriment that the competence deficits of these patients require.

All during the patient's hospitalization we advocate working with the family as both a crisis intervention technique and as a way of inquiring into the pathogenic aspects of the family interactions.

Our postpsychotic treatment techniques emphasize an exploration not only of antecedent conflict—neurotic in content—but also of the complications in the patient's life wrought by the psychosis itself. During this phase much work can be accomplished on the feelings of inner badness, the relationships to the congeries of good and bad introjects, and the experiences of inner emptiness. Yet, we avoid a classical psychoanalytic treatment situation, for the reasons already spelled out by Wexler (1951), Freeman (1970), Fromm-Reichmann (1948), London (1973), and others: the danger of increased feelings of separation and loss of structure, the fear of encouraging regression, and the risk of stimulating uncontrolled fantasies.

The postpsychotic program emphasizes training and habilitation, the learning of new skills, the relearning of old skills, and helps in rebuilding internal structures such as delays over actions, and brakes on fantasies. These, in our opinion, aid in strengthening a sense of stability and of confidence.

The use of all adjuncts is critical. Which work best in which circumstances is an empirical matter. It seems to us that it is blind parochialism to continue to interpret rather than to observe, to rely upon only one mode of intervention defensively advocated, and to ignore other aspects of the social-biological-psychological milieu. A systems approach introduces a dimension of complexity that we are only now beginning to appreciate. Yet maturity, healthy narcissism, if you will, surely can help us to absorb the blow to our self-regard that is represented by the narrower scope given to psychoanalysis in this view of the treatment of the schizophrenias. We can appreciate how ironic it is that Freud's observations and the theory he drew from them—fundamental as they are to an understanding of man's apparent irrationality—should find a limit at the most irrational of all human conditions, the schizophrenias.

SUMMARY

Klein has described how metapsychology obstructs our detailed attention to clinical theory because it is used to explain the clinical theory. The attitude of some psychoanalysts to schizophrenic phenomena underscores the claim that metapsychology is used as a disguised somatic theory. As such, it has become impervious to clinical psychological data, for in its role as a physical-somatic theory, metapsychology obstructs the search for verifiable physical-somatic factors by the appropriate nonpsychological methods required to discover them. A systems view of schizophrenic phenomena marshals data from diverse disciplines—including genetics, biochemistry, sociology, physiology, psychology, psychoanalysis—and a realistic look at therapeutic results. This multiple approach leads to the adopting of a plurality of therapeutic interventions and provides an open channel for the recruitment of additional information sorely needed for a clearer understanding of the schizophrenias.

156 PHILIP S. HOLZMAN

REFERENCES

Arlow, J., & Brenner, C. (1969), The Psychopathology of the Psychoses: A Proposed Revision. *Internat. J. Psycho-Anal.*, 50:5-14.

Bender, L. (1956), Schizophrenia in Childhood: Its Recognition, Description and Treatment. *Amer. J. Orthopsychiat.*, 26:499-506.

Bernfeld, S. (1944), Freud's Earliest Theories and the School of Helmholtz. *Psychoanal. Quart.*, 13:341-362.

Burnham, D. L., Gladstone, A. T., & Gibson, R. W. (1969), *Schizophrenia and the Need-Fear Dilemma*. New York: International Universities Press.

Dyrud, J., & Holzman, P. S. (1973), The Psychotherapy of Schizophrenia: Does It Work? *Amer. J. Psychiat.*, 130:670-673.

Federn, P. (1952), *Ego Psychology and the Psychoses*. New York: Basic Books.

Fenichel, O. (1945), *The Psychoanalytic Theory of Neurosis*. New York: Norton.

Frank, L. K. (1951), Genetic Psychology and Its Prospects. *Amer. J. Orthopsychiat.*, 21:506-522.

Freeman, T. (1970), The Psychopathology of the Psychoses: A Reply to Arlow and Brenner. *Internat. J. Psycho-Anal.*, 51:407-415.

Freud, A. (1969), Difficulties in the Path of Psychoanalysis: A Confrontation of Past with Present Viewpoints. *The Writings of Anna Freud*, 7:124-156. New York: International Universities Press.

Freud, S. (1894), The Neuro-Psychoses of Defence. *Standard Edition*, 3:43-61. London: Hogarth Press, 1962.

_____(1896), Heredity and the Aetiology of the Neuroses. *Standard Edition*, 3:141-156. London: Hogarth Press, 1962.

_____(1905), Three Essays on the Theory of Sexuality. *Standard Edition*, 7:123-243. London: Hogarth Press, 1953.

_____(1911), Psychoanalytic Notes on an Autobiographical Account of a Case of Paranoia (Dementia Paranoides). *Standard Edition*, 12:3-84. London: Hogarth Press, 1958.

_____(1913), The Claims of Psycho-Analysis to Scientific Interest. *Standard Edition*, 13:165-192. London: Hogarth Press, 1955.

_____(1924a), Neurosis and Psychosis. *Standard Edition*, 19:149-156. London: Hogarth Press, 1961.

_____(1924b), The Loss of Reality in Neurosis and Psychosis. *Standard Edition*, 19:183-190. London: Hogarth Press, 1961.

Fromm-Reichmann, F. (1948), Notes on the Development of Treatment of Schizophrenics by Psychoanalytic Therapy. *Psychiat.*, 11:263-273.

Grinker, R. R., Sr., & Holzman, P. S. (1973), Schizophrenic Pathology in Young Adults: A Clinical Study. *Arch. Gen. Psychiat.*, 28:168-175.

Gunderson, J. G., rep. (1974), The Influence of Theoretical Model of Schizophrenia on Treatment Practice. *J. Amer. Psychoanal. Assn.*, 22:182-199.

Hartmann, H. (1951), Technical Implications of Ego Psychology. *Essays on Ego Psychology*. New York: International Universities Press, 1964, pp. 142-154.

Heston, L. L. (1966), Psychiatric Disorders in Foster Home-Reared Children of Schizophrenic Mothers. *Brit. J. Psychiat.*, 112:819-825.

Hogarty, G. E., and the collaborative study group (1973), Drugs and Sociotherapy in the Aftercare of Schizophrenic Patients. *Arch. Gen. Psychiat.*, 28:56-64.

Holt, R. R. (1963), Two Influences upon Freud's Scientific Thought: A Fragment of Intellectual Biography. In: *The Study of Lives: Essays on Personality in Honor of Henry A. Murray,* ed. R. W. White. New York: Atherton, pp. 364-387.

Holzman, P. S. (1970), *Psychoanalysis and Psychopathology.* New York: McGraw-Hill.

Kayton, L. (1973), Good Outcome in Young Adult Schizophrenia. *Arch. Gen. Psychiat.,* 29:103-110.

Kety, S., Rosenthal, D., Wender, P., & Schulsinger, F. (1968), The Types and Prevalence of Mental Illness in the Biological and Adoptive Families of Adopted Schizophrenics. In: *The Transmission of Schizophrenia,* ed. D. Rosenthal & S. Kety. New York: Pergamon Press, pp. 345-362.

Klein, G. S. (1970), Two Theories or One? *Bull. Menninger Clin.,* 37:99-132, 1973.

Lidz, T. (1972), The Nature and Origins of Schizophrenic Disorders. *Ann. Intern. Med.,* 77:639-645.

London, N. (1973), An Essay of Psychoanalytic Theory: Two Theories of Schizophrenia. *Internat. J. Psycho-Anal.,* 54:169-178.

May, P. R. A. (1968), *Treatment of Schizophrenia: A Comparison of Five Treatment Methods.* New York: Science House.

Meehl, P. (1962), Schizotaxia, Schizotypy, Schizophrenia. *Amer. Psychol.,* 17:827-838.

Ricoeur, P. (1970), *Freud and Philosophy: An Essay on Interpretation.* New Haven, Conn.: Yale University Press.

Waelder, R. (1960), *Basic Theory of Psychoanalysis.* New York: International Universities Press.

Weissman, M. M., et al. (1974), Treatment of the Social Adjustment of Depressed Patients. *Arch. Gen. Psychiat.,* 30:771-778.

Wender, P. H., Rosenthal, D., Kety, S. S., Schulsinger, F., & Welner, J. (1974), Crossfostering. *Arch. Gen. Psychiat.,* 30:121-128.

Wexler, M. (1951), The Structural Problem in Schizophrenia: Therapeutic Implications. *Internat. J. Psycho-Anal.,* 32:157-166.

6

DRIVE OR WISH?
A RECONSIDERATION OF THE
PSYCHOANALYTIC THEORY
OF MOTIVATION

ROBERT R. HOLT

Its theory of motivation is at once the glory of psychoanalysis and its shame. What is loosely known as the theory of instincts includes both a number of Freud's most important and lasting insights and some of his most regrettable theoretical failings. It badly needs fundamental revision; but the process must be both radical and conservative—what is not good must be extirpated at the root, but what is good must be retained.

From the beginning, this part of psychoanalytic theory has been the most intensely controversial, the focus of several apostasies and of the most violent and personal attacks on Freud himself: the traducer of innocent children, the slanderer of holy men and women, the sexual monomaniac, and so on, ad nauseam. Analysts therefore have good reasons to view with considerable suspicion any proposals to reconsider Freudian motivational theory, especially one that proposes to do away with the concept of instinctual drive itself. It is only natural to rally round the flag when it is under unfair assault, and to feel that any doctrine so often viciously attacked for so

The preparation of this paper was supported by a U. S. Public Health Service Research Career Award, Grant 5-K06-MH-12455, from the National Institute of Mental Health.

many bad reasons must be not only heroic but true—a conclusion, unfortunately, that is not necessarily accurate. When I used the deliberately overdramatic phrase, "the shame of psychoanalysis," in reference to the theory of instinctual drives, I meant to prepare the way for a demonstration that this central part of psychoanalysis is so riddled with philosophical and factual errors and fallacies that nothing less than discarding the concept of drive or instinct will do. At the same time, just because this concept contains so much of value, we must be quite sure before we abandon it that a viable alternative is at hand which does not sacrifice any of the hard-won gains of psychoanalysis. In particular, there is a danger of repeating the error made in the course of some earlier efforts to revise the theory, which have begun by ignoring or repudiating a number of *facts*.

Let me emphasize, then, that a first necessity of any revised psychoanalytic theory of motivation is that it *save the data of observation*. We must not let any theoretical novelty cause us to deny the facts that people have blind rages, wild lusts, and parasitic infantile longings, any of which may not be present as conscious desires, or that they are also capable of mature interests, genuine altruism, and intense devotion to principle. If it seems that throwing out the dual instinct theory, psychic energy, or the notion of drive as the cause of behavior threatens to turn psychoanalysis into a pallid game of disembodied and feeble cognitive operations, we should ponder long and hard before we make any such radical changes. For these very reasons, I have been hesitating for some years to publish this paper, not because its stance is radical, but because I wanted to be sure that it does not inadvertently undermine any part of the central observational core of psychoanalysis. And I believe that some of these same reasons may account for the fact that George Klein (1967) did not call attention to the truly radical nature of his contribution to a revised psychoanalytic theory of motivation, or explicitly call for abandonment of the prevalent theory.

I shall list briefly some empirical propositions that I believe include the most important motivational facts of psycho-

analytic observation, which must be adequately conceptualized. Often, people are unaware of the goals toward which
their behavior is directed and strongly resist any efforts to help
them become aware of these goals. After psychoanalytic work
(analysis of defenses, interpretation of dreams, etc.) or in
altered states of consciousness (drug states, fever deliria,
hypnosis, etc.), they frequently become aware of previously
denied wishes (positive or negative—longings and aversions)
and offer new confirmatory memories or other material.
People can have somatic symptoms for which no organic cause
can be found, but which can be shown (by the just-mentioned
means) to be the bodily expression of wishes or fears and
defenses against them. When a wished-for form of behavior is
(or seems) impossible, people are capable of getting some
gratification by engaging in other behavior, which at times
seems to them unrelated. Almost everyone is more interested
in getting sexual pleasure than he or she will admit, often
pursuing it in devious and complicated ways. Symptoms and
other forms of puzzling behavior are frequently motivated by
unconscious fears concerning, or wishes for, sensual (including
narrowly sexual) pleasure. Several parts of the body other than
the genitals—notably the mouth and anus—are capable of
yielding pleasure that has a sensuous, exciting quality very
similar to that provided by stimulating the genitals. (Rather
than stating the facts of infantile sexuality and the perversions
propositionally, let me merely allude to them in this paren-
thesis.) If a person is forbidden one form of sexual pleasure, he
will often turn to another. Children living in the Western nuclear family (and in many more or less similar family structures found in other societies) regularly develop sexual attrac-
tion to the adults with whom they come into close, repeated
contact during the first few years of life, as well as jealousies,
fears, and hatreds, many of which feelings (incestuous, parri-
cidal, etc.) are culturally taboo and are not easily avowed; but
they continue to exist and to have demonstrable effects on behavior (especially on dreams, fantasies, and symptoms). Boys
commonly develop fears of bodily mutilation after having experienced and more or less openly expressed erotic wishes

toward their mothers — frequently fears that the father or some surrogate will harm their penises. Girls often develop feelings of having lost a penis and/or envious wishes to get one. There is an intrinsic connection between certain universal types of wishes (for example, sexual and destructive), certain bio-chemical and other organismic states (hormones and catechol amines in the blood), and associated affects (sexual excite-ment and anger). When adults are severely thwarted or exposed to other kinds of intense stress, they frequently abandon goal-seeking behavior of a kind appropriate to their developmental status and re-experience wishes that were characteristic of earlier stages. Much of the time all people experience motivational conflicts; that is, they have mutually incompatible wishes, though these may or may not be wholly conscious. Finally, a great deal of human behavior is moti-vated by one or another form of a need to maintain a satisfactory self-evaluation.

Though I have tried to state this brief inventory of moti-vational observations (which does not aim to be exhaustive) in as untheoretical terms as possible, we are more familiar with most of them as cast in the form of propositions from what Rapaport (1959) called the *clinical theory* of psychoanalysis. Indeed, it is virtually the hallmark of the clinical theory that it is quite close to the factual, observational core of psycho-analysis, as opposed to metapsychology, which Rapaport called the *general theory* of psychoanalysis. I might epitomize the rest of this paper by saying that it is an attempt to recover and rehabilitate the clinical theory of motivation by clearing away the deadwood of metapsychology, which has buried it to a great extent. Indeed, at first it is difficult to decide what aspects of the body of psychoanalytic propositions about motivation belong to the one theory and what to the other. Freud did not make any such distinction: he in fact tended to lose sight of the basic distinction between observations and concepts or theories. For that reason, many analysts believe (mistakenly, in my opinion) that Freud derived the notion of instinct or drive and many of his propositions about it directly from clinical experience, and that this whole segment of psychoanalysis is part of the clinical theory. On the contrary, historical studies (such as those of Amacher, 1965; Spehlmann, 1953; and Ellenberger, 1970) make it plain that the conception of *Trieb,* particularly as set forth in the *Three Essays* (Freud, 1905b) and in "Instincts and Their Vicissitudes" (Freud, 1915a), is a direct outgrowth and elaboration of a physicalistic model of the organism presented by his predecessors and teachers. In my view, then, a large part of what we know as the theory of instincts, including the concept of instinct or drive itself, is part of metapsychology and not of the clinical theory; and my own estimation is that this paper does not make nearly as radical a proposal as anyone who is accustomed to considering instinct theory as being close to the clinical heart of psychoanalysis might think.

METHODOLOGICAL CRITIQUE

In this section, I propose first to push further the distinction between the metapsychology of motivation and clinical motivational theory. Then I shall review the respects in which Freud's metapsychology of instinctual drives contains fallacies, factual errors, inconsistencies, and other philosophical shortcomings. Little of what I will have to say is original, and because many of these criticisms are familiar or have been made by myself or others more fully elsewhere, I shall not document the points extensively. My aim, instead, is to show the cumulative impact of these criticisms.

The two psychoanalytic theories of motivation (see Klein, this volume, Chapter 2) are not only difficult to separate; paradoxically they sharply contradict one another in many ways. In its starkest and clearest form — essentially as stated in the "Project"[1] (Freud, 1895b) — the metapsychology of moti-

---

[1] Even here, Freud characteristically went off in several directions, following up various lines of thought as they arose, even when they made him begin implicitly to postulate another basic model. He was usually confident that synthesis would take care of itself in the long run — truth would prevail — whereas too much concern for consistency could hamper creativity. His was no little mind to be frightened by Emerson's hobgoblin!

vation is an explicit, coherent, but untenably mechanistic theory, which has the virtue of being testable and the misfortune of being mostly wrong. It is demonstrably the result of Freud's effort to remain true to Helmholtz and Brücke, his scientific ideal father imagoes; about all that is original to him in his theory is his synthesis of his teachers' ideas. With nonessential changes in terminology, the same ideas persisted in his various reworkings of metapsychology (see particularly 1915a) until the end. The clinical theory, by contrast, originated in Freud's work with patients, and he never brought it together in any one place. It is partly implicit, partly scattered throughout his writings, and I cannot undertake the task of assembling the bits here. My present concern is not with specific formulations about the kinds of goals people strive for and the regularities of conflict and defense — the kinds of topics with which the clinical theory deals — but primarily with more fundamental, underlying conceptions of an explanatory sort. In the final section, however, I shall return to the task of explicating the clinical theory of motivation and completing its extrication from metapsychological entanglements. In doing so, I hope to hold fast to what is essential and original in Freud's treatment of motivational issues, and to free it from the residues of nineteenth-century physiology, which threaten to conceal the true merits of what he had to teach us.

Let me concentrate now on stating the important testable propositions of the metapsychological theory.

The basic model of the organism is the hypothetical reflex arc, conceived of as stimulus→internal processing→response. That is, all behavior originates in the intrusion of physical energies from either the external world or from intrasomatic sources into the nervous system, which is conceived of as passive, without energies of its own, and functioning so as to rid itself of the noxious input via action. Since the inner processing may be very complex, involving much delay and the apparent violation of the constancy principle in the building up and maintenance of tension over some time in the service of the reality principle, the basic, pleasure-principle functioning may not be apparent though it is assumed to be there. Only adaptive, realistic behavior with biologically adequate objects can reduce tension by removing the inner organic sources of input; hence the necessity of paying attention to the real world and acting in a sensible, purposive fashion instead of making impulsive but futile lunges after direct gratification.

This is a complex first formulation, and there are several testable propositions inherent in it.[2] Item: The nervous system is passive and functions only when stimulated from outside itself. Testable neurophysiologically, and on the whole found wanting. Item: All stimulation is inherently and originally noxious ("primal hate of objects," Freud, 1915a) and becomes of positive interest only when the child has learned that even more painful inner sources of unpleasure cannot be eliminated except by pursuing external need-satisfying objects. Testable from infant observation, and found wanting. There is a large body of contemporary behavioral observation in man and other animals attesting to the independence and elemental nature of curiosity, an exploratory motive, stimulus hunger, or the like; indeed, Freud himself, especially during the decade 1905-1914, made many statements that there were autonomous, nonvoyeuristic sources of curiosity or the drive for research. Item: Increases in intrapsychic tension are unpleasant, and pleasure may be obtained only from reducing tension. Freud explicitly tells us that his observations contradict this proposition, which is clearly demanded by the theory; there is a considerable and growing literature of contemporary observations that confound tension-reduction as a basic principle of motivation; and there is neurophysiological evidence for anatomically separate pleasure and unpleasure centers. In sum, the passive reflex model must be abandoned.

Motivated behavior differs from ordinary reflex action, Freud often asserted, in that external stimuli act as simple impacts, which may be removed or escaped, whereas drive stimuli are internal, act continuously, and cannot be escaped. (At times in later papers, he sharpened this contrast by

---

[2] For more detailed treatment of the following points, with references, see Holt (1965a, 1965b).

contending that there were thresholds protecting against external stimuli, but no thresholds to give shelter even mo-, mentarily against the incessant input of the instinctual drives.) Here the model of the external stimulus seems to be the neurologist's rubber hammer, which Freud had wielded for so many years in eliciting reflexes. But as any experimenter in the field of stimulus deprivation knows, it is virtually impossible to protect a person from physiologically effective, external stimuli and keep him alive. We are bathed in a continuous sea of inescapable stimulation, and in fact our normal functioning seems to be dependent on an average expectable environment of varied stimuli. By contrast, the motives that seem most clearly to fit Freud's drive model — the evacuative needs, hunger, and thirst, as well as genital sexuality — are all capable of satiation and exhibit refractory phases after full consummation.

The facts are, then, that to the extent that internal stimuli can be physiologically detected, they are relatively phasic rather than "always ... constant" (1915a, p. 118), whereas external stimuli may be of all durations, from a microsecond flash of light to the eternal background of noise (except when extraordinary efforts are made to achieve silence). The assertion that we cannot literally run away from inner stimulation is, of course, true, but it is not a fact on which it is possible to build much useful theory.

In attempting to draw that distinction, Freud was leading up to a central proposition in his metapsychology of motivation, which is that instincts involve inputs of stimuli to the nervous system from within the body; indeed, he wrote, "instincts are wholly determined by their origin in a somatic source" (1915a, p. 123). Even though Freud said that "The study of the sources of instincts lies outside the scope of psychology" (p. 123), he made it explicit in several contexts (1905b, 1911) that all motivation originated in bodily stimuli, which meant that complete satisfaction of whatever motive was possible only through commerce with an object (which might be part of one's own body, but which was clearly enough a physical entity) that altered the offending endosomatic inputs. This is a rather extreme formulation, and it is surprising that it has attracted so little questioning from within psychoanalysis. I do not hesitate to say that it is impossible to demonstrate any relevant somatic stimulation connected with the vast majority of human motives; surely, the burden of proof was on Freud to find it, and neither he nor any of his followers has apparently felt it necessary to do so.

It is instructive to read reviews of the contemporary literature on the so-called physiological needs or basic drives (e.g., Wayner and Carey, 1973), which generations of us have unquestioningly assumed, with Freud, intimately involved stimuli to enteroceptors of some kind—for example, stimuli arising in the stomach and buccal mucous membrames have long been thought to play a major role in hunger and thirst. While such sensations undoubtedly exist and are part of the *experience* of being hungry and thirsty, important especially in infancy, they are not necessary to food- and water-seeking behavior; numerous studies (some of which I shall cite shortly) have demonstrated that they play no crucial role in these motives. Which is not to deny the clinical importance of experienced hunger and thirst. The fact that people have no sense of being hungry after they have starved themselves for a few days creates a life-threatening danger for anorectic patients. Quite aside from the nature of their specific unconscious fantasies and their role in interfering with food intake, such patients lack the usual conscious urge to eat.

Please notice that if we reject the passive reflex model and the conception that internal stimuli play a decisive role in motivation, very little is left of Freud's celebrated summary statement in "Instincts and Their Vicissitudes": "from a *biological* point of view, an 'instinct' appears to us as a concept on the frontier between the mental and the somatic, as the psychical representative of the stimuli originating from within the organism and reaching the mind, as a measure of the demand made upon the mind for work in consequence of its connection with the body" (1915a, pp. 121-122). Very little, that is, except one of Freud's baldest commitments to a dualistic interactionism, a solution to the mind-body problem that holds little favor among contemporary philosophers. I am in general agreement with Rubinstein's (1965) paper on "Psychoanalytic Theory and the Mind-Body Problem," and though I think a good deal more could be said about the interesting history of Freud's varying psychophysical stands in the course of his professional and theoretical development, I cannot undertake to do that here. Suffice it to say that, after he left the consistent and defensible parrallelism he clearly enunciated in his book on aphasia (Freud, 1891), Freud did not squarely face up to the issue and attempt to think it through. Rather, he seems to have adopted whatever position seemed expedient in any context where it came up, disarming criticism by a wry self-depreciation—he had, he said, a constitutional incapacity for and antipathy to philosophical thinking, and a predilection to stick to the facts of clinical observation. Or, as in the passage I just quoted, Freud would paper over an issue by a literary device: he would take refuge in a metaphor – here, that of a frontier between territories—instead of committing himself to a conceptual analysis.

However inclined we may be to empathize with Freud in his dilemmas, psychoanalysis as a science cannot avoid the responsibility of adopting a consistent philosophical position. It should be some form of identity theory, I believe, a monistic conception of the body-mind relation in which we think of the biological and the psychosocial as different levels of conceptual analysis of a complex unity: the behaving person in his context. In this frame of reference, there is no "mysterious leap from body to mind," any more than there is either a concrete or a metaphysical chasm to be jumped between electronics and information theory. There is surely no need to assume that a process, such as a physiological need, starts out on the bodily level and then at some point suddenly becomes "psychical," in Freud's term, only to return to a physical level of existence again if a somatic symptom is involved. Rather, the same complex event must be studied from beginning to end on the physiological level, and likewise on the psychological level—that is, in terms of wishes, fantasies, and other meanings. As long as we are consistent and comprehensive on each level, the two analyses are complementary, and both contribute to our total understanding without getting in each other's way.

Part of Freud's difficulty, as others and I (Yankelovich and Barrett, 1970; Klein, 1975; Holt, 1965a) have argued elsewhere, stemmed from his inability to see any way to make a true science in other than physicalistic terms, although he dealt always and almost exclusively with patterns of meanings.[3] That fact poses no insuperable difficulty for the contemporary philosopher of science, nor need it do so for the psychoanalytic theorist.

The disinterested contemporary reader must be struck by another feature of Freud's discussion of motives or instincts — his treating them constantly as if they were real, concrete entities. In short, he reifies (and often, even personifies) concepts that should remain abstract. For example, Freud wrote of the sexual instincts that they are numerous and "*act in the first instance independently of one another.*... The aim which each of them *strives* for is the attainment of 'organ pleasure' " (1915a, pp. 125-126; emphasis supplied). Here, as he was often to do elsewhere, he spoke of an instinctual drive as if it were not only capable of acting — serving as an efficient cause — but as if it were a sentient being capable of exerting effort, of persisting in its need to attain discharge, despite internal defense and external blocking, and even of adopting wily disguises. This charge is anything but novel; psychoanalysts are justifiably weary of hearing it, for the fallacy is not

---

[3] His way of trying to handle meanings was to treat them as "drive-derivatives," a concept that enabled him to go ahead and consider the clinical facts of motivation in more or less their own terms. Some critics of this paper have complained that I have not given adequate stress to this fact. I did not highlight it in the text because it seems to be a theoretically unsatisfactory way of trying to patch up a major deficiency in metapsychology. Meanings still have no recognized place in metapsychology; "drive-derivative" and equivalent expressions are merely a back door by which they are smuggled in despite their lack of proper scientific credentials. For the odd paradox of metapsychology is that despite its apparent reliance on "psychical" concepts, these are modeled after the concepts of physics (energy, force, structure) and physiology (excitation, pathway), and the mere addition of the adjective does not convert them into units or dimensions of semantic, phenomenal, or other meaningful realms.

truly intrinsic to the theory. The psychoanalytic theory of motivation *can* be stated and used without reification or personification. The fact is, however, that almost all of us stumble into these fallacies at least occasionally, and I venture to say that most of the time when psychoanalysts use motivational concepts — instinct, drive, libido, energy, force, cathexis — as if they were causally efficacious entities, they do so fallaciously. Schafer (this volume, Chapter 4) is so much impressed with the insidious pervasiveness of this error that he has embarked on the radical program of doing without substantive nominal concepts almost entirely. The only nouns he allows in his "action language" are words denoting persons, actions (plus classes and modes of action), situations, and to some extent dispositions. I find his proposals for such fundamental changes in our scientific language rather breathtaking, and am reluctant to conclude that radical surgery of this extent is needed. We should reserve judgment on Schafer's new approach, however, until he has had a chance to state it fully, which he is doing in a forthcoming book.

Another curious feature of Freud's various versions of his theory of instinctual drives is his strong preference for only two fundamental motives, to which all others could be reduced. True, in various places he did assert that there were numerous sexual and ego instincts, and the final conception of "life instinct" clearly contains a good many diverse motives. It was as if his conviction about the central importance of *conflict* forced him always to postulate an opposed duality of basic drives, even if it became necessary to lump together disparate motives with anatomically and physiologically quite separate bases. But all we need to do is to hold fast to the clinical facts about conflict, accounting in an alternative theory for its ubiquity and pathogenicity, and then we are freed from the artificial necessity to assume that all motives may be reduced to any two. It is clinically obvious that sex and aggression, in their many manifestations, are overridingly important; but fear, anxiety, dependence, self-esteem, curiosity, and group belongingness (to name only an obvious handful) cannot validly be reduced to sex and aggression, and are motivational themes the therapist cannot afford to ignore. For that matter, I do not believe that love, affection, friendship, and related themes can be satisfactorily reduced to sex either, despite the fact that Freud's authority has made us accept the reduction all too unquestioningly for years. Again, let me emphasize the fact that the dual instinct theory belongs to metapsychology, not to the clinical theory.

If you have followed me so far, you may nevertheless feel that I have disposed of only the most mechanistic version of the metapsychology of motivation. What about the sophisticated version Rapaport (1960) proposed in one of his last papers?[4] "*Motives are appetitive internal forces*," he wrote, going on to define *appetitive* in terms of "(a) peremptoriness, (b) cyclic character, (c) selectiveness, and (d) displaceability" (p. 865). Peremptoriness corresponds to Freud's pressure (*Drang*); Rubinstein (1967) calls this concept the hypothesis of motive pressure, and it has been highlighted in Klein's (1967) paper on peremptory ideation.

If we were to ask, What is the evidence for the existence of such internal forces as Rapaport postulates?, we would find that he adduces none. He merely invokes clinical experience generally and leans on the authority of William James (1890), who pointed out as a basic unsolved problem of psychology the distinction between behaviors we are impelled to carry out and those that are optional. Now, it is surely a fact of observation that some impulses and desires are relatively weak and easily managed by voluntary activity, while other impulses bring to mind vivid metaphors: they erupt from ego-alien sources, take over the organism, and drive it to an inexorable conclusion. But this is a kind of data to be explained, not in itself conclusive evidence for any theory.

The analogy of the sorcerer's apprentice comes to my mind

[4] I deal here with only the basic definition, not the full theory as Rapaport presented it, because it does not seem to me that he made fundamental changes in Freud's conception. True, Rapaport's version of psychic energy does not have some of the confusions of Freud's, but he leans on it and also on the concept—equally dubious, methodologically—of psychic structure as central explanatory constructs, though both concepts are still subject to most of the objections I have cited above.

at this point. Surely, when the obliging broom kept bringing water beyond the point where it was wanted, when it indeed began to be a threat to the hapless apprentice's life, its behavior appeared as inexorable and peremptory as one could imagine. Yet all that was involved was the necessary signal to halt the mechanism that had been started: the magic word that would serve as a negative feedback or switch-off. Or, closer to home, if we consider any machine that is not self-regulating, like an automobile, once it has been turned on it will go until its energy supply has been exhausted. Whether or not it seems "peremptory" is entirely a matter of control—if the car's throttle is stuck and no one is at the wheel, it is as much of a menace, and in much the same way, as a person in an epileptic furor or psychotic rage. A biological phenomenon even more analogous to the runaway car is a cat with a cauterized interpeduncular nucleus: it walks straight ahead, remorselessly and undeterred by any barriers put in its way, until it literally knocks itself out or collapses from exhaustion (Bailey and Davis, 1942). These examples suggest the possibility that the peremptoriness of some kinds of motivated behavior is at least as well explained in terms of defects in the controlling mechanism of negative feedback as by a theory of elusive psychic forces and energies pressing for discharge. Indeed, as Rubinstein (1967) has demonstrated, the existing doctrine of psychic energy lacks any explanatory power and is merely a set of descriptive metaphors. They owe their survival not to enhancing our understanding or providing any new insights into the detailed workings of behavior, thought, and affect, but to their rich literary suggestiveness.

I do not wish to discuss the concepts of psychic energies and forces, however, since their emptiness has been extensively and adequately argued elsewhere, by a number of others (e.g., Kubie, 1947; Rubinstein, 1967; Peterfreund, 1971) and by myself (1967). I want instead to attack a central remaining notion of instinct theory: that motives are a build-up of something—if not energy, perhaps tension[5]—that must be

---

[5] For a critique of the concept of tension, see Holt (1965a).

discharged, goading the person into action. Let me begin by
recalling some relevant developments in the experimental
psychology of motivation, a field worthy of our study despite
the fact that it has mostly used nonhuman subjects.

LESSONS FROM THE EXPERIMENTAL PSYCHOLOGY OF DRIVE

For about 40 years (from approximately 1915 to 1955),
research on the experimental psychology of motivation was
dominated by the concept of drive. This conception arose
from studies of the effects of *deprivation*: when an animal was
deprived of food or water, for example, he would eat and
drink more than a nondeprived animal when he got the
chance, and would work, learn, dare to attempt hazards like
electrified grids, and generally be more active and restless.
Drive was conceived, then, as a state of unpleasant internal
stimulation arising out of the physiological deficits induced by
the deprivation and impelling the organism into some kind of
behavior. It was assumed, further, that consummatory action
with the need-satisfying object led to objective satisfaction of
the tissue needs, so that the noxious drive-stimuli were reduced. As Cofer and Appley (1964) point out, this conception
strikingly parallels that of psychoanalysis, which preceded it
by a few years. (Indeed, to the extent that Freud does talk
about the bodily sources of drive, he treats them in much the
same way.)
    Since this concept of drive seemed so fruitful as an explana-
tion of hunger and thirst, it was extended to all the so-called
physiological needs, including sex. Initially, the experimental-
ists conceived of sex just as Freud had done in his paper on
anxiety neurosis (1895a): deprivation caused the accumulation of sexual products (at least in the male) and an uncom-
fortable state of distention rather than of deficit. Later, with
the discovery of hormonal influences on sexual behavior, the
position adopted by drive theorists was much like Freud's in
the *Three Essays*, particularly the later editions. What accumulated with deprivation was not secretions like seminal fluid,

they now thought, but blood levels of androgens or estrogens. When these hormones were abolished by castrating the animal, sexual behavior tended to stop, only to be dramatically reinstated after injections of the missing substance. But more detailed analysis of the role of sex hormones led to puzzling findings, which did not support the tension-reduction notion at all. In the first place, circulating androgens and estrogens are, if anything, only partly necessary and never sufficient conditions for sexual excitement and activity, and an impressive body of observations on many species, including man, has indicated that libido, the physiological capacity to engage in intercourse, and even orgasm (if not ejaculation) can persist for as long as 30 years after removal of the gonads, and thus without, or at best with extremely low, titers of the presumably necessary hormones. Moreover, it has never been found that orgasm *reduces* blood levels of hormones, nor is there any plausible mechanism by which such swift biochemical change could take place.

What is even more significant is that no infrahuman species shows the expected build-up of sexuality with increasing deprivation. As long as the animal has the general health and bodily preconditions for adequate performance, and leaving aside the phenomenon of estrus in many mammalian females, once a minimal recovery time has elapsed after an orgasm, the overwhelmingly important determiner of subsequent sexual excitement and activity is the presence of a more or less suitable partner.

As the most distinguished authority on the sexual behavior of animals, Frank Beach (1956), has put it:

> To a much greater extent than is true of hunger or thirst, the sexual tendencies depend for their arousal upon external stimuli. The quasi-romantic concept of the rutting stag actively seeking a mate is quite misleading. When he encounters a receptive female, the male animal may or may not become sexually excited, but it is most unlikely that in the absence of erotic stimuli he exists in a constant state of undischarged sexual tensions. This would be equally true for the human male, were it not for the potent effects of symbolic stimuli which he tends to carry with him wherever he goes [p. 5].

Thus, Beach is not blind to the fact that human beings do act
as if they had such accumulations of drive tension, but he
argues that these in fact amount to self-stimulation mediated
by imagery, fantasy, and internal language.

The late Kurt Goldstein used to tell of a striking clinical
demonstration of Beach's point. One of his severely brain-
damaged patients had lost the capacity for imagery, and his
abstract ability was so impaired that he had virtually no
capacity for autonomous thought—he seemed entirely sti-
mulus-bound. Although he was physically healthy and vigorous, he never showed any evidence of sexual desire or spontaneous erections. Even when his wife visited him in a private
room and disrobed him as well as herself, he lacked sexual
interest until she directly touched his genitals. At that point,
he became fully potent and was able to have intercourse with
her to their mutual satisfaction.

After many years of detailed study of sexual motivation in
animals, Beach has concluded that sex is better conceptualized as an appetite than as a drive. There is no evidence that
any physiologically measurable "tensions" build up in or near
the genitals with deprivation; indeed, when the whole genital
area has been denervated, male animals of several species still
become excited by receptive females and successfully copulate
with them, though the mechanism of ejaculation does seem to
depend upon intact sensory feedback from the penis.

What seems to be critical in sexual arousal is sensory awareness of the sexual partner. If inexperienced rats are deprived
of two or more senses, they do not attempt copulation when
they have the opportunity. Sexually experienced rats continue
with success despite the loss of any two senses, and cease only
when three senses are eliminated, a fact that suggests that,
even in the rat, sexual excitement may be achieved to some
degree from memory of previous experiences of gratification.
(Compare, in this context, Fisher's [1966] case of the elderly
castrate with a sexual dream.) Another dramatic demonstration of the importance of external arousal comes from repeated experimental findings that when a male has been

allowed to copulate with a female to the point where he shows
no further interest in her and appears "sexually exhausted,"
his capacity to perform sexually is immediately restored when
a new mate is offered to him. This phenomenon has been
found in the rat, rooster, guinea pig, monkey, and bull, and
anecdotal evidence suggests that it may occur on the human
level as well! It is very difficult to account for these facts by
means of a conception of sex as a drive arising out of an inner
build-up of tension that must be discharged.

There is a good deal of other evidence that external stimuli
play an important role in sex. The frequency of mating is
affected by various environmental conditions, temperature
and illumination, for example. Mammalian mating takes
place more frequently and successfully in familiar as compared to strange surroundings, though any inhibitory effect is
chiefly experienced by the male. This fact is strikingly confirmed on the human level by the observations of Masters and
Johnson (1966) that it was primarily male subjects who were
initially inhibited by being called on to have sexual intercourse
in their laboratory under observation.

Incidentally, in both males and females, much evidence
supports Beach's suggestion that two separate mechanisms
are involved in genital sexuality: one governing sexual arousal,
the other governing ejaculation and orgasm. Thus, there are
two separate thresholds: one for the onset of sexual excitement
and tumescence, which in nonhuman animals is determined
largely by an interaction of internal hormones and external
stimuli, supplemented increasingly at ascending levels in the
evolutionary series by subjective or symbolic self-stimulation;
and a threshold for orgasm, which is determined by sensory
feedback primarily from penis and clitoris. Though only
orgasm reduces sexual tension, there is ample evidence that
preorgastic sexual sensations are pleasurable and are eagerly
sought by all species even if orgasm is denied (Sheffield et al.,
1951; Kagan, 1955).

In short, recent careful observational and experimental
studies of nonhuman animals, which were the classical em-

bodiments of "animal instinct," do *not* support the notion of sex as an internally arising drive or tension that causes the organism to seek out need-satisfying objects.[6]

Let us turn to the evidence on aggression. Though rage, fighting among members of the same species, and other aggressive phenomena are widespread among animals, including many birds, fishes, and other submammalian species, and though such behavior has been meticulously studied, there is little convincing evidence that a need for aggression builds up after an animal has been deprived of it, Lorenz (1963) to the contrary notwithstanding. No animal, after being deprived of fighting, responds to the opportunity afforded by a suitable victim in the way he does to food after being kept hungry for a while. The bulk of the systematic experimental and observational work in man as well as in animals supports the conception that aggression is an innately determined (though extensively modifiable) reaction to certain classes of provocations, chiefly assault, frustration, and threat (including, in animals, trespass on property). In these respects, it closely resembles fear or the avoidance of pain, which seems to be equally "instinctive." It can hardly be a coincidence that that the physiological and biochemical substrates of fighting and flight are extremely similar and at the least closely interrelated, so much so that it seems artificial to consider (as Freud did) aggression a drive and fear merely an affect—a point cogently made by Murray (1938) many years ago. Fear and anxiety have such an obvious outward reference that it is understandable that Freud was even more reluctant to consider them instinctual or motivational in nature; but the attempt to treat them as affects runs into serious difficulty. In "The Unconscious" (1915b), Freud wrote that it was meaningless to speak of unconscious affects, since an affect was by

---

[6] I hope my position is clear: I do not mean to deny the obvious importance of the biological (anatomical, physiological, biochemical, etc.) determinants of sexual behavior, but only the drive concept itself. Even though the concept *instinct* or *drive* is becoming an anachronism, we are so used to it that my attempt to replace it can easily give the false impression that I refuse to face either of two realities: the facts of biology, or the facts of psychoanalytic observation.

definition a conscious phenomenon of energic discharge, yet clinical observations forced him, as they have the rest of us, to speak constantly albeit apologetically about unconscious anxiety.

If neither sex nor aggression is considered by most experimental psychologists and ethologists to fit the drive notion, what about hunger and thirst? Hunger seems to be the original model for the drive concept,[7] in psychoanalysis as well as in experimental psychology (see the "Project" [1895b], and Freud's [1900] hypothesis about the origins of ideation in the hallucinatory gratification of the hunger need in infants). The great physiologist Walter B. Cannon (1929) was much impressed by the role of local, unpleasant stimuli in both hunger and thirst (hunger pangs from the activity of the empty stomach, and oral sensations from dehydration of the mucous membranes); he lent his prestige to this drive conception of hunger and thirst and adduced a good deal of evidence for it. Yet it had long been known that animals might go empty for periods of weeks or months without any food-seeking behavior; and it was known that although stomach contractions might cease with the first bite or even with the sight of food, eating and hunger do continue for a while. Even so, the hungry feeling stops long before the objective tissue need has been supplied.

As I have already suggested, recent years have seen the accumulation of much more evidence undermining the applicability of the drive model to hunger. Eating is governed by strong preferences for specific substances, some of which — like saccharine — may be nonnutritive and thus incapable of providing release from "tension." In a series of experiments, the role of sensations from stomach contractions has been shown

---

[7] That is, the original explicit model. Implicitly, I believe that the model was probably urination, the one activity that clearly does have the alleged course (a build-up of fluid generating an increase of unpleasant internal sensation, followed by a literal discharge and a subjective sense of pleasure through relief). Note that hydrodynamics is even relevant here — literally, not metaphorically — and there *is* a set of the "interconnecting pipes," to which Freud was wont to allude, in the male urinogenital apparatus.

to be minimal; for example, gastrectomy or denervation of the stomach does not have any major effect on hunger. Most patients who had been vagotomized for peptic ulcer, according to a study by Grossman and Stein (1948), "did not recognize any alteration in the character of their hunger sensations as a result of vagotomy."

Both behavioral and neurological findings strongly point to the existence of at least two separate mechanisms controlling food intake: one concerns eating, the other satiety. The whole business turns out to be astonishingly complex: hunger and eating are governed by other areas of the brain besides the lateral hypothalamus and the hypothalamic ventromedial nuclei (the satiety center, which also seems to contain glucostats); brain thermostats may be involved too, for the temperature as well as the glucose concentration of the blood seems to affect the activity of the relevant hypothalamus and eating. Under normal circumstances, sensations from the stomach and other parts of the body do play some role, as do visual, olfactory, gustatory, and other oral sensations from chewing and swallowing. The role of learning in all this is only beginning to be investigated. Even the phenomenon of behavioral restlessness following deprivation of food no longer seems explicable in terms of accumulated tension; rather, there is good evidence that when it occurs (which is by no means all the time) it may be a mechanism for maintaining bodily temperature, which drops in starved animals if they are inactive.

The preceding summary (originally prepared for a panel discussion on drive theory at a meeting of the American Psychoanalytic Association in December, 1967—see Dahl, 1968) is both out of date and too brief to give an adequate account of the complexities of the four classical drives—sex, aggression, hunger, and thirst. But the more recent literature, to the extent that I have been able to follow it, is, if anything, more open in its rejection of the drive concept, which is the main point I have been trying to make by this excursion into an unfamiliar literature.

In sum, the classical "self-preservative" or ego motive of hunger operates in much more complicated ways than was supposed a few decades ago, and does *not* fit the tension-reduction model of drive, which had been originally framed to fit it. Much less can the drive concept be generalized to other types of motives, however peremptory. The metapsychological concept of *Trieb* — of instinct or drive — is thus in all major respects indefensible: philosophically shaky, factually mistaken, and, I believe, often clinically misleading (see Klein, this volume, Chapter 2). We must give it up.

Toward a New Theory

As an alternative to the metapsychological concept of instinctual drive, I propose, first, that we focus attention on its counterpart in the clinical theory, Freud's concept of wish; second, that psychoanalytic theorists consider the potentialities of the model of wishing proposed by George Klein (1967); and third, that it may ultimately be possible to build a systems conception in terms of which Klein's model will be a microscopic look at one sector which, though important, is only part of a larger picture. In the remainder of this paper, I shall expand on each of these proposals.

First, then, wish as a clinical concept. Let me remind you that Freud worked productively for his first fifteen years as a psychoanalyst without the concept of *Trieb*, relying primarily on wish as his motivational term. The main dynamic concept in *Studies on Hysteria* (Breuer and Freud, 1895) — affect-charged, repressed memories — has the major defining properties of wish: it is a cognitive-affective concept, framed in terms of meanings and potentially pleasant or unpleasant outcomes of possible courses of action. The principal motivational concept used in the brilliant case history of Dora (Freud, 1905a) and in Freud's (1900) masterpiece of combined clinical insight and theoretical elaboration, *The Interpretation of Dreams*, is wish. With it, he was able to do almost everything that an analyst needs to be able to do with a motivational concept, and even after introducing *Trieb*, he did not cease to make frequent use of wish. Therefore, substituting wish for drive means coming back to clinical home ground, while abandoning a largely redundant part of metapsychology that has failed to work, despite its popularity among analysts who have the mistaken impression that drive has the better scientific footing.

One of the advantages of wish is that it does not easily lend itself to the reifying and personifying (anthropomorphic) fallacies with which drive is so rife. A wish implies a person doing the wishing, and we are unaccustomed to speaking of a wish as if it had a life and mind of its own, as the Freudian *Triebe* so often seem to. A wish can be conscious or unconscious; it can conflict with another one; it can be countered, blocked, or modified by defenses and controls. Wishes are plainly near cousins to *plans* on one side (secondary process) and to fantasies on the other (primary process); they are concrete, often immediately available to introspection, not lofty or vague abstractions.

With the concept of wish, we can reassert, in answer to the behaviorists and other mechanistically inclined theorists, that behavior *is* purposive, that fears, longings, plans, fantasies, and other mental processes are not epiphenomena, but must be central to any adequate psychology of human behavior, and that the person is often not conscious of what his purposes are. Those who find it hard to shake off reductionistic habits of thought may find these ideas more acceptable if they think of wishes and plans as strictly analogous to the programs of computers.

To those who object that wishes are not biological enough, that they do not readily lend themselves to the explanation of psychosomatic problems, I would say that they can express our limited understanding just as well as the metapsychological language of instincts or drives, and have the advantage of not committing us to a great deal of pseudoexplanatory mythology that does not have satisfactory grounding in fact. Before we can begin to make any more progress in this complicated area, we have to agree to stop pretending that we have answers to insoluble philosophical problems. No matter what metaphysical position you take, there remains an impenetrable mystery in the fact that subjective experience exists in a physiochemical world. Perhaps we shall someday learn what are the sufficient conditions for a physiochemical system to take on attributes we call mental; at present, we just do not know.

In an already long essay, I cannot adequately summarize Klein's proposed model of the way wishes function for those who have not already read his paper "Peremptory Ideation" (1967; see especially his Fig. 1, p. 89). Briefly, Klein diagrams the sequence of events that occur in what he calls a "cognitive unit of motivation," from the initial desire to the final experience of gratification, as a closed feedback loop. It begins with what he termed a "Primary Region of Imbalance" (PRI), an unusual state of affairs in one brain region that facilitates, successively, various components of thought, affect, and action. At the end, the PRI is canceled or "switched off" by an appropriate kind of feedback from experience.

Klein's model is basically a translation into modern terminology of Freud's account (in Chapter VII of *The Interpretation of Dreams*) of the nature of wishing: a wish begins with "the excitations produced by internal needs" (cf. the PRI), and ends when

> an 'experience of satisfaction' can be achieved which puts an end to the internal stimulus. An essential component of this experience of satisfaction is a particular perception ... the mnemic image of which remains associated thenceforward with the memory trace of the excitation produced by the need.... next time this need arises a psychical impulse will at once emerge which will seek to re-cathect the mnemic image of the perception and to re-evoke the perception itself, that is to say, to re-establish the situation of the original satisfaction. An impulse of this kind is what we call a wish [Freud, 1900, pp. 565-566].

Klein has taken the essentials of Freud's account of wishing, has stripped it of its anthropormorphism and its power-engineering economics of energy, and elaborated it in a number of interesting respects. In particular, his representations of the activity of a repressed unconscious fantasy and the various ways it can complicate ideomotor systems constitute an important contribution to the clarification and formalization of the clinical theory of psychoanalysis. Yet, to my ear, his phrase "Primary Region of Imbalance" is an unfortunately vague metaphor implying something very much like the old drive-notion of need-generated "excitations" or "tensions" that must be discharged. Indeed, in an effort not to cut all ties to existing theory, Klein retains the misleading term "discharge" as well, even though he attempts to give it a new meaning. In his examples of thirst (p. 91) and sexual wish (p. 94), he tends to regress to simplistic, tension-reducing conceptions that motives originate in enteroceptive stimuli. I believe that it will strengthen his model if all these remnants of the old drive theory are abandoned.

I propose, then, that we replace "imbalance" by "perceptual-evaluative mismatch"—hardly a gain in euphony, but, I hope, one in explicitness. "Mismatch" implies a process (which may be conscious, preconscious, or unconscious) of comparing *both* a perceptual (input) and a centrally generated pattern (mainly from memory), *and* value judgments attached to each pattern. In more phenomenological terms, that means testing an existing and a potential state of affairs for the degree to which they coincide, as well as for any significant discrepancy in value. When what exists is less valuable than what might be, we usually call the fantasied scenario of closing the gap a wish; when what exists is more highly valued, what might be is usually considered a threat or danger, the fantasy a *fear* or an *aversion*. (I intend the term wish to be understood, most of the time, to include these negative forms.) The (sometimes unconsciously) felt gap between actuality and potentiality can obviously be abolished by a change in reality, so that what exists is what was wanted, or what threatened has been successfully averted; then a discrepancy no longer exists, and the motivational unit goes out of existence. A sequence of the kind Klein diagramed—a wish—is thus initiated not by some unspecified kind of imbalance, but by a cognitive-affective state something like dissatisfaction, which arouses anticipations of pleasure and/or unpleasure (I repeat, not necessarily conscious) as a consequence of various courses of action or inaction.[8] The condition of perceptual-evaluative mismatch typically originates when the person faces some opportunity or threat, or something not itself particularly desirable or undesirable but which is (directly or indirectly) associated with some such valued state.

My use of the term value instead of the more usual pleasure and unpleasure is deliberate: it is to remind us that human beings tend to conceptualize their affective responses, to crystallize them into values and ideals. Eventually, I hope that it will be possible to integrate the wise insights of Schafer's (1967) paper on "Ideals, the Ego Ideal, and the Ideal Self" with Klein's model.

There is a strong and by no means accidental resemblance between this model and Freud's account in the "Project" of what he called judgment, in terms of a wishful cathexis (what might be) and a perceptual cathexis (what exists). Those who are familiar with the work of von Holst and Mittelstadt (1950) may see an interesting similarity to their conception of reafferance; and the concept of mismatch has been borrowed from a contemporary Russian psychologist, Sokolov (1960). In

---

[8] There are some obvious similarities between my reformulation of Klein's model and the conception of motivation advanced by McClelland as long ago as 1951 (see also McClelland et al., 1953). I cannot undertake here to explain in detail why I do not find the McClelland model entirely satisfactory; but in general I agree with the critique of Cofer and Appley (1964, pp. 382-386). Helson's (1959) concept of adaptation level is plainly useful, perhaps necessary, but I believe that the problem of value is far too complex to be reduced to degrees of deviation from adaptation level. For some further parallels to contemporary theories, see my footnotes on p. 91 of Klein (1967). Most recently, I am impressed by a number of striking similarities between the model toward which I have been groping and the elegant, highly elaborated model proposed by Powers (1973). At the time of this writing, I have not yet been able to study and assimilate Powers's book with the care it deserves, but I believe that it will be worth the attention of anyone who is sympathetic to what I have been trying to do. It is a sophisticated cybernetic systems model, protoneurophysiological in Rubinstein's sense, which briefly but explicitly treats unconscious processes, dreams, imagination, conflict, anxiety, and defense. It may well have the potentiality for modeling the observational data and clinical theory of psychoanalysis better than any other contribution from outside the psychoanalytic community. I wish also to call attention to what seem to me striking parallels between the model developed here and the more detailed one recently published by Rubinstein (1975).

what may look like name-dropping, I hope to suggest the fact that Klein's model (and my suggested modifications) have roots in Freud's own thinking and parallels in theories proposed by some major contemporary workers in ethology and neuropsychology.

Let me turn now to a consideration of what seem to be the next steps in the building of Klein's model into a complete motivational theory. At present, of course, I cannot do more than put up a few signposts pointing in some necessary directions for further theoretical work.

One of the immediate consequences of Klein's starting point, his intention to conceptualize peremptory ideation, is the fact that his model is limited to negative feedback systems. Here is another bit of heritage from the tradition of drive theory, which takes as the type case of motivation self-limiting sequences like that of urination. Yet it is obvious that a great deal of behavior in everyday life does not have this episodic character; most of us spend most of our time in continuing, long-term activities, many of which have no logical stopping points. We have to add the conception of *positive* feedback systems, which do not involve any "discharge" or even "switch-off." Rather, our theory must recognize that as long as a pattern of behavior yields a balance of gratification over negative affect it will tend to be continued. In terms of the model, the transmissions from the final stage to the primary region are not inhibitory but facilitating, and the cycle continues until it is interrupted by something external to it — for example, considerations of scheduling, or the intrusion of demands from other people. The fact that the person resumes the behavior in question when it is opportune to do so usually makes it plain enough that there had been no cancellation of an initiating perceptual-evaluative mismatch by an experience of match, but only a temporary interruption. Concrete instances of behavior undoubtedly will at times require both types of explanation (positive and negative feedback systems, or perhaps complex hybrid types).

A closely related issue was only briefly touched on in Klein's 1967 paper: the relation between momentary trains of motivated thought (or wishes) and the long-run ideals, fears, defensive strategies, career plans, persistently recurring symptoms, and sustained repetitive strivings of human beings. The model he set forth is best adapted to explain the behavior of the moment, especially self-terminating segments of behavior. A more generally useful system will have to explain how such temporary systems come into being (Klein accounts well enough for their disappearance) and how they attain the varying degrees of specificity as well as personal consistency that observation compels us to assign them. Here again I hope for a link-up with Schafer's (1967) paper on ideals.

Another direction of needed theoretical work is one in which Klein often moved: constantly to keep in mind, and make theoretical allowance for, individual variations of all kinds on the general theoretical themes. Psychoanalysis has justly been criticized for presenting too monolithic a conception of personality, as if people were all organized in very much the same ways and developed along standard lines. Here is another locus of great discrepancy between theory and practice, for while metapsychology states the general case so insistently as to seem to allow no room for a psychology of personality, the psychoanalytic method allows the working clinician to get to know the unique individuality of each patient as few others can. It is time for theory to catch up with practice. I believe that Klein's model can account for many types of individual differences in motives, but its potentiality needs to be actualized.

A related direction is a developmental one. Klein's model presupposes a mature person; of course, we must eventually be able to model motivation at all levels of personal development, and account for the ways in which growth takes place. The capacity to entertain simultaneously a present percept of the world and an imagined image of what it might be is a developmental cognitive achievement of no mean order. Piaget has presented in useful detail the sequential stages through which relevant cognitive operations pass, but the motivational implications of each stage have hardly begun to be worked out. The nearest approximation may be found in the work of Jane

Loevinger (1966; Loevinger et al., 1970) on ego development; she describes different kinds of goals and of goal-seeking behavior at each of the nine or so levels of development she has isolated, working largely with sentence-completion test data from girls and women. I can mention only a couple of ways in which her work suggests fruitful reconceptualization of motivational issues. Much of what has been treated in the psychoanalytic literature as degrees of ego autonomy can be viewed as parts of specifiable stages of development. Freud, being a highly autonomous and mature person himself, tended at times to write as if other people were much like himself; he may not have realized how much less freedom to choose among alternative courses of action was possessed by the great majority of otherwise normal persons.

I have found it interesting to extract from the case of Dora (Freud, 1905a) the implicit, common-sense theory of motivation Freud used when dealing with ordinary, nonpathological behavior (Holt, 1975). He never thought to make this theory explicit or take it seriously, since his emphasis was always on going beyond it to explain puzzling behavior; but intelligible behavior is motivated too, and a comprehensive theory must account for it. Freud's implicit view was that healthy, normal people typically act in rational ways; that is, they foresee the consequences of available courses of action and choose the one realistically likely to result in the most gratification and the least unpleasantness. Elsewhere, to be sure, he did describe the secondary process as characterized by delay and the experimental action of thought rather than by an impulsive reach for immediate gratification; but it was not always obvious that these discussions are relevant to motivation as well as to thought. And though Freud clearly stated that a developmental sequence is involved, he did not extend the phasic model of psychosexual development beyond the first few years of life. We can and should do so; I am convinced that the facts of motivation will lend themselves to a sequence of phase changes such as Kohlberg (1969) has described in the area of moral judgment. The structure of wishing as Klein has diagramed it undoubtedly grows more complex stage by stage, and his scheme will lend itself, I believe, to the conceptual clarification of wishing at each developmental level. His developmental hypotheses about types of pleasure (Klein, 1972) can fruitfully be drawn on in this effort.

Another way in which Klein's model needs to be evolved is to take into account self and self-evaluation, the importance of which I believe analysts are increasingly appreciating. One of the most painful kinds of mismatch is that between a person's sense of his present self and his desired self. As we know clinically, self-loathing can reach the point where suicide seems necessary to put a stop to intolerable pain. Yet this entire, highly important realm of motivation is at present only crudely conceptualized under the cloudy heading of narcissism. We know something about how the negative self-feelings of shame and guilt develop, but I believe that the whole area of self-evaluation and feelings concerning the self stands in great need of developmental reconsideration. If it is to be as useful as I believe it potentially to be, Klein's model must find an explicit place for an explanation of self-esteem, self-hatred, narcissistic self-love, mature self-respect, and all the other varieties of self-evaluations. Though I cannot demonstrate it here, I believe that this requirement is much more than a specification of content and that it will entail a substantial extension of the model.

Finally, it should be evident that Klein's model, like most antecedent psychoanalytic theories, is concerned almost entirely with psychological, intrapersonal matters. To use one of his favorite metaphors, it is a glimpse through a reduction screen, which artificially — but usefully — restricts our vision to a sector small enough to conceptualize. Klein would surely not have maintained that it was a sufficient account of motivation, or that motivation could for long be considered without reference to most of the rest of psychology. For years, Klein understood and taught the complex and many-layered nature of human concerns, and he steadily urged that we look on behavior as a seamless unity. We might for our convenience abstract emotion from thought, or perception from motivation, but we should do so at a risk of forgetting their ultimate integrity. From this standpoint, we should not proceed to develop one model for motivation, one to explain memory, and another for each of the traditional divisions of the old elementary texts, in the vain expectation that the unity of observed human functioning will somehow emerge from the joint, even "interactive," operation of these several models. Nature may be orderly, but it is not the creation of an obsessive-compulsive God who created thought one day, motivation another, and saw to it that there were proper boundaries between all such categories. As a motivational model grows more adequate, it begins to look like a complete theory of personality. If we ask of this ultimate model, "How does the person get to know his surroundings?," the answer will be in a set of perceptual propositions; if we ask, "How can we understand the directional, goal-seeking nature of the person's behavior?," the answer will be put in a set of motivational propositions; but the model of the behaving person remains the same.

Perhaps at this point it might be useful to restate the obvious: that behavior is a complex function of internal determinants: genic, biochemical, hormonal, and other biological determinants, the residues of past learning and maturation; and external determinants: the social structure and culture within which the person lives, tonic supports (Holt, 1965b), and the immediately present press (potential harms, benefits, and opportunities). If this full range of behavioral determinants is to be taken into account, nothing less than the most comprehensive theoretical framework available today will do — a systems conception. This framework can satisfactorily coordinate the resources of the other human sciences that are plainly needed for a complete and generally useful psychoanalytic theory of motivation.

Among the most relevant neighboring disciplines are many of the branches of biology. We cannot content ourselves with having disposed of the notion that the body makes its contribution merely by bombarding the brain with enteroceptive stimulations; there are many important somatic aspects of sex and aggression (as well as the so-called physiological drives). Let us begin with the difficult problem of aggression.

Behavior genetics is as yet a new science, and though it is well established that we are not blank slates on which experience can write whatever she likes, the detailed structures and processes through which behavioral predispositions are inherited are far from being well understood. Nevertheless, as Moyer (1973) puts it, "the brain contains inborn neural systems that, when active *in the presence of particular stimuli*, result in aggressive behavior toward those stimuli" (p. 35). The only change I would make in that formulation would be to substitute press for stimuli (see below). Electrical inputs to certain areas in the amygdala can set off aggressive behavior, which demonstrates the point. The thresholds for the production of anger and hostility can be lowered biochemically, or by the pressure of tumors in or near the amygdala.

In terms of our model, people have an inborn readiness to value positively *either* escape from or inflicting harm on persons, animals, or objects that harm them, threaten to do so, or block the attainment of important goals, and a readiness to act in these same ways. (What seem to be separate cases may in a way reduce to one, since injuring an enemy is a way of putting a stop to his inflicting harm on you, just as running away is. It all comes down to the negative valuing of being injured or frustrated—which has obvious survival value—and the consequent need to have a variety of response patterns to prevent being injured or blocked from attaining gratifications—a capability that is also obviously adaptive. I can see no need to postulate any direct pleasure in causing or perceiving injury to another unless that other is perceived as threatening or thwarting.)

Whether a given person will tend to choose aggression or flight as a means of coping with threat or frustration seems to be in considerable part a matter of intrauterine hormonal setting of the nervous system. A great deal of fascinating work is currently going on concerning the effects of hormones and other biochemical agents on both sexual and aggressive behavior (and, more generally, on sex-linked "masculine" and "feminine" behavior). The impression with which I come away from reading accounts of this research is that the effects seem to be of two kinds: First, parts of the CNS may become programmed during fetal development with a readiness to produce certain patterns of behavior—most strikingly, greater aggressiveness, general activity, interest in rough games and sports, and possibly career-oriented achievement motivation—in boys and in girls who were virilized in utero because their mothers had had injections of progestins or had suffered from the adrenogenital syndrome (Money and Ehrhardt, 1972). (Boys are virilized by their own fetal testosterone.) Second, granted that the capacity for producing a form of behavior is present in the brain, the threshold for its production may be raised or lowered by the biochemical *milieu intern*—notably, by the amount of circulating testosterone. (Other biochemical influences, like the degree of hypoglycemia, or the responsiveness of the adrenals, are also important, but the details are less important for present purposes than the basic principles.) Past learning also plays an enormously important role. If in early life a person is consistently and severely punished for any display of aggressiveness, later provocations will obviously tend to evoke fear and avoidance. If his aggressiveness has been ignored or encouraged, he will later probably fight rather than take flight.

Notice, however, that the role of a biologically adequate external releaser is still crucial. When, for example, 6-hydroxydopa was injected into the ventricles of rats' brains, fighting as a response to being electrically shocked was greatly increased and the rats also tried to bite the experimenter when handled, but there was "little or no intraspecific aggression when the animals were in their home cages"—i.e., no aggression without provocation (Thoa et al., 1972, p. 76).

At a first approximation, then, the modified Klein model links up with the biological in this way: any particular situation is more or less likely to arouse a perceptual-evaluative mismatch and thus a wish depending on the hormonal (and, more generally, the biochemical) history and contemporary state of the person's body, which also influence the availability of various behavior sequences as elements in the completed wish-cycle or ideomotor system.

As I have argued elsewhere (Holt, 1965b), the phenomena that psychoanalysts have long conceptualized in purely intra-psychic (or intraorganismic) terms must be accounted for in a way that takes serious account of the person's environment, especially the threats and opportunities it presents. Once we replace imbalance by valued mismatch between a perceived and an imagined world, it becomes evident that the single feedback loop Klein diagramed and discussed is only part of a larger, more complex system comprising the person and his environment. One of the incidental by-products of the current ecological movement is the rise of environmental psychology, a slogan that may help redirect the attention of psychologists to behaviorally relevant aspects of man's surroundings other than obvious positive and negative reinforcers. Again, Murray (1938) is proved to have been unusually foresighted: after 35 years, his concept of *press*—the motivationally relevant aspects of a person's environment—and his pioneering classification of its major types remain virtually without competition.

Since I am surely not ignorant of the notorious emphasis of behaviorists, social-learning theorists, and in fact most American psychologists on "stimulus control of behavior," the just-preceding statement must sound like a willful perversity. If so, which of these colleagues has produced a psychologically useful or systematic classification of "stimuli"? If any such exists, it has remained obscure. The trouble is our old heritage of physicalism: stimuli are almost never *clearly* defined by psychologists in any but physical terms. Outside of psycho-physics, where it is appropriate and necessary to define sounds (for example) as pressure waves measured in herz and dynes/cm², it is misleading to talk about situations, people, and other interesting features of a person's environment in terms of stimuli. Even when you attempt to define the word in psychological terms, it still carries a physicalistic, submeaningful connotation.

It was part of Murray's genius to grasp this point, to reject the misleading term "stimulus," and to substitute for it a new term clearly defined in terms of meaning, to serve as a unit for the analysis of the psychological environment. If you imagine that press are nothing more than a classification of stimuli in terms of response, let me commend to you Murray's wise exposition (1938, pp. 116 ff.). Press are not defined by reference to the subject's response to them, but in terms of consensually established meanings—essentially the same approach as that of sociologists and anthropologists. Indeed, these disciplines may be said to be the principal ones concerned with press, though they do not use the term, and psychologists have left systematic treatment of the environment almost entirely to them, to architects, geographers, climatologists, and other social scientists.

By way of summary, let me give very briefly the present status of the model as I see it. It is protoneurophysiological (Rubinstein, 1967), in that the operative concepts are stated in generalized terms suitable for eventual translation into anatomical and physiological language, on the one hand, and into terms that are meanings, on the other. The relation between the two sets of terms is one of encoding: it is assumed that all subjective, phenomenological events are coded assemblages of information being transmitted and processed in the nervous system in biochemical and biophysical form. Some degree of isomorphism is thus assumed (if a phenomenal unity appears, there is in some sense a corresponding unity of process in the biological substrate). Units are defined predominately in terms of meanings,[9] but care is taken constantly

_____

[9] The human being is designed and functions so as to process and produce meanings. That being the case, so long as the person is alive and well, he cannot help but deal with meanings and make meaningful sense out of his experience. To say that he has a *need* to find meaning is thus no more accurate than, and is as misleading as, to say that an automatic knitting machine has a need to knit or that a seed has a need to germinate. Those activities are simply what they do, each in its own fashion, carrying out the function its structure makes more or less inevitable. I believe that the structure of the human nervous system, in its organismic setting, makes the generation of meanings as natural as the generation of sweat from sweat glands. In a certain sense it is true that we do need to sweat, but that sense is simply

not to postulate anything that conflicts with the contemporary state of knowledge in the neurosciences.

All behavior is caused, but not necessarily (and not in all its details) determined, by wishes.[10] Much of it is determined simply by the detailed structure of a person's body, by the adequacy of his physiological functioning, and by genetic programs. The activity of the gastrointestinal system, for example, can be accounted for in the terms of the preceding sentence, and no doubt for such reasons is not usually considered "behavior." But consider a boy playing baseball: his native strength, coordination, and state of bodily vigor at the moment obviously have a lot to do with the style and adequacy of his playing, and even with whether he plays at all or not. Ordinarily, when we say that all behavior is motivated, we imply a definition of behavior as the part of the person's total activity that is caused by identifiable motives. I see no need to get into that kind of game here. Let us simply note that some aspects of the most obviously wish-determined behavior are caused nonpsychologically, and also that activities ordinarily considered to be "purely physiological" may be affected in some respects by wishes. Psychosomatic medicine teaches us, for example, that unconscious wishes to be filled up or emptied out can greatly interfere with the normal functioning of the GI tract.

As part of the normal functioning of the sensory organs and the CNS, healthy people continually construct a phenomenal world while awake. Part of that activity is a continuous matching of inputs against stored memories of past perceptual experience. Satisfactory matching results in the sense of recog-

---

that sweating is useful, adaptive, even necessary to the maintenance of a steady temperature within the body, just as we need to have something solid to walk upon without our necessarily wishing for it more than occasionally.

[10] This unpsychoanalytic-sounding proposition needs some amplification. I think it is safe to say that all *extended* behavior sequences are determined by wishes, usually by a number of them with varying degrees of consciousness. But viewed more microscopically, behavior is at times automatized, in Hartmann's sense of the term, or habitual; as Rapaport (1960) put it, to consider that *all* behavior is in all components motivationally determined is to return to the old and fallacious "seething cauldron" conception of Freud's early writings.

nition, and it appears that a general silent precondition for normal behavior is a steady background of such implicitly reassuring matches: the person is oriented, he finds most aspects of his experience at least generally familiar. Let us assume, following Piaget (1936) and a good many other contemporary theorists, that moderate degrees of mismatch arouse mild degrees of pleasure and interest, which we call curiosity, and which initiate and sustain exploratory behavior. Let us assume, also, that when mismatch is sudden and considerable in extent (passively suffered) the person experiences startle and some innately programmed unpleasure.

In the foregoing, I am assuming that there are brain centers the activity of which is accompanied by positive and negative affective experiences, and which are genetically "wired into" various innate programs (for example, the pleasures associated with stimulation of the various erogenous zones). When the infant or child happens to experience something that is in this way innately gratifying, he uses whatever sensorimotor schemas he has at his disposal to prolong the pleasure — a positive feedback system (or, in Piaget's terminology, a circular reaction).

Such positive feedback systems are the main supplementation required by Klein's model, which deals only with negative feedback loops. With these two types of systems, we can explain most of the kinds of motives with which psychoanalysts are concerned. When we get more ambitious and hope to cover all aspects of behavior and inner life, what began as a systematization of clinical theory starts to look like an attempted replacement for metapsychology. Indeed, the program for theoretical development already sketched out here is ambitious enough to betray the fact that I share yearnings that Freud recognized as speculative and philosophical. Like him, however, I shall at least for the moment suppress them and break off.

In conclusion: drive is dead; long live wish! Freud's concept of *Trieb* served a useful function in his own theoretical development, but for us it is an anachronism beyond hope of rehabilitation. With relatively few terminological changes, however, his earlier but never abandoned concept of wish can be made a clinically usable substitute. And as it has been sharply restated by Klein, the theory of wish promises to become the nucleus for a fully developed, recognizably psychoanalytic and generally useful theory of human motivation.

REFERENCES

Amacher, P. (1965), Freud's Neurological Education and Its Influence on Psychoanalytic Theory. *Psychol. Issues,* Monogr. No. 16. New York: International Universities Press.

Bailey, P., & Davis, E. W. (1942), The Syndrome of Obstinate Progression in the Cat. *Proc. Soc. Exper. Biol.,* 51:307.

Beach, F. (1956), Characteristics of Masculine Sex Drive. In: *Nebraska Symposium on Motivation, 1956,* ed. M. R. Jones. Lincoln: University of Nebraska Press, pp. 1-32.

Breuer, J., & Freud, S. (1895), Studies on Hysteria. *Standard Edition,* 2. London: Hogarth Press, 1955.

Cannon, W. B. (1929), *Bodily Changes in Pain, Hunger, Fear, and Rage.* New York: Appleton.

Cofer, C. N., & Appley, M. H. (1964), *Motivation: Theory and Research.* New York: Wiley.

Dahl, H., rep. (1968), Psychoanalytic Theory of the Instinctual Drives in Relation to Recent Developments. *J. Amer. Psychoanal. Assn.,* 16:613-637.

Ellenberger, H. F. (1970), *The Discovery of the Unconscious: The History and Evolution of Dynamic Psychiatry.* New York: Basic Books.

Fisher, C. (1966), Dreaming and Sexuality. In: *Psychoanalysis: A General Psychology,* ed. R. M. Loewenstein, L. M. Newman, M. Schur, & A. J. Solnit. New York: International Universities Press, pp. 537-569.

Freud, S. (1891), *On Aphasia.* New York: International Universities Press, 1953.

———— (1895a), On the Grounds for Detaching a Particular Syndrome from Neurasthenia under the Description "Anxiety Neurosis." *Standard Edition,* 3:85-139. London: Hogarth Press, 1962.

———— (1895b), Project for a Scientific Psychology. *Standard Edition,* 1:283-387. London: Hogarth Press, 1966.

———— (1900), The Interpretation of Dreams. *Standard Edition,* 4 & 5. London: Hogarth Press, 1953.

———— (1905a), Fragment of an Analysis of a Case of Hysteria. *Standard Edition,* 7:3-122. London: Hogarth Press, 1953.

———— (1905b), Three Essays on the Theory of Sexuality. *Standard Edition,* 7:125-245. London: Hogarth Press, 1953.

———— (1911), Formulations on the Two Principles of Mental Functioning. *Standard Edition,* 12:218-226. London: Hogarth Press, 1958.

———— (1915a), Instincts and Their Vicissitudes. *Standard Edition,* 14:109-140. London: Hogarth Press, 1957.

———— (1915b), The Unconscious. *Standard Edition,* 14:159-215. London: Hogarth Press, 1957.

196   ROBERT R. HOLT

Grossman, M. I., & Stein, L. F., Jr. (1948), Vatogomy and the Hunger-Producing Action of Insulin in Man. *J. Applied Physiol.*, 1:263-269.
Helson, H. (1959), Adaptation Level Theory. In: *Psychology: A Study of a Science,* Vol. 1, ed. S. Koch. New York: McGraw-Hill, pp. 565-621.
Holt, R. R. (1965a), A Review of Some of Freud's Biological Assumptions and Their Influence on His Theories. In: *Psychoanalysis and Current Biological Thought,* ed. N. S. Greenfield & W. C. Lewis. Madison: University of Wisconsin Press, pp. 93-124.
_____ (1965b), Ego Autonomy Re-evaluated. *Internat. J. Psycho-Anal.*, 46:151-167.
_____(1967), Beyond Vitalism and Mechanism: Freud's Concept of Psychic Energy. In: *Science and Psychoanalysis,* 11:1-41. New York: Grune & Stratton.
_____(1975), The Past and Future of Ego Psychology. *Psychoanal. Quart.*, 44:550-576.
James, W. (1890), *The Principles of Psychology.* New York: Smith, 1962.
Kagan, J. (1955), Differential Reward Value of Incomplete and Complete Sexual Behavior. *J. Compar. & Physiol. Psychol.*, 48:59-65.
Klein, G. S. (1967), Peremptory Ideation: Structure and Force in Motivated Ideas. In: Motives and Thought: Psychoanalytic Essays in Honor of David Rapaport, ed. R. R. Holt. *Psychol. Issues,* Monogr. No. 18/19:80-128. New York: International Universities Press.
_____(1972), The Vital Pleasures. *Psychoanalysis and Contemporary Science,* 1:181-205. New York: Macmillan.
_____ (1975), *Psychoanalytic Theory: An Exploration of Essentials.* New York: International Universities Press.
Kohlberg, L. (1969), Stage and Sequence: The Cognitive-Developmental Approach to Socialization. In: *Handbook of Socialization Theory and Research,* ed. D. A. Goslin. New York: Rand McNally, pp. 347-380.
Kubie, L. S. (1947), The Fallacious Use of Quantitative Concepts in Dynamic Psychology. *Psychoanal. Quart.*, 16:507-518.
Loevinger, J. (1966), The Meaning and Measurement of Ego Development. *Amer. Psychol.*, 21:195-206.
_____ , Wessler, R., & Redmore, C. (1970), *Measuring Ego Development.* San Francisco: Jossey-Bass.
Lorenz, K. (1963), *On Aggression.* New York: Harcourt, Brace & World.
Masters, W. H., & Johnson, V. E. (1966), *Human Sexual Response.* New York: Little, Brown.
McClelland, D. C. (1951), *Personality.* New York: Sloane.
_____ et al. (1953), *The Achievement Motive.* New York: Appleton-Century-Crofts.
Money, J., & Ehrhardt, A. (1972), *Man and Woman, Boy and Girl.* Baltimore, Md.: Johns Hopkins University Press.
Moyer, K. E. (1973), The Physiology of Violence. *Psychology Today,* 7:35-28.
Murray, H. A. (1938), *Explorations in Personality.* New York: Oxford University Press.
Peterfreund, E. (1971), Information, Systems, and Psychoanalysis: An Evolutionary Biological Approach to Psychoanalytic Theory. *Psychol. Issues,* Monogr. No. 25/26. New York: International Universities Press.
Piaget, J. (1936), *The Origins of Intelligence in Children,* trans. M. Cook. New York: International Universities Press, 1954.
Powers, W. T. (1973), *Behavior: The Control of Perception.* Chicago: Aldine.

Rapaport, D. (1959), The Structure of Psychoanalytic Theory: A Systematizing Attempt. *Psychol. Issues,* Monogr. No. 6. New York: International Universities Press, 1960.

_____(1960), On the Psychoanalytic Theory of Motivation. In: *Nebraska Symposium on Motivation, 1960,* ed. M. Jones. Lincoln: University of Nebraska Press, pp. 173-247. Also in: *The Collected Papers of David Rapaport,* ed. M. M. Gill. New York: Basic Books, 1967, pp. 853-915.

Rubinstein, B. B. (1965), Psychoanalytic Theory and the Mind-Body Problem. In: *Psychoanalysis and Current Biological Thought,* ed. N. S. Greenfield & W. C. Lewis. Madison: University of Wisconsin Press, pp. 35-56.

_____ (1967), Explanation and Mere Description: A Metascientific Examination of Certain Aspects of the Psychoanalytic Theory of Motivation. In: Motives and Thought: Psychoanalytic Essays in Honor of David Rapaport, ed. R. R. Holt. *Psychol. Issues,* Monogr. No. 18/19:20-77. New York: International Universities Press.

_____(1975), On the Role of Classificatory Processes in Mental Functioning: Aspects of a Psychoanalytic Theoretical Model. *Psychoanalysis and Contemporary Science,* 3:101-185. New York: International Universities Press.

Schafer, R. (1967), Ideals, the Ego Ideal, and the Ideal Self. In: Motives and Thought: Psychoanalytic Essays in Honor of David Rapaport, ed. R. R. Holt. *Psychol. Issues,* Monogr. No. 18/19:131-174. New York: International Universities Press.

Sheffield, F. D., Wulff, J. J., & Barker, R. (1951), Reward Value of Copulation without Sex Drive Reduction. *J. Compar. Physiol. Psychol.,* 44:3-8.

Sokolov, E. N. (1960), Neuronal Models and the Orienting Reflex. In: *The Central Nervous System and Behavior: Transactions of the Third Conference,* ed. M. A. B. Brazier. New York: Josiah Macy, Jr. Foundation, pp. 187-276.

Spehlmann, R. (1953), *Sigmund Freuds neurologische Schriften: Eine Untersuchung zur Vorgeschichte der Psychoanalyse.* Berlin: Springer. English summary by H. Kleinschmidt in *Annual Survey of Psychoanalysis,* 4:693-706. New York: International Universities Press, 1953.

Thoa, N. B., Eichelman, B., Richardson, J. S., & Jacobowitz, D. (1972), 6-Hydroxydopa Depletion of Brain Norepinephrine and the Facilitation of Aggressive Behavior. *Science,* 178:75-77.

von Holst, E., & Mittelstadt, H. (1950), Das Reafferenzprincip (Wechselwirkungen zwischen Zentralnervensystem und Peripherie). *Naturwissenschaft,* 37:464-476.

Wayner, M. J., & Carey, R. J. (1973), Basic Drives. *Annual Review of Psychology,* 24:53-80. Palo Alto, Calif.: Annual Reviews, Inc.

Yankelovich, D., & Barrett, W. (1970), *Ego and Instinct.* New York: Random House.

7

PSYCHOANALYSIS AS A SCIENCE: ITS PRESENT STATUS AND ITS FUTURE TASKS

ROBERT S. WALLERSTEIN

In the field of psychoanalysis, few theoretical issues are more constantly and passionately argued — among both adherents from within and observers and critics, friendly and otherwise, from without — than the status of our discipline as a science. Its position is widely defended in debate, often against powerful arrays of outside scientist and philosopher of science, skeptics, as in the distinguished company, pro and con, gathered under the chairmanship of Sidney Hook for the New York University Institute of Philosophy in 1958, whose proceedings were published under the title *Psychoanalysis: Scientific Method and Philosophy* (Hook, 1959). But psychoanalysis is also called upon to defend itself against the less strident but equally concerned questions from within, which are given expression under the alternative notion that our discipline and our technique are, after all, yet more art than science, and and taking strength from the individual artistic mastery achieved. And yet, at the same time, even among the most convinced and most knowledgeable proponents of psychoanalysis as a science, both its theory and its method *as science* seem continuously to require justification, because of our admittedly peculiar subjectivistic data, and our essentially private methods for gathering and validating that data, the latter

---

Presented as Plenary Session Address at the Fifth Regional Conference of the Chicago Psychoanalytic Society, March 31, 1974.

ostensibly needed in the service of creating and fitting the observational and investigative method that is (uniquely) appropriate to the particular nature of the phenomena that constitute that science—in our case, we add, that peculiar science.

It would take us too far afield from our purpose here for me to essay any comprehensive historical review of these many arguments. The historian John Burnham (1967), in his far-ranging monograph on, among other things, the history of psychoanalysis as science, summarized these questions about the scientific status of psychoanalysis under the following headings: (1) its theoretical formulations, with their terms too loosely defined for the theories couched in them to be verifiable by usual scientific means; (2) the nature of the evidence used in psychoanalytic expositions, based as it is on the *private* data of the consulting room, with insufficient opportunity for fair counterevidence or alternative evidence; (3) the linked question of the dubious scientific credentials of evidence often drawn from nonscientific fields, folklore, mythology, even the arts, etc.; (4) the interpretations of the evidence, with alternative interpretations often equally possible and plausible, and without adequate safeguards against the suggestion of the evidence through the interpretation; and (5) the undue reliance on analogical and metaphoric thinking, often with built-in creeping reifications. These selfsame questions have also been addressed in numerous presentations by research-minded analytic practitioners, with varying emphasis on the balance between assertion and doubt, between statement of secured or claimed status, and with concerned questions about the complex and difficult conceptual, technical, semantic, and even epistemological issues at stake. I want only to call attention, for example, to contributions focused on this particular area within the past decade by Lustman (1963), Brenner (1968), Harrison (1970), and Ritvo (1971).

I myself have also been long identified with these concerns, and it is within the comforting belief that we are indubitably a science—albeit one that has not been as scientific in its investigative and research endeavors as it might be, or as the evolving technology of scientific method (by which I mean, of course, scientific method appropriate to the observational field of the science at issue) would permit — that I have myself (together with my research collaborator, Harold Sampson [Wallerstein and Sampson, 1971]) made a long and detailed exposition of the range of issues, from the conceptual to the methodological, that beset research into our central interest and activity, the process of psychoanalytic therapy, and that have kept this research from being as firmly scientific as I think it today can be.

Our arguments there were concerned, that is, to make *better* science out of the research study of our activities as a science. These arguments took their impetus from a guiding conviction that the traditional case-study method innovated by Freud, though it has provided a truly extraordinary range of insights into the structure of the mind, the organization of mental illness, and the forces that are at work and that make for change in the treatment situation, is not by *itself sufficient* to the present and future scientific needs of our field. We argued, therefore, for the need to formalize (i.e., to go beyond) the clinical case-study method as the *central* research instrument and research access to the therapeutic process in analysis. We were concerned with the need for more formal systematic research on the psychoanalytic process, while being at the same time properly mindful of the many problems and issues thereby raised in devising and executing such research in a manner at once meaningful and responsive to the subtlety and complexity of the phenomena and while still scientific in the best sense of that term (of loyalty to the reality principle, as it is embodied in appropriate canons of scientific inference).

At the same time, we expressed ourselves as fully cognizant of the extraordinary reach of the classical case-study method and of its still enduring power to effect the advancement of scientific knowledge in our field. The whole corpus of psychoanalysis, the closest in existence to a general psychology, comprehending the phenomena of both normal and abnormal personality development, attests brilliantly to the explanatory power of the theory derived from the data of the consulting room. And we know that, by contrast, whatever spectacular growth the more formal research method and research inquiry have undergone recently, they have *to this point* exerted but very slight influence on either theory or practice in our field.

One of the, to me, less significant issues — and controversies — concerning our field as science is the question of the appropriate mix of these *two avenues* of continuing approach to new knowledge within and about psychoanalysis. A good many fear that the classical method of psychoanalysis has been reaching a point of rapidly diminishing productivity, and there is considerable talk about the sterility of much of the literature in our field (Kubie, 1966), and the dearth of new ideas (Bak, 1970) and creative activity (Kohut, 1970) within classical analysis. Kohut (1970), in describing the inquiry of the Ad Hoc Committee on Scientific Activities of the American Psychoanalytic Association into the concern that "all was not well with present-day scientific research in the field of psychoanalysis, in particular . . . a lack of original contributions, i.e., of genuine accretions to our knowledge" (p. 462), voiced the double suspicion "that (a) there is a dearth of new psychoanalytic insights in the *central* areas of psychoanalytic knowledge, and (b) present-day original contributions and the research enthusiasm of analysts tend to be devoted to the application of psychoanalytic knowledge to peripheral areas" (p. 463; emphasis added).

Kurt Eissler (1969) in his provocative paper "Irreverent Remarks about the Present and the Future of Psychoanalysis" has developed this viewpoint furthest with his thesis that perhaps Freud, the founding genius of psychoanalysis, had exhausted in his own lifetime its major probabilities for fundamental new discovery, at least via its classical method. Eissler stated his view very directly: "It is breathtaking to review what Freud extracted during the course of four decades, from the free associations of eight subjects who each lay on a couch for 50 minutes per day. The input-output quotient was here truly enormous. This question, however, remains: Did Freud extract from his patients' associations all the knowledge that is to be gained from the psychoanalytic situation? With one qualification, to be dealt with presently, I would say that the answer is yes" (p. 465). Or, to quote again, "the psychoanalytic situation has already given forth everything it contains. It is depleted with regard to research possibilities, at least as far as the possibility of new paradigms is concerned" (p. 469). "With [Freud's] death, psychoanalysis entered the phase of 'normal science'; it has stayed in it since then (here Eissler is using the words *paradigm* and *normal science* in the sense made familiar to us in the work of Thomas Kuhn, 1962) (p. 465).

It would be a digression here to list the qualifications (actually more than one) with which Eissler sought to balance somewhat the views that he very deliberately stated so sweepingly, or to defend, as Gitelson (1964) did so cogently, the social and the scientific importance for any science of its phase of "normal science" as problem-solving activity par excellence, representing in endeavors and accomplishments the productive incremental labors of the whole organized scientific community. For the purpose of exposition, I want rather to focus on Eissler's over-all conclusion (representing, as I think it does, the viewpoint of many) that "all that can be learned by way of the couch Freud had already learned—at least, in terms of the paradigms that this knowledge called for. Research will now move away more and more from the treatment room to other scientific loci" (p. 468).

I know how invidious it can be to point to any single contribution at the implied risk of slighting others of comparable merit, but leaving aside all contributions that rest, in part at least, on data other than that generated in the psychoanalytic consulting room, such as Mahler's (1968) major expansion of our developmental theory and our knowledge of developmental process, I do want to note, from within the confines of the classical psychoanalytic method alone, the culmination of Kohut's investigations of the structure and the treatment of the narcissistic personality disorder in his book, *The Analysis of the Self* (1971), which has impressed so many as a landmark addition (albeit surrounded still by lively controversy) to our knowledge of the psychopathology and the psychoanalytic therapy of this important category of stubbornly refractory patients. I cite Kohut in part because he makes my point of the continuing vigor of the so-called traditional psychoanalytic enterprise, in response not only to the rather widespread view expressed in the quoted article by Eissler, but also to its echoing to some extent even by Kohut (1970) himself in the survey from the work of the Committee on Scientific Activities of the American Psychoanalytic Association.

My over-all point is that we are a science which, *aside* from its growth at its interfaces, at its interactions with adjacent and/or applied areas and with the kinds of data generated by the particular phenomena and methods of those areas—for example, the data of cognitive and affective developmental process from direct child observation, the psychophysiological correlative data in the realm of psychosomatics, or the implications for our dream theory of the experimental psychological data of the dream laboratory—has internally two main investigative methodologies: its classical method, which, since Freud, has remained its chief wellspring, and the recently developing, more formalized and systematized, specifically psychoanalytic research on and about psychoanalysis as a process for the exploration of the human mind in depth (see, as examples, Gill et al. [1968] and Wallerstein [1968]).

I do not propose at this point to discuss the methods and the related conceptual and practical issues involved in formalizing, or going beyond, the traditional case study as our chief research instrument. I hope it is clear, however, that I do *not* refer to experimental manipulation of the psychoanalytic process in any way. Paul Meehl (1973) is the most recent to remind us, as Lustman (1963), Brenner (1968), and Harrison (1970) did before him, that "An enterprise can be empirical (in the sense of taking publicly observable data as its epistemic base) *without* being experimental (in the sense of laboratory manipulation of the variables)" (p. 106), and he adduces such respectable sciences as astronomy, geography, ecology, paleontology, and human genetics as obvious examples. What I refer to as formalizing and "going beyond" is the process of obtaining the data of the consulting room (of course with due safeguards for the privacy and the confidentiality of the patients involved) and studying those data in ways that are simultaneously clinically and scientifically relevant. This process requires systematized attention to such issues as: (1) the need to make the basic phenomena or primary data of psychoanalysis available to shared study, whether by use of systematically kept process notes or verbatim recordings, with all the problems of each; (2) the importance of reducing, ordering, and summarizing the data with attention to their relation to our inferences about them, and to what Seitz (1966) has called the "consensus problem" in psychoanalytic research—the issue of handling differences in inference or judgment among clinical experts; (3) the problem of the circumvention of circularity of clinical judgment, the handling of the danger of smuggling in confirmations of our predictive judgments through our interpretations of the subsequent data; (4) the problem of generalizing from very few cases; and (5) the problem of devising scientific controls where control groups in the usual senses are for the most part not appropriate and often not ethical.

All of these issues are surveyed *at length* in my paper with Sampson, "Issues in Research in the Psychoanalytic Process" (1971), which I have already referred to. But what I do want to state and emphasize here (which was also stated in that paper though it was not its main thrust) is that the *disciplined* use of the case-study method itself, though without the same overt conceptual paraphernalia of explicit "controls, dependent and independent variables, hypotheses, and predictions," is not just our traditional science and road to science as bequeathed to us by Freud, but a necessary vital and continuing part of our current and ongoing scientific march.

I do not refer here to the more extreme position, advanced by some (see Ramzy, 1962, 1963), that every clinical analysis is after all not only a search but in its essence also a research, that "every psychoanalyst who merely follows the method he was taught to follow will discover that he has been doing research, just as Monsieur Jourdain, of Molière's *Le Bourgeois Gentilhomme*, suddenly discovered that he had been speaking prose for forty years without knowing it" (1963, p. 74). I *do* refer, rather, to the *scientific* understanding and therefore the scientific use of the "peculiar" (i.e., different from that of other sciences) nature of our data and the self-conscious exposure of our shared assumptions about how one acquires knowledge of the phenomena within our clinical field and the intellectual reach and limitation of those assumptions.

It may be useful in this context to—very briefly—remind ourselves explicitly of these usually unremarked assumptions. Erikson (1958), in a little-noticed article, spelled out most precisely the nature and the role of what he called "*disciplined subjectivity*" in the handling of clinical evidence and clinical inference. Waelder (1962) delineated this concept further in defending the role of "introspection or empathy" in this regard, arguing that though introspection and empathy are not infallible ways to know, they are certainly not negligible and give our science, *qua* science, at least one *advantage* over physics. This knowing process takes place by what Home (1966) has called "cognitive identification," in which the "meaning is known to us through an *act of identification* and not through an act of sense perception [in the usual sense] ..." (p. 47). Kris (1947) has averred that the interpretation of meaning (understood in this context) works not by "producing" recall, but rather by completing an incomplete memory, thereby implying that validation within analysis consists of the judgment of goodness of fit. That is, "the situation existing previous to the interpretation, the one which 'suggested' the interpretation, must be described as one of incomplete recall (and therefore, as in some measure similar to the situation in which the memory trace was laid down)" (p. 246). It was Schmidl (1955) who developed this concept of validation within the system most fully, arguing for the fit of the specific Gestalt of what is interpreted with the Gestalt of the interpretation, in which not only are inferences made from a general empirical rule to a specific case but, additionally, certain elements of the specific life experience of the patient come to be connected with each other (a homely analogue being the unerring fit of the two halves of the torn laundry ticket).

At the same time, persuasive as we analysts find this chain
of reasoning from "disciplined subjectivity" through to "goodness of interpretive fit" as respectable and appropriate science,
it is precisely at this point that friendly philosophical critics
like Meehl (1973) pose methodological caveats or at least
methodological limits to what we can claim as substantiated
(and agreed upon) scientific status. On just this issue of the
evidential value of the verbal productions in psychoanalytic
hours (how we decide we know what it is that has transpired),
Meehl reminds us that the pendulum can swing between two
opposed methodological errors:

> One mistake is to demand that there should be a straightfor-
> wardly computable numerical probability attached to each sub-
> stantive idiographic hypothesis, of the sort which we can usually
> compute with regard to the option of rejecting a statistical hy-
> pothesis. . . .
>   [But] the opposite error is the failure to realize that Freud's
> "jig-saw puzzle" analogy does not really fit the psychoanalytic
> hour, because it is simply not true (as he admits elsewhere) that
> all of the pieces fit together, or that the criteria of "fitting" are
> tight enough to make it analogous even to a clear-cut criminal
> trial. Two points, opposite in emphasis, but compatible: Any-
> one who has experienced analysis, practiced it, or listened to
> taped sessions, if he is halfway fair-minded, will agree that (1)
> there are sessions in which the material "fits together" so beauti-
> fully that one is sure almost any skeptic would be convinced, and
> (2) there are sessions in which the "fit" is very loose and under-
> determined (fewer equations than unknowns, so to speak), this
> latter kind of session (unfortunately) predominating [p. 108].

Again, Meehl reminds us, with his statements of methodological qualifications, that whichever way we turn on each
of our *two* major avenues of access to new clinical or theoretical discovery in the central core of our psychoanalytical
enterprise, it is hedged by problems and difficulties — as is all
new accretion of knowledge in science. That psychoanalysis
has, however, earned the sophisticated attention of hardheaded philosophical positivists from without is external confirmation, if such be needed, that we are indeed to be considered a scientific enterprise, one in the state of "normal

science" (again in Kuhn's sense) so staunchly described by Gitelson (1964) as that mixture of problem-solving activities within the prevailing paradigm or scientific world-view carried on by a scientific community at one with itself as a social movement. This is what Harrison (1970), in the title of his article, called "*Our* Science."

This kaleidoscopic and I hope not overly condensed overview of the present status of psychoanalysis as science is, I would trust, reasonably familiar terrain, on which we can have a reasonable degree of consensus, albeit with the varying emphases that reflect our individual scientific predilections for study and research. Given this assessment of our present position, let me now outline, if not our ordained future course as a science, for none can claim predictive prescience in such undertakings, at least what I see as some of our crucial scientific tasks ahead. Here we are confronted by highly personal choices. A goodly number of analysts, including several of the authors of articles I have already cited (Bak, 1970; Brenner, 1968; Eissler, 1969; Harrison, 1970; Kohut, 1970, 1973; Ritvo, 1971), have spoken and written with differing, individual voices in this arena, some with the word "future" central to their title. But I would like for my essay in this realm to take a step backward in our conceptual developmental progression, if not in time, and take my point of departure from a phrase I used to describe the basis of our very justification as a scientific enterprise—the phrase "if such be needed." For I think my best entry into what I see as the essential conceptual tasks facing our science in its coming development and extension lies in my starting with the consideration of the position advanced by the philosopher and analytic scholar Home, who, in 1966, questioned fundamentally many of the assertions made here by myself (and by the others whose views I have here collated) about the nature of the propositions of our field as constituting science.

Home's argument is embedded in what he calls the distinction between two fundamentally different ways of studying man: the scientific enterprise built in each of its various branches on the accumulation of lawful regularities and gen-

eralizations across the instances of the natural phenomena
studied, and the humanistic enterprise built on the intensive
unraveling of the historically bound, the uniquely creative,
and the idiosyncratic. Within the framework of this distinction he asks, " 'What is psychoanalysis about?' 'What essentially characterizes its subject matter?' 'What sort of theories
can validly be constructed about it?' " (p. 42). He feels that we
analysts have difficulties in being clear or in being in clear
agreement about such fundamentals, not because we speak
different languages — Freudian, Kleinian, etc., minor differences for the purpose of his argument — but because of "lack of
clarity about the *kind of thing* we are discussing and therefore
about the *kind of logical framework* in terms of which it can
be understood and discussed" (p. 43; emphasis added).

To Home, the answer *is* clear. Freud's fundamental discovery, his basic insight, was that the neurotic symptom has
meaning. But this discovery carried unexpected and usually
unnoticed logical consequences. According to Home, "In
discovering that the symptom had meaning and basing his
treatment on this hypothesis, Freud took the psycho-analytic
study of neurosis *out of the world of science* into the world of
the humanities, because a meaning is not the product of
causes but the creation of a subject. This is a major difference;
for the logic and method of the humanities is radically
different from that of science, though no less respectable and
rational, and of course much longer established" (p. 43). This,
however, was not the perception of Freud, the natural-scien-
tist product of the physicalistic school of Helmholtz. As Home
puts it: "it is not surprising that, in the excitement of so great a
discovery and one that opened up such vast new territories,
Freud should have overlooked the logical implications for
theory of the step he had taken" (p. 43). And so Freud
proceeded to attempt a *science* of psychoanalysis built on the
operation of a succession of *models of the psychic apparatus*,
from the original neurological model of the "Project for a
Scientific Psychology" (1895) through the reflex-arc or "pick-
et-fence" model of Chapter VII of *The Interpretation of
Dreams* (1900) through to the full-blown tripartite structural

model of *The Ego and the Id* (1923) and *Inhibitions, Symptoms and Anxiety* (1926).

But here is the crux of what Home feels to be the confusing intermingling, within the one conceptual arena of psychoanalysis, of the premises, the phenomena, and the logical structure of the fundamentally differing humanistic and scientific modes of thought, leading often to statements in our discourse that Home feels do not "in a strict sense, mean anything" (p. 42) — and he gives examples of such statements.

What is this fundamental logical distinction that Home would have us focus upon?[1] It is basically the difference between the humanistic act of interpretation and the scientific act of explanation. For a science basically asks "how" questions and receives answers in terms of mechanisms and causes; but a humanistic study asks "why" questions and receives answers in terms of reasons, i.e., motives. And it is this last which Home avers is the *only* proper business of psychoanalysis — to discern individual meanings. This it does through specific acts of "cognitive understanding" or "cognitive identification." "In this mode of cognition [through identification], which is that used by the analyst in analysis, the observation of facts [i.e., the phenomena, the verbal and nonverbal behaviors of the consulting room] subserves the purpose of establishing an identification from which an interpretation can be made. The interpretation is a new kind of fact whose factuality depends on the accuracy with which the evidence has been interpreted and on the completeness of the evidence. Unlike a scientific fact, it cannot be demonstrated ..." (p. 44).

A corollary to all this is the assertion that the mind, though a noun, is clearly not a thing, and every nounlike, thinglike

---

[1] This issue of the extent to which psychoanalysis is a scientific enterprise versus a humanistic enterprise is *not* the same question as the extent to which psychoanalysis as a science (if we take the side of the argument, to be developed further in this presentation, that it *is* science) is biologically rooted — though the questions are felt by some to be related. For a comprehensive perspective on the natural-science bent and biological framework within which such a seminal thinker as Hartmann viewed and placed psychoanalysis, see Schafer's (1970) article "An Overview of Heinz Hartmann's Contributions to Psychoanalysis."

attribute with which we endow it is nothing else than the play of metaphor. Caught up in this wholesale metaphoric bag, then, is of course not only our instinct theory, but also our whole theory of the mind in terms of the model id, ego, and superego, our conceptualized explanatory world of mental structures and functions and mechanisms and processes—in short, all of metapsychological theory, and much, if not most, if not all, of the level of clinical theory as well (as set forth in the layerings described by Rapaport [1960] and Waelder [1962])—the level, that is, of defense mechanism, of repression, and of the return of the repressed. All this must be abjured in order to purify psychoanalysis and rid it of its currently built-in, irreconcilable contradiction that "on the one hand in clinical practice, and especially through the technique of free association, it assumes a spontaneous subject; on the other it reifies the concept of mind and elaborates a scientific type theory in terms of causes" (Home, 1966, p. 47). Indeed, this basic contradiction leads to a compounding of the confusion because the metapsychological words like instinct and energy and tension inevitably get used in relation to clinical experience and acquire a second clinically defined meaning that overlaps the first. Parenthetically, however far we are each individually willing or unwilling to go in support of Home's argument, we are all unhappily reminded of the many confusions between the clinical and metapsychological levels of theorizing that do beset our literature in just the ways that Home suggests.

What is the total thrust of this exposition of Home's position? That "psycho-analysis, growing up amidst the triumphant application of scientific method, understandably adopted the method for itself without considering whether it was logically appropriate. It has landed itself [thereby] in a morass of reified concepts; for scientific method demands the kind of facts which it can use" (p. 49). Let us not misunderstand Home to mean thereby that if psychoanalysis is not science, it is therefore any the less, for (as a final quotation from this provocative paper), "My aim has been to make the point that science is not just an improved version of humanistic thinking;

it is a different kind of thinking with a limited field of reference, with different basic axioms and a different logical form" (p. 45).

I have quoted at such length from Home's paper, not just to explore the implications of the argument over the nature of psychoanalysis as science pushed to the extreme (I should say to the antiextreme, or rather opposite extreme), but also to state this argumental *direction* as the congenial, conceptual haven for a growing movement among psychoanalytic thinkers away from the decades of development of modern-day ego psychology in its aspiration toward a general psychology, a comprehensive and comprehensible description and explanation of the function and structure of the human mind in health and in disease — a development that reached its apogee in the works of Hartmann and his collaborators and of Rapaport. For example, and far less extremist in its position, is the growing disenchantment among some of our most influential theoreticians, and among some of those who have been most directly influenced by Hartmann and Rapaport, with the often overgrown and overelaborated, clinically remote and experience-distant structure of our metapsychology. Differing from that of Home, this is an argument usually advanced not against psychoanalysis as science, but ostensibly on its behalf as a science, that is, making the effort to divest itself of *aspects* of, or even of all of its metapsychology, which is declared to be more a metaphysics than a (scientific) psychology.

In this regard, most has been written and argued over energy theory and the economic point of view, which Lustman (1969), who has been one of its staunchest defenders, says "has certainly been the single most attacked formulation in the literature" (p. 95).[2] I do not want to digress here into a dis-

---

[2] The arguments pro and con are familiar and do not require repetition in this context. On the one side is the call by Rosenblatt and Thickstun (1970), who speak for a host of others (Kubie, Rubinstein, Holt, Gardner, Klein, etc.) in calling for the abandonment of psychic-energy theory as being hopelessly incongruent with any of the conceptualizations or usages of energy concepts in the realms of natural science, and as being additionally hopelessly unable, in terms of the tension-

cussion of these various viewpoints on energy theory and the closely related instinct theory which, as I have indicated, are both defended and attacked within psychoanalysis under the banner of differing views of what constitutes the essence of our science and of the theory appropriate to it. Rather, I want to call attention to a recent article by Schafer (1972) entitled "Internalization: Process of Fantasy?," which carries the assault on metapsychology, and by extension on the totality of the theory of the structure of the mind and its functioning, to a point that I feel approximates Home's assertion of psychoanalysis as fundamentally (and perhaps only) an individual and artistic enterprise. In this most thoroughgoing and radical critique of all metapsychological—or structural—or spatial—constructions in our theorizing, Schafer begins with the concept of internalization as representing some kind of "insidedness"; and by asking "Inside of What?," through successive approximations, he logically dissects the concept to where the meaning is declared to be only fantasy and metaphor—

---

reduction model, really to deal with the phenomena it must be designed to explain, for example, the existence of pleasurable tensions. These authors call for the replacement of energy-theoretical models by information-processing models built in accord with previously learned affective expectations which then act as inducers, facilitators, or inhibitors of subsequent behaviors. They try to show how this alternate (putatively more scientific) theory is better theory, and better science, because it is more *translatable* into terms congruent with modern neurophysiological thinking (though not necessarily so translated yet); and how also the other metapsychological points of view, the structural, the dynamic, etc., can survive intact enough when the energy-dependent aspects and interactions are dropped out. (The argument they advance as to how the *dynamic* point of view, dependent as it is on the interplay of psychic forces, can be altered and still survive enough to maintain its essential structure and usefulness within the over-all theory of the mental apparatus after energy theory is dropped out, is not, however, an altogether convincing one.)

The opposite argument, equally familiar, is that made, for example, by Lustman (1969): that Freud was less influenced (or at least less misled) by the prevailing physicalistic theories of science of his day than is nowadays assumed in many quarters, and was rather more occupied with building the theory required to cope with the clinical problems that derived directly from his empirical observations. In this framework, the body of concepts called the economic point of view (psychic energy, cathexis theory, the pleasure-pain principle, etc.) was developed because of certain characteristics which Freud noted (and which still hold good) in symptoms, dreams, parapraxes, jokes, and in the course of psychoanalytic therapy. That is, Freud developed the concepts—and Lustman believes them to be still signally useful—to deal with (instinctual) phenomena, phenomena characterized and therefore misleading if it is proposed or used as part of science. In this progression, not only do such constructs as psychic energy and drive theory, force and instinct, disappear, but literally so does all of metapsychological (i.e., general psychological) conceptualizing via such terms as structure, space, locus, superficial and deep, psychoanalysis as a depth psychology, levels and layers, underlying factors and causes, hierarchic organizations (as of impulse and defense), mental process or mechanism, regulatory structures, functions and relationships. All this is eschewed as metaphor that states a fantasy (i.e., internalization is a "bloodless statement of an incorporation fantasy"; p. 412), but when posing as science it carries all the dangers of pseudoexplanation, of reification, of concreteness of thought, of making nouns out of adjectives and adverbs, and mistaking fantasies for things (processes). What we have left, according to Schafer, are but classes of mental events, and if we translate past what he calls the "simple (though not naïve) descriptions" (p. 435) into, for

---

by increase, diminution, displacement, and discharge. More recently, Kohut (1971, 1972), that chief articulator of introspection and empathy as our central clinical tools, has at the same time compellingly articulated metapsychological theory *in toto,* including instinct and libido theory, as central to his theoretical explanatory system for the understanding and the treatment of narcissistic personality disorder. In his paper on narcissistic rage (1972), he defends this effort as follows: "As my final task I shall now attempt to explain narcissistic rage in metapsychological terms—even though I know that metapsychology has fallen into disrepute and is considered by some to be hardly more than a sterile thought exercise" (pp. 394-395). And he goes on to deploy such concepts as exhibitionistic libido, flow and discharge, psychoeconomic unbalance, and ego-regulatory capacities.

And to round out this array of arguments pro and con, I want only to call attention to Applegarth's (1971) scholarly review of the issues and her mediate position abandoning the complex psychoanalytic conceptualizations of different types of instinctual energies in favor of a conception of sexual and aggressive drives that differ not in their kinds of energies but in their pattern of mediating structures. She says: "The most extreme criticism of the energy theory takes the form of suggesting that all energic explanations be abandoned. It would seem to be difficult, however, to account for variations in intensities and for the very existence of conflict if we did not assume forces to be at work in the mental apparatus.... It is when we come to the idea of different qualities in energy, i.e., neutralization, fusion, binding, separate sexual and aggressive energies, that we are plunged into difficulties.... these apparently qualitative differences in the energy can all be explained by differences in the controlling structures, so that the energy behaves differently not because it is changed in itself but because it is differently directed" (p. 441).

example, the language of internalization and of introject, "have we [he asks] understood or conveyed anything more? If anything [he states] we are working with less" (p. 435).

Here Schafer presses the argument perhaps even further than Home, for the latter at least has declared the essential act of psychoanalysis to be the act of interpretation, which he has called an ascription of meaning in terms of motivation. Schafer questions even the use of motivation words in the psychoanalytic process as also carrying the dangers of pseudo-science. Of this, he says: "Further considerations ... would require formulating fundamental doubts concerning the logical necessity and legitimacy of using *motivation words* to explain behavior. This is so because the term 'motive,' for example, refers to a mover of action that is prior to it in time and 'interior' to it as an inner or behind-the-scenes entity that is personlike in its comprehension and activity" (p. 431fn.). In so stating it, has Schafer brought psychoanalysis close to losing its distinctive character, moving it almost to an identity with the existentialist psychology that, translated into an approach to psychotherapy, regards the goal of therapy as but the assessment of experience in its moment-to-moment quality and texture, rather than, as traditionally in psychoanalysis, seeing the mind's experience as the backdrop for wishes and intentions, conscious or unconscious, in short the world of avowed or hidden meanings as motivations?[3]

In elaborating this thinking among psychoanalytic theo-reticians in both hemispheres, I am not making the point that their views are on all fours with one another. Home speaks for the view that psychoanalysis is but an individual humanistic enterprise, accounting for the individual as creator of his own destiny in accord with the established and honored rhythm of the humanities. The many American authors (of whom

[3] Since writing this paper, I have had the opportunity of studying Schafer's recent series of articles (1973a, 1973b, 1975), in which he seeks to develop the fabric of an *action language* that will encompass and adequately describe the clinical phenomena of psychoanalysis, and stand in place of the whole of *psycho-dynamic* language, which is declared to be an anachronistic hindrance to our status and development as both a discipline and a science. The argument made in this series of articles, however, is very comprehensively represented in Schafer's earlier work, from which I have drawn in my presentation.

Schafer is but the most radical exemplar) who would perform various degrees of major surgery upon the corpus of our meta-psychology, and who, I think, thereby give up our efforts and our claims to a general psychology of the operations of the human mind in health and in illness, do so not in the name of the humanities but out of their particular conception of the nature of psychoanalysis as a science. They follow Bertrand Russell's definition of psychology as the science of those occurrences which by their very nature can only be observed by one person. As this kind of science, then, it too has its own proper (scientific) questions and its own rules of evidence and inference that guide judgments about the adequacy and propriety of the answers.

Whatever the scope of difference between these two views, what they do have very much in common is the sharp delimitation of the proper domain of psychoanalysis as a human enterprise. They say in effect that psychoanalysis has essayed far too much. It has attempted to be both an explanation of the mind of man, how it works, as well as an interpretation of the history of an individual man, why he believes as he does. In this is has been far more ambitious in one sense than physics. For physics attempts only to explain the behavior of particles in the mass, the huge agglomerated mass. It looks at any single particle as but the random variation within the lawful regularity that very precisely describes the behavior of the totality of the particles that constitute the mass. Psycho-analysis has historically caught itself up in trying both to describe the mind of man as a creature of nature across the mass (to answer what Home calls the "how" questions) and to understand the mind of each individual man under its scrutiny in its historically motivated determination (the "why" questions).

That the two endeavors have proceeded *pari passu,* and in ways that conceptually are not always distinguished one from another has been a source of great complexity and unending confusion for us. It has led to what George Klein (1973), looking at this same dilemma, has called "two traditions of psychoanalysis," again two different kinds of science. Of these he says,

the important differences between the two traditions of psycho-
analsis is not the energy-discharge model of the one—the so-
called "metapsychology"—which is absent in the other. The
more profound point of distinction is that they derive from two
different philosophies of inquiry and explanation. Each leads
to different conceptions of what psychoanalysis is all about, of
where efforts at discovery should be directed, how psychoanalytic knowledge should be systematically organized, on what
problems and in what settings we should do research, what objectives of explanation should be served in doing research. The
tragedy is that the two orientations have often been confounded,
creating theoretical and empirical havoc [p. 10].

Klein's answer, and here he is at one with Home and
with Schafer, is to declare the one area totally out of bounds
for our science, as but an impossible burden and confusion to
the other. It is this trend that is the crux of the present major
conceptual confrontation within our literature about our
status as a science. I trust that it is clear at this point that,
though I have used the exposition of this trend as a questioning base and a taking-off point, it is with the intention to
propose a different, and opposite, path toward the resolution
of these dilemmas—one that to me poses the coming conceptual task and therefore the future arena of activity for psychoanalysis as a science.

This problem was grappled with, in just these terms, in a
panel discussion at a meeting of the American Psychoanalytic
Association on "Models of the Psychic Apparatus" (Abrams,
1971). On that panel, Modell took his point of departure in
the same distinction between the two aspects, the two traditions, of psychoanalytic endeavor. He called it the two
"contexts." In the one context, Freud, trying in his successive
theoretical formulations and model-building to demonstrate
general "laws" of psychic functioning, analogous to the established "laws" of the physical sciences, placed man as a part of
nature and subject to the same regularities that influence all
other natural phenomena. But Freud also established another
context of man as molded by civilization and not merely as a
product of nature. And the products of culture do not have
the same high generalizability (universality) as do the pheno-

mena of nature. Here we are in the world of man's created environment: the psychosocial process and the idiosyncratically unique perspective that psychoanalysis as the unfolding of the history of a life shares with history in the collective, the assignment of meaning by the placing of observation into its given individual historical context.

Modell affirmed psychoanalysis to be that unique science that lives in *both* orientations—that of natural science and that of individual history—and simultaneously studies phenomena within both contexts. On that same panel, Brenner underscored that the historical approach is also, or can be, a scientific endeavor, subject to its own proper rules of evidence and of inference, despite the fact that historians of the past were often simply storytellers or perhaps patriotic deceivers, basically not yet trained in any scientific methods. What Modell and Brenner do here, of course, is to maintain the tension of keeping psychoanalysis in both its contexts, both its universes of discourse (unlike Home and Schafer and the many others who, in the service of conceptual clarification or perhaps of heuristic simplification, force it, or at least declare it, to be tenant in only one). But they do so, and here I believe their step is insufficient, without pointing to the kinds of canons of correspondence or of relationship that would make the double tenancy into a coherent theoretical (scientific) enterprise.

Such an effort toward seeking relationships within an overarching conceptual framework has been begun by Sandler and Joffe (1969) in their statement "Towards a Basic Psychoanalytic Model," in which they make a basic distinction between the experiential and the nonexperiential realms of the mind. The experiential comprises what we call the contents of the mind: "The realm of subjective experience refers to the experience of the phenomenal content of wishes, impulses, memories, fantasies, sensations, percepts, feelings and the like.... experiential content of any sort, including feelings, *can be either conscious or unconscious*" (p. 82). This is the realm of the phenomena of mind that Schafer and Home declare to be the whole of the proper business of psychoanalysis, the realm of the "why" questions, where answers come in terms of meaning, or, in the language of George Klein (1973), of "intentionality" or "directional tendency." As stated, it is a world of both conscious and unconscious *experiences*, and the established work of psychoanalysis is to bring more fully into the ken of the individual whatever experiences he has, for whatever defensive or adaptive reasons, disavowed. I would only add at this point what I will state more fully further along: that it is a world that has its own proper rules of evidence and inference and is therefore part of our domain as science.

In sharp contrast to this experiential realm is what Sandler and Joffe call the nonexperiential realm: "This is the realm of forces and energies, of mechanisms and apparatuses, of organized structures, both biological and psychological, of sense organs and means of discharge. The non-experiential realm is intrinsically unknowable, except insofar as it can become known through the creation or occurrence of a phenomenal event in the realm of subjective experience. From this point of view *the whole of the mental apparatus* is in the non-experiential realm, capable of becoming known to us (only to a limited extent) via subjective experiences of one sort or another" (p. 82). This is the realm, then, not of the *phenomena* of the mind, but of the explanatory constructions that order and establish sequences of regularity and interdependency among those kinds of phenomena. Such constructions represent the efforts of Freud and the ego psychologists who came after him to develop a comprehensive scientific theory of the mind, or, as it is usually called, a structure of the psychic apparatus. How can we, then, establish the relevance and the usefulness of this body of conceptualization in the face of those who declare it to be a mass of both unnecessary and confounding doctrine that forces psychoanalysis to ask the wrong kinds of questions: "how" questions that seek answers in terms of "causes" and lead to the elaboration of a theoretical explanatory superstructure (as in the metapsychological points of view) that seems to involve theoretical models—for example, energy models—which few find wholly satisfactory and many find to be confusing metaphysics rather than science at all?

Sandler and Joffe build their presupposition of the interrelatedness of the two realms into the very language of the distinction between the experiential and the nonexperiential realms of the mind. They put this relationship thus: "There is an intimate relation between the experiential and the nonexperiential realms.... Apart from the maturational influences, the mental apparatus develops only through conscious or unconscious awareness of changes in experiential content and related attempts to control that content. Thus the elements in the non-experiential realm are employed, mobilized and changed — all outside the realm of experience — although changes in the non-experiential realm are mediated by experience and their employment or modification provides, in turn, new experiential data" (p. 82).

As an example, they use *fantasying* as an organized mental functioning that falls wholly within the nonexperiential realm, and they contrast this with *fantasies*, "The image and feelings which are the products of fantasying [which] fall within the realm of experience (conscious or unconscious)" (p. 83). This distinction (and relation) between fantasying (in the nonexperiential realm) and a fantasy (in the experiential) is incidentally very akin to that made by Seymour Kety, the biochemical researcher in psychiatry, in his oft-quoted statement that "there can someday be a biochemistry of memory but never of memories." It is from this same position that I want to specify more fully my own perspective on the present and future tasks of psychoanalysis as science. For my paradigm instance, I would like to take the issue of defensive functioning because of its comparative simplicity, its centrality to all psychoanalytic conceptualizing, and its solid anchoring in the relatively experience-near level of clinical theory that is an essential element of theorizing, even among those who are most radical in eschewing the metapsychological superstructure of the psychic apparatus as superfluous and pseudoscientific.

I will begin by following Gill, who in his monograph on

topography and systems in psychoanalytic theory (1963) draws the distinction between defense mechanisms (clearly in the nonexperiential realm) and defenses (equally clearly—to me— in the experiential realm). For a defense mechanism is nothing but a construct that denotes a way of functioning of the mind. It is a construct invoked to explain how behaviors, affects, and ideas serve to inhibit, avert, delay, or otherwise modulate unwanted impulse discharge. Defenses, on the other hand, are the actual *behaviors, affects,* and *ideas* that serve defensive purposes. Their functioning as defenses is explained *in terms of* the operation of the defense mechanisms—and it is the clarification of what we mean here by *in terms of* that is the locus of inquiry into what I call the explicit establishment of the canons of correspondence or relationship between these two realms of discourse, the experiential and the nonexperiential. For example, an exaggerated sympathy can be a defense against an impulse to cruelty. The postulated operative mental mechanism by which this is explained is called reaction formation. Defenses can range from discrete attributes or aspects explicable by reference to the simple operation of a single defense mechanism (as in the example just cited) to complex behavioral and characterological constellations that are likewise specific, recurrent, and serve defensive purposes, like clowning, whistling in the dark, sour-grapes attitudes, etc. These more complex configurations are variously called *defensive operations, patterns, maneuvers,* etc. They are made up of various combinations and sequences of behaviors, affects, and ideas, the operations of which are explicable by reference to a variety of the classically described defense mechanisms, and mixed with other ego activities.

Using this model of defensive functioning (i.e., this distinction between defense and defense mechanism), our psychoanalytic scientific task as I conceptualize it is, then, threefold. One aspect is the systematic *clinical* examination, within the psychoanalytic situation (and through study, with whatever degree of research formalization, of the data generated in that situation) of the phenomena that we know as *defenses*. This is the systematic exploration of the experiential realm, the world of mental contents or events. In this instance, it comprises the study of the behaviors, affects, and ideas that, whether simply or complexly, hierarchically serve as defenses, that are usually unconscious in their defensive working and defensive purpose, though they are capable of being rendered conscious by psychoanalytic work. It is the realm of the "why" question that seeks answers in terms of ascriptions of meanings unique to the unfolding of the history of a single individual. It is this realm that Home and other like-minded thinkers I have quoted consider to be the whole of the proper business of psychoanalysis. But, to me, this exploration of the experiential realm constitutes only part of the domain of psychoanalysis, and likewise only part of the *science* of psychoanalysis — and here I refer to the rules of clinical evidence and interpretive fit that mark the methodology of the classical method of clinical case study and also to the rules of the more systematized formal research organization of the clinical data yielded by the consulting room. When successfully accomplished, study in this realm yields a comprehensive mapping of the defensive behaviors of the individual under study, in all their configural meanings, over time, and in relation to the shifting press of circumstances from within and without.

The second, companion task is the concomitant study and elaboration of the constructed organizations that we know as *defense mechanisms*, the conceptual substrate that expresses the regularity and the expectability that we discern as the integrity and identity of a recognizable and identifiable defense organization (and over-all character organization) in the individual, as well as the generalizability and universality across individuals that leads to the lawfulness of the world of nature as studied by science. This, then, is the systematic development of the nonexperiential realm partaking of commonalities of process, mechanism, and structure. It is not a realm of experience; it therefore cannot be conscious, since, to quote Gill (1963), "logically speaking, one can become conscious only of a content which is the *outcome* of the working of the mind, not of the working itself." It is the realm of "how" questions, of the alignment of causes, forces, that determine processes and mechanisms that apply to the understanding of the operation of the psychic apparatus, the minds of all men, individually and in the mass. It is the world that Home and the others have ruled out as an improper and misconceived universe of discourse and of exploration for psychoanalysis— but to me it is the essence of what gives psychoanalysis its claim to be a *general* psychology of the mind in its normal as well as its disordered functioning (and this is quite apart from the question of how much of our metapsychological structure as currently developed we wish to subscribe to, alter, or replace).

And then there is the third scientific task, already alluded to in this presentation: the study of the linkages and the regularities in the juxtaposition between the "how" questions and the "why" questions, between the explanatory constructions of the nonexperiential realm (the conceptualized operation of the defense mechanisms) and the observed and inferred phenomena of the experiential realm (the historically determined and evolved configuration of defensive behaviors unique to that individual). In the example chosen, that of defense mechanisms and defenses, the correspondences subsumed by the phrase *in terms of*—that is, the idiosyncratic patterning and deployment of defensive behaviors accounted for *in terms of* the operation of particular combinations and permutations of the generally available armamentarium of possible defense mechanisms in human character—seem generally self-evident, simple, and nonproblematic. This is so because the example is drawn from the most directly clinical— that is, experience-near—level of mental functioning. As the examples relate to constructions and observations further from immediate experience (and I shall later indicate such examples), the task becomes correspondingly more difficult. But it is in the establishment of such canons of correspondence at all levels of construction and of inference (however remote from direct experiencing) that I see the scientifically necessary burden of making psychoanalysis truly a science which is both a general psychology, a study of the general and lawful functioning of the human mind in health and disease, and also an idiosyncratic genetic unfolding of the succession of meanings and reasons, overt and covert, that the individual at study lives by and imposes upon his being in the world.

Having said all this, I need add several caveats. First, it must be understood that I agree wholeheartedly with the concern of Home, Schafer, Klein, etc., as to the mischief and havoc that can arise from the haphazard intermingling and confounding of the two realms of discourse, the confusions that can arise between "how" questions answered in terms of mechanism (how does reaction formation work and where does it draw its strength?) and "why" questions answered in terms of reasons (why is there such an exaggerated cloying sympathy in this individual and what is its history?). But I differ from the authors just mentioned in considering both questions to be separately necessary (why this behavior at this time, and how, or through what operations, is it brought about?); both are separately necessary to a full psychological, i.e., psychoanalytic explanation, as Freud was the first to tell us. For proper explanation, the two realms must be kept conceptually separate, yet at the same time they must be seen in their interrelatedness — and this last, of course, is the task of specification that psychoanalysis as science has hardly begun to face and systematically undertake.

Closely related to this is the point that much of the frequent confounding of the two realms results from the fact that, to a large extent, they share an undifferentiated language whose context does not always make clear — perhaps the author himself is unclear — the realm of reference of the particular usage. A familiar example is the usage of the phrase pleasure-unpleasure to signify either hypothesized libidinal tension discharge and arousal states (clearly in the "how" realm), or, often in the same paragraph, experiences of shifting affects (clearly in the "why" realm). Such semantic confusion through shared languages renders the task of maintaining proper conceptual separation between the realms of the "how" and the "why" even more difficult.

The final related caveat has to do with the kind of science that the psychoanalytic endeavor creates for us. What I want to make clear, if I have not already done so, is that the general psychological theory (the metapsychology, if you will) that I am talking about is truly appropriate to (i.e., is consonant with) the particular nature of our subjectivistic data and the introspective and empathic methods by which we derive those data — relying, then, in our explanatory network on such necessary (to us) psychological constructions as, for example, those of overdetermination and multiple function. Thus I am not talking about a science modeled on physics or any other of the natural sciences, or any derivations via physicalistic physiology, that of Helmholtz or otherwise; I trust I am as ready as others to modify (even discard) aspects of our general theory, for example the tension-reduction energy model, whose place may derive more from roots in scientific analogy than from an appropriate explanatory fit to our particular data. I am referring, that is, to what has here been called throughout, "our" science or our peculiar science.[4]

Let me now pick up from the example I have been using of the relation between defenses or defensive behaviors and defense mechanisms. The task of properly guiding observation and inference in the experiential realm and explanatory construction in the nonexperiential realm, and of establishing appropriate and adequate rules of correspondence between them, clearly becomes progressively more difficult the more remote from immediate experience is the level of organization and of conceptualization being dealt with. For example, in the sense used here, the concepts of self and of identity as psychic organizations coherent in space and continuous over time, yet

___

[4] Central, of course, to this statement of position is the conceptualization I have of the nature or meaning of *metapsychology*. To me, metapsychology is *not*, as it is to some, equivalent to a biological or neurobiological explanatory framework imposed upon the data and the phenomena of psychology. The degree of neurologizing of psychology that may be placed within the corpus of metapsychology, for example, via aspects of energy theory, *can* be removed from it — see Applegarth (1971) and Rosenblatt and Thickstun (1970) — without harm to the essence of metapsychology. Rather, to me metapsychology is a *kind of generalizing,* of constructing general psychological explanatory systems via a variety of vantage points, simultaneously and systematically, the various metapsychological points of view — out of the conviction that only through the simultaneous and systematic deployment of these various perspectives can behavior be fully comprehended in its overdetermination and its multiple functions.

subject always to growth and change, are more complex and more remote from the direct, immediately comprehended data of experience than the concepts dealt with from the more directly clinically anchored level of repression and defense and return of the repressed. Concomitantly, the corresponding experiential organization that these concepts of self and of identity relate to, the self (and the object) representations and the positive and negative identity formations, is also more inferential and at a greater remove from their observational base in what is directly experienced and comprehended — and with this there is a greater spread of conceptual distance and explicating to be bridged between the explanatory constructs and the experiential representations they are invoked to give coherence to. The problem, then, of establishing the proper rules of correspondence, the placement of the correct (more complex) "hows" in juxtaposition to the correct (more inferential) "whys" and the minimization of slippage, confounding, and confusion in so doing increases almost geometrically in complexity.

To jump still further from the direct data of experience, when we talk not of self and identity and their corresponding experiential representations but of the level of ego organization (or id or superego organization), we are again at an even greater conceptual distance from the constructs that make up the ego as a system of regulatory devices, structures, thresholds, and discharge channels and the experience-based inferences that comprise the ego as a class of aims or directional configurations of behavior and experience (see Klein, 1973, p. 12).

But to chart this arena systematically with a logical theory of the mind, *how* it works, appropriate to and coordinate with a logical ordering of the observed and inferred data of individual history and experience, *why* it does what it does — these are the coming tasks as I see them, and therefore the future of psychoanalysis as a science. To me, it is the complexity and the special peculiarity of psychoanalysis as a science that it pursues its inquiry simultaneously in each of the two realms, the general and the individual, the how and the why, and in so doing forges concurrently the logic of their interrelationships. This set of tasks is the same whatever the substantive areas on which the psychoanalytic investigative searchlight is focused, whether in the areas of applied psychoanalytic study (literature, art, history, group process, and collective behavior, etc.), correlative psychoanalytic study (psychosomatics, child development, etc.), or within the core of psychoanalytic endeavor — the psychoanalytic situation. It is for this reason that I have made no effort in this presentation on the status of psychoanalysis as science to survey the present state of scientific activity in each of these substantive arenas.

I want to add, moreover, that the proper resolution of these scientific tasks for psychoanalysis will rest, and here I circle back to the beginning point of this presentation, on the fullest development and the simultaneous pursuit of each of the avenues of continuing approach to new knowledge and new conceptualizing within and about analysis — on both the classical method of the clinical case study and the more formalized and systematized research study built upon the basic data of the psychoanalytic process. Here, as elsewhere in analysis, we have the issue of two attitudes, two scientific predilections and scientific stances, each of which, in the integrity of its own pursuit, will serve as a needed corrective to the potential deficiencies of the other. While in the one approach we see a possible excess of concern with scientific rigor and publicly replicable data at the potential expense of psychological perceptivity and clinical feel, in the other approach there is danger of a possible excess of concern with subtle perceptivity and insight via empathic identifications at the potential expense of exactitude and confirmability. But it is my hope that between the two, an appropriate admixture will be found — not necessarily in any single investigator or practitioner — an admixture that I trust, with the growth over this present generation of a more formalized and systematized research endeavor in its proper relation to the whole body of psychoanalytic activity, will be found within and across the field as a whole. With this development, we can predict a healthy and vigorous future for psychoanalysis as a science in the pursuit of the difficult scientific tasks that I have tried to visualize.

REFERENCES

Abrams, S., rep. (1971), Panel on Models of the Psychic Apparatus. *J. Amer. Psychoanal. Assn.*, 19:131-142.

Applegarth, A. (1971), Comments on Aspects of the Theory of Psychic Energy. *J. Amer. Psychoanal. Assn.*, 19:379-416.

Bak, R. (1970), Psychoanalysis Today. *J. Amer. Psychoanal. Assn.*, 18:3-23.

Brenner, C. (1968), Psychoanalysis and Science. *J. Amer. Psychoanal. Assn.*, 16:675-696.

Burnham, J. C. (1967), Psychoanalysis and American Medicine, 1894-1918: Medicine, Science, and Culture. *Psychol. Issues,* Monogr. No. 20. New York: International Universities Press.

Eissler, K. R. (1969), Irreverent Remarks about the Present and the Future of Psychoanalysis. *Internat. J. Psycho-Anal.*, 50:461-471.

Erikson, E. H. (1958), The Nature of Clinical Evidence. *Daedalus*, 87:65-87.

Freud, S. (1895), Project for a Scientific Psychology. *Standard Edition*, 1:283-397. London: Hogarth Press, 1966.

——(1900), The Interpretation of Dreams. *Standard Edition,* 4 & 5. London: Hogarth Press, 1953.

—— (1923), The Ego and the Id. *Standard Edition*, 19:3-66. London: Hogarth Press, 1961.

—— (1926), Inhibitions, Symptoms and Anxiety. *Standard Edition*, 20:75-175. London: Hogarth Press, 1959.

Gill, M. M. (1963), Topography and Systems in Psychoanalytic Theory. *Psychol. Issues,* Monogr. No. 10. New York: International Universities Press.

——, Simon, J., Fink, G., Endicott, N. A., & Paul, I. H. (1968), Studies in Audio-Recorded Psychoanalysis. I: General Considerations. *J. Amer. Psychoanal. Assn.*, 16:230-244.

Gitelson, M. (1964), On the Identity Crisis in American Psychoanalysis. *Psychoanalysis: Science and Profession.* New York: International Universities Press, 1973, pp. 383-416.

Harrison, S. I. (1970), Is Psychoanalysis "*Our* Science"? Reflections on the Scientific Status of Psychoanalysis. *J. Amer. Psychoanal. Assn.*, 18:125-149.

Home, H. J. (1966), The Concept of Mind. *Internat. J. Psycho-Anal.*, 47:42-49.

Hook, S., ed. (1959), *Psychoanalysis: Scientific Method and Philosophy: A Symposium.* New York: New York University Press.

Klein, G. S. (1973), Is Psychoanalysis Relevant? *Psychoanalysis and Contemporary Science,* 2:3-21. New York: Macmillan.

Kohut, H. (1970), Scientific Activities of the American Psychoanalytic Association: An Inquiry. *J. Amer. Psychoanal. Assn.*, 18:462-484.

—— (1971), *The Analysis of the Self.* New York: International Universities Press.

—— (1972), Thoughts on Narcissism and Narcissistic Rage. *The Psychoanalytic Study of the Child,* 27:360-400. New York: Quadrangle.

—— (1973), The Future of Psychoanalysis. Presentation following Chicago Symposium on "Psychoanalysis and History."

Kris, E. (1947), The Nature of Psychoanalytic Propositions and Their Validation. In: *Freedom and Experience: Essays Presented to Horace M. Kallen*, ed. S. Hook & M. R. Konwitz. New York: Cornell University Press, pp. 239-259.

Kubie, L. S. (1966), A Reconsideration of Thinking, the Dream Process, and "The Dream." *Psychoanal. Quart.*, 35:191-198.

Kuhn, T. S. (1962), *The Structure of Scientific Revolutions*. Chicago: University of Chicago Press.

Lustman, S. L. (1963), Some Issues in Contemporary Psychoanalytic Research. *The Psychoanalytic Study of the Child*, 18:51-74. New York: International Universities Press.

———— (1969), Introduction to Panel: The Use of the Economic Viewpoint in Clinical Analysis: The Economic Point of View and Defense. *Internat. J. Psycho-Anal.*, 50:95-102.

Mahler, M. (1968), *On Human Symbiosis and the Vicissitudes of Individuation*. New York: International Universities Press.

Meehl, P. E. (1973), Some Methodological Reflections on the Difficulties of Psychoanalytic Research. In: Psychoanalytic Research: Three Approaches to the Experimental Study of Subliminal Processes, ed. M. Mayman. *Psychol. Issues*, Monogr. No. 30:104-117. New York: International Universities Press.

Ramzy, I. (1962), Research in Psychoanalysis: Contribution to Discussion. *Internat. J. Psycho-Anal.*, 43:292-296.

———— (1963), Research Aspects of Psychoanalysis. *Psychoanal. Quart.*, 32:58-76.

Rapaport, D. (1959), The Structure of Psychoanalytic Theory: A Systematizing Attempt. *Psychol. Issues*, Monogr. No. 6. New York: International Universities Press, 1960.

Ritvo, S. (1971), Psychoanalysis as Science and Profession: Prospects and Challenges. *J. Amer. Psychoanal. Assn.*, 19:3-21.

Rosenblatt, A. D., & Thickstun, J. T. (1970), A Study of the Concept of Psychic Energy. *Internat. J. Psycho-Anal.*, 51:265-278.

Sandler, J., & Joffe, W. G. (1969), Towards a Basic Psychoanalytic Model. *Internat. J. Psycho-Anal.*, 50:79-90.

Schafer, R. (1970), An Overview of Heinz Hartmann's Contributions to Psychoanalysis. *Internat. J. Psycho-Anal.*, 51:425-446.

———— (1972), Internalization: Process or Fantasy? *The Psychoanalytic Study of the Child*, 27:411-436. New York: Quadrangle.

———— (1973a), Action: Its Place in Psychoanalytic Interpretation and Theory. *The Annual of Psychoanalysis*, 1:159-196. New York: Quadrangle.

———— (1973b), The Idea of Resistance. *Internat. J. Psycho-Anal.*, 54:259-285.

———— (1975), Psychoanalysis without Psychodynamics. *Internat. J. Psycho-Anal.*, 56:41-55.

Schmidl, F. (1955), The Problem of Scientific Validation in Psychoanalytic Interpretation. *Internat. J. Psycho-Anal.*, 36:105-113.

Seitz, P. F. D. (1966), The Consensus Problem in Psychoanalytic Research. In: *Methods of Research in Psychotherapy*, ed. L. A. Gottschalk & A. H. Auerbach. New York: Appleton-Century-Crofts, pp. 209-225.

Waelder, R. (1962), Psychoanalysis, Scientific Method, and Philosophy. *J. Amer. Psychoanal. Assn.*, 10:617-637.

Wallerstein, R. S. (1968), The Psychotherapy Research Project of the Menninger Foundation: A Semifinal View. In: *Research in Psychotherapy*, ed. J. M. Shlien. Washington, D.C.: American Psychological Association, 3:584-606.

———— & Sampson, H. (1971), Issues in Research in the Psychoanalytic Process. *Internat. J. Psycho-Anal.*, 52:11-50.

8

ON THE POSSIBILITY OF A STRICTLY CLINICAL PSYCHO-ANALYTIC THEORY: AN ESSAY IN THE PHILOSOPHY OF PSYCHOANALYSIS

BENJAMIN B. RUBINSTEIN

The thesis that a strictly clinical psychoanalytic theory is possible has in recent years been emphatically stated by the late George S. Klein (1970, 1973). In essence, his point is that the clinical theory of psychoanalysis is self-sufficient and that what Freud (1915) called metapsychology may, at least in principle, be a branch of natural science but serves no discernible clinical purpose. Klein's basic idea is not new. It has its roots in a claim, originally formulated by Dilthey in the early years of this century, that our understanding of human beings and their affairs is a special form of understanding that is independent of the methods and concepts of natural science.

To determine whether a strictly clinical theory is indeed possible, we must first determine the nature and functions of the statements making up this theory. An examination of the nature of these statements has to include an examination of the views of Dilthey and some of his followers. This is particularly important inasmuch as these views, while rejected by Hartmann (1927a), are at least up to a point consonant with views expressed by the Hungarian psychoanalyst Imre Hermann (1934) and, as just indicated, by Klein. So far as I can see, the most unequivocal characteristic of clinical psychoanalytic statements is that they refer to persons. We must therefore examine the concept of a person in some detail. Next to be examined is the problem of clinical inference and confirmation, which define the functions of the statements making up the clinical theory. After a discussion of the existential implications of these statements, we come finally to the question whether a strictly clinical psychoanalytic theory is possible, i.e., whether this theory can stand on its own, without support from extraclinical hypotheses.

This is the basic question to which I address myself in the present study. In my view, to understand it properly, we must approach this question in the roundabout way I have just outlined. I hope the reader will have forbearance with what at first may seem like a series of unrelated topics, loosely strung together.

The Understanding of Human Beings and Their Affairs

In natural science we often speak about understanding an event if we can identify the cause of its occurrence. Ultimately, the understanding, which is a psychological phenomenon, is here a reflection of seeing the observed connection as an instance of an accepted cause-effect generalization or other theoretical statement. In other words, whenever it occurs, understanding in this sense is intimately related to the specific formal derivation, which we call an explanation, of a particular statement from other more general ones. Dilthey (1962),[1] who is primarily interested in history, makes a sharp distinction between this form of understanding and the understanding of human beings and their affairs. Part of the process involves the understanding of a mental content by its expression (p. 69; see also Rickman, 1962, p. 39). The relationship here, according to Dilthey, must be understood, not in terms of cause and effect, but only in terms of *meaning*. In Dilthey's

[1] The book referred to is an English translation of excerpts from Vol. 7 of Dilthey's work which was published in German several years after the author's death in 1911.

view, it is through its meaning that "Experience in its concrete reality is made coherent" (p. 74).

It may be of interest to note briefly some of the ways in which Dilthey speaks about meaning. In many instances, he regards an event as having meaning in the sense of its being a *sign* of the presence of another event, as in the case of an expression and the mental content of which it is an expression (p. 75). In other cases, Dilthey speaks about meaning in a sense related to *significance*, as when he considers the meaning of a life, particularly the life of an important historical personality (pp. 74-75). It would seem that, in instances such as these, recognizing meaning may be analyzable in terms of other processes. Rickman (1962), however, claims that, as Dilthey uses these words, "Understanding, 'the process of grasping meaning, is a mental operation which can be defined in terms of other mental operations as little as can seeing and reasoning" (p. 39).

Max Weber, the influential sociologist, and the psychologist Eduard Spranger are the best known among Dilthey's followers. In the first, methodological, chapter of his study of adolescence, Spranger (1925) writes that, in its most general sense, to understand is to see mental connections as meaningful (p. 3). He contrasts this general form of understanding, which he (apparently with some hesitation) regards as penetrating into the inner essence of the connections, with explanation, such as the causal explanations derived from laws of merely external succession. In Spranger's view, meaning is intimately connected with value (p. 4). We should note that, according to him, a merely descriptive psychology is not yet understanding. The experiences of others are understood only when we are able to perceive order and meaning in the profusion of mental states and sequences that are somehow presented to us (pp. 6-7).[2]

Although not a direct follower of Dilthey, the psychiatrist-philosopher Jaspers has clearly been influenced by him. His

[2] For a further discussion of both Dilthey and Spranger from a psychological point of view see Allport (1938), pp. 539-542.

concept of understanding is closely related to that of Dilthey. But, at least in the German edition with which I am acquainted, Jaspers (1923) does not explicitly propose a relationship between understanding and meaning. He distinguishes between static and genetic understanding, the former being the envisioning in their actual givenness (*Sich-zur-Gegebenheit-Bringen*) of the mental states of others, the latter the understanding of the emergence of one mental content from another (p. 199). Jaspers claims that genetic understanding is immediate, self-evident, and not further analyzable. He mentions as an example what he regards as Nietzsche's immediately understandable thesis that moral principles and demands emerge from a sense of weakness, "because the mind in spite of its weakness in taking this detour seeks to satisfy its will to power" (p. 199; translation mine). Jaspers terms understanding by reference to unconscious mental events, as in psychoanalysis, *as-if* understanding: i.e., the connections are understood *as if* they were conscious. In his opinion, it has not been demonstrated that what is thus understood is actually the case (pp. 204-205).

Hartmann (1927b, 1927c)[3] refers to Dilthey's psychology as merely descriptive (1927b, p. 38), thus contradicting (without mentioning it, although he repeatedly refers to him) Spranger's characterization, cited above, of understanding psychology. Hartmann may, however, use the word descriptive in a sense different from Spranger's. He thus pays scant attention to the concept of meaning, which he, contrary to Dilthey and Spranger, thinks has little psychological relevance (1927c, pp. 394-397). Indeed, according to Hartmann, Freud regarded a mental event—say, a neurotic symptom—as meaningful if it could be assigned "a place in the (causal) relationships of the mind" (p. 400).

Hartmann discusses Jaspers' views at some length. He believes that understanding in Jaspers' sense may be of value as a preliminary step toward the establishment of causal relationships (pp. 376-377), which, he emphasizes, is the aim of an

---

[3] These papers are English translations of the first chapters of Hartmann's book (1927a) on the fundamentals of psychoanalysis.

explanatory psychology such as psychoanalysis. He criticizes
Jaspers for being content to recognize understandable connections (p. 378), but does not consider his view of *as-if* understandable connections (i.e., connections involving unconscious
mental events) and the lack of proof for their reality.[4]

Hermann (1934) is one of the very few analysts to treat the
concept of meaning in a systematic way. According to him,
something (an idea that occurs to a patient, an attitude, an
analytic hour) is meaningful if it can be integrated with the
psychic continuum of the person in question. Psychoanalytic
understanding is the identification of meaning. Accordingly,
"To understand something analytically means to know the
place this something occupies in the psychic continuum of the
person" (p. 54; translation mine). Hermann speaks *metaphorically* about a *Sinn-Organ*, or meaning-perceiving organ
(p. 71). He claims that in the absence of distorting factors it
will "perceive" meaning as something immediate (p. 73)—an
idea that seems closely related to Dilthey's concept of the
process of grasping meaning. The functioning of this "organ,"
however, is not always reliable, and the meanings it "perceives" must be checked with other methods, including empathy (pp. 76-77).

We may notice that, in Hermann's thinking, cause and
meaning do not seem to be mutually exclusive categories.
Thus, according to him, the occurrence of a mental event may
be *caused* by a particular psychological constellation (p. 68).
On the other hand, however, he emphasizes that strict causality exists only in the realm of metapsychology, for which
meaning is irrelevant (p. 70) and which he regards as basically
a translation of meaningful connections into the language of
physics (p. 93). This last statement in particular indicates that

[4] In a paper considering, among other things, Dilthey's views on understanding
and Hartmann's criticism of them, Eissler (1968) does not clearly distinguish
between the two meanings of the word "understanding" as used by these authors:
viz., the sense of understanding a scientific explanation, on the one hand, and
Dilthey's sense of immediate understanding, which (seemingly at least) is in no way
related to explanation, on the other. Eissler also fails to recognize that *logically* an
explanation is an explanation, whether true or false, newly discovered or obsolete.

Klein's conception of meaning is rather closely related to
Hermann's.

It is important to note that Hermann goes beyond the quite
general definition of meaning just outlined. Specific meanings, he thinks, emerge in a number of ways, all of them
representing functions of the "meaning-perceiving organ."
Among the ways he lists are: (1) *transposition,* which leads to
our seeing the purpose of one activity as the purpose of
another; (2) *interpolation,* the rendering of an event understandable by positing an unconscious motive to which the
occurrence of the event may be related; and (3) *extrapolation,*
the rendering of an event understandable by positing an
external situation to which the occurrence of the event may be
related (pp. 74-75). It seems that in Hermann's view the
meaningfulness of the thus established connections derives
from the fact that certain events that otherwise would have no
place in the "psychic continuum" of the person in question can
thus be integrated with this continuum as (hypothetical)
elements of it.

The following example will give a more concrete idea of
what Hermann may mean by the concepts of a psychic
continuum, the integration into it of an otherwise puzzling
event, and meaning. According to Nietzsche's thesis, referred
to above, we observe that there are moral demands which do
not fit into a "psychic continuum" that is generally assumed to
be dominated by a will to power. If we now "interpolate" a
sense of weakness and a desire, flowing from the will to power,
to overcome the weakness, then it will appear that the
observed moral demands serve as the means to fulfill this
desire, namely, by curtailing the strength of the strong, thus
rendering the weak comparatively less weak. With this construction, we have established a connection between the will to
power, the sense of weakness, and the moral demands by
which the latter (including the activity of expressing them)
have become integrated into a psychic continuum to which at
first glance they did not seem to belong.

As this example indicates, we cannot speak about the integration of an event into the psychic continuum of a person

without specifying the way in which the event in question is integrated. It seems that it is through the way in which it is integrated that an event may be spoken about as having meaning. When the moral demands, including the activity of expressing them, come to appear as the means to an end, they are suddenly seen to have a *purpose*. This is the crucial point. In a commonly used meaning of "meaning," the meaning of an activity (as, for example, the activity of expressing moral demands) is defined precisely in terms of the purpose the activity serves.

Another point the example brings out is that the understanding of a psychological connection, contrary to what Jaspers and Hermann claim, is neither immediate nor is it, contrary to Jaspers' claims, self-evident and, once stated, further unanalyzable. The apparent immediacy, self-evidence, etc., of our psychological understanding in a case like the one just considered may well be a consequence of our facility, perhaps the outcome of a number of relevant experiences, to see events that can possibly be seen that way as means to ends. My main objection to Jaspers' view rests on the assumption I am making that the *structure* of a connection (such as the structure we refer to as a means-end relationship) is a decisive factor in psychological understanding. If indeed it is, and if we are familiar from previous experience with a certain structure no matter how it has been manifested, then a newly discovered connection exhibiting this structure will be immediately understandable, seem self-evident, and, on the face of it, further unanalyzable.[5]

A means-end relationship, obviously, is not the only structure on which psychological understanding, specifically in psychoanalysis, is based. Other structures include the relationship between a dream symbol and what it is a symbol of and the relationship between current and in some way analo-

---

[5] I have borrowed the term structure from modern linguistics. It seems to me that the use of this term in linguistics is analogous to the way I use it here. But my use of it is also related to the way Lévi-Strauss (1963, esp. Chap. 11; 1966) uses it. This is of course not surprising, since, in his thinking, Lévi-Strauss is admittedly influenced by linguistics.

gous past situations. I have recently (Rubinstein, 1974) discussed these relationships in greater detail and have tried to
show that in the three cases the relationship may be expressed
in terms of meaning and that, when it is, the concept of
meaning is used in each in a different meaning. I may
mention that the relationships of the last two types mentioned
are akin to but not identical with the types of relationship
yielded by what Hermann calls transposition and extrapolation.

I must briefly consider what, at least superficially, seems to
be yet another concept of meaning. According to Klein
(1973), "The central objective of psychoanalytic clinical explanation is the *reading of intentionality;* behavior, experience, testimony are studied for meaning in this sense" (p. 10;
Klein's italics). To properly understand the import of this
statement in the present context, we must try to examine the
meaning of the word intention as this word is commonly used.
We note, to begin with, that a sentence like, "I intend to do
such and such," may have the meaning expressed in the
sentence, "Unless the circumstances prevent it, I *will* do such
and such." Here, "intending" stands for something like "being
set on," and is not in any obvious manner related to meaning.
Assume, however, that I am doing something that seems
puzzling to an onlooker. If the onlooker asks, "What are you
doing?" and I reply, "Although it perhaps may not seem so,
my intention is to do such and such," my reply indicates what I
mean (i.e., what I have in mind) to do. Now, to *mean* to do
something obviously has very little in common with the
meaning of doing it. The relationship between intention and
meaning is most clear-cut in cases where intention is related to
purpose. Thus the purpose of an action is commonly thought
of as the *intended effect* of that action, to achieve its purpose,
as I indicated in a general way above, being describable as the
meaning of a person's performing it. In this usage, the relationship between "intention" and "meaning" is clearly predi-
cated on the relationship of both to "purpose."

UNDERSTANDING IN TERMS OF MEANING:
ITS AMBIGUITY AND LIMITED SCOPE

According to Klein (1970, 1973), the outstanding characteristic of clinical psychoanalytic statements is that they
concern meaning, significance, purpose, intention, etc. We
have seen that these concepts are related to one another and
that some of them, particularly the concept of meaning, are
quite ambiguous. Accordingly, when we speak about meaning
we should specify in what sense we use this word. There are
some uses of meaning that I have not—or at least not
explicitly—considered above, among them the most common
one, namely, the meaning of verbal expressions. The sentence, "It is raining," has a very precise meaning, which—
somewhat simplifying analyses of "meaning" by Strawson
(1950), Wittgenstein (1953), and Ryle (1957)—may be said to
be essentially a function of the way the sentence is *used* to refer
to a state of affairs. The sentence, "He did A because he
wanted to achieve B, and A ordinarily leads to B," clearly has
a meaning in this sense. But in a different sense of "meaning,"
doing A has a very specific meaning, which is to achieve *B*. In
its reference to this meaning, the sentence expresses the structure of the Nietzsche example discussed above. As is readily
seen, it is important to distinguish between the linguistic and
nonlinguistic meanings of "meaning" just indicated.

We should note that, whereas a causal relationship can exist
without any one knowing about it, no sentence, event, etc.,
can have a meaning without a somebody *to whom* it has this
meaning. A meaning cannot be a meaning unless it is understood as such. This is implicit in every meaning of "meaning."
In some cases, particularly when we speak about *unconscious
meanings*, we cannot avoid the question whether the something—say, a dream symbol—to which we attribute a meaning can be fairly said to have this meaning to the acting
individual (in this case the dreamer) himself or whether it has

meaning *only* to another person, who functions as an inter-
preter. Klein's exposition is marred by his failure to pay
sufficient attention to this fact.

Psychoanalytic writers are interested primarily in nonlinguistic meaning. Considering only this meaning of "meaning,"
we find that clinical psychoanalytic statements do not always
refer to the meanings of events. Some statements of this type
have reference to causal relationships. An example is the
statement, "His love for her, which she did not reciprocate,
drove him to this desperate act." To define clinical psychoanalytic statements as statements referring, not to causal
relationships, but to the meanings of events thus would not be
true to fact. Rapaport (1960) implicitly brought out this point
in his discussion of causes and motives.

The Concept of a Person

Since clinical psychoanalytic statements cannot be said always to refer to the meanings of events, and since the very
concept of having a meaning is ambiguous in the ways just
noted, we should look for an attribute of these statements that
is both unambiguous and truly criterial. At least on the face of
it, it does not seem that we have to look far. Directly or indirectly, each of the statements in question has reference to a
person: as an actor, as entertaining an emotion or being driven
by one, as the object of actions by other persons, as the victim
of circumstances, etc. Systematic (direct as well as indirect)
references to persons thus are a common feature of statements, such as those of Dilthey, Spranger, Hermann, and
Klein, which refer to the meanings of events, and those of
Jaspers, which do not. Fully to appreciate the significance of
this fact, we must examine in detail the concept of a person
and what it means when we say that a person does such and
such.

As Strawson (1959, Chap. 3) has emphasized, the concept of
a person is part of our common-sense conceptual scheme (see,
e.g., p. 109). It is not easy to define, but we all know what we
have in mind when we use the word "person" and its cognates,

such as personal pronouns and proper names. In an informal sort of way, we may, however, considering both Strawson's views and Englebretsen's (1972) modification of them, regard a person as an entity that is exhaustively defined by a particular, normally indissoluble combination of bodily and mental attributes. I use the word attribute in a wide sense, so that "having legs" and "thinking about Y" are both attributes, whether permanent or temporary, of a person. Contrary to what some people believe, mental attributes, according to the best currently available evidence, cannot exist by themselves (e.g., after death), nor can they, in contrast to bodily attributes, disappear to any appreciable degree from the combination without the person's ceasing to be a person. Therefore, someone whose arms and legs have been amputated is still regarded as a person, while someone who is demented is not. We should note, on the other hand, that, at least to its owner, a dog, too, is a person of sorts. To most people, however, a jellyfish is not.

We could go on listing examples of living things that are not persons. It is more interesting, however, to consider some of the things a person is not. When we speak about somebody as a person, we do not at the same time think of him as an organism, although from a certain point of view he is that also. But in our everyday dealings with persons, this fact is perfectly irrelevant. It thus seems fair to say that from the point of view from which somebody appears as a person, he is not an organism, and from the point of view from which he appears as an organism, he is not a person.

I shall have more to say about that later. In the present connection, however, I want to call attention to the fact that, as soon as we eliminate references to a person from our statements and speak instead about the wishes, feelings, thoughts, etc. that have been abstracted from the person whose wishes, feelings, thoughts, etc. they are supposed to be, we have taken a first step toward description in the mode of natural science, i.e., toward seeing a person as an organism. This first step, however, does not necessarily commit us to take a further step in that direction. On the other hand, as we shall see shortly, if we want to understand more fully what it means to say that a person does certain things, such a first step may be unavoidable. And, indeed, we find indications of this step's having been taken in the writings of Dilthey, Spranger, Jaspers, Hermann, and Klein. In the case of these authors, however, the focus soon shifts back to the person — at least implicitly. To Hartmann, by contrast, the first step is unequivocally a first step toward a "depersonalized" metapsychological description, i.e., a description in the mode of natural science.

But let us return to the main point of the present discussion. It is practically a matter of definition that ordinary language is the natural vehicle for speaking about persons. Typical examples of references to a person are sentences like, "He loves his wife," "He walks," "He thinks," "He lifts a stone," "He is not as smart as he believes he is," "He is too heavy." These sentences point to another thing a person is not. I have said that, looked at from one point of view, he is not an organism. There is, however, no point of view from which he, as Strawson has emphasized, will appear as a Cartesian Ego or as in any way comparable to an Ego of this sort. The "he" in the sentence, "He thinks," is the same "he" as the "he" in the sentence, "He lifts a stone," and the "he" in the sentence, "He is too heavy." To Descartes's way of thinking, on the other hand, the "he" in "He thinks" (as the "I" in "I think") is of an entirely different species than the "he" in the two other sentences given. What he had in mind is perhaps best rendered in some such grammatically anomalous sentence as, "His I thinks."

Although the claim that it is the same "he" that appears in all three sentences is consistent with the above informal view of a person as an entity exhaustively defined by a particular, normally indissoluble combination of bodily and mental attributes, a few additional words may help to clarify it. Descartes's Ego concept may be regarded as based on two premises: (1) thinking is an activity that, although unobservable, is strictly comparable to activities like those of walking and lifting stones; and (2) like walking and lifting stones, the activity of thinking requires a subject performing it. According to Russell (1921, pp. 17-18; 1945, p. 567), both premises are mistaken. When we think, we are not aware of an activity (or act) of thinking. Hence, he concludes, there is no such activity and, accordingly, no need to posit a subject performing it. Russell claims that what an individual is aware of is only that *there are thoughts in him.*

That he certainly is aware of. It seems, however, that, apart from this *specific* awareness, when we think, we also have a *general sense* of continuous activity. It is not that the specific thoughts we are aware of always occur in an uninterrupted series. Quite the contrary. For the most part, we are not aware of the unfolding of the activity of thinking in every one of its details. In other words, the *specific* thoughts that occur in us occur only at certain intervals, which may be extremely brief or quite prolonged. In the case of problem solving, for example, among the thoughts that occur, one may represent what looks like a solution to the problem, to be followed in the same "session," although often not right away and without a distinctly articulated transition, by a rejection of this solution. Obviously, we would not say that, in any given "session" during the intervals, whether short or long, between the occurrence of thoughts like these, we are not thinking. It follows that our sense of continuous activity is not illusory, that thinking is indeed a continuous activity; however, we experience it in specific detail only in part. In a more general way, Lashley (1958, p. 4) has made the same point.

Having refuted Russell's claim that thinking is not an activity, must we conclude now that, since thinking is after all an activity, this activity must have a subject? I take the fact that it is consistent with our common-sense conceptual scheme as justification for provisionally affirming this conclusion and see where it leads us. The next question is, then, how the presumptive subject is to be defined. Let us compare thinking with walking. Offhand, it would appear that, since walking is an observable activity, the subject of walking must also be observable. What is observable about somebody, however, is his body; but we would not say, for example, "His body walks around the block." It is true that his body is prominently involved in the activity of walking. His body, however, is merely the sum total of the (permanent) bodily attributes that in normally indissoluble combination with a set of mental attributes make up the person he is. And it is the person, of course, who is the subject of the activity of walking.

Similarly with thinking. Since thinking is an unobservable activity, Descartes, to match what he believed to be the observable subject, say, of walking, posited an unobservable subject of thinking. But just as we do not say, "His body walks around the block," we also do not say, "His mind thinks about how to solve this problem." It is true that his mind is prominently involved in the activity of thinking. But his mind is merely the sum total of the mental attributes that in normally indissoluble combination with a set of bodily attributes make up the person he is. And again it is, of course, the person who is the subject of the activity of thinking.

Somebody may object that it is really the individual's brain that does the thinking. It is, however, not his brain as a piece of his body, but his brain as the embodiment, so to speak, of his mental attributes that is supposed to do the thinking. Although his brain most likely is prominently involved in the activity of thinking, it is, however, not more meaningful to say, "His brain thinks about how to solve this problem," than it is to say, "His mind thinks about how to solve this problem."

These considerations make the person appear at least *as if* he were the subject of his various observable as well as unobservable activities. The way in which he may perform the latter is, however, quite mysterious. Is it then, as Russell (1945, p. 567) has intimated, merely a linguistic convention that makes it appear that the activities in question are in fact performed by him? I do not think so. We can define "being a subject" not only syntactically, but also in terms of the individual's experience. It seems that a person genuinely has a sense of performing the activities in which he is involved and that at any given moment this sense in part defines him to himself as the person he is at that moment. We may say that generally a person has a sense-of-being-a-person (often referred to as a sense of self) and that when he does such and such he has a sense-of-being-a-person-doing-such-and-such—for example, a sense-of-being-a-person-thinking. This sense, obviously, is not identical with the sense of the activity of thinking I referred to above. Whereas the sense of the activity of thinking is "depersonalized," the sense-of-being-a-person-thinking clearly is not. It is of interest that the sense-of-being-a-person involves a sense of being in part a body. I shall not, however, pursue this question further.

I am trying to make two points. The first is that the sense-of-being-a-person-thinking is reflected in, not induced by, linguistic expressions such as the sentence, "I think." The second is that the sense-of-being-a-person-thinking does not reveal anything about the processes of thinking. Indeed, from the point of view from which somebody appears as a person, these processes are irrelevant. On the other hand, to speak about a sense-of-being-a-person-thinking is to say that *in his own experience* it is the person who performs the activity of thinking—or, for short, who *does* the thinking. And in his view this meaning of "does," although—if we start to reflect about it—it seems quite nebulous, is perfectly acceptable to common sense. To our common-sense way of thinking about ourselves, a question like, "What precisely does the word 'does' mean in this context?" simply does not arise.

I shall consider the question why a person believes that what he experiences about himself will apply to others as well. In the present connection, it suffices to note that ordinarily he has no doubt that it does.

It is apparent that in this discussion of thinking we have taken the first step (but only the first step) toward description in the mode of natural science. I have sought to illuminate some of the features of the concept of a person, considering particularly the things a person is said to do. One conclusion we have come to is that thinking, although experienced *as such* only in part, is an unobservable activity attributable to a person. A further conclusion is that the person may be said to be the subject of this activity in two different meanings of the word subject. To our common-sense way of looking at things, the person is the subject in the sense of being the one who literally *performs* (or does) the thinking. From a critical point of view, on the other hand, to say that the person is the subject of the activity of thinking is not to imply anything about the precise nature of the relationship between the person and the thinking. Looked at from the same critical point of view, his conviction that he is the subject of this activity, in the sense of being the one who literally performs it, appears as most likely derived from an experience I have referred to as a sense-of-being-a-person-thinking. In a very general way, we may thus characterize thinking as an *unobservable activity associated with experiences of particular kinds*. Other unobservable activities, such as wishing, doubting, loving, may be characterized in a similar manner.

We may note that the common-sense view of a person as subject pervades everyday speech, literature, history, ethics, and so-called philosophies of life. For proper understanding of the clinical theory of psychoanalysis, however, we must abandon it in favor of the critical point of view I have tried to indicate above.

Ordinary Language and the Particular Clinical Hypotheses

We come now to the most crucial point of the discussion so far. When we speak about patients in psychoanalysis, we refer to them in sentences of the same type as those listed above, i.e., sentences such as "He loves his wife," "He went out for a walk," "He thinks." I shall preliminarily speak about these as sentences of type 1. We do, however, also refer to patients in sentences that seem to be of a different type, for example, "Unconsciously he hates his father," "He has repressed the wish," "Without being aware of it, in talking about his concern that his girl friend may want to leave him, he is also expressing concern about the analyst's impending vacation," etc. Sentences of this general type are not only used to speak about patients, they also serve as vehicles for the interpretations that an analyst, at appropriate points in the analysis, may present to a patient. I will preliminarily speak about these sentences as sentences of type 2.

One thing is immediately apparent. The "he" in the sentences of type 2 refers to the same entity, namely, a person, as the "he" in the sentences of type 1. One difference between the sentences of the two types is that the sentences of type 2 do not reflect a sense-of-being-person-doing-something. It would be a contradiction in terms of speak about a sense-of-being-a-person-unconsciously-wishing-such-and-such or a sense-of-being-a-person-repressing. The corresponding sentences, apparently, have been constructed by analogy with sentences of type 1.

Another difference between the two types of sentences is that, whereas those of type 1 may refer to both observable and unobservable activities as well as to other mental events (such as being sad), external causes of mental events (such as being rejected), and dispositions (such as being stubborn, intelligent, etc.), the sentences of type 2 refer *only* to *unobservable activities*. The outstanding characteristic of these unobservable activities is that they are *not associated with experiences of any kind*. Being thus neither observable nor associated with experience, the occurrence of these activities is strictly a matter of inference. From a purely linguistic point of view, the introduction of references to hypothetical activities of this sort may be regarded as an *extension of ordinary language* brought about in part by adding specific qualifiers, such as the term unconsciously, to the verb phrases of certain ordinary-language sentences.

It is of interest to note that, although offhand they may appear somewhat questionable, we may feel more inclined to accept the possibility of unobservable activities not associated with experience if we keep in mind (a) that, as I have tried to show above, thinking is an unobservable activity that we only in part experience in specific detail; and (b) that the precise nature of the relationship between a person and the unobservable activities associated with experience we ascribe to him, unproblematic though it may seem to common sense, eludes us when looked at from a critical point of view.

I shall refer to sentences of type 1 as *regular ordinary-language sentences* and to sentences of type 2 as *sentences of the extended ordinary language.* I will say that the latter, regardless of how they are used (i.e., whether to speak about patients or as vehicles for interpretations presented to patients), express *particular clinical hypotheses.* Particular clinical hypotheses may, however, at times also be expressed in type-1 sentences.

A Note on the Clinical Psychoanalytic Theory

The particular clinical hypotheses do not form part of the clinical psychoanalytic theory, but represent statements derived from the application of this theory to certain observations. The theory is constituted of two sets of statements that may be referred to, respectively, as *general* and *special clinical hypotheses.* Both sets include *motivational, situational,* and *genetic* hypotheses.

An example of a *general motivational hypothesis* is the hypothesis that all observable and unobservable activities in which a person may be said to engage are motivated, consciously or unconsciously. Among the unobservable activities, apart from those mentioned above, are dreams, parapraxes, and certain neurotic symptoms. Another *general motivational hypothesis* is that of the activity and tendency to indirect expression of unconscious motives. Examples of *special motivational hypotheses* are hypotheses about particular so-called defense mechanisms.

An example of a *special situational hypothesis* is the hypothesis that, if insulted, a person will feel hurt. The *general situational hypothesis* under which this hypothesis is subsumed is one we may refer to as the hypothesis of situation-specific responses. The *general genetic hypotheses* refer to developmental sequences and to the long-range effects of specific early experiences. Transference reactions are inferred in accordance with a genetic hypothesis stating that under certain conditions a present situation may become in part functionally equivalent with situations in the past that are in some way similar.

There are a number of general and special clinical hypotheses that do not fit into the categories mentioned. Among the most important of these are hypotheses adduced for the interpretation of dreams.

Clinical psychoanalytic theory has two functions: (1) to explain our observations; and (2) to contribute to the confirmation of these explanations. The actual explanations are embodied in the particular clinical hypotheses derived in accordance with one or several of the general and/or special clinical hypotheses constituting the theory. For the most part, these hypotheses concern what Klein (e.g., 1970, p. 114) referred to as the "why" of behavior. But some of them are more relevant to what in his view is the "how" of behavior. General clinical hypotheses underlying dream interpretation are examples.

To get an idea of how the general clinical hypotheses operate in explanation, let us briefly consider some of the most commonly adduced general motivational hypotheses. We infer that an activity is related to a motive if it can be seen as the fulfillment, or as a substitute fulfillment, or as a means to the fulfillment of this motive. The inference is here from what an activity can be *seen as being* to its *possibly being in fact* what it can be seen as being. We should note that, as I indicated above, the general clinical hypotheses functioning as premises in this inference may also be regarded as expressing the *structure* of the particular clinical hypotheses thus inferred. Since this structure, although not consciously identified as such, is in most instances immediately recognizable, clinical inference does not subjectively have the earmark of a logical operation.

In the present connection, these few hints about the nature of clinical explanation must suffice. Because of the limited space at my disposal, I must discuss the confirmation of our explanations in an even more cursory manner. The most important point is that the same general and special clinical hypotheses that function in the derivation of clinical explanations function also in the confirmation of these explanations. In clinical confirmation, we proceed from the establishment of a possibility to the assessment of *probability*. The procedure is roughly as follows. Suppose we have inferred that an observed (or reported) behavioral event B may be a substitute fulfillment of an unconscious wish W. The next steps are (a) to postdict in accordance with appropriate general and/or special clinical hypotheses the occurrence in the recent or remote past of situations that may have led to the establishment of W as an active unconscious wish; and (b) to predict in accordance with a different set of general and/or special clinical hypotheses the occurrence of events qualifying as indirect expressions of W. In most instances, these predictions are merely implicit. Clearly, the particular clinical hypothesis that B is a substitute fulfillment of W will be confirmed to the extent that our postdictions and predictions come true.

If this analysis is correct, it seems that *in principle* the confirmation of particular clinical hypotheses does not differ from the confirmation of hypotheses in other scientific disciplines. The main differences are that (1) the predictions, as just mentioned, are usually merely implicit; (2) they are not of particular events, but of any one or several of a particular *class* of events; (3) the conditions for the occurrence of these events are for the most part not specifiable. Properly modified, the second of these points applies to postdictions as well.

The belief that Popper's so-called falsifiability criterion is needed to determine the scientific status of hypothetical statements rests on the *assumption* that we can find supporting evidence for practically every hypothetical statement we care to make (see, e.g., Popper, 1962, p. 36). As far as particular clinical hypotheses are concerned, Popper's assertion notwithstanding, this is simply not true. As every analyst knows, in the course of an analysis a number of particular clinical hypotheses are formulated and subsequently dropped (and usually forgotten) because of lack of evidence. It follows that whatever evidence we gather in favor of particular clinical hypotheses is significant for the confirmation of these hypotheses.

I may mention, before proceeding, that both Jaspers and Hermann, at least by implication, refer to the necessity of clinical confirmation of particular clinical hypotheses. In his criticism of Jaspers' view of the self-evidence of understandable connections, Hartmann (1927c, p. 380) likewise alludes to this point.[6]

The Existential Implications of the Statements of the Clinical Psychoanalytic Theory

I have distinguished between a common-sense and a critical view of a person as subject. These views pertain specifically to the person as the subject of his unobservable activities. To simplify matters, I shall in the following speak about a common-sense and a critical view of the person. So far as I can see, both are compatible with the view of a person I formulated in accordance with Strawson's concept.

I indicated that properly to understand the clinical theory of psychoanalysis we have to adopt the critical view of a person. There are, however, two points we must consider in this connection. One is that the particular and special clinical hypotheses and most of the general clinical hypotheses are, or can be, formulated as statements about persons, as these appear to common sense. The second point is that the critical view of a person merely poses a problem but offers no solution. What it does is to reveal the mysterious nature of the relationship between a person and the unobservable activities of which he is said to be the subject. It seems that, if we are to find a solution to our problem, we must approach human beings from the point of view of natural science. This is particularly important when we consider unconscious mental events and, as we will see, the validity of the general clinical hypotheses.

[6] These authors do not speak about particular clinical hypotheses; but their reference is to statements for which I use this designation. I may mention that in a paper to be published shortly (in *Psychoanalysis and Contemporary Science*, Vol. 4) I have discussed in greater detail the various points considered in this section.

The way we look at these issues is crucial to the question of the possibility of a strictly clinical psychoanalytic theory. Before discussing them, I must outline, unavoidably, at some length, what I believe to be a proper context for the discussion. Let me begin with the particular clinical hypotheses. Each of these, as I just indicated, typically concerns a person—more specifically, what a person wishes, feels, does, etc., and what happens to him. I have also indicated that we can eliminate from our statements explicit references to a person and speak instead about the wishes, feelings, thoughts, etc., that may be abstracted from the person whose wishes, feelings, thoughts, etc., they are supposed to be, and that in taking this step we have moved toward description in the mode of natural science, i.e., toward seeing the person as the human organism he, apart from being a person, is also. Without trying to defend this position, I shall adopt the identity theory of the mind-brain relationship.[7] Following the procedure just indicated to its last consequence, we eventually come to a point where the mental attributes we ascribe to a person will appear as states of the organism this person is also or, more specifically, as states of its brain, or of parts of its brain. When we do that, the person, who this organism is also, vanishes from view. He, of course, still remains a person; but, from the point of view of natural science, this fact is as irrelevant as it is irrelevant, when we see a person as a person, that he is also a human organism.

In what sense do we say that a person is also an organism? Are these merely two ways of referring to the same entity? Certainly not in the sense in which the English word *moon* refers to the same entity as the French *lune*. It seems more to the point to say that the relationship between a person and the corresponding human organism is analogous to the relationship between the color red and electromagnetic waves with a a wave length of 7×10^{-5} cm.

[7] Quite apart from the fact that it seems to me the most likely of currently existing theories, the adoption of this theory makes for simpler description. What I have to say, however, is also compatible with a merely correlative approach to the mind-brain relationship.

Let me pursue this question a little further. We are clearly not making the same assertion when we say, "This object is red" and "This object reflects electromagnetic waves with a wave length of 7 x 10^{-5} cm." We do, however, believe that the same objective state of affairs presents itself to us, *although in different ways*, when we—with sufficient reason—say about an object O (a) that it is red; and (b) that it reflects electromagnetic waves with a length of 7 x 10^{-5} cm. The two attributes are functions of two different methods of observation, and it would be nonsensical to say that the one attribute is more real than the other. It would be just as nonsensical to say, "O is not *really* red," as it would be to say, "O does not *really* reflect electromagnetic waves with a wave length of 7 x 10^{-5} cm." It is, on the other hand, not nonsensical to claim that the redness of O is contingent on a particular relationship between O and a sentient being, whereas O's reflecting waves of a certain wave length presumably is not. Disregarding other sentient beings, we can say that the redness of O is a feature of our *everyday human world* while O's reflecting waves of a certain wave length is a feature of the *world of natural science* or, more specifically, *of physics.* [8]

We can say in a quite similar way that a person is an entity of our everyday human world, while the human organism he is also is strictly a biological entity, i.e., an entity of the world of natural science. In the case of redness, we require particular instruments to discover that any red object in our everyday human world in the world of physics is a something that reflects waves of a certain wave length. In the case of a person, on the other hand, we do not need particular instruments to discover that he is also an organism. What we require is merely a different way of looking at him, namely, the way we look at things from the point of view of natural science.

If the words person and organism, as I claim, are not

[8] It is obviously incorrect to speak about an object as if it were describable in the same way in our everyday human world and in the world of physics. It is, however, simpler to do so and, in the present connection, it is not likely to lead to misunderstanding.

synonymous, then the concepts they stand for must be defined in different ways. Largely following Strawson, I have regarded a person as an entity that is exhaustively defined by a particular, normally indissoluble combination of bodily and mental attributes. An organism, on the other hand, may be regarded as an entity defined by bodily (i.e., anatomical and physiological) attributes, some of which are *also* mental. We can hardly doubt that the bodily attributes of an organism that are also mental are certain processes in the brain of this organism. I shall refer to these processes as *M-processes*. They include (1) *ME-processes,* which correspond (in a sense of "correspond" that I shall not try to define here) to the experiences and unobservable activities associated with the experience of the person this organism is also; and (2) *MI-processes* (or inferred M-processes), which are the unobservable activities not associated with experience we by inference ascribe to the person in question.

We can now take a further step. I have said that the "he" in a sentence like "He walks" is the same "he" as the "he" in the sentence, "He thinks." If we turn now from the person, the "he" in these sentences refers to, to the organism this person is also, i.e., if we "depersonalize" the sentences in question, we find that they cannot simply be transposed to apply to the organism, for example, by substituting an "it" for the "he." It sounds awkward to say about an organism that it walks and even more so to say about it that it thinks. In the case of walking, we can say (very roughly) something like "Sequences of specific, finely coordinated neuromuscular events occur, which have the effect that the organism as a whole is moved from one place to another." In the case of thinking, on the other hand, we might claim that, whenever it is true to say about a person that he thinks, it is also true to say that certain M-processes, some of which qualify as ME-processes, occur in the brain of the organism this person is, apart from being a person. We should note, however, that the ME-processes that are included among the (physiologically defined) M-processes of thinking are only part of the larger group of ME-processes included among the larger group of M-processes in the brain of the organism that, to the person, who is also this organism, are his sense-of-being-a-person-thinking. We, of course, do not know anything about the neurophysiological nature of these processes or about the ways in which they are integrated with one another. For our present purpose, however, this lack of knowledge, although regrettable, is unimportant.

In the case of wishing, say, of wanting A, we can similarly distinguish between the ME-processes included among the (physiologically defined) M-processes of wanting A and the larger group of ME-processes, of which they form a part, which are included among the M-processes in the brain of the organism that to the person, who is also this organism, are his sense-of-being-a-person-wanting-A. Suppose now we have reason to say about a person that *unconsciously* he wants A. If this is the case, we must also have reason to say that certain MI-processes occur in the brain of the organism this person is also. If we have no reason to make the second of these statements, then *either* the referent of the statement that a person unconsciously wants A is unrelated to what goes on in the brain of the organism that is also this person, *or else* we *only believe* that we have reason to say that unconsciously the person wants A. From any but a dualistic point of view, to say that a person unconsciously wants A amounts to ascribing MI-processes of a particular type to the brain of the organism that is also this person — and nothing more. It seems obvious, but nevertheless is important to emphasize, that these MI-processes occur in complete isolation from the M-processes in the brain of the organism that, to the person in question, are his sense-of-being-a-person.

I want to bring out two further points about ME- and MI-processes. The first is that, whereas ME-processes present two sets of data, MI-processes present data of only one set. The two sets of data presented by the ME-processes are (1) the experiences, etc., of the person, who is also the organism in the brain of which these processes occur; and (2) the experiences of another person who (with some presently unfathomable instrument) watches what at the same time happens in the brain of the organism in question. The data presented by the

MI-processes, on the other hand, are the experiences of the (mythical) person who watches the brain in which these processes are supposed to occur when we ascribe, say, an unconscious wish to the person who is also the organism the brain of which is being watched. It seems fairly clear that, in contrast to ME-processes, MI-processes are analogous to electromagnetic waves in the invisible part of the spectrum.

The second point is that, to an outside observer, ME-processes are as much a part of the world of natural science as are MI-processes. On the other hand, in contrast to experiences and unobservable activities associated with experience (such as wanting something), unobservable activities not associated with experience (such as unconsciously wanting something) are part of our everyday human world *in name only,* i.e., we may speak about them *as if* they were a part of this world, fully knowing that really they are not. Since there are no data, and no possibility of ever obtaining data to support the opposite claim, these activities, assuming that they do occur, have no reality beyond that of the corresponding MI-processes. If we admit them to our everyday human world, we in fact admit what is only a label, disregarding whatever the label is a label of.

THE SIMPLE AND THE EXPANDED CLINICAL PSYCHOANALYTIC THEORY

Having come to this conclusion, we must stop and recall what I said earlier about the person and his various unobservable activities associated with experience. The point I was trying to make is that from a *critical point of view* — which is not identical with the viewpoint of natural science — it is quite mysterious how a person goes about being the subject of these activities in the sense of actually "doing" them. The mystery, if anything, is augmented by the fact that, in regard to thinking, we are aware of the actual process only in part.

To our common-sense way of looking at things, on the other hand, the concept that a person is indeed a subject in the indicated sense presents no problem. It seems that what lends unity to the person's experience of thinking, and what may lead him to conclude that he is indeed the subject of this activity, is what I have referred to as his sense-of-being-a-person-thinking.

As I have indicated, since they are not given in the experience of the person who is also the organism in the brain of which they occur, MI-processes, such as unconsciously wanting A, cannot be integrated with the sense-of-being-a-person of this person. Nevertheless, when I say, for example, about a patient that unconsciously he wants to do such and such, I would claim without hesitation that in ascribing the unconscious wish to this patient I do not cease to see him as a person — not even at the moment I ascribe the wish to him. As to the wish itself, accordingly, I do not have a sense of it as not being describable in terms of our everyday human world. To common sense, although temporarily hidden from view, it is as much a part of this world as any conscious wish. It is only when we adopt a critical point of view that we become aware of the fact that it really exists *only* in the world of natural science, namely, in the form of MI-processes of a certain type in the brain of the organism that is also the person to whom we impute the unconscious wish in question. As I just indicated, from a critical point of view, in our everyday human world the term "unconscious wish" is merely a label, an indicator of the presence of an *as-if* wish, to borrow Jaspers' term.

On the other hand, as I indicated earlier, the fact that we are only partly aware of the processes involved in thinking — which means that from a physiological point of view thinking is a specific sequence of ME- and MI-processes — may make us, reasoning by analogy, feel more inclined to accept the possibility that the label "unconscious wish" actually signals the presence of a specific set of MI-processes.

One consequence of this discussion, it seems to me, is that we must make a sharp distinction between a *simple* and an *expanded clinical psychoanalytic theory.* In the simple psychoanalytic theory, our common-sense way of looking at things is unchallenged. When we turn to the expanded theory, on the other hand, we come up against questions that are not only alien to common sense, but unanswerable in its terms. The curious thing, as I have indicated, is that we can, apparently without (at least too obviously) going beyond common sense, infer and confirm particular clinical hypotheses. But, when we look critically at what we are doing, we will realize that, as phrased in ordinary language, our inferences and confirmations represent merely a first step.[9] Having taken this step, we are faced with the choice of whether to accept it as final or take yet another step which will reveal the ordinary-language descriptions we have inferred and confirmed as being merely labels for MI-processes of particular kinds. In contrast to the simple clinical psychoanalytic theory, the expanded clinical psychoanalytic theory thus straddles, as it were, two worlds—our everyday human world and the world of natural science. Another way of saying this is that, with regard to unconscious mental events, the expanded clinical theory, in however general terms it may be phrased, makes use of what we traditionally refer to as metapsychology.

This point is brought out even more clearly in the case of the general clinical hypotheses we adduce both for the inference and the confirmation of particular clinical hypotheses. I have indicated that these hypotheses may be regarded in two ways: (1) as expressions in general terms of the *structure* characterizing certain classes of particular clinical hypotheses; and (2) as *premises* entering into the inference and confirmation of particular clinical hypotheses. There is, however, yet another, perhaps more fundamental way of looking at the general clinical hypotheses. In a quite specific sense of this word, the question is of their status. It appears that in the simple clinical psychoanalytic theory these hypotheses function essentially as postulates that are taken either to be

---

[9] The "first step" here is not to be confused with the first step toward "depersonalized description," which I referred to above.

true or merely useful. I will shortly discuss the first of these alternatives. As to the usefulness of the hypotheses, it is determined by how well they "work" in the sense of enabling us to
organize our data into as coherent and simple a system as
possible. According to this interpretation, the hypotheses can
hardly be said to have a truth value defined in any way other
than in terms of their usefulness. Thus, for example, while it is
not necessarily true it is nonetheless useful to think that there
may be something to which the term "unconscious motive"
applies.

Let us see what happens if we take the general clinical
hypotheses to be true. They may then be regarded as the
(unproven) presuppositions on which the whole of clinical
theory is based. If we consider the points made in the earlier
section on the clinical psychoanalytic theory, it is obvious that,
viewed this way, the general clinical hypotheses can contribute
to the confirmation, in the ordinary sense of this word, of
particular clinical hypotheses. In these cases, however, even
though we may not spell it out, we must always add a reservation to a confirmatory statement. We can thus say about
a given particular clinical hypothesis that it is confirmed to a
such and such degree, but *only* if the general clinical hypotheses involved in the confirmation are assumed to be true.

One may object to this conclusion that, if we accept certain
data as confirmatory of a particular clinical hypothesis, then
these data must confirm also the general clinical hypotheses in
accordance with which the data in question were (implicitly)
predicted or postdicted, as the case may have been. This is
part of a scientific procedure that, as expounded, for instance,
by Ayer (1946), is generally accepted. Take the prediction,

If h & K & L, *then* d,

d being a datum, h a particular clinical hypothesis, and K and
L general clinical hypotheses. If, now, d occurs, its occurrence
confirms h, K, and L in the same measure.

This objection, however, loses much of its force if we
consider that, at least in some instances, even a fair number of
confirmatory data do not preclude alternative hypotheses,
particular as well as general. In just how many instances

alternative hypotheses are possible I do not know. But, considering the several schools of psychotherapy that currently flourish, each with its own set of (often merely tacitly accepted) general as well as special clinical hypotheses, the number of instances in which alternative hypotheses are actually used may be quite impressive. I will consider only the general clinical hypotheses. Even though the various schools may have some general clinical hypotheses in common, the complete sets are, notwithstanding, quite different. We need only think of the difference between Freudian and Jungian dream interpretation to appreciate this point. Thus, while the view of the dream as a wish fulfillment is the most basic hypothesis in accordance with which all other general clinical hypotheses underlying Freudian dream interpretation are derived, the most basic hypothesis of Jung's is, in MacIntyre's words (1967, p. 296), that dreams are "compensations for deficiencies in the dreamer's waking life" or, as Fromm (1951), p. 109) — closer to Jung's own mode of expression — has put it, "revelations of unconscious wisdom." From this basic hypothesis, general clinical hypotheses are derived in accordance with which dreams are interpreted, among other things, as "indicating the goals and aims of the dreamer" (p. 95). Although somewhat one-sided, these are fair characterizations. We are, therefore, not surprised to find that, according to Jung (1943), "Misled by the so-called dream mechanisms of Freudian manufacture, such as displacement, inversion, etc., people have imagined they could make themselves independent of the 'facade' of the dream by supposing that the true dream-thoughts lay hidden behind it" (p. 100). Jung, however, is far from taking dreams in their literal meanings. But, where Freud sees displacements and (among others) sexual symbols, he sees "poetic metaphors" (p. 104) and "archetypal images" (such as the image of the wise old man) derived from the "collective unconscious" (pp. 108-110). Certain similarities in particular interpretations notwithstanding (see, e.g., Jung's interpretation of a dream of his own on p. 112), the two approaches to dream interpretation, Freud's and Jung's, could hardly be further apart.

Let me try to amplify this point. Suppose that a set of general clinical hypotheses, H_F, and the corresponding particular clinical hypotheses are confirmed by a set of data, d_F, and that another set of general clinical hypotheses, H_J, and the corresponding particular clinical hypotheses are confirmed by a set of data, d_J. Suppose further that in a number of cases, in which members of both H_F and H_J are adducible, members of d_F as well as of d_J are clearly identifiable and carry *roughly* the same weight as evidence *in the sense* that the identified members of d_F may reasonably said to represent *satisfactory evidence* for the adduced members of H_F (and for the corresponding particular clinical hypotheses) and the identified members of d_J may reasonably be said to represent *satisfactory evidence* for the adduced members of H_J (and for the corresponding particular clinical hypotheses). In these cases we would have no way on strictly clinical grounds to choose between the two sets of adducible general clinical hypotheses.

Even if, generalized, this argument merely claims that alternative sets of—in the indicated sense—clinically equally well-confirmed hypotheses may exist, though not necessarily demonstrably at the present time, it considerably weakens the evidence for the general clinical hypotheses identified in accordance with the formula "*If* h & K & L, *then* d." What the argument shows is that each set of general clinical hypotheses, apart from generating corresponding particular clinical hypotheses, also has the power *selectively* to single out relevant evidence *without in any way affecting* the possibly identifiable evidence for competing sets of general clinical and corresponding particular clinical hypotheses. It is thus at least logically conceivable that we may end up with two or more interpretive systems pitted against each other without any method of choosing among them.[10]

It follows that the general clinical hypotheses with which we are concerned may still be regarded as ([largely] unproven)—or, more simply, as (unproven)—presuppositions. Things

---

[10] This point forces us to introduce a reservation into the argument against the applicability of Popper's falsifiability criterion presented above. I shall, however, reserve a full discussion of this question for another occasion.

would be different if these hypotheses could be confirmed directly, i.e., independently of the particular clinical hypotheses in the confirmation of which they participate. It is at this juncture that the expanded clinical psychoanalytic theory becomes relevant. Although analysts hardly ever stress this point (and Klein, too, has overlooked it), it seems clear that, as seen from a clinical point of view, the function of metapsychology is precisely to *justify* the presuppositions the general clinical hypotheses represent. This is particularly obvious with regard to the hypotheses mentioned earlier that, in Klein's terms, refer to the "how" of behavior. The predicament of the "why" hypotheses, however, is in no way different. For instance, the hypothesis of the activity and tendency to indirect expression of unconscious motives is in the traditional theory formulated in terms of the pressure for discharge inherent in psychic energy, whereas at least some of the general clinical hypotheses adduced for dream interpretation are in the traditional theory formulated in terms of the properties of unbound, freely mobile energy. In a sense, the general clinical hypotheses, as they have been indicated above, express the *structure*, not only of classes of particular clinical hypotheses, but also in regard to their clinical relevance of a number of metapsychological hypotheses. Although not in themselves metapsychological, they may, viewed from the angle of metapsychology, be said to express nothing but this structure.

In the example just given, the hypotheses involving the concept of psychic energy are testable physiologically, and, if confirmed, they would — in accordance with what I have just said — also confirm the general clinical hypotheses exhibiting the same structure. It is fairly commonly agreed that, for all practical purposes, the hypotheses involving the concept of psychic energy have been refuted physiologically. This does not mean, however, that the corresponding general clinical hypotheses have now also been refuted. The latter hypotheses are formulated in a way that makes them compatible with a great number of *structurally* similar but *materially* entirely different physiological hypotheses.

I want to make three additional points. The first is that many analysts who use metapsychological hypotheses knowing them to be physiologically invalid — or at least questionable — really use them as metaphorical expressions for what I am referring to as general clinical hypotheses. When these analysts claim that the question of physiological validity or invalidity is irrelevant, they mostly use their hypotheses in the same way as the general clinical hypotheses are used as (unproven) presuppositions in the simple clinical psychoanalytic theory. One does, however, occasionally hear that it is not the truth of the metapsychological hypotheses that counts, but merely their usefulness.

The second point is merely an amplification of some of the points already made. Suppose it is conclusively shown that the brain cannot function as assumed by some of the general clinical hypotheses. The clinical confirmation of particular clinical hypotheses that is based on these general clinical hypotheses is then clearly invalid.

The third point refers to how at the present state of knowledge we can go beyond the simple to an expanded clinical psychoanalytic theory. All I have to say is that we can construct models that are compatible with current neurophysiological knowledge. Klein (1967) and Peterfreund (1971; Peterfreund and Franceschini, 1973) have constructed such models, and I have also recently made an attempt to do so (Rubinstein, 1974). None of these models is complete. But they all include, among others, hypotheses that, although materially different from the traditional hypotheses involving psychic energy, are structurally similar to them (or at least to some of them) and, accordingly, to the corresponding general clinical hypotheses. Klein's hypothesis (1967, p. 90) of the significance for motivational functioning of a "primary region of imbalance" giving rise to a "self-closing pattern of excitations" illustrates this point. In a general way we can characterize the mentioned models as positing, not only specific M-processes, but also the organization of, including the interaction between, such processes. In their degree of physiological specificity, the hypotheses constituting models of this type must, of course, go beyond that of the general clinical hypotheses to which they are structurally similar, or else they cannot be tested physiologically. If a particular model is shown to be physiologically implausible, new models have to be constructed. The, at least potential, physiological testability of any model or hypothesis is obviously crucial for its admission into the expanded clinical theory. I may mention in passing that only if we construct such models can we take into account the possible effect on the M-processes we have posited of abnormal non M-processes, such as may occur, for example, in schizophrenia.

I think we can conclude that, although apparently possible, a strictly clinical psychoanalytic theory is merely a partial theory. I have referred to a theory of this kind as a simple clinical psychoanalytic theory and contrasted it with what I call an expanded clinical psychoanalytic theory. Only the latter is truly scientific in that it precludes the substitution of, at least in principle, testable hypotheses by (unproven) presuppositions, which in the last analysis differ from dogma in name only. On the other hand, however, an expanded clinical psychoanalytic theory can hardly be said to exist today. What exists is essentially a search for such a theory, deriving whatever force it has from a refusal to accept as final the existing simple clinical theory, no matter whether it is presented in the rather dry factual way indicated above or shrouded in the nostalgically old-fashioned, somewhat fanciful garb of current metapsychology.

We have moved a long way from Dilthey and his followers. We have found that the crucial difference between the view of man presented by natural science and by the sciences of man as a sentient, striving, purposive being is not the difference between causal understanding and understanding in terms of meaning, but in the way man is seen by us, as a human organism or as a person. In clinical practice we see man unequivocally as a person. However, to justify our hypotheses about unconscious mental events, we must turn our attention to the organism this person is also. Psychoanalysis as a science must thus combine the ways of looking at man, say, of history and literature with those of neurophysiology and other biological sciences. That is the challenge our discipline faces us with, but also its fascination.

REFERENCES

Allport, G. W. (1938), *Personality: A Psychological Interpretation.* London: Constable.

Ayer, A. J. (1946), *Language, Truth and Logic,* 2d ed. New York: Dover.

Dilthey, W. (1962), *Pattern and Meaning in History,* ed. and introd. H. P. Rickman. New York: Harper Torchbook.

Eissler, K. R. (1968), The Relation of Explaining and Understanding in Pyschoanalysis. *The Psychoanalytic Study of the Child,* 23:141-177. New York: International Universities Press.

Englebretsen, G. (1972), Persons and Predicates. *Philosoph. Stud.,* 23:393-399. Dordrecht: Reidel.

Freud, S. (1915), The Unconscious. *Standard Edition,* 14:159-215. London: Hogarth Press, 1957.

Fromm, E. (1951), *The Forgotten Language.* New York: Rinehart.

Hartmann, H. (1927a), *Die Grundlagen der Psychoanalyse.* Leipzig: Thieme.

_____ (1927b), Concept Formation in Psychoanalysis. *The Psychoanalytic Study of the Child,* 19:11-47. New York: International Universities Press, 1964.

_____ (1927c), Understanding and Explanation. *Essays on Ego Psychology.* New York: International Universities Press, 1964, pp. 369-403.

Hermann, I. (1934), *Die Psychoanalyse als Methode.* Vienna: Internationaler Psychoanalytischer Verlag.

Jaspers, K. (1923), *Allgemeine Psychopathologie,* 3d ed. Berlin: Springer.

Jung, C. G. (1943), On the Psychology of the Unconscious. In: *Two Essays on Analytic Psychology,* trans. R. F. C. Hull. Princeton, N.J.: Bollingen Paperback Edition, 1972.

Klein, G. S. (1967), Peremptory Ideation: Structure and Force in Motivated Ideas. In: Motives and Thought: Psychoanalytic Essays in Honor of David Rapaport, ed. R. R. Holt. *Psychol. Issues,* Monogr. No. 18/19:80-128. New York: International Universities Press.

_____ (1970), Two Theories or One? *Bull. Menninger Clin.,* 37:102-132.

_____ (1973), Is Psychoanalysis Relevant? *Psychoanalysis and Contemporary Science,* 2:3-21. New York: Macmillan.

Lashley, K. S. (1958), Cerebral Organization and Behavior. In: *The Brain and Human Behavior,* ed. H. C. Solomon, S. Cobb, & W. Penfield. Baltimore, Md.: Williams Wilkins, pp. 1-18.

Lévi-Strauss, C. (1963), *Structural Anthropology.* New York: Basic Books.

_____ (1966), *The Savage Mind.* Chicago: University of Chicago Press.

MacIntyre, A. (1967), Jung, Carl Gustav. In: *The Encyclopedia of Philosophy,* ed. P. Edwards, 4:294-296. New York: Macmillan and Free Press.

Peterfreund, E. (1971), Information, Systems, and Psychoanalysis: An Evolutionary Biological Approach to Psychoanalytic Theory. *Psychol. Issues,* Monogr. No. 25/26. New York: International Universities Press.

_____ & Franceschini, E. (1973), On Information, Motivation, and Meaning. *Psychoanalysis and Contemporary Science,* 2:220-262. New York: Macmillan.

Popper, K. R. (1962), *Conjectures and Refutations.* New York: Harper Torchbook, 1968.

Rapaport, D. (1960), On the Psychoanalytic Theory of Motivation. In: *Nebraska Symposium on Motivation, 1960,* ed. M. Jones. Lincoln: University of Nebraska Press, pp. 173-247. Also in: *The Collected Papers of David Rapaport,* ed. M. M. Gill. New York: Basic Books, 1967, pp. 853-915.

Rickman, H. P. (1962), General Introduction to W. Dilthey, *Pattern and Meaning in History.* New York: Harper Torchbook, pp. 11-63.

Rubinstein, B. B. (1974), On the Role of Classificatory Processes in Mental Functioning: Aspects of a Psychoanalytic Theoretical Model. *Psychoanalysis and Contemporary Science,* 3:101-185. New York: International Universities Press.

Russell, B. (1921), *The Analysis of Mind.* London: Allen & Unwin.

_____ (1945), *A History of Western Philosophy.* New York: Simon & Schuster.

Ryle, G. (1957), The Theory of Meaning. In: *Philosophy and Ordinary Language,* ed. C. E. Caton. Urbana: University of Illinois Press, 1963, pp. 128-153.

Spranger, E. (1925), *Psychologie des Jugendalters,* 15th ed. Leipzig: Quelle & Meyer.

Strawson, P. F. (1950), On Referring. In: *Essays in Conceptual Analysis,* ed. A. Flew. London: Macmillan, 1956, pp. 21-52.

_____ (1959), *Individuals.* Garden City, N.Y.: Anchor.

Wittgenstein, L. (1953), *Philosophical Investigations.* New York: Macmillan.

9

ORIGINS OF CONSCIENCE

JANE LOEVINGER

George Klein, in one of his last essays (this volume, Chapter 2), compared Freud's clinical theory of sexuality with his drive-discharge or metapsychological theory. Both are based on, and are meant to account for, the same clinical observations; indeed, Freud was almost certainly unaware of the discrepancies between the two theories. The clinical theory stays close to and accounts for the observed facts; it also serves as the foundation of psychoanalytic practice. The drive-discharge theory, which equates pleasure with a reduction of tension and which is most often emphasized in psychoanalytic writing and teaching, does not even save the phenomena. That is to say, the most salient characteristic of sexual experience, in the wide meaning Freud gave to sexuality, is a distinctively piognant experience of pleasure. There is hardly room for this phenomenon in the drive-discharge model. As Klein and others have pointed out, psychoanalysis is pervaded at many ponts with a conflict between its clinical and its metapsychological theories. But since sexuality is the heartland of psychoanalysis, Klein's essay is far more than simply a case in point.

In this paper I shall examine a different topic — conscience — from a point of view similar to that of Klein's in his paper on sexuality. Unlike sexuality, which was seen as falling distinctively within the purview of psychoanalysis from the

The preparation of this essay was supported by Research Grant MH-05115 and Research Scientist Award K5-MH-657, both from the National Institute of Mental Health, U.S. Public Health Service.

beginning, conscience commanded Freud's attention only during his last period. My approach differs from Klein's in its greater emphasis on developmental origins. I propose also to alter the terms of discourse. Being no clinician, I would prefer not to describe my approach as clinical. It is a phenomenological approach, as was Klein's. I shall not, however, write another critique of the drive-discharge theory, for that has been done often enough by now.

THE PHENOMENA OF PSYCHOLOGY

Phenomenology is primarily a method, not a body of received information (Spiegelberg, 1965). The commitment of the phenomenological movement is to approach the world in general and the world of human experience in particular in such a way as to save the phenomena, that is, to preserve as terms of observation and analysis the things of experience. Klein was advancing a phenomenological argument when he noted that Freud's metapsychological theory of sexuality did not have room for the most distinctive of sexual experiences, a poignantly pleasurable arousal. The phenomenological method is opposed, on the one hand, to reducing experience to elements, particularly elements that bear the stamp of particular sense organs, and, on the other hand, to interposing nonexperienced theoretical entities between the scientist-observer and the observed world.

An interest in psychological theory may appear to be incompatible with a phenomenological commitment. The phenomenological method, however, prescribes the initial approach, not the final outcome, which may be highly inferential and theoretical, at least insofar as many members of the movement are concerned (Spiegelberg, 1965). My own commitment, which I believe to be compatible with a phenomenological method, is to examine and describe the data of psychology *in the first instance* at a minimal inferential level. One criterion for describing behavior at the minimal inferential level is that the subject and the observer agree on the terms of the description. An alternative criterion is that most reasonably intelligent, perceptive, educated people without special training in psychology, philosophy, or related disciplines agree on the description itself. The reservations are necessary. There is no one as incapable of observing and describing the phenomena of psychology as a psychologist wholly committed to his own particular theory. The issue is not the correctness of the theory, but the validity of the observation, report, and reflection on the phenomena as they are experienced. Let us look at some examples of the interference of theory with observation.

Rotter (1966), a social-learning theorist, has proposed a test for "internal versus external control of reinforcement." Presumably, this test yields data about a person that have something to do with conscience; surely conscience has something to do with internal control of behavior. However, Rotter evidently believes conscience too inferential a term; "internal control of reinforcement" seems to him closer to what is actually being observed. No doubt he is aware that in changing terms he has also redefined the limits of the construct. What he probably does not acknowledge is that "internal control of reinforcement" is itself a highly inferential construct, far removed from any observations made by means of his test and even more remote from the human experience of conscience. Edward Tolman used to point out that the very term "reinforcement" has a whole theory built into it, one that he, of course, believed to be mistaken.

Another example of such inference comes from the psychoanalytic school. Sandler et al. (1962) have provided a format for classification of clinical observations related to the superego, hence presumably also related to the formation of conscience. Consider the following example of an observation, quoted in its entirety:

> Her mother has been the most important figure in her world. She appears to be the superego figure much more strongly than the father.

Her superego in general seemed strong as indicated by her use of compliance as a response resulting from introjection of the castrating mother.

She attempts to do what mother wishes even in the treatment room where she now knows many activities are permitted. She is very frightened that the therapist might tell her mother about "forbidden" or "important" activities and conversations so that before one of her mother's visits, she always behaves in a controlled fashion in treatment [p. 112].

In this "observation," it is not at all clear what in fact has been observed and what inferred. Certainly the third sentence contains so may layers of inference as to be dubiously included under the heading of data. Indeed, I believe that the use of the term superego in recording observations of conscience formation is an example of the interposition of theoretical constructs between the observer and the experience. The phenomenological movement is addressed to this problem.

The philosophical difficulties in defining an "observation" are not to be gainsaid. The primacy of the abstract category versus the primacy of the particular instance is related to some of the oldest problems of philosophy, going back to Meno's paradoxes, as Weimer (1973) has pointed out. The present point is a somewhat different and more superficial one. In beginning my discussion of conscience, I am determined to use the term as persons do in accounting for their own behavior to themselves.

Matters are made complex by the fact that the world of human behavior as man experiences it is not the same for all. Any particular person's way of perceiving is relatively stable, at least after infancy, but when changes occur, they are consequential. The way of perceiving the behavioral world is at the core of the ego, and its changes are the substance of ego development.[1] Thus to arrive at a consensual picture of the experienced world of behavior is difficult or impossible. That, nonetheless, is one task of phenomenological psychology.

[1] There are, of course, other ways of describing the ego and ego development; I believe they are more or less equivalent to this one, but a discussion of them is beyond the scope of this article.

The Phenomena of Conscience

What, then, are the experiences to which we assign the name conscience, according to common sense and common speech? We must include both what is meant by "my conscience" and what is meant by "his conscience," what is implied in a "bad conscience," and, in addition, what is conveyed by "conscientiously." My ultimate aim is to study the origins of conscience reflectively, empirically, and theoretically, and I begin by reflecting on the experience of conscience. Conscience may, however, have different meanings at different stages. Although its developmental course cannot be excluded completely from our consideration, we are concerned primarily with articulating a conception of a mature conscience. But it is clear that at the same time the necessary antecedents of conscience may include some behaviors or attitudes that appear antithetical to those of a mature conscience. At what developmental point one says, "Here conscience begins," may prove to be arbitrary.

The elements of conscience include a sense of accountability for past actions and feelings and obligation in regard to future ones, a capacity for self-criticism, and well-articulated standards and ideals. All of these attributes seem directly implied by the notion of conscience, but that is not to say that they are logically independent. They may prove, however, to have different historical origins. They may not be exhaustive of the elements of conscience, but they provide a start.

Conscience has no meaning unless one is accountable for one's behavior, which may include thoughts or feelings. Perhaps the closest term for accountability in common speech is "blame." In the vocabulary of conscience, it is also probably one of the first words acquired. Blame has reference to the past and responsibility for it. It also has the connotation of blaming others, but blaming oneself is not excluded. In addition to responsibility for the past, accountability implies present and future obligations. Accountability, responsibility, and obligation have both cognitive and motivational aspects. A set of concepts is involved, that of rights, duties, privileges, and the like. In addition, there must be some pull, call, or commitment. Whether one can have a clear conception of rights and duties without feeling obligated to fulfill one's duties and to allow others their rights is not clear a priori.

Whereas conscience always implies blame, blame does not always imply conscience. Conscience is, above all, a reflexive concept. It implies self-criticism, which in turn implies at least rudimentary self-observation. In common speech, the term self-consciousness is more frequent than self-observation. Perhaps self-consciousness is an early, somewhat unfocused version of self-observation. All such reflexive terms apply only to a person with some articulated sense of self. One might say that reflexive traits imply and are preceded by selfhood. Differentiation of self and nonself, which is the earliest problem in ego development, is thus the forerunner of all reflexive aspects of conscience. Even if we include in the realm of conscience the fear of punishment for disobeying rules, an articulated sense of self is still implied.

One reflexive trait that may be included in conscience, as it is sometimes carelessly defined, but which cannot be integral to its definition, is self-control. Some minimal self-control is prerequisite to the sequence of development that culminates in mature conscience, but lapses may occur at any stage. What is essential is the ability to distinguish impulse from control. Infallible control is good conduct, a different matter from conscience. (The topic of overcontrol will be omitted from this discussion.)

Perhaps the most essential and most discussed aspects of conscience are the emotional components of self-criticism, including shame, being ashamed, and guilt. Erikson (1950) has described the feeling of being shamed, of feeling naked, exposed, and "put down" by rivals or by hostile critics. Although the distinction is not a usual one, one can distinguish being shamed from being ashamed. To be ashamed implies a more self-administered put-down than to be shamed. Typically, one is ashamed before those one loves.

Thinking in terms of the small child, what changes as he progresses from being shamed to being ashamed are not the persons before whom he stands, probably his parents in either case, but rather his ability to integrate them as loved persons at the same moment he feels himself blamed or shamed.

One can be ashamed, not only of actions for which one is responsible, but also for characteristics, such as a clubfoot or illegitimacy, for which one is not responsible. One feels guilty for actions one might have performed differently and often enough for thoughts or feelings that one has rejected. Guilt is very different from being shamed, but not so different from being ashamed. Guilt is one step further in the internalization and evolution of conscience. The presence of an audience or of onlookers, actual or potential, is essential to the idea of being ashamed, but it is absent in or less important to the feeling of guilt. The judgment of others is the core of being ashamed; self-judgment is the core of guilt feelings.

A different element of conscience is involved in upholding standards and striving for ideals. Here, the emphasis is on the "ought" rather than on the "ought not," on striving rather than on constraint. There is no sharp divide, for one may criticize oneself for not upholding standards or for not living up to ideals. The origins of self-criticism and of ideals are different, however. The ultimate ideal to which a mature conscience gives its allegiance is the ideal of justice. The term "sense of justice" implies both an ideal of justice and a feeling that justice must be made to prevail—thus there are both a standard and a call or commitment. This leads us to the next element.

A complete account of the phenomena of so rich and varied an experience as conscience may be impossible. One additional element of a mature conscience must be added, however: disinterestedness. A person with a truly mature conscience has the possibility, even the proclivity, if not to love others exactly as he loves himself, at least to take their standpoint into equal account with his own. This involves treating others as ends rather than as means, but more than that. It involves transcending both egocentrism and the orientation that allows conscience to be satisfied by mere obedience.

SUPEREGO AND EGO IDEAL

Let us turn now to some related psychoanalytic ideas. In doing so, I abandon the phenomenological approach, which has now defined our purview, in favor of one more in keeping with current usage within psychoanalysis. Contemporary psychoanalytic writing presents more or less conflicting usages of the terms conscience, superego, and ego ideal as a result of the fact that Freud sometimes used the terms interchangeably and at other times with varying connotations. It is not my aim to provide another review of the psychoanalytic literature on these concepts. I have taken conscience primarily in terms of its connotations from common speech, with only such alteration as fidelity to things as they are required. The terms superego and ego ideal will be used in what I take to be their most usual contemporary meanings. The solution of theoretical problems is, in any case, not found in arbitrarily imposed definitions. Rather, the person who understands the ideas sees beyond definitions to the things symbolized. The terminology should be as transparent as possible. If the things talked about are real, the words should not be crucial. I seek clarity and insight into developmental origins, but not necessarily originality; still less do I attempt a comprehensive review of the literature.

Chein (1972) summarizes his version of the psychoanalytic structural theory: the ego and the superego are moral, ego and id seek gratification of wishes, superego and id are archaic and primitive. This formulation by itself is sufficient to explain why none of the three concepts—id, ego, and superego—can be dispensed with. Let us leave open for the moment whether the development of the superego is an aspect of ego development or pursues an independent course. For now, it suffices that the concept of the superego cannot be dispensed with.

Perhaps the most comprehensive discussion of the varied origins of a mature conscience is that of Flugel (1945). He delineates four essentially independent sources, though granting that specific behaviors reflect the influence of several sources simultaneously. One source is the ideal self or ego ideal, to which a portion of one's narcissistic libido becomes directed, a concept obviously drawn from Freud's (1914) essay on narcissism. A second source is the incorporation of moral attitudes and precepts of others, particularly one's parents. Flugel tends to call these two sources of conscience the ego ideal, in contradistinction to the superego; both of these sources were known before Freud, particularly to Baldwin (1897) and McDougall (1908), as Flugel points out. The third source is aggression turned against the self. Flugel describes the fourth source primarily in terms of sadomasochism, but at times he sees it in terms of the need for mastery; I shall emphasize the latter aspect in my account. The last two sources of conscience are generally termed the superego; they represent unique contributions of psychoanalysis. The root sources of conscience, then, are narcissism, parental standards, aggression, and the drive for mastery. I shall presently take up these four sources of conscience in terms similar to, but not limited to those of Flugel, and in what I take to be their developmental order. To them, I shall add a fifth, mutual love.

Other psychoanalysts have differed over what functions are ascribed to ego ideal and superego, but even more sharply over whether they see ego ideal as the precursor of superego or vice versa (Schafer, 1968).

In a brief but pithy essay, Lampl-de Groot (1962) traces the origins of the superego and the ego ideal. The ego ideal begins with the infant's "hallucinatory wish fulfillment," in the stage of primary narcissism. As the infant becomes aware of the distinction between inside and outside, hallucinatory wish fulfillment is replaced by fantasies of omnipotence and grandeur. Following his experiencing of relative powerlessness, these fantasies are replaced by fantasies of his parents' omnipotence. After he is disillusioned in this regard also, he forms ideals and ethics. For Lampl-de Groot, the entire sequence remains primarily one of wish fulfillment.

Equating conscience with superego, Lampl-de Groot traces its origins in a separate sequence. The original experience is one of unpleasure. Some of the experiences of unpleasure later become structured as restrictions and demands of the parents, which the child obeys to retain their love. At the next stage, some of these demands are internalized via identification. Finally, the child accepts the restrictions and forms a conscience in order to safeguard his social relations with parents and the wider group in which he now finds himself. Throughout, the superego remains primarily an agency of restriction.

Lampl-de Groot asks: As different as these two sequences are, how were they ever seen as one sequence, establishing a single agency or substructure within the ego? Her answer includes the observation that parental images are crucial in both sequences, though in different ways; that is, the ego ideal is related to being like parents, while the superego is related to living up to their demands. Moreover, although their aims are opposite—wish fulfillment is served by the ego ideal, and restriction and prohibition by the superego—in practice both agencies unite into one substructure and influence each other's function. Thus, ultimately ideals can be experienced as demands.

Lampl-de Groot apologizes for speaking of the ego ideal both as an ego function and as a substructure within the ego. This is a core problem, and one that has troubled other writers. Surely, the solution is that the course of ego development must always lie in the direction of structuralization, which entails the creation of substructures within the ego. Formally, what else can ego development mean? The differentiation of functions and the formation of structures are two ways of describing the same set of phenomena; only concrete habits of thought make them sound like different things.

One difficulty with all expositions of early development is that the words of adult life do not fit. Hallucinatory wish fulfillment seems to imply three elements: a wish, perception of its nonfulfillment, and then the false perception of its fulfillment. In speaking of the mental life of the early infant, such a sequence is not meaningful. Rather, it is clear that wish and perception must be merged: to wish for the breast is at first not different from imagining it there. The disappointment of the merged wish and fulfillment is what structures the wish as separate from the perception of its fulfillment (see Shapiro, 1970).

Psychoanalysis is a developmental theory through and through. Flugel makes the point that nothing so complicated as the superego can arise at one fell swoop, as Freud's statement (1923) that the superego is heir to the Oedipus complex — currently (or at least for long) the received wisdom of psychoanalysis — may seem to imply. In the light of the more detailed tracing of developmental origins by Lampl-de Groot, the truth of Flugel's assertion is emphasized. Is it any more valid to set the origin of conscience at the beginning of latency than to set the origin of sexuality at the beginning of puberty? From a developmental view, what we take as point of origin can only be arbitrary. There is always an earlier precursor until we arrive at the earliest and most obscure mental stages.

THE EVOLUTION OF CONSCIENCE

I propose now to reconstruct the evolution of conscience, drawing on all of the foregoing as well as other sources, including my own reflections. I cannot claim here to be rigorously phenomenological. The growth of conscience is not available to direct observation; one cannot open the discussion without at least low-level theoretical terms. But I shall try to fly as close to the ground as possible, that is, to use only concepts with specifiable and fairly obvious observational referents. To be theoretical at all, one must go beyond purely dispositional concepts to concepts that indicate diverse dispositions. Freud's conception of narcissism, which rests on a variety of observations, is an example.

The infant at first has the ability to wish only by imagining his wish as fulfilled. That gratification does not always ensue leads to the distinction between wish and perception and, simultaneously, between the inner world and the outer. For a long time thereafter, however, it is primary-process thinking that largely prevails, now taking the form of fantasy fulfillment of grandiose and other wishes. The child who announces that "there was an alligator at nursery school today" or that he "can run faster than anyone" can, if pressed, acknowledge a version closer to an adult's idea of the truth. He does not, however, have side by side a correct perception of himself and a fantasied omnipotent grandiose self, as some perhaps careless accounts of the idealized self might seem to suggest. His thoughts are more fluid and less structured than that. What characterizes the mind of the child is precisely that he does not distinguish reality and fantasy, his real self and his idealized or wished-for self. To establish the distinction is exactly the same as to recognize the unreality of his idealized or wishful picture of himself.

Similarly, as he consoles himself for his own perceived smallness and weakness by ascribing all power to his parents, he does not entertain simultaneously an idealized and a realistic image of them; he cannot make this distinction, though he may from time to time see their faults with enormous perspicacity, as he shows by exploiting them. To make the distinction between parents as they are and parents as they ought to be is more or less the same thing as forming rules and standards to which parents (and others) must subordinate themselves. Before the child has some abstract standards of conduct, it is power itself that confers rightness (Kohlberg, 1971). Hence it does not seem to be meaningful to ask which comes first, disillusionment with the omnipotent parents or the formulation of rules; ordinarily they are part of a single process. Granting always that archaic forms persist and continue to have some influence, true ideals and ethics are founded on the demise, that is, take the place of, idealization of self and parents.

So far, we have traced only the structural or formal aspect. The content of the child's standards continues to change long after the structural aspect of his ethics is fairly well established. Beginning at first with what Ferenczi called "sphincter morality," the child proceeds to a morality of authoritarian conformity, then, in favorable instances, to self-evaluated standards, and in unusual cases, to disinterested standards of justice, an evolution that has been traced in greater detail by Kohlberg (1971).

NARCISSISM

In his essay on narcissism, Freud (1914) proposed a psychodynamic explanation of crucial steps in the foregoing sequence. The child transfers a portion of his self-love from his real self to his ego ideal, which can retain the perfection that reality forces him to admit he does not have, in order to save his narcissism from disappointment.

Another dynamic explanation comes from Ausubel (1952), who states that the child faces disastrous loss of self-esteem when he comes to recognize his own smallness and dependence. In order to save his self-esteem, he becomes a satellite of his all-powerful parents, shining in their reflected glory. One can, in fact, accept both Freud's and Ausubel's explanations; they do not seem to be contradictory, nor do they contradict the purely cognitive explanation that is implied in the exposition of the sequence. Indeed, is not the self-esteem of which Ausubel writes itself a version of narcissism?

It is in relation to narcissism that the present essay comes closest to paralleling one feature of Klein's essay on sexuality, namely, his critique of Freud's drive-discharge theory. One of the many observations on which Freud based his concept of narcissism was that lovers feel abased; that is, the more one loves others, the less one loves oneself. This observation was not a necessary part of the concept; of all of the elements of the essay on narcissism, it is the one most often disputed. Indeed, one may wonder whether this supposed "observation" had a part in the conception. Was it not rather that Freud's, by then, long-standing theory of a fixed quantity of libidinal cathexis generated a false "observation"? Drop cathexis theory and drop the hypothesis that the lover's self-love is lowered, and the conception of narcissism is in no way weakened.

The essay on narcissism does more than display the weakness of cathexis theory. It marks both the highest achievement and the beginning of the end for Freud's construction of a psychology derived from instincts or drives. Of all aspects of human psychology, conscience would appear to be the least amenable to explanation by or derivation from drives. Indeed, from the beginning of his psychoanalytic work, Freud conceived of psychopathology as originating in conflict between drives and conscience. With the essay on narcissism showing that the ego ideal, an essential element of conscience, was itself an outgrowth of narcissism, Freud was on his way to a drive-derivative version of conscience. This remarkable tour de force, however, subtly altered the meaning of the term drive or instinct. In an important sense, a drive is defined by the envelope (to borrow a term from Sullivan) of its possible gratifications. A sexual drive that can be gratified by setting up within oneself an ego ideal cannot be a tissue need; one may dispute even whether it is still a demand made by the body on the mind, as Freud defined "instinct" in his 1915 edition of *Three Essays on the Theory of Sexuality* (1905). Such a drive is something more like a human urge, an idea Freud was to carry forward in *Beyond the Pleasure Principle* (1920), though again with some obscurities and again leaving loose ends for subsequent theorists to tie up.

AGGRESSION

Just as nonfulfillment of wishes is the point of origin of the developmental sequence that culminates in ideals and ethics, so it is the starting point for a second line of development that follows a different course, but also ultimately contributes to conscience—to wit, turning aggression against the self. Presumably, we can speak of a neonate as having wishes, or impulses, if we are careful not to impute too much meaning to the term wishes. The frustration of those wishes, even though temporary, must lead to something akin to aggression. By the time one can speak appropriately of an aggressive impulse, the infant has gone beyond the first inchoate state of merged impulse and fulfillment. The baby's reaction to frustration, like that of the older child, presumably is often aggressive. Indeed, what appears to be rage can be observed in babies. As Flugel observes, the one target of a baby's aggression that is always present and within reach is himself. In addition, control of impulses, even control motivated by self-interest, comes later than the structuring of impulses as such. So long as expression of impulse, per se, is experienced as more compelling than any calculated self-interest requiring control, directing aggression against the self is likely to occur. Normally, as the child advances in motor abilities, most of his aggression is directed outward. But there are risks there, too, since others may retaliate. Parents, furthermore, though frequent sources of frustration, are also needed and loved and may be intolerant of their children's aggression against them or against others. Since impulse predominates over control for a long time in childhood,[2] a time that varies from child to child, the path back to aggression against the self may remain open for a long time. Indeed, self-rejection and naked aggression against the self are more or less diagnostic of low ego levels (Loevinger and Wessler, 1970). Control of impulse is in part the heir of such aggression directed against the self. Differentiation of impulse from control implies a split or doubling of self, representing a higher degree of structure than uncontrolled impulsivity; by providing for delays when necessary or advantageous, it opens the way to more gratification. Impulse control remains the most important transmutation of aggression turned against the self in the evolution of conscience. Later versions of aggression against self are shame, being ashamed, and guilt feelings, each playing its stage-appropriate part in the evolution of conscience. These sensibilities are acquired in that order over a period of years, and none is totally lost. A mature conscience is likely to be robust with respect to all of these negative emotions, however, and thus is tolerant of self as well as others.

[2]Some psychopathic characters are so described even in adult life.

MASTERY

The third element identified by Flugel is the drive for mastery. The fundamental terms of psychological theory are not settled and agreed on; hence, we cannot say for certain whether this element is closely allied to or derived from the aggressive drive, or whether a drive for mastery exists separate from the aggressive drive, each capable of being turned inward. Indeed, it is problematic whether the ego need for mastery is comparable to a drive or instinct such as sex, though it certainly has a driven quality. But these metapsychological questions need not be answered before we can pursue our interest in the origins of conscience.

The specifically psychoanalytic version of the need for mastery is that one must do what one has suffered, that experience is mastered by actively repeating what one has passively undergone (Loevinger, 1966b). Freud (1920) first clearly enunciated this principle after watching his little grandson throw away his favorite toys. He concluded that this was the boy's way of mastering the greatest deprivation he suffered, namely, the periodic disappearance of his beloved mother. He could not control his mother's coming and going, as he could control the disappearance of his toys. (The little boy in a poem by Milne handled the problem in a different way: "'Mother,' he said, said he: 'You must *never* go down to the end of the town without consulting me.'") The universal baby game of peekaboo is another example of what Freud was observing. At any rate, Freud referred repeatedly to that principle thenceforth. In *Beyond the Pleasure Principle*, where he first expounded it, it was used to explain children's play and the repetition of unpleasant experiences in the transference and traumatic events in dreams. Freud later used the same principle to explain aspects of impulse control and superego formation, as have also, in various ways, Anna Freud, Flugel, Erikson, Loewald, and Ricoeur, to name a few. But let me indicate what my own conception of mastery is, a formulation that has profited from the contributions of those writers and others.

It makes no sense to speak of mastering experience by actively repeating what one has passively undergone at the time of hallucinatory wish fulfillment, that is, of the inchoate impulse-gratification image. Even such structuring of impulses as to permit a definite perception of nongratification followed by aggression or anger does not suffice. Experience must be structured in some more coherent format for one to speak meaningfully of mastering it. Thus, we are not talking of the neonate at this point.

What experience does the baby or young child feel the need to master? Freud's examples are the trip to the doctor and the temporary or permanent loss of a beloved person or thing. According to Fenichel (1945), whenever the child is flooded with a large quantity of excitation, he will attempt to master the situation by actively reproducing it in his play. The child also endlessly repeats newly acquired but not wholly automatic skills in what appears to be a related need (drive? instinct?), as Hendrick (1942) has pointed out. Whatever may be the limits of the operation of this principle, it appears to be a central mode of ego functioning.

It is also a driving force in the evolution of conscience. The child's impulses are such that he must be restrained by his parents. The child would like to restrain and control his parents, as they restrain and control him, but he cannot and dare not. This situation is doubly frustrating, in that the child is both controlled and then prevented from making the natural response to being controlled. Fortunately, the needs involved are plastic, and the child readily substitutes a new victim for the ones whose use he is denied. This may be at times a younger sib or playmate, but usually he is restrained in this direction also, and the ultimate victim must be the child himself. He masters the situation by assuming the role of the parents toward himself or a part of himself. That is the origin of self-control and, at the same time, of the distinction between impulse and control. It is as if the child were saying, "What they have done to me, I must do to it." Substituting for "I" and "it" the German *das Ich* and *das Es*, the sentence becomes (approximately) "What they have done to me, my ego must do to my id." Blessedly, no child talks so, but that is in principle the dynamic formula for the origin of impulse control (Loevinger, 1966b). At the same time, it is at least part of the dynamics of ego structuring and of superego formation (Freud, 1923, 1930).

Before leaving the theme of doing what one has suffered, let us note its similarity to the primitive mechanism of undoing. More than similarity, what is involved is an evolution of more or less reflexive undoing in the direction of active and often constructive mastery of experience. A distinctive outcome of these impulses is a sense that accounts must be balanced. At first this takes the form of revenge and of the law of the talion. The part that the law of the talion plays in the development of conscience is acknowledged by few authors, two exceptions being John Stuart Mill and, among psychoanalysts, Odier (1943).

Mill (1861) pointed out that the desire to punish those who have done harm is a natural sentiment that derives from two impulses that "either are or resemble instincts; the impulse of self-defense, and the feeling of sympathy" (p. 306). We share our desire for revenge or retaliation against those who have harmed us with lower animals, who try to hurt those who have hurt them or their young. But, by virtue of our intelligence, our range of sympathy may be even broader, extending not merely to our children but to tribe, country, or mankind. Thus, Mill sees what he calls the "sentiment of justice," which includes the desire to punish, as not moral in itself; what is moral is its exclusive subordination to the social interest. The law of the talion is a favored principle of a primitive and spontaneous sentiment of justice and remains a secret-hankering in most minds: "When retribution accidentally falls on an offender in that precise shape, the general feeling of satisfaction evinced bears witness how natural is the sentiment to which this repayment in kind is acceptable" (p. 313).

PARENTAL STANDARDS

The fourth element of conscience identified by Flugel is the incorporation, or acceptance as one's own, of the prohibitions, standards, and ideals of one's parents. A child about whom one can speak in such terms has again taken a large step forward in the organization of his experience. Although terms such as impulse and aggression are applicable to young infants, they do not require much in the way of personality organization. Mastery through active repetition is closely related to undoing, primitive as a defense mechanism, though still implying more complex organization than mere impulse or aggression. To take over parental standards and prohibitions and make them one's own requires a rudimentary notion of rules, and that in turn requires a degree of mental development going beyond that required for mastery through activity. I hesitate to put an age on this achievement, not only because there are conspicuous individual differences, but also because there is an inherent ambiguity in assigning a date to a slowly evolving conception. That, indeed, is one of the major points of this essay.

To pursue further the meaning and mechanism of the adoption or incorporation of parental standards would lead us back over ground already covered here and in many other places, in terms similar to Anna Freud's (1936) discussion of identification with the aggressor.

MUTUAL LOVE

The fifth element of conscience, which I wish to add to Flugel's four, has been expressed in various ways: valuing another person equally with oneself; valuing another person as an end in himself rather than as a means toward one's own ends; the ability to see from another person's point of view. At its highest and rarest reach, this becomes disinterestedness, the opposite pole from the egocentricity of childhood and youth, the achievement of what lawyers call the "judicial temperament."

The origin of this fifth contributor to conscience lies in love, or, if you will, the human bond. In explaining altruism, love and conscience are alternatives. Sacrificing one's own interests so as to further the interests of one's own children or spouse is a less decisive evidence for conscience than doing so for some person more remote. At the same time, it is hard to believe that a person would develop much, if any, conscience without love for other people. Obviously, the child's love for his parents is involved in acceptance of their standards and ideals, and it is involved somewhat less directly in the other aspects of the formation of conscience that have been outlined. The love of a child for his parents is, however, intrinsically and ineradicably an asymmetrical relation. Symmetrical love, the love for a peer, appears to be essential for the development of a mature conscience. This is truly a new element in late childhood and early adolescence. It is by no means an inevitable development.

One of the most valuable contributions of Harry Stack Sullivan to our theory of conscience lies in his observations on the role of the chum in the preadolescent era. According to Sullivan (1953), juveniles in the early school years show "a shocking insensitivity to feelings of personal worth in others" (p. 230). The relation of a preadolescent youngster to a chum of the same sex provides a unique opportunity to advance from such egocentricity to a truly social state. In the chumship the youngster learns for the first time to value another as he values himself, to identify himself with another's interests, to cherish his friend's triumphs and happiness as if they were his own. He experiences love in its true depth. To rejoice in the happiness of one's beloved chum is not at all like disinterestedness, but it is an essential precursor. It is through the affective tie to another person seen as one's equal that the capacity to experience from another's point of view matures and opens the way for a few to achieve disinterestedness. The highest altruism and idealism have their origins in these experiences; they are less likely to develop in a sexual relationship not preceded by a relation with a chum of the same sex, according to Sullivan.

Piaget, in one of his earliest volumes, *The Moral Judgment of the Child* (1932), is concerned with the same pivotal point of development, though in entirely different terms. Piaget sees the origin of morality in the repetitive motor schemas of the playing infant. These motor schemas evolve into rituals, which are the forerunners of rules. The child at first uses rules egocentrically. With regard to Piaget's chief paradigm, the game of marbles, the child begins by imitating use of rules, only later catching on to the notion of winning. There is a paradox in the initial competitive stage. The child regards the rules of the game as sacred and immutable; at the same time, he feels free to violate them when it is to his advantage to do so. Later on, when he realizes that the rules are agreed on by children and can be changed by mutual consent, he also becomes more dependable in obeying them. Piaget refers to this as the change from heteronomous morality to autonomous morality. He sees the key to the change in the transition from the unilateral respect of child for parent to the mutual and egalitarian respect of the child for other children.

Sullivan stresses loneliness as the emotional impetus that drives the youngster into an exclusive relation with a chum; Piaget stresses the cognitive aspects, including the need to communicate with a group of equals. Both authors locate the transition in preadolescence, or at about twelve years of age.[3] As different as the approaches of Piaget and Sullivan are, they bring us to the same point: essential to maturity of conscience is the ability to advance beyond authoritarian conformity to seeing and feeling oneself as a member of a society of equals.

By itself, mutuality does not suffice to create the "judicial temperament"; it is but a step or prerequisite. The point is rather that the morality of obedience cannot, failing such transformation to mutuality, lead to the highest estate of conscience. One of the paradoxes of the growth of conscience is exposed at this point. We may desire to create or encourage in our charges maturity of conscience, but in the nature of things there is no direct way to lead them beyond the morality of obedience. Disinterestedness, even more than responsibility, must grow; it remains radically unreachable by tuition, with or without sanctions.

[3] My own data suggest this as the earliest but not the latest age for the transition.

DYNAMIC PRINCIPLES

Since the development of conscience is a matter of internal or intrapersonal differentiation, a major task of a dynamic theory of conscience formation is to account for the origin of intrapersonal schemas. Although the term "schema" may sound more like Piaget and subsequent cognitive psychologists than like Freud, the concept of schema, and particularly the concept of the transposition of schemas, is pervasive in Freud's writings. In all of Freud's thinking about symptoms, dreams, and parapraxes (*Fehlleistungen*), there is an implicit premise that interpersonal schemas give shape and impetus to intrapersonal schemas. This principle was made explicit in "Mourning and Melancholia" (1917), where loss of a love object was declared to be the source of internal differentiation within the ego, a theme that Freud elaborated to account for impulse control and superego development in later writings.

Closely allied to the principle of deriving intrapersonal schemas from interpersonal schemas is the principle, discussed above, that experience is mastered by actively repeating what one has passively undergone. This is an extraordinary psychological principle, one that appears to be a unique discovery by Freud. One anticipation is Preyer's (1881) notion of "joy in being a cause," but while that captures something of the flavor of the idea, it is far from having the dynamic impact of Freud's version. James Mark Baldwin, as we shall see, also anticipated this principle. Let us restate Freud's principle of mastery once more: whatever someone has done to me, I must do to someone (or something) myself. We can view this principle as an interpersonal schema, that is, as a formula governing the child's relations with other people. As we have seen, it enters into the formation of impulse control and superego development. We have, then, derived intrapersonal schemas from interpersonal ones. Can we push back any further the question of where this fundamental interpersonal schema comes from? I would like to speculate on this matter.

The principle asserts that the child must do to someone or

something more or less what has been done to him; this is formally similar to saying that action and reaction must be equal and opposite. That is, Newton's third law bears an abstract resemblance to this most fundamental principle of ego functioning. Every child from the moment of birth, indeed from before birth, is surrounded by instances of the workings of Newton's third law. If he hits his bed or the floor, the bed or floor hits him with equal and opposite force. If he is playing under a table and stands up, the table hits his head with the same force that his head hits the table. Some sort of appreciation of this physical principle is bound is to come at an early stage in the child's development.

For the small child, even at a much older age than what we are now concerned with, physical principles, psychological principles, and moral necessity are simply indistinguishable. Thus it is at least conceivable that the (inchoate) observation that action and reaction are equal and opposite would generate some obscure sense that events require balancing or undoing. The primitive law of the talion of which Mill wrote may have originated in this way. Obviously, there is no way to bring up a child in a non-Newtonian world so that we can see what would change, nor is there any obvious way to watch in more detail how such primitive mechanisms develop. That intrapersonal schemas are given shape and impetus by interpersonal schemas is clear and traceable. That interpersonal schemas in turn owe their shape to sensorimotor schemas and physical principles is logical but not easy to render in a convincing way. That is about as far as we can go.

We have now used two dynamic principles, both drawn from Freud's writings: the first, the principle of mastery, states that one masters experience by actively repeating what one has passively undergone. The second principle states that intrapersonal schemas are given form and impetus by interpersonal schemas; this might be called the structural principle. Indeed, this principle is at once dynamic, structural, and genetic (which is one reason I do not find such distinctions useful). .

The third dynamic principle of psychoanalytic ego psychology has never been formulated rigorously. It may be stated something like this: Psychic progression may be grounded on regression. The original version of this principle is put forth in Freud's essay on narcissism, in which he shows that setting up an ego ideal is grounded on regression to narcissism. There are many references in psychoanalytic literature to a relation between regression and progression. Perhaps every progression is in some sense a regression, though that general form has not been proved. Every regression is presumably a solution to some problem, but if we attempt the symmetrical form, that every regression is also a progression, then words are in danger of losing their meaning. Whether it is true or not that every progression has within it some element of regression, recognizing the potentially intimate link between progression and regression can have practical as well as theoretical consequences. The regressive signs in adolescence and in psychotherapy might be more tolerable if understood as preconditions for growth.

Ego Development

Freud once wrote that the superego is a differentiated level within the ego; he also used superego more or less interchangeably with conscience and ego ideal. Today we are required to be more careful in our usage. Conscience is a term from common speech that has its own phenomenological referents, not to be substantially altered by the dictates of professional psychologists. Although we can study conscience phenomenologically, there is no such thing as observing the superego. The superego is a technical term, a hypothetical construct covering certain archaic and largely unconscious components of conscience formation. Let us grant that the terms conscience, superego, and ego each has its own distinguishable meaning and sphere of reference. What does this imply about the relation of ego development and superego development to the development of conscience?

Elsewhere I have described in detail the stages of ego development, basing my description on a wide survey (mostly unpublished) of relevant theoretical and empirical literature as well as extensive original research with my colleagues (Loevinger, 1966a; Loevinger and Wessler, 1970; Loevinger et al., 1970). A brief synopsis must suffice here.

The first stage in ego development can be called presocial; it is the period in which the ego comes into existence. This stage begins with a normal autistic period, then moves to a symbiotic period. The central problem is the delineation of self as opposed to nonself.

The next stage[4] can be called impulsive. In this stage, the child is preoccupied with his own wishes and impulses, which serve to consolidate and affirm his sense of self. In this stage, too, he depends on the environment for control. The central problem can be stated as impulse versus control.

The next stage we call self-protective. The child is preoccupied with safeguarding himself against inner and outer dangers. One task is to gain control over his own impulses, postponing gratification when it is expedient to do so. Thus, one central issue is vulnerability versus security. Another central issue, perhaps developing a little later, is that of domination versus submission in relation to others. As the child gains control over his own impulses to the extent of being able to tolerate temporary delays, he becomes less vulnerable and more secure. He is at the same time submitting to the control of others and at times making himself feel secure by dominating others.

The next stage is usually called conformist. Here the child has resolved the problem of self-protection and the problem of domination-submission by identifying himself with authority, at first his parents, later school authorities, and ultimately civic authority. Thus, he submits to authority's rules, but, by identifying himself with the controlling powers, he shares in their domination. The conformist stage is reached by most but by no means all children. Evolution beyond this stage is more

[4]Because of the ambiguity and possibly shifting conception of what constitutes a stage and what constitutes a transition between stages, I prefer to describe stages in words rather than numbers. There is also a hazard in giving names to stages, since a literal-minded person can always draw wrong inferences from the titles.

problematic, with diminishing numbers ever reaching successively higher stages.

The following stage we call conscientious. Internalization of rules has proceeded further to include self-administration of sanctions, self-evaluation, and self-selection of the rules to be followed. Ideals having reference to a wider social unit than one's immediate family are characteristic. The obligation to conform to rules, regardless of consequences, is ultimately replaced by an obligation to consider the consequences of one's actions for others. Interpersonal relations move beyond cooperation and reciprocity to a deeper mutuality.

The small child begins by depending entirely on the environment for control of his conduct. As he moves along the scale of ego development, he learns to control his own behavior in response to sanctions: at first to the sanctions of overt punishment and reward, later to the attenuated reward and punishment of approval and disapproval, and finally to the internalized rewards and punishments of guilt and self-respect. Although none of these sanctions ever become totally ineffective, external sanctions become progressively less necessary for the achievement of good conduct, and also progressively less efficacious. At the highest ego levels, which we call autonomous and integrated, we find a relatively small number of people who have mature consciences that are relatively free of guilt and of moral condemnation, able to tolerate moral ambiguity, and capable of a disinterested balancing of their own welfare with that of others.

Let us return now to the topic of the growth of conscience. We have seen five more or less independent sources that contribute to the evolution of a mature conscience. These are, in their developmental order: (1) the formation of a sense of self, (2) the turning of aggression against the self, (3) the need for mastery, (4) the adoption of parental precepts and standards, and (5) the enjoyment of mutual love and respect. Each of the sources of conscience has its origin in one of the stages of ego development.

(1) The ideal self, originally better called an idealized self, has its origin in the sense of self that dates back to the earliest

narcissistic period; ultimately this strand of development becomes the ego ideal.

(2) The turning of aggression against the self is observable in many infants and is characteristic of the impulsive stage; the inability to delay acting on impulse long enough to calculate advantage is precisely one of the marks of this stage. Impulse control gets at least some of its force from aggression turned against the self, as do, later, shame and a sense of guilt.

(3) The need for mastery, including self-mastery as a protection against inner and outer dangers, is characteristic for the self-protective stage.

(4) The adoption of and identification with parental and other rules and standards obviously characterize the conformist period.

(5) Finally, mutual love and respect are characteristic potentialities of the conscientious stage. From them develop the toleration of individual differences and devotion to disinterested justice that mark the highest estate of conscience.

While these several strands make quasi-independent contributions to the formation of conscience, they are not independent lines of development. On the contrary, my main point is that the growth of conscience and ego development are so intimately intertwined that they constitute a single complex sequence of events. The key to this conception is the idea of structure: The ego is, above all, a structure or organization. At any given moment it is an organic unity, though to others and possibly even to a person himself inconsistencies in his character are evident. The ego develops through time as an organically growing form. As must be apparent, wherever we pick up the thread of the growth of conscience, we will be led back to the same sequence of events, including, though not confined to, those summarized by the psychoanalytic slogan, "The superego is heir to the Oedipus complex" (Freud, 1923).

In one important respect, my conception of ego development differs from most or all of the received psychoanalytic versions, particularly that of Erikson (1950). For me, it appears to be both empirically true and theoretically plausible that people arrive at an identical level of maturity of conscience and of other aspects of ego development at widely different times of life. Some people have advanced as far as the conscientious stage in preadolescence; others will not advance to the conformist stage until late adolescence. These facts require a conception of ego development that is free of any age-specific contingencies. By telling the story of ego development only in the "average expectable" version, as most psychoanalytic accounts do, one conceals a whole series of questions: What is the earliest possible age for a given transition? The latest possible one? The optimal one? The usual one? What conditions other than age are optimal, necessary, or sufficient for a given transition to take place? In order to cope with such issues, one must have an abstract conception of ego development, with each level described, not by the characteristics it assumes at the age where it is most common, but by the characteristics it assumes regardless of chronological age. Such an abstract conception does not emerge by accident.

Although this conception of ego development is not the received psychoanalytic version, it is neither antagonistic to nor inconsistent with the body of the psychoanalytic script. Indeed, I believe it is necessary for its completion. Lampl-de Groot (1949), for one, speaks of conscience development as an aspect of ego development; she simply takes it for granted, rather than expanding it as an argument.

In a recent volume, Ricoeur (1970) holds a "debate with Freud." His argument is somewhat as follows: The original thrust of psychoanalysis was to unmask the hidden, archaic sources of behavior, including as behavior dreams, symptoms, slips, and jokes. Freud thus found meaning in apparently meaningless behavior. The theoretical explanation that Freud offered was couched in terms of discharge of instinctual energy. At variance with the terms of that explanation, however, were some elements of Freud's theory. Identification was never reducible to an instinctual or energic explanation.

Moreover, psychoanalytic therapy has from the start been essentially interpersonal. The transference is not only a transaction between a psychoanalyst and a patient but is itself the medium of the transaction; further, the childhood experiences revived and repeated in the transference are also invariably interpersonal.

In the ego psychology of Freud's later years as well as in his works on artistic creation, there are elements that Freud admits are not completely accounted for in terms of their archaic sources. What shall we make of Freud's aphorism (1933, p. 80), "Where id was, there ego shall be," if we are thinking only in terms of unmasking instinctual origins? In order to complete Freud's script as well as to understand human development, one must complement Freud's archaeology of the subject with a teleology of the subject: so Ricoeur.

The conception of ego development that my colleagues and I have worked out has logical and empirical grounding independent of psychoanalysis. One need not accept the tenets of psychoanalysis to follow the essential elements of our conception. Ricoeur's argument, however, leads to the conclusion that psychoanalysis requires for its completion a "teleology of the subject," which can hardly be other than a theory of ego development. The conception of ego development I have sketched is, in broad outline if not in specific detail, a candidate for this niche in psychoanalytic theory.

CONSCIENCE AS PACER

The origins of conscience are, then, intimately intertwined with ego development. That is not to say that ego and conscience are one, or that either term is dispensable; indeed, they are terms from different universes of discourse. Stages in the development of conscience, however, closely parallel stages of ego development, and the dynamic principles that one needs to account for the development of conscience are the same as, or overlap, those needed to account for ego development. There is one final turn to the argument, and that is to show that conscience, or perhaps the ego ideal, is itself a moving principle in ego development.

The operative word is "pacer," and it is most clearly defined in a paper by Dember (1965) on recent experimental work in cognitive psychology. When given a choice, people seek out intellectual problems of an appropriate level of difficulty for themselves, not too hard and not too easy. They tend, moreover, to sample various levels of difficulty, but to concentrate on that level just a little above their current level of functioning. Problems at that level Dember refers to as "pacers." "It is the pacer, if one is available, that enables the individual to change.... As he maintains active contact with the pacer and eventually masters it, his own level of complexity grows, and he is ready for a new pacer" (p. 421).

The construing of conscience as pacer goes back at least to James Mark Baldwin (1897). Baldwin saw the young child as having two selves, an accommodating self that seeks to learn from parents and older persons, and a habitual self that practices on younger sibs. The former will often appear to be altruistic, the latter often aggressive. Here Baldwin seems to anticipate the principle that Freud later clarified in terms of mastery through transition from passive to active. Ultimately, the child evolves a third self, an ideal self, originally representing the standards set up by parents and teachers as a "copy for imitation." With growth, the child incorporates the ideal self into his habitual self, but as he progresses, new patterns are set for him. Thus his "ethical insight must always find its profoundest expression in that yearning which anticipates but does not overtake the ideal" (Baldwin, 1897, p. 166).

A similar but more sophisticated view has been worked out within the framework of psychoanalytic theory by Loewald. Loewald's version (1960, 1962), much condensed, runs like this: The condition for psychological growth is the tension between a more organized or more mature psychic structure and a less organized, less mature one. Originally, the mother fulfills the function of creating this condition, reflecting to the child both his existence as a person and the potentialities she sees in and hopes for him. As the child grows, this tension between the more organized structure and the less organized one becomes internalized, as the tension between the (unconscious) id and the (conscious and preconscious) ego or as the tension between the ego and the ego ideal or superego. In psychoanalysis as therapy, ego development is resumed, with the analyst in the parental role, representing in his relation to the patient the more developed psychic structure; the analyst reflects back to the patient both how he appears to another and how the analyst envisages his potential growth.

The superego embodies hopes, ideals, and aspirations for the future—that is not only its function but its nature. As those aspirations are realized and became habitual, they become part of the ego, and the child or adult has new aspirations. Thus the superego does not present a fixed program of aspirations and injunctions, constant throughout life. It is rather a name for the function of formulating ideals and aspirations. The superego is the future as embodied in the present.

Loewald is apparently talking primarily about normal superego develoment, not the rigid superego of the neurotic. He writes of the conscience as the "voice" of the superego. On the whole, his usage of the term superego approximates that of the term conscience in the present paper.

Summary

Although this essay has not stressed the point, writers as far back as Nietzsche (1887) have noted that, seen from the viewpoint of man as animal, conscience is a sickness; yet it is also a sublime achievement and the beginning of all culture. Various authors have pointed out that the sources of conscience lie in both conscious and unconscious mental life. Conscience is grounded on narcissism and on interpersonal relations. Conscience has its origins in love and in aggression. Conscience reproduces and memorializes the inequality of station of parent and child; yet, in its fullest and rarest reach, conscience transcends all inequalities of station. In sum, in conscience abides much of the mystery that is man.

REFERENCES

Ausubel, D. P. (1952), *Ego Development and the Personality Disorders.* New York: Grune & Stratton.
Baldwin, J. M. (1897), *Social and Ethical Interpretations in Mental Development.* Excerpts in: *The Self in Social Interaction,* ed. C. Gordon & K. J. Gergen. New York: Wiley, 1968, pp. 51-59.
Chein, I. (1972), *The Science of Behavior and the Image of Man.* New York: Basic Books.
Dember, W. N. (1965), The New Look in Motivation. *Amer. Scientist,* 53:409-427.
Erikson, E. H. (1950), *Childhood and Society.* New York: Norton.
Fenichel, O. (1945), *The Psychoanalytic Theory of Neurosis.* New York: Norton.
Flugel, J. C. (1945), *Man, Morals, and Society.* New York: International Universities Press, 1970.
Freud, A. (1936), The Ego and the Mechanisms of Defense. *The Writings of Anna Freud,* 2. New York: International Universities Press, 1966.
Freud, S. (1905), Three Essays on the Theory of Sexuality. *Standard Edition,* 7:125-247. London: Hogarth Press, 1953.
_____(1914), On Narcissism. *Standard Edition,* 14:67-102. London: Hogarth Press, 1957.
_____(1917), Mourning and Melancholia. *Standard Edition,* 14:237-260. London: Hogarth Press, 1957.
_____(1920), Beyond the Pleasure Principle. *Standard Edition,* 18:3-64. London: Hogarth Press, 1955.
_____(1923), The Ego and the Id. *Standard Edition,* 19:3-66. London: Hogarth Press, 1961.
_____(1930), Civilization and Its Discontents. *Standard Edition,* 21:59-145. London: Hogarth Press, 1961.
_____(1933), New Introductory Lectures on Psycho-Analysis. *Standard Edition,* 22. London: Hogarth Press, 1964.
Hendrick, I. (1942), Instinct and the Ego during Infancy. *Psychoanal. Quart.,* 11:33-58.
Kohlberg, L. (1971), From Is to Ought: How to Commit the Naturalistic Fallacy and Get Away with It in the Study of Moral Development. In: *Cognitive Development and Epistemology,* ed. T. Mischel. New York: Academic Press, pp. 151-235.
Lampl-de Groot, J. (1949), Neurotics, Delinquents and Ideal-Formation. In: *Searchlights on Delinquency,* ed. K. R. Eissler. New York: International Universities Press, pp. 246-255.
_____(1962), Ego Ideal and Superego. *The Psychoanalytic Study of the Child,* 17:94-106. New York: International Universities Press.
Loevinger, J. (1966a), The Meaning and Measurement of Ego Development. *Amer. Psychol.,* 21:195-206.
_____(1966b), Three Principles for a Psychoanalytic Psychology. *J. Abnorm. Psychol.,* 71:432-443.

———— & Wessler, R. (1970), *Measuring Ego Development. I: Construction and Use of a Sentence Completion Test.* San Francisco: Jossey-Bass.

————, Wessler, R., & Redmore, C. (1970), *Measuring Ego Development. II: Scoring Manual for Women and Girls.* San Francisco: Jossey-Bass.

Loewald, H. W. (1960), On the Therapeutic Action of Psycho-Analysis. *Internat. J. Psycho-Anal.,* 41:16-33.

————(1962), The Superego and the Ego-Ideal. *Internat. J. Psycho-Anal.,* 43:264-268.

McDougall, W. (1908), *An Introduction to Social Psychology.* London: Methuen, 1961.

Mill, J. S. (1861), Utilitarianism. In: *Utilitarianism, On Liberty, and Essay on Bentham,* ed. M. Warnock. Cleveland: World, 1962, pp. 251-321.

Nietzsche, F. W. (1887), *A Genealogy of Morals,* trans. J. Gray. New York: Macmillan, 1897.

Odier, C. (1943), *Les Deux Sources, consciente et inconsciente, de la vie morale.* Neuchâtel: De la Baconnière.

Piaget, J. (1932), *The Moral Judgment of the Child.* Glencoe, Ill.: Free Press, 1948.

Preyer, W. (1881), *Mind of the Child.* Excerpts in: *The Child,* ed. W. Kessen. New York: Wiley, 1965, pp. 132-147.

Ricoeur, P. (1970), *Freud and Philosophy: An Essay on Interpretation.* New Haven, Conn.: Yale University Press.

Rotter, J. B. (1966), Generalized Expectancies for Internal versus External Control of Reinforcement. *Psychol. Monogr.,* 80 (1, Whole No. 609).

Sandler, J., et al. (1962), The Classification of Superego Material in the Hampstead Index. *The Psychoanalytic Study of the Child,* 17:107-127. New York: International Universities Press.

Schafer, R. (1968), *Aspects of Internalization.* New York: International Universities Press.

Shapiro, D. (1970), Motivation and Action in Psychoanalytic Psychiatry. *Psychiat.,* 33:329-343.

Spiegelberg, H. (1965), The Essentials of the Phenomenological Method. In: *The Phenomenological Movement: A Historical Introduction.* The Hague: Nijhoff, pp. 653-701.

Sullivan, H. S. (1953), *The Interpersonal Theory of Psychiatry.* New York: Norton.

Weimer, W. B. (1973), Psycholinguistics and Plato's Paradoxes of the *Meno. Amer. Psychol.,* 28:15-33.

10

PERSPECTIVES ON MEMORY

HANS W. LOEWALD

I.

Memory, for the psychoanalyst, is not just a faculty or function of the intellect by virtue of which the mind registers, retains, and may remember experiences, events, and objects. For him, memory also has something to do with separation, loss, mourning, and restitution, and often carries with it a sense of nostalgia, especially as we get older. The words commemoration and memorial remind us of such connotations.

The past would be irretrievably lost without memory; in fact there would not be any past, just as there would not be any present that has meaning or any future to envisage. The fact that memory lets us have a past means that we experience loss and the irretrievability of the past and yet can recover the past in another form.

Memory, however, does not simply enable us to hang on to the past in some way; it gives meaning to the present and helps to shape a future. Memory is connected with our whole experience of time. It is not merely a faculty of reviving or reproducing the past, nor is it simply the faculty of recording and retaining present but fleeting perceptions so that they may last in some other form. By virtue of memory, our experiences become connectible, are woven into a context, and extend into a past and a future. In an important sense, memorial

This paper was presented as the Brill Memorial Lecture to the New York Psychoanalytic Society on November 14, 1972.

activity is linking activity. A before, now, and after are created in this linking and become mutually influential, continuity of our life as individuals comes into being. By these memorial processes, what would otherwise be at best bits of impressions, only to perish immediately, are made to remain as inner state, image, or idea to be linked with fresh impressions and experiences. To move from one eventful moment to the next without having lost the first one — so as to be able to link and match one with the other — requires memorial activity. Without the mind's activity of holding and rebuilding its impressions and its own acts, affects, perceptions, ideas, images, and fantasies, an activity in which present reality is organized by matching and comparing with what has been and what, in anticipation, might be — without all this there would be for us neither past nor present nor future. These are the modes of time, the mutually dependent articulations of experience that arise through memorial activity. Without such inner reproductive holding, in which consists the linking together of before, now, and after, we would experience neither duration nor change. Memory, in this broadest sense, is the activity by which, above all, some sort of order and organization, some sense of permanence as well as of movement and change, come into our world.

Such a broad conception of memory, in which the word refers to that central, all-pervasive activity of the mind by which our world and our life gain breadth and depth and continuity in flux, and change in continuity, by which, in other words, our life and world acquire dimension and meaning, makes memory virtually synonymous with mind itself. This broad definition, however, is not so much an arbitrary overextension of the accepted sense of the word, but rather a return to an ancient close relation, if not identity, of the two words mind and memory, a relation documented by their common root and still visible in such English words as mindful and remind, or in the German *Gedachtnis* (from *Denken,* to think). To stay with language for another moment, memory and mourning are also closely related etymologically. And the other German word for memory, *Erinner-*

ung, derives from inner, internal, the same inner that appears in *Verinnerlichung,* internalization, which, considering its motivational aspects, brings us back to loss, mourning, and restitution.

In many ways, the following discussions, as will be apparent, owe much to the work and thought of others. Apart from Piaget and Freud himself, I mention only a few: Bartlett, Kris, Mahler, Spitz, Winnicott, Rapaport, George Klein, I. H. Paul, and Heinz Werner. It would be most useful and would contribute greatly to the clarification of my own formulations if my considerations could be correlated with their research, but the limitations of time and mental energy make this impossible here.

The genetic-motivational aspects of memorial processes (I use the plural to stress their variety, and in order to avoid the notion of a monolithic "memory function")—including their instinctual-affective roots and genetic derivations—are of particular relevance to a psychoanalytic study. It is important to emphasize again that memorial processes are activities, despite the fact that they may, on the one hand, become automatic (operating then without needing added cathexes) and, on the other hand, evolve into enduring process patterns which we tend to call structures.

By thinking of memory as active process—and not only in regard to unconscious or conscious and intentional remembering, but specifically also in regard to the more deep-seated memorial processes we call registration and retention—we will avoid the temptation to visualize the latter two aspects, and especially registration, as some sort of record that lasts by virtue of the inertia of matter, like indentations on a phonograph disk or on the wax slab of Freud's (1925) famous mystic writing pad. It is necessary, if these processes deserve the name of memory at all, also to conceive cf registration-retention as activities, as patterned forms of low-key cathectic processes, which will resonate to corresponding new cathectic processes (as in recall) and may be amplified, as it were, or modified and restructured by them. Something can be revived only if it is still living or if, as with the phonograph disk, activity can be simulated by setting the system in motion by artificial means. The principle of the insusceptibility to excitation of uncathected systems (Freud, 1917) applies here. Freud, of course, always assumed the activity of "the unconscious," including unconscious "memory traces." It is precisely the fact that the wax slab of the mystic writing pad cannot reproduce the writing from within that makes the analogy with memory break down. If the wax slab could make writing on the celluloid visible from within, it would, as Freud said, be a mystic pad indeed (1925, p. 230). The recall of a childhood memory, for example, is to be understood as a reinforcement or restructuring, by virtue of new cathectic processes based on new experiences, of the reproductive activity constituting the unconscious registration-retention of that infantile experience; and that unconscious reproductive activity itself, like the unconscious wish in dreams, continues to determine the character of the present experience, in fact helps it to be significant and not meaningless. This applies, I believe, not only to those intermediary memorial process-structures called unconscious ideas or fantasies, but also to the underlying so-called mnemic images or memory traces that in psychoanalytic theory have tended to be taken as ultimate givens or mechanical replicas of sensory data.

In passing, I should like to mention a difficulty regarding the conventional distinction between registration and retention. Freud was repeatedly preoccupied with the question whether anything ever registered by the mind could be truly destroyed. If we are inclined, as Freud was, to assume that such destruction does not occur, then the distinction between registration and retention is difficult to maintain. The reasons not to assume such destruction have to do with the very notion of unconscious memory and its continuing effect on subsequent mental life, and with the coexistence of early and later stages of mental development in the structure and dynamics of the mind. If nothing recorded in the mind is ever truly destroyed—i.e., extinguished rather than merely altered— and if through the alterations the psychoanalyst can still perceive or guess the original text that continues to be active

and have its own impact, then registration amounts to retention. One meaning of the timelessness of the unconscious
depends on this consideration. The term retention, then,
would be reserved for those subsequent memorial processes
that elaborate and alter original registrations.

I have so far not specifically mentioned that aspect of
memory which is called remembering. Remembering, for
psychoanalysts, is an equivocal term, insofar as Freud has
distinguished, notably in his paper "Remembering, Repeating
and Working-Through" (1914b), between remembering and
repeating, while pointing out at the same time that repeating,
as in acting out, is the patient's way of remembering. He
subsumes both under reproducing and speaks of reproduction
in action (repeating) versus reproduction in the psychical field
(remembering in the narrower sense). But there can be no
question that both acting out (or hysterical reminiscences and
transference manifestations in the analytic situation) and
remembering "in the old manner" — as Freud (1914b) calls
it — are memorial processes. Their differences and their relations to each other will have to occupy us later on. A character
common to both, and to other memorial processes, is that they
are reproducing something.

Let me now return to the motivational aspects of memorial
processes and specifically to what I have called their instinctual-affective roots and genetic origins. My exposition and
discussion in what follows will of necessity be condensed and
schematic and will leave many misgivings, doubts, and questions which either cannot be resolved or answered within the
present context, or which are complex theoretical issues
beyond my capacity for further organization and penetration
at the present time.

When I speak of instinctual forces and of instincts or
instinctual drives, I define them as motivational, i.e., both
motivated and motivating, and as being the most primitive
psychic forces in the motivational, hierarchically organized
network of psychic forces. As intrapsychic motivations, they
arise within and develop from a psychic matrix or field
constituted essentially by the mother-child unit. Instincts are

here defined as what Freud has called psychic representatives, not as biological forces, and as forces which *ab initio* manifest themselves within and between what gradually differentiates into individual and environment (or ego and objects, or self and object world — allowing these terms for the moment to be equivalent). Instincts remain relational phenomena, rather than being considered energies within a closed system, to be "discharged" somewhere (see Loewald, 1971). The differentiation, within the original matrix, of individual and environment involves the differentiation of narcissistic and object cathexis. Here, narcissistic cathexis means instinctual currents between elements within the emerging individual (or ego system); object cathexis means instinctual currents between individual and environment (or objects). Narcissistic and object cathexes, once portions of instinctual cathexis have thus been differentiated — other portions remain undifferentiated — react with and influence each other; they do not simply each go their own way. It is the instinctual interactions within the ego system that deserve par excellence to be termed narcissistic, although the state prior to the differentiation of object cathexis and narcissistic cathexis is referred to as primary narcissism, a designation that is justified insofar as we consider that prior state in regard to the prospect of intrapsychic development. It is true that, once an ego system or internal world has developed, it may itself be cathected as a totality, and we speak of this process, too, as narcissistic. For our present purposes, let it be clear only that one has to distinguish, on the one hand, between cathectic processes *within* the system that give it its character as an organization, and, on the other, cathectic processes that are deployed *upon* the system by itself.

A few terminological comments are unavoidable. I use the word ego here in the sense in which Freud has used it, for example in the paper "On Narcissism" (1914a) and again in *Civilization and Its Discontents* (1930) (*after* the formulation of the structural theory), i.e., in the general sense of the totality of the psyche as an organization, and not in the sense specified when we speak of id, ego, and superego as sub-

structures of the total psyche. Despite that ambiguity, I prefer
ego in the present context, because the term self, which
Hartmann has used in the definition of narcissism, in my
opinion is equally if not more ambiguous and is in need of
much further clarification as an analytic concept. I wish to
stress again that I have in mind primarily the cathectic
interactions *within* the ego (or self) system. To me, it seems
preferable to reserve the term self for a stage in the individual's development when the structuralization into id, ego, and
superego is rather definitively established. To my mind, the
word object is the most problematic term but so ingrained in
psychoanalytic language that it is difficult to circumvent it. If
the ego is a unity that has to develop and not something
"there" from the beginning of psychic development, this is also
true for the object. It is misleading to speak of objects when
referring to stages in development where the differentiation of
inside and outside, or ego and object, is at best *in statu
nascendi,* where, in other words, there is as yet no subject as a
psychic unity that may cathect or interact with something that
is differentiated as an external unity.

I believe that Freud did not come to distinguish clearly
between instinctual narcissistic cathexes in interaction with
the ego system as a whole and narcissistic cathexes that
constitute and organize that unity, i.e., which are employed in
the ego's internal organization. It is the latter, I suggest, that
are involved in the genesis of memory. But I believe this thesis
to be in accord with Freud's own ideas regarding the role of
introjection-identification in ego and superego formation,
although he does not explicitly speak of memory in this
connection. It should be clearer now why I have gone into
some detail about the differentiation of narcissistic and object
cathexis. This differentiation runs parallel to that of memory
and perception in early psychic life. Possibly it is the selfsame
differentiation as considered from the instinct side. It seems to
me that there have been two parallel theories in psychoanalysis, one in terms of perception and memory (the "topographic" model), with a tendency to equate perception with
consciousness and memory with the unconscious, and the

other in terms of instincts and motivation and libidinal development. I believe that the concept of narcissistic libido (and its aggression complement, masochism) provided a bridge between the two theories and led to an attempt at unification in the structural theory.

Considering memory with regard to the distinction between it and perception, we may ask what it is that is registered and how it is registered. In reply to the first question, one might be inclined to say: perceptions are registered. It is now generally agreed that perception is not a passive process, not something that happens to a "perceptual apparatus," but a process that involves activity on the part of the perceiver. The act of perception is an interaction, and what is registered would be that interaction. The mental activity involved in perceiving, its modification in the interaction with the perceptual stimulus, is reproduced, or rather one should say, is continued, in the registering act. This is an act which, seen from the standpoint of an outside observer, reproduces or continues internally a process that has occurred between the subject and an object or stimulating agent. Perceiving, in the beginning of mental life, is an instinctual activity, and the stimulus perceived is by that very fact an instinctual stimulus. The internal reproduction of that instinctual interaction is equally an instinctual activity. Indeed, from the standpoint of that bundle of instincts which is the primitive infantile psyche, interaction with something outside and internal interaction are indistinguishable; nor does the infantile psyche differentiate a perceptual act (having occurred) from a memorial act (occurring now). Memory, as registration or recording, and perception are identical for the infant.

Let us consider the primitive experience of satisfaction, an instinctual-perceptual experience in which cognition and conation have not yet fallen asunder. This experience is reproduced, we assume, in the process of hallucinatory wish fulfillment, a first sign — again viewed only from the observer's point of view — of memory. For the infant, there is no difference between the actual event of satisfaction and its reproduction. But the exigencies of life are such that the hallucinatory experience does not remain satisfying, i.e., the instinctual urge eventually has to be satisfied again by the repetition of the perceptual experience. Its internal reproduction does not last for long or remain strong enough without further external reinforcement. This latter fact remains true, to a much attenuated degree, for the rest of one's life, but it is the more obvious the farther back we go into the origins of mental life. This consideration may throw some new light on the problem of the destructibility of memory that I mentioned earlier: Is the indestructibility of the unconscious contingent on a minimum degree of nourishment from object-libidinal interactions?

As mentioned before, the internal interaction called registration (to be understood in the same active sense as perception) is best viewed, it seems, as a continuation of the perceptual experience, a reproduction in the sense in which a reverberating echo is a reproduction, and not as the resumption of a process that has come to an end. Memory would basically be an instinctual, narcissistic activity modulated and patterned by interactions with environment, which gradually gains a high degree of autonomy, but which, in order to become preconscious or conscious, requires periodic reinforcement through perceptions (object-cathecting activity) which "revive memories."

The experience of satisfaction, brought about by a mutually responsive interaction with environment, would be continued, at least for a while, as a "registration." The hypothetical hallucinatory wish fulfillment, as an inner revival of the experience of satisfaction, is based on such registration and is conceivable only inasmuch as a renewed wish may now be temporarily satisfied through the internal interaction called registration, which is a continuation of the experience of satisfaction. If registration is the continuation, internally or mentally, of a satisfying interaction with environment, it is at the same time a continuation of the system's intrinsic instinctual activity *as modified by the satisfying response*. The perceptual experience tends to pattern internal excitation in the experiencing system in novel ways, so that internal processes gain in complexity and richness.

Our preoccupation with the fact that renewed "specific action" on the part of environment eventually becomes necessary has perhaps led us to neglect a consideration of the psychic activity that takes place during the period between the satisfying experience with environment and the renewed necessity for it. The general quiescence of the baby in a state of satisfaction does not mean that psychic activity has ceased. Instead of assuming that during such periods the psyche has returned to a state of rest (as postulated by the constancy or inertia principle), it is, in my opinion, far more reasonable to assume that the interactions with the world continue to reverberate, are reproduced, and thus lay the foundations for the development of an internal world, in the form of memorial processes. Instead of thinking of static memory traces or mnemic images as the model for registration — traces which then supposedly are utilized by a function called memory — registration and its elaborations in retention are seen here as an active (although "silent") process of continued reproduction of interactional activities that is in itself a linking. It is in the process of internal reproduction that the identity, and later the similarity, with the initial stimulating experiences comes about. The similarity does not reside in static traces which then may be used by memory. The terms memory trace or mnemic image already *contain* the problem of memory; they do not explain or elucidate it.

The controversy over schema versus trace in memory theory may perhaps be clarified, if not resolved, in the following way: schema refers to the intrinsic instinctual activity of the system, whereas trace refers to the modifying or patterning influence brought to bear on that activity by the responsive environmental activity. The proponents of schema insist on the observation that perceptual material is in some way organized by memory and not just passively received. On the other hand — and this refers to trace — the perceptual material undoubtedly modulates and organizes the intrinsic activity into certain process configurations. What is registered — i.e., reproduced — is just that mutual organization. This reproduction — and here we go a step further in our discussion of perception and memory, and object cathexis and narcissistic cathexis—this memorial product, while being itself further organized by new perceptions, in its turn further organizes perceptual material. That perception and memory have a reciprocal influence on each other is a clear implication of my reminder that perception is an active process and not a purely passive reception. The mental "schemata," themselves increasingly articulated by perceptual material, increasingly participate in the organization of perceptions, so that percepts more and more acquire structure. Perception, rather than being the forever fresh and pure receptivity that Freud often claimed it to be, is shot through with memory. Because this memorial element in perceptions is for the most part unconscious and automatic, we take the so-structured material as what we call objective external reality. That mode of schematizing which is objectivation of reality appears to us to be encountered in external reality, as though it were contained already in the material itself and not the product of the meeting between mind and world. That this meeting may produce other ways of experiencing reality is well known to us from our observation of children, from primitive mentality, and from creative moments in ourselves and in others— creative in the sense that mental schemata are not rigid and lose their automatic character. But the largely automatic objectivation of experience makes us view that particular schematization as the unquestioned standard of truth.

In a similar way, when thinking of memory traces, we have already built into their countenance that objectifying schematization which our mental, memorial processes only gradually develop. We tend to visualize the original primitive "memory traces" as more or less faithful tracings of what we, dominated as we are by secondary-process mentation (a highly complex form of schematization), have come to see as objective data given us by nature. These traces, however, in which experiences are reproduced, cannot be reproductions or continuations of anything other than quite primitively organized interactions between a primitively organized mind, dominated by primary process, and a therefore primitively organized or schematized environment—where, in addition, a distinction between individual and environment, between memory and what is memorized, is barely in the making, and where sense impressions are likely to be global, all-engulfing, and engulfed coenesthetic receptions. (I am referring here to Spitz's [1965] distinction between coenesthetic and diacritic perception.) We must assume that at early developmental levels registrations, being continuations, reproductions, reverberations of interactions between mind and world, are subject to the laws of primary process no less than these interactions themselves.

The development of diacritic perception is related to the distinct sensory modalities that arise out of a welter of undifferentiated global sensory experiences; and any registering-retaining activities would have the same global character at such stages. We have reason to assume that in early psychic stages (as well as in certain exceptional or abnormal "ego states" that hark back to them) the child does not distinguish between his mouth and the mother's breast, or between the activity of sucking and mouth and breast. Also, one moment is not distinguished from the next, or memory from the remembered event, nor, even at a somewhat later time when we can begin to speak of emotions, is the mother's smile or assuring appearance distinguished from the baby's own delight.

In sum, what is perceived and can be registered in reproductive activity is determined on the one hand by material, insofar as it is available and needed, and on the other by how and to what degree this material is differentiated and integrated. The kind of mind, so to speak, that organizes the material, the fashion and degree of schematization—including even that degree of minimal schematization where neither is the perceiver distinguished from the perceived nor the moment of initial interaction ("perception") from the moment of reproduction ("memory")—these are the conditions to be considered, together with the properties of the material for memorial processes, i.e., the kind of environmental responsive stimulation. In primitive hallucinatory wish fulfillment, i.e., in the recathexis of the registration of an experience of satisfaction, there would be no distinction between the past or present state of being or between external and internal reality.

I will mention only in passing that Freud's (1895) early
concept of motor or kinesthetic image (*Bewegungsbild*) and
Rapaport's (1942) distinction between drive organization and
conceptual organization of memories are related to these
considerations. But two points have to be emphasized and
integrated here, although I am unable to do more than
mention them in this presentation: (1) the development from a
minimal degree of schematization in "coenesthetic reception"
to the various differentiations implied in "diacritic perceptions" is itself codetermined by the higher schematizations
provided by the environment, schematizations that are embedded in the manner in which the environment encounters
and interacts with the developing individual. (2) Insofar as
schemata are considered as constituents of memory, that is, of
the mind that organizes and reproduces material at the same
time it is being organized by it, memorial processes, as
mentioned before, enter into the very fabric of perception. If
memory is that aspect of our activity as humans which links
events and phenomena together so that they are more than
unrelated bits and pieces, namely, by holding an experience in
reproductive continuation while the next one occurs, then
perceptions as organizations of stimulation events cannot exist
without memory.

I have said that we cannot assume a cessation of psychic
activity during the period of general quiescence that occurs
when a baby is in a state of satisfaction. During such periods,
it seems plausible to assume, the foundations for the development of an internal world are built in the form of unconscious
memorial processes by which the satisfying interaction with
environment is continued, without any need for further
external interaction. Maternal "cathexes" leading to satisfaction, by being continued or reproduced after they have ceased
externally, pattern or structure hitherto undifferentiated instinctual activity in such a way that the maternal stimulating
responses become part of the internal repertoire. Not only
does the baby have instinctual needs, but the mother also
stimulates the baby in many ways and thus increases and
enriches his instinctual-perceptual capacities and activities.

These, in turn, if appropriately responded to, further contribute to internal, memorial activity. The quiescent periods during which memorial processes continue — which in fact are needed to provide a chance for memorial activity to evolve an internal world without interference by unceasing or over-stimulating external interactions — might be compared to the latency period of childhood, when the consolidation and elaboration of the internal world in the wake of the Oedipal period takes place.

If nothing else would, the resolution of the Oedipus complex, with its relinquishments and the internalization-repression of Oedipal object relations, reminds us that we have so far left out a most important aspect of the problem of memory. Memory seems to be inextricably interwoven with experiences of separation, loss, object withdrawal, or cessation of satisfying external interactions. Loss or separation from a love object appears to be a most powerful stimulus for the activation of memorial processes. I mentioned in the beginning that the words memory and mourning are closely related etymologically. Memory and "object loss" are so intimately connected and yet so much in an oppositional relation to each other that it often looks as though they are the two sides of the same coin. Although memorial processes often appear to be motivated by object loss, there would be no loss but only emptiness if the object were not already remembered in some form. And yet, one must also say that, in a deeper sense, only by virtue of the differentiation of subject from object — which is the primordial separation — does memory arise.

It would seem that those memorial processes which are set in motion by loss, whether they are conscious recollections or unconscious remembering as in the identifications of the mourner, are revivals of deeper memories. On the basis of retention, that is, of the internal, continuous, though unconscious, reproduction of interactional experiences, what otherwise would be inner emptiness or rage due to disruption, may become a longing that produces the experience of missing or realizing the absence of something, under the impact of renewed instinctual pressures. This something has continued in inner reproduction and therefore may be longed for and missed and sought again on the outside or revived inside. For the very young infant, the absence of the needed mother is not so much an experience of separation or loss as one of total helplessness and emptiness, insofar as memorial processes are only fleeting and seem to cease or fall below a threshold of effectiveness without reinforcement by interaction with the mother. It is for this reason that I began the discussion of memory development with the satisfying experiences of infancy. At a later level, only sufficiently gratifying Oedipal experiences lead to further psychosexual development through the resolution (internalization) of Oedipal relationships. There can nevertheless be no question that external deprivation and consequent inner conflict and pain are powerful determinants in promoting, although probably not founding, memory development, that is, the elaboration of an internal world. Memory is the child of both satisfaction and frustration.

I have said there would be no (experienced) loss if the object were not remembered in some form. The object, or rather the infant-mother interaction, is "narcissistically" continued into what we call memorial reproduction. Would this not occur if external interaction were to continue? Such a hypothetical case plays havoc with what we know about the periodicity of biological and psychic processes. The infant at some point, which ideally coincides with the mother's withdrawal of the breast, is satisfied and goes to sleep. Instinctual activity, however, no less than vital biological processes, continues within the infant. It does not cease, but is transposed to a different arena, as it were. Biological processes, digestion, assimilation, etc., continue within the infantile organism to maintain and develop the internal processes and structures that constitute biological growth. From the point of view of the infant's growth, the aim and purpose of the biological interactions between infant and mother are his maintenance and development, and it is these internal biological processes and their results that count; from this viewpoint, the mother-infant interactions are means to an end. Similarly, those reproductive memorial processes that take over and continue internally what was external interaction are, from the viewpoint of individual mental growth, the end to which early "object ties" are the means. The infant becomes satisfied and — speaking from an outside observer's standpoint — withdraws from the external world as much as the mother "withdraws" from the infant. The infant no longer avails himself of the mother, except as a continued "internal" presence; in his sleep he digests and reproduces internally what had transpired in the actual feeding event.

Here we have to remind ourselves of the fact that such reproduction is more than a continuation: it is a continuation in which something changes. It increasingly involves a metamorphosis analogous to biological metabolism. Retention involves more or less profound changes, restructuralizations, elaborations, and integrations with other interactional processes. The initial registrations become integrated into the total context and dominated by it. This perpetual reorganization materially influences how we perceive and how we interact with the world, even as new external interactions influence internal reorganizational processes by continuing to alter memorial processes.

The relation between initial registrations and their retention may be compared to a musical theme and its variations; the latter may become so complex and elaborate that the theme is hardly recognizable in them, yet it remains the basic structure. At times the theme is repeated at the end in all its simplicity, highlighting the complexity and richness of the whole composition and making more explicit the transformational relations between the theme and the variations as well as amongst variations themselves. At the same time, the theme repeated at the end seems to say: this — despite all the artistry and grandeur in between — is what it all comes down to in the end.

Memorial activity appears to be, if not initiated, at any rate promoted or activated by experiences of deprivation as well as by experiences of satisfaction. The same problem comes up in regard to identification and its motivation. For instance, many identifications leading to superego formation are thought of as the result of renunciations forced upon the child by external prohibitions and frustrations; and this is true as well in the work of mourning. But we know also that early identifications with the parents occur under circumstances that have nothing to do with deprivation or loss, but with a closeness amounting to lack of separateness, as though what is perceived or felt in this intimacy, by that very lack of distance, becomes an element in the child or helps to form his character — as though the parent's trait is continued into the child, without his having to give up anything. Insofar as this state of affairs, this felt identity, cannot permanently be maintained, due to unavoidable "untimely" separations and disruptions of intimacy, what we call the internal world or character of the child — although for him it is neither inner nor outer but still undifferentiated — becomes strengthened if the conditions are not too disruptive. That is, the memorial processes that were promoted by the intimacy (which was "satisfying") gain prominence, begin to predominate *due to the disruption*, and increasingly acquire the status of inner versus outer. The satisfying original identity is renounced to a degree, or the importance of sensory contact as a condition for identity recedes. It looks as though the experience of satisfaction leads to or permits the giving up of intimacy or identity with environment if it alternates with experiences of deprivation or loss. Most likely, the alternations and combinations of experiences of satisfaction and deprivation that occur in life under ordinary circumstances make it possible that either and both may have the same result: experiences of satisfaction may lead to renunciation and internalization under the impact of experiences of deprivation which alert to that danger, while experiences of deprivation may lead there too, under the sway of experiences of satisfaction, which permit the former not to become truly traumatic and alert the psyche to the possibility of satisfaction by internalization. Neither one nor the other experience alone would eventuate in psychic development.

What I have said implies something I have so far not specifically mentioned: experiences of deprivation themselves

are continued in memorial reproduction, once the foundations for memory have been laid by sufficient satisfying
intimacy. Let me also mention again a factor one tends to lose
sight of: the infant's inherent tendency toward withdrawal
from sensory contact as a result of satisfaction, which under
optimal conditions is reciprocated by the environment and
which is a component element in the alternations I have
spoken of.

I have so far mainly discussed aspects of memory which have
to do with its genesis and have maintained that memorial
processes deserve to be called narcissistic, in contrast to
object-cathecting processes. I have tried to describe briefly the
differentiation of narcissistic and object libido out of the undifferentiated matrix of an instinctual force-field constituted
by the mother-child psychic unit. And I have suggested that
the differentiation of memory and perception in early development runs parallel to that of narcissistic and object
cathexis; perhaps at bottom is the same differentiation process viewed from the cognitive side. This would imply an
original unity of instinctual and cognitive mental processes
and would accord with the conception of an undifferentiated
phase out of which id and ego develop, with one — to my mind
ineluctable — amendment: at the level of that phase there also
is no differentiation of subject and object or inside and outside
or of temporal modes. Only when there is developed in mental
life something like an experience of internality and externality
and of temporal modes, only then can we distinguish between
memory and perception and between narcissistic and object
cathexis.

II.

When something is reproduced that in some form has
become part of the inner life, either in action or affect or in
imagination and ideation, we speak of remembering. Since
recording and retaining themselves reproduce experience and
are reproductions in the sense delineated earlier, remem-

bering is a way of reproducing reproductions, a potentiated form of memory.

I have already mentioned Freud's (1914b) distinction between reproduction in action and reproduction in the psychical field as two forms of remembering. I propose to go beyond Freud's formulation, which was geared to considerations of psychoanalytic technique, and to speak of enactive and representational remembering. The first includes not only acting out and transference repetitions, but also identificatory reproductions, as in the following example. In contrast to offering recollections of his father's overbearing behavior toward him, a patient may at times behave in just that overbearing fashion toward his son, or he may show such behavior toward the analyst in the analytic hour. He may even first *describe* his father's behavior toward him in more or less objective terms and then subtly shift to *enacting* the father's behavior in what I have just called identificatory reproduction. Such shifts from representational to identificatory reproduction are not uncommon during analysis, although we are perhaps more familiar with shifts from enactive to representational reproduction, the latter being the analyst's aim when he interprets the patient's behavior as an identification with his father. Perhaps it would be more correct to say that the analyst's aim is to establish links between the two forms of memorial reproduction, to allow one to be illuminated by the other in a mutual recognition which leads to higher psychic organization (cf. hypercathexis).

Characteristic for the enactive form of remembering is that, as remembering, it is unconscious, i.e., the individual is not aware that he is reproducing something from the past. But this is only a superficial way of looking at it: the remembering is unconscious in a much deeper, dynamic sense, inasmuch as it shares the timelessness and lack of differentiation of the unconscious and of the primary process. In my example of the patient's identification with his father, the patient re-enacts what we assume to be his earlier identification, his earlier dedifferentiation from object relation, involving secondary process, in the direction of primary-process mentation; and in this re-enactment there is no past as distinguished from present. From the point of view of representational memory, which is our ordinary yardstick, we would say that the patient, instead of *having* a past, *is* his past; he does not distinguish himself as rememberer from the content of his memory. In representational remembering, the mind presents something to itself as its own past experience, distinguishing past from present and himself as the experiencer from what he experienced.

It is to be noted that any significant degree of affect present in representational remembering brings it closer to re-enactment: the patient may, as we say, be overcome by his memory so that the index of pastness and the distinction between himself as the agent of reproduction and the remembered content are diminished. The inner distance required for representational remembering appears to decrease in proportion to an increase in affect. I will not be able to enlarge here on the important relations between affect and memory, but can only stress that affective states and moods may often be understood as forms of nonrepresentational remembering (cf. anniversary reactions).

We have encountered characteristics of the nonrepresentational, enactive forms of memory before: we discussed original registrations as reproductive continuations of interactional experiences and said that in its primitive beginnings there is no differentiation of an internal process ("memory") from an interplay of primitive psyche and environment ("perception"), and no distinction between present (the moment of reproducing) and past (the time when what is reproduced occurred). This, of course, also means that there is as yet no difference between the agent and the product of his activity, between registering and its content.

Let me now attempt to fit these various considerations into a larger metapsychological framework. In doing so, I am fully aware of the unsolved theoretical difficulties that remain and of the fact that the following condensed conceptualizations are not always in keeping with accepted psychoanalytic theory, and may raise new problems. But I believe that progress in our field, and especially advances in psychoanalytic theory, will depend on formulating new propositions and on reorganizing available psychoanalytic knowledge and observation.

The distinction between enactive and representational memory resolves itself into that between unconscious and preconscious memory. Unconscious memory follows the laws of primary process, whereas preconscious memory is determined by secondary process. There is thus a primary memorial system, which consists in the aggregate of identifications and internalizations that enter into the organization of the psychic substructures id, ego, and superego. From this point of view, the latter are memorial structures on different levels of organization. Representational or, more generally speaking, preconscious memory constitutes a secondary memorial system, which arises and branches off from the primary system on the basis of the organization of the ego and as a result of that organization. I distinguish between the ego's structure as a self-organizing system of narcissistic interactions, and the ego's functions in relation to the world and to itself, which its structure makes possible. Similarly, a biological structure like the lung comes about by various intrauterine developmental processes which enable it to function as a respiratory organ after birth. The developmental processes leading to the organization of the ego as a psychological structure, however, begin at birth and come to their relative completion only during and through the Oedipal period. The secondary, preconscious memorial system is a function of the ego insofar as secondary-process mentation characterizes the ego's functioning in relation to the outer and inner worlds.

Leaving out of consideration the id (the structure resulting from the organization — to an extent separate and autonomous — of instinctual life), both ego and superego are creatures of the internalization processes described by Freud (1923) although not so termed by him. In that respect they are memorial structures. Without going into any detail here about internalization, I should say that I conceive of it, broadly speaking, as the process by which interactions within the original mother-child psychic matrix, and later between the growing individual and his environment, become transmuted into internal interactions constituting the individual psyche and creating, maintaining, and developing an internal world. This internal world has to be distinguished from the representational world (Sandler and Rosenblatt, 1962) or inner world or "map" (Rapaport, 1957, pp. 696-697) constituted by mental representations of objects and their relations to each other. The latter is the secondary or representational memory system; it arises on the basis of the development of the ego and as a function of it. Internalization in the sense intended here is not a process involving the representation of objects and object relations, but it involves, to speak in Freud's language, their dissolution or destruction. In the identification that may lead to internalization, it is precisely the object character of a person that is either not yet established (as in those early identifications preceding object cathexis), or is suspended or annihilated by a process of dedifferentiation of subject and object. The object is not represented by the ego to itself, but it becomes deobjectified and depersonified, and the former object relation becomes a dynamic element of the reorganized ego.

I have said that unconscious memory follows the laws of primary process while preconscious memory is determined by secondary process. A clarification of the terms primary and secondary is in order. I suggest that a deeper meaning may be discovered in these terms, deeper than merely indicating that the former is more primitive and comes first and the latter develops out of it and comes second. Mental and memorial processes are primary if and insofar as they are *unitary,* single-minded, as it were, undifferentiated and nondifferentiating, unhampered, as Freud (1933) has described it, by laws of contradiction, causality, and by the differentiation of past, present, and future and of subject and object, i.e., by the differentiation of temporal and spatial relations. Condensattion and displacement, considered as indications of the influence of primary on secondary process, are regressive influences in the direction of an original density where all our distinctions and dichotomies do not hold sway. Mental processes are primary to the extent to which they are nonsplitting, to the extent to which they do not manifest or establish duality or multiplicity, no this and/or that, no before and after, no action as distinguished from its agent or its goal or its object. It is clear that into this category fall what we call magical thinking, omnipotence of thought and movements and gestures, as well as identification, coenesthetic reception, and many other phenomena of so-called primitive mentality such as the "oceanic feeling" and ecstatic experiences.

The secondary process is secondary insofar as in it *duality* becomes established, insofar as it differentiates; among these differentiations is the distinction between the perceiver and the perceived. The ego as agency of the secondary process presents something to itself, whether this is material from the outer or the inner world. Mental processes, in the development from primary to secondary process, undergo a splitting of themselves by which an inner encounter arises, which leads to all the distinctions and dichotomies characteristic for secondary process. This dichotomous reflexion—I am not speaking here of conscious reflection—is set in motion or made possible by the fact that the parents actively reflect the child to the child by their responsive encounters with him, encounters that become elements in the child's eventual inner reflexiveness. It is this mirroring of the child on the part of the parents, a mirroring which inevitably, due to the parents' higher mental development, reflects "more" than the child presents, that leads to the development of secondary process. Words provided by the environment are one prominent example of this mirroring "hypercathexis" which, according to Freud, makes it possible for the primary process to be succeeded by the secondary process. The interpretations given to the patient in analysis, especially, in our context, when enactive remembering is interpreted in terms of representational memory, are highly developed forms of such hypercathecting reflection, which the patient may then make his own.

I believe that these considerations, sketchy and incomplete as they are, are in accord with Freud's (1933, for example) ideas about the intimate relations between the ego and the preconscious system and "external reality." The unconscious and preconscious, considered from the viewpoint of memory, are primary and secondary memorial systems. (This, incidentally, is consistent with Freud's diagram of the psychic apparatus in Chapter VII of *The Interpretation of Dreams* [1900].) I adhere to the term preconscious here because the word indicates something about the character of secondary process. The essential characteristic of preconscious mental processes is not that they lack conscious awareness, but that they involve that internal splitting by which what I would call an inner *con-scire* is established in mental life. We are most familiar with this *con-scire*, with this splitting into different psychic elements which thereby may encounter and know each other, from consciousness. But it is not conscious awareness of such things that establishes that knowing. In consciousness, we only become aware, in a reflective movement of a higher order, of representational or, as I will call it, *conscient* mentation. The latter is recathected in conscious recall.

In primary memorial activity, such inner splitting and *con-scire* is lacking. If memory is linking reproduction of experience, in primary memory activity the links are links of action, or, from another viewpoint, links of the continuity and urge of instinctual process. Through "hypercathexis," of which Freud's "word presentations" joining with "thing presentations" (1915) are an example, and which originates in the mother's mirroring interpretation and organization of the child's urges, feelings, and actions—through such processes the links of action and feeling become links of meaning. The various elements of action and feeling begin to encounter and "know" each other; they become a context of meaning, which is one way of describing the organizing function of the ego. Freud increasingly insisted on the ego's character as a coherent organization. In his later writings, he more and more tended to the view that the main characteristic of the repressed is that it is excluded from the coherent ego, i.e., excluded from an over-all context of meaning, thereby regressing toward primary process, toward a nondiacritic, nonrepresentational form of mentation. As such, the repressed is a reservoir of primary memorial processes which, through interpretation (meaning-giving on the part of the analyst), may combine with or again become part of a context of meaning.

With all this, the status of unconscious fantasies and unconscious ideas remains problematic. Similar to the latent dream thoughts, they appear to be combinations of elements from the two realms, the primary and secondary memorial systems, or the unconscious and the preconscious. Perhaps the most we can say is that a so-called unconscious idea, like a latent dream thought, is a construction or reconstruction of something dynamically unconscious in terms of, or in the language of, preconscious thought processes. An unconscious idea would not be something that as such has an existence in the primary memorial system. The unitary, enactive memorial process-structure, for an empathic observer, corresponds to a dual, secondary memorial structure that is isolated from the former and readily available only to the analyst as agent of secondary-process mentation. The unconscious structure, in and through the act of interpretation as a hypercathectic act, again becomes, in the case of derepression, an "idea," i.e., a secondary-process structure.

Becoming an idea means that the unconscious structure loses its unitary, instinctual, "single-minded" character and becomes reinserted into a context of meaning, i.e., into a context of mutually reflecting and related mental elements. The linking is no longer merely one of reproductive action; it is one of representational connection. The loss involved in the transformation of the unitary, single-minded character of primary memorial activity is, I believe, the cause for what Freud has called the resistance of the id. This loss is fended off by the "compulsion to repeat" which forever remains an active source of conflict between id and ego.

We are led back to the intricate relations between memory and mourning. In some sense, the sadness and grief of mourning perhaps also concerns that loss, that giving up of the unitary single-mindedness of instinctual life which tends to preserve in some way the primary narcissistic oneness from which we have to take leave in the development of conscient life and secondary-process mentation. That development involves being split from the embeddedness in an embracing totality, as well as that internal split in which we come to reflect and confront ourselves. The development of conscient, representational memory is a departure from that inner unity and replaces the original unity prior to individuation. Individuation is our human way of memorializing and thus re-creating those origins.

The ego is, as Freud thought—and I believe this is his deepest insight into its psychology—the precipitate, the internalization of what goes on between the primitive psyche and its environment; it is an organization of reproductive action, but action on a new stage, the stage of internality. This interplay on the internal stage of action constitutes the process-structure of the ego. The ego, in its further elaboration and articulation of this reproductive action, which takes place in continuous interaction with the world, then develops toward that more remote, divided, and abstract form of mentation we call the secondary process or representational memory. It is at the same time more distant and self-divided, and more lucid and free—shall we say: sadder and wiser? By virtue of the secondary process, the ego exercises its functions, including that function by which the individual becomes an object of contemplation and care and love to itself and can encounter others as objects in the same spirit.

Before closing, I wish to say a few words about a prime function in human life—and in psychoanalysis as an exquisitely human undertaking—of fully matured memorial activity. Through psychoanalysis man may become a truly historical being. In contrast to the ahistorical life of primitive societies and primitive man, including the primitive man in ourselves, the higher forms of memorial activity make us create a history of ourselves as a race and as individuals, as well as a history of the world in which we live. Rudiments of this history-creating activity are present even in primitive mentality, but it comes into its own in the individual in those higher forms of reflective memory wherein we encounter our-

selves in all our dimensions. This is the thrust of psychoanalysis, of the endeavor to transform unconscious or automatic repetitions—memorial processes in which we do not
encounter ourselves and others—into aware and re-creative
action in which we know who we and others are, understand
how we got to be that way, and envisage what we might do
with ourselves as we are. In such memorial activity, which
weaves past, present, and future into a context of heightened
meaning, each of us is on the path to becoming a self. For
most of us, such self-aware organization and conduct of life
with others and ourselves remains a potential rather than an
actuality, except for brief moments or periods. Understanding
this potentiality, however, can help us to strive toward a more
human life.

REFERENCES

Bartlett, F. C. (1932), *Remembering: A Study in Experimental and Social
    Psychology.* Cambridge: Cambridge University Press, 1967.
Freud, S. (1895), Project for a Scientific Psychology. *Standard Edition,* 1:283-387.
    London: Hogarth Press, 1966.
_____ (1900), The Interpretation of Dreams. *Standard Edition,* 4 & 5. London:
    Hogarth Press, 1953.
_____ (1914a), On Narcissism. *Standard Edition,* 14:67-102. London: Hogarth
    Press, 1957.
_____ (1914b), Remembering, Repeating and Working-Through. *Standard
    Edition,* 12:145-156. London: Hogarth Press, 1958.
_____ (1915), The Unconscious. *Standard Edition,* 14:159-215. London: Hogarth
    Press, 1957.
_____ (1917), A Metapsychological Supplement to the Theory of Dreams.
    Standard Edition, 14:217-236. London: Hogarth Press, 1957.
_____ (1923), The Ego and the Id. *Standard Edition,* 19:3-66. London: Hogarth
    Press, 1961.
_____ (1925), A Note upon the "Mystic Writing-Pad." *Standard Edition,*
    19:227-232. London: Hogarth Press, 1961.
_____ (1930), Civilization and Its Discontents. *Standard Edition,* 21:59-145.
    London: Hogarth Press, 1961.
_____ (1933), New Introductory Lectures on Psycho-Analysis. *Standard Edition,*
    22:3-182. London: Hogarth Press, 1964.
Klein, G. (1966), The Several Grades of Memory. In: *Psychoanalysis—A General
    Psychology: Essays in Honor of Heinz Hartmann,* ed. R. M. Loewenstein,
    L. M. Newman, M. Schur, & A. J. Solnit. New York: International Uni-
    versities Press, pp. 177-389.
Loewald, H. (1971), On Motivation and Instinct Theory. *The Psychoanalytic
    Study of the Child,* 26:91-128. New York: Quadrangle.

Mahler, M. (1968), *On Human Symbiosis and the Vicissitudes of Individuation.* New York: International Universities Press.

Paul, I. H. (1967), The Concept of Schema in Memory Theory. In: Motives and Thought: Psychoanalytic Essays in Honor of David Rapaport, ed. R. R. Holt. *Psychol. Issues,* Monogr. No. 18/19:218-158. New York: International Universities Press.

Rapaport, D. (1942), *Emotion and Memory,* rev. ed. New York: International Universities Press, 1950.

_____, ed. (1951), *Organization and Pathology of Thought: Selected Sources.* New York: Columbia University Press.

_____ (1957), A Theoretical Analysis of the Superego Concept. In: *The Collected Papers of David Rapaport,* ed. M. M. Gill. New York: Basic Books, 1967, pp. 685-709.

Sandler, J., & Rosenblatt, B. (1962), The Concept of the Representational World. *The Psychoanalytic Study of the Child,* 17:128-145. New York: International Universities Press.

Spitz, R. A. (1965), *The First Year of Life.* New York: International Universities Press.

Werner, H., & Kaplan, B. (1963), *Symbol Formation.* New York: Wiley.

Winnicott, D. W. (1958), *Collected Papers.* New York: Basic Books.

11

NOTES ON THE STUDY OF THE CREATIVE PROCESS

MARGARET BRENMAN-GIBSON

Let us begin by exploring what scientists usually call "methodological considerations," that is to say, the study of how to go about studying something. At the International Symposium on the Science of Creative Intelligence held in 1972 at the Massachusetts Institute of Technology, a distinguished professor of chemistry commented that "our vision of science must become a world view not limited to the West of the last 300 years." The response to his comment was the following:

> The Western scientific approach to knowledge is based on the nonvariability of the *objective* means of observation. The Eastern approach to knowledge is based on the nonvariability of the *subjective* means of observation.... Western science has continued to contribute to the advancement of civilization because good minds in the West have persistently applied the *objective* methodology of gaining knowledge; whereas Eastern civilization has not continued to contribute to the advancement of civilization, because good minds in the East have not persistently applied the *subjective* methodology of gaining knowledge.

This paper was first presented on August 15, 1973, at the Eleventh International Symposium for teachers on the Science of Creative Intelligence, held at the University of Maine under the auspices of Maharishi International University. It is part of a long-term inquiry into the nature of the creative process, supported in part by the Austen Riggs Center, the Robert P. Knight VFR Fund, the Foundations' Fund for Research in Psychiatry, the Foundation for Research in Psychoanalysis, the National Endowment for the Humanities, the Guggenheim Foundation, the Grant Foundation, the Lederer Foundation, the Whitney Foundation, and the American Association of University Women.

This was the view of Maharishi Mahesh Yogi, first a physicist, now a monk teaching the "science of creative intelligence" in every country of an increasingly embattled planet.

The essential point I want to make here is that in this, our twentieth century, these two approaches to knowledge are rapidly converging even within the scientific establishment, and that the time is overdue for good minds in the West consistently to apply the *subjective* as well as the *objective* method of gaining knowledge. In fact, not long ago during the course of an informal but exceedingly serious discussion of these heavy matters, a physicist of my acquaintance, the author of what is probably the best textbook on concepts and theories in the physical sciences, commented to me, "Perhaps you pioneers of inner space, not we of outer space, will be responsible for man's next step forward in universal knowledge. After all, are you psychoanalysts not past masters of the subjective means of observation, and is not man's consciousness the ultimate frontier?" I congratulated him, a hardheaded natural scientist, on thus coming to so radical an insight, and confessed that I had been for some time whispering the same idea to myself. I hastened to add, however, that, pleased as I was with his bouquet, I had to decline it, both for myself and for my colleagues, since the only "past masters" of the subjective means of observation that I knew anything about were not to be found among the members of my profession nor indeed of my civilization, but among those great teachers of the distant past, who were truly masters and who had made wide-ranging observations of consciousness — and of the mechanics of the thought process itself. I referred, of course, to authors of great Eastern bodies of thought such as the Vedas (a Sanskrit term whose root relates, please bear in mind for later consideration, to both *vis*ion and *wis*dom). Having made this large disclaimer, I went on to say that I was nevertheless convinced that the wheel of emotional, social, and intellectual history had come — in some desperation — full circle and that some of us in the much-maligned "soft sciences" of psychology, history, and sociology were beginning to explore, as a bona fide method, the approach to gaining knowledge that Erik Erikson (1969) has called "disciplined subjectivity." I then added that I myself—in the course of trying to study the complex and subtle creative process—saw no way other than the subjective to explore initially these states of consciousness. I made clear that I was not excluding the repeatable, quantifiable experiment, but that I regard this as probably a later—and not even an inevitable—phase of such a study. "Indeed," I added (quoting Jane Loevinger), "as in the battle of the sexes, so in the clinical research dialogue, if either side wins, the cause is lost" (see Loevinger, 1963; Brenman, 1947, 1948, 1952, 1959; Brenman et al., 1950; Wallerstein and Sampson, 1971).

My physicist friend interrupted, wondering whether I was aware that the growing significance in this century of the subjective aspect of gaining knowledge is by no means restricted to the "soft sciences" and that, at least since the renovation of quantum physics in the mid-twenties, the relationship of subject and object is increasingly taking center stage in all approaches to the gaining of knowledge. Moreover, he added, physicist Niels Bohr's concept of "complementarity" is unthinkable without the premise that *the means* of observation changes the phenomenon itself. In the course of the process of knowing, the knowledge obtained is clearly influenced by the structure and quality of the subject's consciousness as well as by the nature of the objective process.

In fact, in September of 1927—almost a half-century ago—at an International Congress of Physics in Como, Italy, Niels Bohr introduced for the first time in a public lecture his concept of complementarity. (The root of this word is completeness or wholeness.) He stressed that he wanted to make use in his presentation of only simple considerations and "without going into any details of technical mathematical character." The deceptively modest essay he delivered had indeed only a very few simple equations, and he stressed that he wanted merely to describe a general *point of view* which he hoped would bring harmony to the seemingly conflicting views taken by his fellow scientists. The heart of his "general point of view" lay in the implication that *"it is impossible to make any sharp separation between the behavior of atomic objects and the interaction with the instruments which serve to define the conditions under which the phenomena appear"* (Holton, 1970). Consequently, the totality of evidence obtained under different conditions must be fitted together as in a jigsaw puzzle and regarded as "complementary" (each element completes the other to comprise a total configuration) if we are to emerge with a picture of an object (Brenman, 1947, 1948). The scientist's own self—for example, a psychoanalyst's or a historian's personal relation to the life story or the piece of history he is studying (especially if he is an instrument in the actual gathering of data)—is then *part* of the totality of evidence.

As is so often the case in the history of ideas, no vocal objections were raised against Bohr's paper on complementarity, for few people appreciated its significance. One scientist was heard to mutter, "It will not induce one of us to change his own opinion about quantum mechanics." Needless to say, this threatened scientist was mistaken. Bohr himself, on the other hand, was so profoundly committed to the idea of complementarity that, when he was asked twenty years later to design a coat of arms for an award he was receiving, he put, at the center, a circle consisting of the mutually interlocked forms of Yin and Yang with the legend above it, "Contraria Sunt Complementa"!

Holton (1972) makes the arresting comment, "What Bohr was pointing to in 1927 was the curious realization that in the atomic domain, the only way the observer (including his equipment) can be uninvolved is if he observes nothing at all!" Bohr sums up the heart of the matter when he says:

> The study of nature is a study of artifacts that appear during an engagement between the scientist and the world in which he finds himself. And these artifacts themselves are seen through the lens of theory. Thus, different experimental conditions give different views of nature.... Our knowledge of light is contained in a number of statements that are seemingly contradictory, made on the basis of a variety of experiments under different conditions, and interpreted in the light of a complex of theories. When you ask, "What is light?" the answer is: the

observer, his various pieces and types of equipment, his experiments, his theories and models of interpretation, *and* whatever it may be that fills an otherwise empty room when the lightbulb is allowed to keep on burning. All this, together, is light [in Holton, 1972, pp. 385-386].

This is an extremely bold position, and it becomes increasingly so when it is carried into the behavioral sciences.[1]

Although Einstein remained overtly hostile to Bohr's point of view for many years, his own thought (in his nonscientific writings) basically shares much common philosophic ground. In 1930, only three years after Bohr's tentative Como statement, Einstein wrote: "The individual feels the vanity of human desires and aims, and the nobility and marvelous order which are revealed in nature and in the world of thought. He feels the individual destiny as an imprisonment and seeks to experience *the totality of existence as a unity full of significance*" (in Holton, 1972; italics mine).

In describing the "philosophical pilgrimage of Albert Einstein," with all its many radical reorganizations and powerful polarities, Holton has left no doubt that Einstein's guiding position was that the world of empirical observation must be subjugated by, and based in, the intuitive *wordless* leaps of intuition, and that an *aesthetic* attachment to "persuasive internal harmony as the warrant of truth" lay at the heart of his means of gaining knowledge. Although Einstein is on the one hand an "apostle of rationality," he steadily warns us not to "look in vain for logical bridges," but to make, when necessary, the great "leap" to basic principles: "To these elementary laws there leads no logical path, but only intuition supported by being sympathetically in touch with experience" (Holton, 1971-1972). A more beautiful way of saying the same thing — I quote now from the Rig Veda — is, "Knowledge is structured in consciousness.... He who knows it not, what can the word accomplish for him?"

The underlying meaning of these ancient sentences is

[1] Toward the end of his life, Bohr tried to apply his concept of complementarity to psychology and to sociology. These efforts remain in Danish, untranslated (G. Holton, personal communication).

repeatedly echoed in the discussion of the most methodologically sophisticated contemporary scientists, who are aware of the significance of the intuitive, holistic (lately called "nonlinear") functions in all creative processes, not simply in those of artists. Thus, Poincaré (1908) says: "The scientist does not study nature because it is useful; he studies it because he delights in it, and he delights in it because it is beautiful.... I do not speak here of that beauty which strikes the senses ... I mean that profounder beauty which comes from the harmonious order of the parts and which a pure intelligence can grasp" (pp. 366-367).

This statement is far more than a *façon de parler*. It goes to the core of the relationship between, on the one hand, the "logical, analytic-verbal" and, on the other, the "nonlinear" approach (Ornstein, 1972). It has equal implications for the relation of "fact" to "interpretation." Holton (1952) says, "... there is nothing more deceptive than facts," adding "... the pattern we perceive when we note 'a fact' is organized and interpreted by a whole system of attitudes and thoughts, memories, beliefs, and learned constructs. *It is thought that gives us eyes"* (p. 650; italics mine).

Michael Polanyi (1958), research physicist and chemist, and one of the most sweeping inquirers into the "nature and justification" of knowledge, also takes a sharp stand very early in his extraordinary work, *Personal Knowledge.*

> I start by rejecting the ideal of scientific detachment. In the exact sciences, this false ideal is perhaps harmless, for it is in fact disregarded there by scientists. But we shall see that it exercises a destructive influence in biology, psychology and sociology, and falsifies our whole outlook far beyond the domain of science. I want to establish an alternative ideal of knowledge, quite generally....
>
> I have used the findings of Gestalt psychology as my first clues to this conceptual reform. Scientists have run away from the philosophic implications of gestalt; I want to countenance them uncompromisingly. I regard knowing as an active comprehension of the things known, an action that requires skill. Skilful knowing and doing is performed by subordinating a set of particulars, as clues or tools, to the shaping of skilful achieve-

ment, whether practical or theoretical. We may then be said to become "subsidiarily aware" of these particulars within our "focal awareness" of the coherent entity that we achieve....

Such is the *personal participation* of the knower in all acts of understanding. But this does not make our understanding *subjective*. Comprehension is neither an arbitrary act nor a passive experience, but a responsible act claiming universal validity. Such knowing is indeed *objective* in the sense of establishing contact with a hidden reality; a contact that is defined as the condition for anticipating an indeterminate range of yet unknown (and perhaps yet inconceivable) true implications. It seems reasonable to describe this fusion of the personal and the objective as Personal Knowledge [pp. vii-viii].

In a later discussion, he goes even further:

We owe our mental existence predominantly to works of art, morality, religious worship, scientific theory and other articulate systems which we accept as our dwelling place and as the soil of our mental development. Objectivism has totally falsified our conception of truth, by exalting what we can know and prove, while covering up with ambiguous utterances all that we know and cannot prove, even though the latter knowledge underlies, and must ultimately set its seal to, all that we *can* prove. In trying to restrict our minds to the few things that are demonstrable, and therefore explicitly dubitable, it has overlooked the a-critical choices which determine the whole being of our minds and has rendered us incapable of acknowledging these vital choices [p. 286].

In view of this fiery manifesto, it has long been a source of puzzlement that Polanyi, who so well understands the dynamic relation of the "intellectual passions" of the knower to the object he contemplates, does not include the word *complementarity* in the index of this most beautiful and comprehensive discussion, nor is it to be found in his *The Tacit Dimension* (1966).

Equally surprising is the fact that the word appears neither in the index of any of Erikson's books nor in Robert Coles's (1970) excellent and careful summing up of the monumental edifice structured for the behavioral sciences by Erikson, whose theories constitute a quantum jump comparable to that of Bohr in physics, and for whom, similarly, the concept of complementarity is central. Perhaps it is inherent in the very nature of this sweeping point of view (so elusive that Einstein complained he could not fully get hold of Bohr's notion) that its overriding significance is only lately coming into focus.

That Erikson, himself, was aware (at least by 1968) of the importance of this point of view is evident from the fact that, in his distilled four-page entry "Identity, Psychosocial" in the *International Encyclopedia of the Social Sciences* (Erikson, 1968b), the word *complementarity* occurs three times: first, when he describes the relation between individual synthesis and the roles available in the community:

> The gradual development of a mature psychosocial identity, then, presupposes a community of people whose traditional values become significant to the growing person even as his growth assumes relevance for them. Mere "roles" that can be "played" interchangeably are obviously not sufficient for the social aspect of the equation. Only a hierarchical integration of roles that foster the vitality of individual growth as they represent a vital trend in the existing or developing social order can support identities. Psychosocial identity thus depends on a *complementarity of an inner (ego) synthesis in the individual and of role integration in his group* [p. 61; italics mine].

Secondly, when he touches on the relation between life history and history:

> Historical processes in turn seem vitally related to the demand for identity in each new generation; for to remain vital, societies must have at their disposal the energies and loyalties that emerge from the adolescent process: *as positive identities are "confirmed," societies are regenerated.* Where this process fails in too many individuals, a *historical crisis* becomes apparent. Psychosocial identity, therefore, can also be studied from the point of view of a *complementarity of life history and history* [p. 61; italics mine].

Finally, when he touches upon the relation of identity to collective ideology:

> In conclusion, however, we must remind ourselves that the *complementarity and relativity of individual and collective ideology* (which no doubt has emerged as part of man's socio-

genetic evolution) also bestows on man a most dangerous
potential, namely, a lastingly immature perspective on history.
Ideologies and identities, it is true, strive to overcome the
tyranny of old moralisms and dogmatisms; yet, they often revert
to these, seduced by the righteousness by which otherness is
repudiated when the conditions supporting a sense of identity
seem in danger. Old ideologists equipped with modern weapon-
ry could well become mankind's executioners. But a trend
toward an all-inclusive human identity, and with it a universal·
ethics, is equally discernible in the development of man, and it
may not be too utopian to assume that new and world-wide
systems of technology and communication may serve to make
this universality more manifest [p. 65; italics mine].

These considerations,[2] then, supply the matrix within which
my explorations of the universal creative process—and in
particular of the relation of playwright to audience[3]—occur.

It is not possible to discuss the relation of the playwright to
his audience without a long look back at the beginnings of the
sense of reality. Erikson, in his Godkin Lectures, delivered in
the spring of 1972 at Harvard, discusses the important observations of René Spitz (1965) on the role of vision as a prime
integrator of the as yet unconnected stimulations of taste,
audition, smell, and touch. According to Spitz's Denver
research team, by the third month the child's visual discrimination has matured enough so that he remembers a total
configuration.

Erikson comments:

> The motherly person, by letting her face, as it were, shine upon
> the newborn's searching eyes, and by letting herself be verified as
> a comprehensible image, thus may be called the first reality.
> And indeed, once infants can nurse with open eyes, they are apt
> to *stare continuously at the mother's face while at her breast.*
> Thus vision becomes the leading perceptual modality for the
> organization of the sensory space, for reality testing and for
> adaptation. To believe this, we only need to enumerate what

[2] This train of thought in general, and the significance of Polanyi's work in
particular, was initially stimulated in me by George Klein.

[3] In conjunction with my study of the creative process, I am currently completing
a three-volume psychohistorical biography of the late American playwright,
Clifford Odets, to be published in part in 1977.

vision manages to confirm: simultaneity in time as well as continuity in space, permanence of objects as well as coherence of the perceived field, the foreground figure and the fusion of the background, *the motion of some items against the stationary presence of others*. But there is also a strong suggestion that the perception of the mother as one who can be recognized even as she ever again loudly recognizes the infant by name, is indeed basic to the establishment of the rudiments of hope. As Joan Erikson [1966] puts it in an essay called "Eye to Eye," "We began life with this relatedness to eyes.... It is with the eyes that concern and love are communicated, and distance and anger as well. Growing maturity does not alter this eye-centeredness, for all through life our intercourse with others is eye-focused: the eye that blesses and curses."[4]

Our language consistently reflects the central evolutionary importance of vision in all of our being and living: man is the farsighted animal as well as the one with foresight and hindsight (Erikson, 1972). When he thinks and understands something, he has an "insight" and exclaims, "I see!" He is "blind" to things he wants to ignore, but "amazing grace" — as the folk hymn has it — opens his eyes. We call someone who appears to comprehend the totality of life experience a "rishi" which means "seer," a great "seer" as being a "maharishi."

A trip to two dictionaries brings, moreover, the news that the words "theater" and "theory" are first cousins, both deriving from words that mean "to see, to view" (*theasthai*) or "to look at" (*theorein*). Both derive from a root "referring to a *visualized* sphere which arouses fascination, belief or wonder" and which was termed "a beholding, a spectacle." One branch became *theater*, where we watch the enactment by players of

---

[4] Let me point out here the relationship between the first-person singular pronoun ("I") which houses the central core of the self-identity, and the word "E-Y-E," which appears developmentally to do the same. The eye is the intermediary between outer and inner light. Indeed, *the* narrative commences with, "Let there be light." Christ adds, "The eye is the light of the body; if therefore thine eye be single, thy whole body shall be full of light" (Matt:6:22). In contemporary and less beautiful terms: if thine "I" be "single," that is to say, if you have succeeded in integrating (compare the word "integer") the civil strife within yourself into a harmonious unity, a cohesive self-identity, you will be "actualized," realized. In the language of ancient wisdom, you will be an "enlightened" person, a whole person lit from within.

an unfolding *make-believe* reality, an order or a form created by the playwright; the other became *theory*, where we "look at" ("speculate" upon) a body of facts to determine what "is" the already-existing order governing their relations to one another. In both theater and theory, thus, the form is initially *created* by the visionary, be he theater-man, theologian-prophet, or theoretician. Indeed, the prefix, "theo" ("thea" is the feminine form) is defined as "a combining form meaning God."[5] Clearly, here—with vision as the early prime integrator—is something at the heart of both the "creative" and the "religious" impulse.[6]

Erikson (1972) continues with the early development of our visionary propensity: "I would postulate that the infant's *scanning* search with his eyes and his recognition of what is continuously lost and found again, is the first *significant interplay* (just consider its later dramatization in peek-a-boo)."

For my purpose here, this first dramatization in the game of peekaboo is the paradigm for the transaction between playwright and audience. Their mutual recognition is critical to the transaction. Erikson's epigenetic model continues:

> It is crowned by the smile aroused at twelve weeks of age by the mother's face and, of course, itself a potent evocatory stimulus in that it enhances the parental person's wish for finding such recognition (in every sense of the word) as only the newborn can confirm. The smiling infant has the power to make us feel central and new, for it gives us, too, hope for a new beginning. . . .

[5] When a greeting is offered in India—palms together in prayer—the greeter is saying, "I perceive the God in you." This greeting goes beyond the Western handshake, which demonstrates only, "I have no weapon." The Indian greeting is a quiet gesture, similar in form to an audience's applause. Members of an appreciative audience also bring their palms together, loudly enough, however, to be heard by the performer or playwright, to whom they are also saying, "We perceive the God in you." Biologist René Dubos (1972) reflects the same view in *The God Within*.

[6] Further confirmation of this fact is Webster's listing of the words miracle (*mirar* means "to look") and wonder as synonyms. Like the word theater, both of these are direct descendants of words referring to that earliest zone of intake (besides the mouth), the eyes.

All this, however, is basic not only for a sense of reality giving meaning to what we are "in touch with" and what we are learning to "grasp" but also for a certain *visionary propensity,* by which man in all subsequent stages imagines, dreams of, and plans situations which restore to him a measure of feeling central and at home in his sphere of living (rather than peripheral and alienated), active and effective (rather than inactivated and helpless), selectively aware (rather than overwhelmed by impressions) and, above all, chosen and confirmed (rather than bypassed and abandoned).[7]

That last is a long and weighty sentence, and I should like to go back through it slowly: Let us start with the word imagines: at once, we see in it the word image, again a visual word, which means, according to the dictionary, "that faculty of the mind by which we conceive the absent as if it were present," or alternatively, "the creative faculty." The word dream is defined as a *"vision* during sleep," and the words dreamer and visionary are interchangeable in ordinary usage. The word plan moves us forward into *logical activity.* Thus, Erikson's sentence adds up to the fact that it is man's nature, by way of his *visionary propensity,* to try in a multitude of forms to resolve dualities and to dissolve boundaries, in order to restore a measure of that harmonious earliest reality (with its sense of unified wholeness and centrality), which we can presume was all-encompassing in the warm waters of the womb and thereafter re-experienced in the relation of the nursing infant to his mother as he looks at her face beaming down upon him. This boundaryless unity is perhaps the prototype of feeling "at home with everything" and in harmony with the universe. Subjectively, it is what Freud called an "oceanic consciousness." We cannot set up critical or quantifiable experiments with such hypotheses. We can only ask, "How does this all hang together?"

A last word about the clause "which *restore[s]* to him a measure of feeling central and at home in his sphere of living": This presumes (as did Freud when he asked what happens to

---

[7] Dr. Norman Reider points out the ancient Hebrew prayer, "May the Lord make his face to shine upon thee" (personal communication).

the shining intelligence of the child) that this initial, innocent sense of unified wholeness and freshness of perception is lost — at least temporarily — by most of us as we grow older. In fact, the Denver researchers have reported a specific "eighth-month anxiety" in which the infant reacts to strangers with a "tearful outburst" or an "apprehensive frown," an early fear of the unfamiliar that is likely an "infantile form of alienation" (Erikson, 1972). It is a mixture of anxiety and rage at being abandoned by what is familiar — or, on a more complex level, the fear of being "alone in a universe which does not care, a universe without a divine counterplayer, without charity." This anxiety at having to organize the unfamiliar into the safely familiar — a task usually begun at eight months — reaches an acute and often painful peak during young adulthood when we are called upon by the developmental process to reorganize into a new whole within ourselves an unprecedented number of complex identity elements and fragments.

Indeed, the poet and painter William Blake saw the Fall of Man not in original sin but in just this *loss of unified wholeness,* rent by successive subdivisions into a battleground for what we call "identity elements" (Erikson, 1968a, 1968b). In his creative struggles to restore that sense of being central and "at home in life," Blake's mythological personages "struggle in a primeval world of frozen depths, tormenting fires and globules of blood." When he believed the French Revolution promised to reclaim for mankind a transcendent spiritual harmony, he wrote his "Songs of Innocence" ("The vegetative universe opens like a flower from the earth's center in which is Eternity"). Five years later, despairing about the failure, as he saw it, of the French Revolution, he wrote the disillusioned "Songs of Experience" ("Is this a holy thing to see / In a rich and fruitful land / Babes reduc'd to misery / Fed with cold and usurous hand?").

All his life Blake struggled with the Christian religion: he could not abide the notion of a vengeful God and saw the essence of man's existential struggle precisely in his persistent efforts to free himself from the suffering bondage of these warring inner subdivisions by evolving a new gestalt, a new edition of the self. It is no accident that in recent years, when there appears to be a discernible trend toward a new and all-inclusive human collective identity, Blake has become so beloved a poet, especially among young people.

Like all artists, he used his external perceptions as a kind of trigger to permit the flow of his creative intelligence to make an aesthetic form that would, first, resolve the dualities within himself: a process called by this generation of the young, "Getting it together." One must interject here that when such efforts succeed in re-establishing a man's inner wholeness — and his consequent peace and freedom — *only* for himself, we wish him well, but we do not call him an artist. It is no more than a "self-wholing" (or self-healing) process: The *Oxford English Dictionary* and the *Dictionary of Etymology* tell us that the words whole, holy, and heal derive from a common root, referring to a complex unity which is "uninjured" or undivided. "Go in peace and be whole," said Mark. It is when a man's creativity transcends his individual necessities and offers the rest of us a vision whereby we, too, can restore such wholeness — with its attendant surcease, however temporary, from the civil war *within ourselves* — that we attend to his theories or his spiritual visions, make pilgrimages to look at his paintings, or sacrifice money and time to listen to his teachings, hear his music, or watch his plays. *The creator achieves for us what we struggle (often in vain) to achieve for ourselves: a form which supplies that freedom from a painful duality (conflict) and that restoration of inner unity toward which we steadily strain.* His gift enables him to integrate, at least for a time, not only his own stressed energy system, but ours. The playwright, in particular, projects visually onto the stage all of the steps, including, of course, the climax, in the resolution of that system-in-conflict.

By techniques that students of language are barely beginning to find words for, the playwright controls the sustained dynamic tension we call "suspense," as he sees to it that his audience is kept dangerously hanging, and hoping that neither pole of his externalized conflict will be arbitrarily or prematurely ploughed under. If the playwright cannot endure either the *content* of the risky struggle or the ambiguity of keeping both sides of a conflict alive, he schematically suppresses one side of the contest and a deadly stasis occurs: now there is no longer a creative process. This is what happens in an "agit-prop" play, that is to say, a work primarily designed for "agitation and propaganda," the usual art form of any "totalistic" solution, be it fascist or communist. In such message plays, the playwright works with only a fraction of himself, and the audience-onlooker also responds fractionally.

Only, for example, when a representative playwright of rare talent, like Clifford Odets, writes such a propaganda play— like his *Waiting for Lefty,* dashed off over a weekend—does the audience remember it. Although writers of college texts have routinely chosen *Lefty* to immortalize Odets as the American "playwright of the thirties," he was in fact at his aesthetic worst in a work such as this. *Lefty* is a prime instance of a simplistic play in which one pole of the contest is suppressed, thus precluding the depth and richness of a genuinely creative production. Its initial impact doubtless stemmed from the fact that its representative message for the Depression era contained archetypal meanings and lively human color.

In his later plays, Odets sustains, like an expert juggler, not only the opposite poles of a protracted struggle, but also those *within* a single character, giving each actor the rich wholeness of an entire person, not a "part-aspect" or an identity fragment, and giving the work the fullness of life, a process that steadily reintegrates on successive levels. Unlike "improvisers" in the contemporary theater[8] or children who—in the

---

[8] The uncurtained contemporary improvisatory theater is understandable—as one expression of the current revulsion against traditional art forms and theories alike—as a desperate effort to return to the innocence of play in the sandbox, where the participants alone are involved in their creations and destructions and where it does not matter that an onlooker may be indifferent to this experimental problem-solving.

In a time that shows all the earmarks of a civilization on its way out, the improvisatory theater has the merit of not yet having lost all hope, as the theaters of "absurdity" and "cruelty" clearly have. (Cf. Langer [1958]) on cruelty at the end of the Roman empire.) Like all apocalyptic visionaries, the latter delight in the

course of resolving a conflict—move *themselves* about in their sandbox dramas, a canny playwright is able to sustain, through his "make-believe" characters, the vicarious participation and emotional involvement of his audience in the contest he has created. Throughout, the audience's engagement in the created contest is imaginary and *symbolic,* taking place strictly on the level of what Freud described as "experimental action," that is to say, thought.[9]

---

destructive side of the fantasy. The gifted and intrepid Peter Brook, however, in his ambitious International Center for Theater Research, is trying institutionally to sustain and renew hope both for the theater and for life itself, by creating a form that is at once an effort to return to an archetypal theater—simultaneously epic and religious—and to anticipate a future in which Man has at last evolved a unified multinational peaceful brotherhood. It is not coincidental that Brook and his collaborator, poet Ted Hughes, conceive their productions within an Eastern vision of life, which seeks "self-perfection through self-knowledge and in the union of the mind with the Divine."

In his initial experimental piece, staged outdoors by actors from all corners of the earth, at the top of the "Mountain of Mercy," overlooking ancient Iranian ruins, once the imperial capital of Persia (and viewed by Brook as the meeting place of the Occident and the Orient), he has staged what he called "an experiment in pure communication." Deliberately inventing a new verbal and nonverbal language called "Orghast," Hughes has constructed a modern passion play—without linear plot—which includes all the archetypal themes of Man: conflict of father and son, promethean hubris, retribution by gods and by women, existential dread, and ultimate redemption. This lavish impulse, simultaneously theatrical and religious in intent (and no less desperate than the off-Broadway sandbox improvisations), has received generous financing from several foundations in its attempt to explore further, in what they consider still-innocent areas of Africa, the possibilities of passing naturally, even as children play, from the world of everyday to the world of imagination and back (*New York Times,* 4/18/71). The Brook-Hughes experiments appear to be significantly different, however, both from the impoverished contemporary theater as well as from traditional theater, which commences with a clear boundary between audience and players, a boundary that progressively disappears as, by dint of the playwright's gift, the audience passes willingly, indeed eagerly, with him *from one level of unconscious conflict to another,* until, at the end, players and audience have merged, an equilibrium is reached, and, as Odets put it, "the proscenium arch disappears." In Brook's work, the dividing lines between players and audience are, from the outset, fluid. *He is reaching toward a state of consciousness qualitatively different from the one to which we are accustomed.*

[9] It is noteworthy that the word actor refers not only to one who takes *real* action but also to one who "makes believe" he is taking real action. The same word has thus opposite meanings. (Cf. Freud, 1910.)

The paradigm of the duality that underlies *all* conflict is the "contest"—be it between cocks,[10] gladiators, pugilists, a bull and a man, a god and a man, lions and Christians, football teams, cops and robbers, mythic heroes, armies of Good and Evil, between those parts of one's developing self called "identity elements" (Erikson, 1968a, 1968b), or between the protagonists in a play. This duality has universally found a place in man's adult, often ritualized, re-enactments of his part and his anticipations of the future (Manuel and Manuel, 1972). As a problem-finding, problem-making, problem-solving animal he takes pleasure early in life in setting up such contests, nonverbal and verbal, in which he may particpate directly or, vicariously, as spectator. We have seen that, as he moves from "child's play" to adult "plays," his requirements for intricacy, subtlety, embellishment, and complexity in externalized conflicts develop with the sophistication of his experience; these needs are closely tied to his own personal stage of verbal and moral development, to his sensitivity to form, and to the prevailing symbols of his culture. Thus, whereas a child's wish to prove superior to his own sense of helplessness is realized in the drama of Superman, who "flies through the air with the greatest of ease," the resolution of *this* hero's conflicts offers no relief, no reassurance, no pleasure, no transcendence to an audience who cannot identify with the simple poles of the primitive yearning and the evil forces opposing it. The child, who can accomplish this identification, is as transfixed by this vision of reality as is his father by a football game.

The resolution of *any* contest (inner or outer) may lie in victory, defeat, mutual withdrawal, or in an expansionary synthesis of the antagonists. Any one of these outcomes, as in comedy, may issue in a heightened sense of well-being or aliveness, or in a more interesting or a funnier reality. The ultimate outcome of any such "unity in diversity" is the

[10] Clifford Geertz's (1972) account of "The Balinese Cockfight" beautifully pulls together the hierarchical range of psychosocial integrations that converge in this bloody drama, regularly staged by these dreamy, beautiful people whose culture otherwise expresses a revulsion against violence.

achievement of equilibrium, however, and the only one *finally free of conflict* (of duality) occurs when all contestants perish; only then is there a state of no-contest.[11] Thus, Aristotle's classic definition of art as purgative, by the way of the "pity and terror" of tragedy, becomes finally understandable: all possibility of suffering ends if the conflict cannot continue. If all the contestants are dead, it is clear the struggle is over. The catharsis in tragedy or the purgative "discharge of affect" occurs only when the playwright succeeds in extracting from this manifest absurdity of life (that is to say, from a "play" whose end is inevitably the death of all the characters) some antidote for the archetypal despair over mortality, some redemptive meaning that transcends the dumb, brutish ugliness of death,[12] and offers what Lifton (1968) calls a "symbolic immortality."

Only a great playwright — and it is no accident there are so few of these in the public and communal art form of theater — dares seriously to create this kind of final resolution, which resolves all internal conflict. In all of history, so grave an undertaking has been left largely to writers of scripture, whose visions of reality — initially orally transmitted — are usually recorded later as poetry. By its very nature and form, poetry (like music) also provides archetypal meanings, a potent antidote to the anticipation of an end to bounded individual consciousness.

When the playwright usurps such "divine leeway" for the creation and destruction of personages in conflict, he inevitably risks an aggravation within himself of the archetypal guilt, terror, and vulnerability which beset him when, of old, he fantasied replacing, or did in fact impersonate, the all-

[11] After writing this section, I came upon Frank and Fritzie Manuel's (1972) scholarly and insightful "Sketch for a Natural History of Paradise," in which, according to Zoroastrian doctrine, the conflictless "paradise of the other world," known as the final "Apatiyarakih," has been translated as "the state-of-no-more-being-contested."

[12] Dr. James Thatcher (personal communication) points out that such transcendence in Greek tragedy was seen as flowing from the classic doctrine "Know thyself." If such counsel could be taken seriously, the "tragic flaw" in man might eventuate not in ultimate despair but in an ennobled sense of meaningfulness.

powerful creator (originator) in his child-world, namely his father. The artist's propitiations are not, as Emerson (1841) says, like those of "common souls," in what he *does*. Being a "nobler soul," he pays with what he *is*. Prometheus is doomed to eternal torture for stealing Zeus's precious fire of creation.

It appears that this successive creating and destroying is fundamental to all creative processes, whether in the natural universe or within the artist. To be sure, the degree of conflict attached to assuming such responsibility for creating and destroying is linked to the social role of the artist in his own time and to the communality and cohesiveness of the forms and symbols in his culture.[13] Thus, when the vitality of Christianity as a social institution was at its height, painters and sculptors, who were directly "serving God" in their work, had little need for strictly personal expression or innovation in their symbols and forms. At the other end of this continuum stands a romantic artist like Beethoven, of whom Leonard Bernstein says, "The man rejected, rewrote, scratched out, tore up, and sometimes altered a passage as many as twenty times . . ."—a bloody record of a tremendous *inner battle*. In pages upon pages of worked-over "feverish scrawls," his abandoned thematic ideas illustrate precisely—as in a play's unfolding—the same necessity to find the "inevitable" passage from one level of conflict to another. An initial symmetry is, for example, rejected for it permits of no climactic "build." Toward the end of the first movement of Beethoven's manuscript score for his Fifth Symphony, one ending is rejected as "too abrupt," another as "too pretentious"; but the final form is then "right as rain" (Bernstein, n.d.).

In great music, however, unlike great drama (with few exceptions), the stage is *not* left "strewn with corpses." The final movement of a symphony—usually preceded by the slow, sad, struggling movement—brings it all together in allegro affirmation. It is not clear why there should be this dif-

---

[13] In a provocative and lively article, Lifton (1973), from another point of view, discusses the process of "communal resymbolization" in the struggle for cultural rebirth.

ference between music and drama. Perhaps it is easier to provide a joyous and redemptive transcendence — whether of death or of life's pain — in sounds than in words or staged actions. Indeed, it is more than a little awkward to read *in words* Conductor Josef Krips's (1954) description of his experience of Beethoven's Ninth Symphony, in which he says that in the Scherzo and in the finale (the Ode to Joy), he sees Beethoven "entering Heaven, free at last." Nonetheless, he is describing the listener's experience.

Those contemporary painters who have not yet given up to despair talk also of their successive creations, destructions, and re-creations on canvas. Some permit the residues of this struggle to remain visible in the final product. Others, like the Dutch classicist Piet Mondrian, having reached an ultimate and satisfying resolution of forces, *want no sign of the preceding struggle visible on the canvas.* Mondrian, for example (in his later work), always made a precise copy of the final arrangement of his areas, taping the components of the original in place. No bumps, overpainted layers, erasures, or jarring signs of underlying struggle were allowed to remain. The final painting, like that of his esteemed ancestor Vermeer, must be serene, cool, and self-contained. The only example in existence of a Mondrian in which the underlying struggle remains visible is an unfinished work presently owned by the Museum of Modern Art, a painting on which he was at work just before he died. It is thickly overpainted and scarred. A Picasso or van Gogh on the other hand — like all romantic artists fully intends that all the signs of the painful struggle *be* visible, and their overpainting is never obliterated. Leo Garel has called my attention to a letter to James Johnson Sweeney in which Mondrian wrote: "My style of painting is this: First I had to annihilate the form by reducing it to lines, colors and circles . . . then I had to destroy the color. . . . Then I had to tear out the circles to leave only the planes and lines . . . My art consists of the purest possible line and proportion."

Expressions like annihilate, destroy, tear out, confirm Mondrian's experience of the destructive phase of the creative

process, which then concludes in the creation of his characteristic appearance of order and serenity.

The price for the hubris of taking into his own hands such
godlike powers of creation and destruction is often experienced by the romantic artist—that is, by a creator who works
essentially from his *individual* state of being—as exorbitant.
His chronic, usually unconscious, guilt—often expressed in
alcoholism or in psychosomatic difficulties—combines with
the "unreality," or what he himself often regards as the
"detachment" or "shallowness," in his ordinary human relationships. Aware, however, that he is most himself, most alive,
most whole, *only* when engaged in such creations and destructions of universes, the guilt is frequently compounded, leaving
him feeling, *between creations,* not only drained, but isolated
and (worst of all) fragmented and meaningless.

In eras when social institutions have a communal and
cohesive vitality, it is likely that such postpartum depressions
are less frequently seen in creators. Obviously, this is a
difficult problem for study. Playwright Clifford Odets (1950?),
in a scribbled note, wrote: "If, as an artist, a contradiction did
not exist in myself, I would invent one. In fact I have. True of
romantic artist. He is his own material. His art is autobiographical, unlike the classicist. Romantic has to hold oppo-
sites in balance . . . centripetal and centrifugal and possibility
of destruction."

He often deplored the chasm between his incapacity to
manage his transactions with ready-made living persons in
"real life" and his ability, as playwright-creator, to "bring to
life" characters on the stage. When, however, he not only
created his Adams and his Eves as playwright but, as director,
also *controlled* each of their onstage "moves" within the grand
and expansive design of his Heaven and Earth, he felt, he said,
"truly like a God."[14] During such brief intervals, the price

---

[14] Poet Robinson Jeffers has celebrated that "divine leeway," that elbowroom
within a psychic system in which there is this kind of "play and dis-play"
(Maharishi, 1972); it allows for precisely that excess, that rich, free, plenteousness
that characterizes a cornucopia, a land of milk and honey, an art work or, indeed,
any unified, free, energy system that can move or overflow in any direction because

appeared not too high. In times of fullness and creative fertility, the expansive and prodigal overflow of lovingly created characters, of the ornamentation of poetic image, irony, metaphor, and humor issued in a sense of power and affluent well-being he knew at no other time.

We do not yet know what are the *necessary and sufficient* conditions that create sufficient "play" in a system to permit this "divine leeway" which issues in so free and extravagant a flow of an artist's gift. That the same artist has cycles of sterility and of productivity can be made, however, more comprehensible by the pursuit of a general hypothesis: *When the artist's capacity to tolerate internal incompatibilities or polarities is high—while seeking a formal integration that will synthesize and resolve them—he can afford to "open channels."*

There is then a free flow in two directions: first in the intake of "raw material" by way of his (probably genetic) especially porous perceptual apparatus; and then in an outpouring of creative intelligence from a variety of integrative synthesizing levels, unconscious fantasy and conscious craft, often described as "playful." When he is "full" and these channels are open, he is prodigally inventive, a veritable spendthrift who can afford the luxury of flinging "secret rainbows" even on the cones of shells so deep in the sea that no one sees them. When,

---

nothing is bound or "locked in." Illustrating this very fullness, the extravagance of which he sings, Jeffers (1941, p. 16)* writes:

Is it not by his high superfluousness we know
Our God? For to equal a need
Is natural, animal, mineral: but to fling
Rainbows over the rain
And beauty above the moon, and secret rainbows
On the domes of deep sea-shells,
And make the necessary embrace of breeding
Beautiful also as fire,
Not even the weeds to multiply without blossom
Nor the birds without music:
There is the great humaneness at the heart of things,
The extravagant kindness, the fountain
Humanity can understand, and would flow likewise
If power and desire were perch-mates.

*Copyright 1941 and renewed 1969 by Donnan Jeffers and Garth Jeffers. Reprinted from *Selected Poems*, by Robinson Jeffers, by permission of Random House, Inc.

however, *his capacity to tolerate ambiguity or conflict (or, actively to seek its resolution by way of form) is for any reason weakened, the entire system freezes, it loses its "play," and the "divine leeway" necessary for creation is temporarily lost. He lacks anchorage and is creatively adrift. Everything is defensively "locked up tight" and rigidly in its place. There is no free play" in the system.*[15] Channels close, again in both directions: little gets in and little gets out. The very thought patterns that make for creative solutions are unavailable. The artist may, in such a time, produce impoverished, constipated, or diarrheic art and feel he is in danger of death from starvation or self-poisoning. Impulsive action or a ritually compulsive making of order, a tightening of rules, replaces creativity. Much the same methods are used on a collective basis in totalitarian states, none of which will be remembered for their art works.

The immediate stimulus for such an opening or closing is little understood in its detail. There is no doubt, however, that the artist's need for confirming response *from some audience* plays a central role in the re-establishment of lost "free play" in a psychic system.[16] The child need satisfy *only* himself in his play construction: the potential psychotic is successful if he can ward off—with his delusional constructions—an affect storm; the well-dreamed dream can be forgotten, but the art work, by the way of form, must transcend its origins and find resonance in other human beings. This is especially true for the playwright, an artist who works, as it were, with his audience looking over his shoulder. He can afford fewer risks and rarely takes the chance, as does the poet, of being

[15] It is worth pursuing here the roots and usages of the word free. The most general meaning (as in a freely moving part in a mechanical system) is when one part of the system is not rigidly bonded (not bound) to another, or "not subject to control from the outside." Thus, the part moves easily, freely; it is not "fixed." To move to another level: an Old English word for love is "freon," from which derives the word freend or, later, friend, that is to say, "a beloved person *freely* joined to another in mutual benevolence," not like a slave to master in bondage!

[16] These issues are close relatives of the problems discussed under "automatization" and "deautomatization" by Gill and Brenman (1959).

ridiculous. It is possible this is a significant factor in the relative paucity of great work in this medium.

Thus we frequently hear from an artist that a work usually gets started not at all by way of "emotion recollected in tranquillity," but from the discovery of a wedge, a "way in," a formal container for the underlying struggle: an image, a rhythmic word-pattern, a single metaphor. Mallarmé quipped, when Degas complained to him that he would like to write a poem but had no ideas: "Poems are not made of ideas, my friend, but of words."

Each medium, each material, has its own life, its own inherent properties and natural laws, be they in the very nature of space, time, light, sound, motion, language, rhythm, or tensile strength. *A mastery of the "laws" of his medium—about which we can say little, but without which there can be no form—is thus inseparable from the artist's effort to synthesize the incompatibilities steadily seeking union within him.* Clearly, I speak here of the work of sophisticated artists, not of naïve primitives whose very lack of skill allows them to work spontaneously "in tune" with their medium.

A painter "playing with two greens," or fascinated with the quality of light on identical haystacks at half-hour intervals, or even exploring a new texture of canvas or paper—or a composer setting up for himself the "technical" problem of writing an entire piece for the left hand—may only thus insure the safe passage of otherwise intolerable affect. *The characters in a play "come to life" only when the playwright sees a way to contain them.* If, for whatever reason, he cannot find a sufficient "container" for the flood of feeling to be released in *him,* they remain puppets or what Clifford Odets called "my matchsticks." When Odets's "matchsticks" rose up from his desk and confronted one another in the language provided them by his infallible ear, he knew he had found the *form* for a new play.

In a diary, he wrote (1958), "I will reveal America to itself by revealing myself to myself." But it was far more than simple revelation. It was a matter also of restoration. Odets became a culture hero in the thirties not simply because he *revealed* a generation to itself, but because his plays restored a lost sense of "at home-ness" to that generation; he provided the same joyful, mutual recognition between his characters and his audience that we earlier described as that first fundamental "interplay": between mother and infant. Alfred Kazin (1965) has put it well:

> ... watching my mother and father and uncles and aunts occupying the stage in [Odets's] *Awake and Sing* by as much right as if they were Hamlet and Lear, I understood at last. It was all one, as I had always known. Art and truth and hope could yet come together—if a real writer was their meeting place ... I had never seen actors on the stage and an audience in the theater come together with such a happy shock.[17] The excitement in the theater was instant proof that if a *writer* occupied it, the audience felt joy as a rush of power....
>
> The unmistakable and surging march of history might yet pass through me. There seemed to be no division between my effort at personal liberation and the apparent effort of humanity to deliver itself [p. 82].

The fulfillment of this dissolution of the boundaries separating the playwright from his audience (as Odets put it, "I want to make the proscenium arch disappear") issues from the fact that existential separateness is transcended in both playwright and audience; as he breathes life into each of his own fragmented and conflicted identity elements, thus creating on the stage a *distribution of himself* in a cast of characters whose conflicts and resolutions with one another are projections of his inner drama, the playwright is providing an antidote for the archetypal alienation described in the baby, the fear of

---

[17] Four decades later, American blacks would experience a similar shock of recognition toward black playwright Lorraine Hansberry. A black actress performing in one of the plays has written of the audience response: "Oh Yes! We knew each other. We were with family. They laughed easily and gratefully in recognition and, though the cast of *To Be Young, Gifted and Black* is composed of both black and white actors, there was an additional dimension in the communication between the blacks in the audience and the blacks on the stage. So we, as Black artists expressing the Black experience, accepted their laughter easily and gratefully in recognition, and the joy, joy, joy of recognition was almost overwhelming...." (*New York Times*, April 18, 1971, p. 3).

being "alone in a universe which does not care, a universe without a divine counterplayer, without charity" (Erikson, 1972). It is of the nature of love.

In a body of work only lately being rediscovered, Odets steadily *seeks this mutual recognition between playwright and audience* by way of a steady reiteration of his faith that man can realize his boundless potential, that he *can* achieve fulfillment "in conformity with the laws of his Nature," if he will but see what it is that blocks natural fulfillment and allows suffering to continue. Like Freud, he mourned the transformation of the child's "shining intelligence" into the dullness of the average adult.

Early in his career as a playwright, he saw the roadblocks to such fulfillment in rather simple economic and political forms. In the previously mentioned *Waiting for Lefty,* for example, union members await their leader, who is found shot through the head. In a surge of hopeful activity, they decide to strike for their demands. The production of this simple play is one of the landmarks in the history of American theater. Odets's by now classic sentence, "Life shouldn't be printed on dollar bills," from his more complex work *Awake and Sing!,* is a more significant distillation of the beginning of the end of the American materialist dream—what Arthur Miller has called the dream of "a nest of peddlers." Again, however, its very title, *Awake and Sing!,* carries a positive and hopeful resonance of a wakeful, aware life—filled with morning light and the creative self-expression of music.[18]

In his well-known *Golden Boy,* written two years later, depicting the highly representative American struggle be-tween creative self-realization and the values of material success, the hero is promised he will "eat the best, sleep the best and wear the best" if he will stop protecting his creative

[18] It is remarkable how often the words night and darkness and sleep begin to come into the titles created by American writers since 1940, as we have moved into a time of building stress in the seats of power and authority, continuous war, and threats of nuclear and ecological disaster. Odets himself contributed three such titles: *Night Music, Clash by Night,* and *I Can't Sleep.* (Compare *Long Day's Journey Into Night, There Shall Be No Night, Darkness at Noon.*)

musician's hands and enter wholeheartedly into the brutal, indeed, the murderous, competition of the well-paid prize-fight ring. The protagonist chooses to become a well-paid fighter-killer, and is incinerated at the play's end in his fast, new, expensive car. It is clear from this work that on some level of consciousness Odets knew his own creativity was now in highest jeopardy.[19]

Two decades later, after finally surrendering his creative powers to the motion-picture industry, Odets (1958) scribbled a note in his diary:

Art as mitigation and location of self. To construct an art work, a novel, play or symphony is to construct an ideal world. It is to build (domain, domicile) an ideal society, home or place, and while, it is true, ideal events may not take place there, the abstracting of material, placing of events, the shaping and constructing, the god-like functioning and clarity, the unhampered activity, the joining and putting together—all these and more represent ideality and ideal behavior—the artist functioning at his most fruitful and human level. Then, may we not say that the creative person is time and again creating a place or home in which he fits himself both inside and out in every sense. And is it not perhaps true that the romantic artist, usually deprived and homeless in the early years is thus a home-maker? *But* that when the art work fails (is rejected or unaccepted) he has again lost his original "home"? And that, even when it is accepted and "successful" that it is in one way or another taken away from him?
A director takes the play (or movie) out of his hands and some-one else has taken over or invaded the home and one is as bereft and as empty as before.
In my case I do not start well or do start well, but the nearer to completion I get the slower and more reluctant and begrudging I become of time spent on that work. I tend not to finish the work! Don't I feel that this too will be taken from me and that I who have constructed the home or nest will be pushed out—that others or another will occupy and run it and that once again oh,

[19]In another place (1971) I have developed several hypotheses regarding the creative process in playwrighting: (1) that whatever else a play is "about," it reflects the playwright's deepest views and struggles regarding *his own* creativity; (2) that the characters are projections of the playwright's identity elements and fragments; and (3) that the themes or meanings may be deciphered on an archetypal, a representative, and an idiosyncratic level.

God, I am homeless and lonely and no work will change my status of dispossession.
Finally, does not very hope itself sicken and die and one can no longer lift his arms in the task of construction since the end-time is always and forever so abortive?

This suffering statement of the artist struggling to be a "homemaker" (no longer able to construct a stable home) does not simply sum up the accumulated stress of an individual artist. It is a representative distillation of a mounting *collective* stress during one of the recurring periods of "times out of joint." It is a historical, communal resurgence of the alienation of the eight-month-old infant who finds himself cut off (Erikson, 1972).

In my effort, over the last several years, to put together the jigsaw puzzle of this artist's life crises and his work, it has become increasingly clear that both epitomize one phase of an American collective identity that is slowly drawing to an end, creating a psychological and moral (or better, an ethical) vacuum — and in this instance, a terror — that history repeatedly creates.

We have learned from Erikson's (1958) study of Martin Luther that, when such a vacuum occurs, there arises a person with highly specific personal gifts whose solutions to his own spiritual crises (that is, his restoration of unity and freedom to himself, whether temporary or permanent) are sufficiently representative for the hungers and thirsts of his contemporaries that he is elevated to a position of leadership, often achieving historical "greatness." It is my conviction that the leader's transactions with his followers are not *qualitatively* different from the exchange I have been describing between a playwright and the audience to whom he "gives voice." In both instances, it is a *vision* of life which is communicated with a singular form and conviction.[20] Now, we are launched into

[20] There is no doubt that what Alfred Kazin called the "gift of conviction" in the artist is matched by the total belief of the leader in himself as a chosen instrument. He typically radiates a buoyant confidence and faith. Kierkegaard said, "Purity of heart is to will one thing." When one's identity has come together around a central significant *meaning,* it issues in a kind of purity — even at times a righteousness — unmuddied by doubt (Tucker, 1968).

the highly controversial subject of the nature of charismatic leadership, a subject for another paper. I cannot resist, however, before I close, adding a few words about it here.

Not long ago, I attended a conference of historians, met to discuss the nature of what they called "the charismatic process." In attendance were scholars who had studied the lives and times of a variety of political and religious leaders (some prophets, some activists). The task of the conference was first to discover what specific talents, gifts, or graces these leaders shared and then to explore their relationship with their followers.[21] For the first two days, we were heaped with fascinating biographical and historical information about several historical personages, and on the third day we were to discover what they had in common. At this point, the conference fell into a paralyzed despair. It was only (at least so it seemed to me) when we abandoned the search for a list of specific traits or talents and sought the answer to our riddle in a holistic, "complementary" approach that we once more took heart.[22] In each instance, the leader had undergone a profound personal struggle with a sense of fragmentation and bondage. When he had managed creatively to solve his personal crisis of identity (often after a period of great agony—Giuseppe Mazzini called his own experience a "tempest of doubt") and to establish a cohesive, "one-pointed" unity within the diversities of himself, he experienced a joyous

[21] *Charism* literally means "talent of grace," or, alternately, the "power to heal."

[22] In other words, instead of trying to "explain"—for example—the success of the Russian revolutionary leader Lenin simply in terms of his self-confidence, his tactical ingenuity, his stubbornness, or his extraordinary intelligence, we must look, rather, at the following sequence: before 1914, his following was limited to members of the radical Russian intelligentsia; by 1917, however, World War I had produced such collective stress among the workers, peasants, and soldiers of Russia that substantial numbers of them became responsive to his leadership. There was now a "fit," as there had *not* been before, between his gifted, impassioned vision— on one level a solution to his own personal conflicts—and the needs of a significant segment of his society. A biographer trying to "explain" Lenin's leadership would thus need to explore not only Lenin's life history (longitudinal) and the moment in *his* life cycle when he ascended to leadership (cross-sectional), but also the history of his country and the cogwheeling moment of its "life cycle" (Erikson, 1968a, 1968b). Here, again, the point of view of *complementarity* is indispensable.

"coming together" and, at the same time, an unprecedented freedom.

But the leader's own reorganization represents only one piece of the jigsaw puzzle. Until it is met by a communal response, born of collective need, he does not become a charismatic leader. Nor can the aspiring artist be fulfilled without *some* audience, however small. In each instance, to be sure, the man under scrutiny has been gifted. But, beyond his personal gifts, the crucial secret of his leadership appeared to lie in the "fit"—the mutuality—between his own mobilization of capacities (in response to a sensed need or danger) and the needs of a significant portion of his society. Thus, whether it is Martin Luther reforming Western Christendom, Giuseppe Mazzini envisioning a mythologically liberated city of Rome at the center of a "free and united Italy," Charles de Gaulle restoring "unity and self-esteem to a free France," or Reverend George Whitefield preaching religious freedom in the coalfields to 20,000 American colonists trembling on the verge of *political* freedom, the quest of the *followers* of all these men is the same: to dissolve the boundaries between them and the leader so that each can share in his *liberation and unification*—in short, in the deliverance he has promised. Just as the playwright's inner civil war is externalized onto the stage, offering (by his dramatic resolutions) unification and liberation to his audience, so does the "stage of history" again and again offer, by way of its leaders, collective resolutions to collective aspirations and conflicts. This is not to say that the actions recommended and taken by the leader and his movement (for example, a revolution to unseat an autocracy or to divide the arable land) cannot be understood *also* on their manifest level, but that the "charismatic process" cannot be understood *solely* in terms of these external economic or political objectives.

A last word: with all the attendant difficulties, it is easier to study creative processes in great artists, scientists, or charismatic leaders—because there are more data available about their lives than about the lives of average people. The teacher whom we remember—and we all have at least one in a

lifetime—is a person who brings about, by that same mutuality, the same joyful affirmation and recognition created by
the artist or leader.

We now live in a time when suffering has grown to a point
when in the words of the Bhagavad-Gita it becomes necessary for "the invincible force of Nature . . . to set man's *vision*
right and establish a way of life which will again fulfill the
high purpose of his existence." We teachers must all be part of
such a new generational force, dedicated to setting right our
own vision and purpose and inevitably then, the vision of
everyone we touch.

REFERENCES

Bernstein, L. (n.d.), Omnibus Series, CL 918, Columbia Records.
Bhagavad-Gita, trans. Maharishi Mahesh Yogi. New York: Penguin Books, 1969.
Brenman, M. (1952), On Teasing and Being Teased: And the Problem of "Moral Masochism." In: *Psychoanalytic Psychiatry and Psychology: Clinical and Theoretical Papers, Austen Riggs Center,* Vol. I, ed. R. P. Knight & C. R. Friedman. New York: International Universities Press, 1962, pp. 29-51.
_____ chm. (1947), Problems in Clinical Research: Round Table, 1946. *Amer. J. Orthopsychiat.,* 17:196-230, esp. pp. 214-222.
_____ (1948), Research in Psychotherapy: Round Table, 1947. *Amer. J. Ortho-psychiat.,* 18:92-118, esp. pp. 100-110.
_____ (1959), Discussion of Bellak, L. "The Unconscious." *Ann. N.Y. Acad. Sci.,* 76:1081-1086.
_____ Gill, M. M., & Knight, R. P. (1950), Spontaneous Fluctuations in Depth of Hypnosis and Their Implications for Ego Function. In: *Psychoanalytic Psychiatry and Psychology: Clinical and Theoretical Papers, Austen Riggs Center,* Vol. I, ed. R. P. Knight & C. R. Friedman. New York: International Universities Press, 1962, pp. 330-350.
Brenman-Gibson, M. (1971), The Creation of Plays: With a Specimen Analysis. Presented in rough draft at the Stockbridge end of the Wellfleet-Stockbridge axis, November 6.
Coles, R. (1970), *Erik H. Erikson: The Growth of His Work.* Boston: Little, Brown.
Dubos, R. (1972), *The God Within.* New York: Scribners.
Emerson, R. W. (1841), History. In: *Emerson's Essays.* Munroe, first edition.
Erikson, E. H. (1958), *Young Man Luther: A Study in Psychoanalysis and History.* New York: Norton.
_____ (1968a), *Identity, Youth and Crisis.* New York: Norton.
_____ (1968b), Identity, Psychosocial. In: *International Encyclopedia of the Social Sciences,* 7:61-65. New York: Macmillan & The Free Press.
_____ (1969), *Gandhi's Truth.* New York: Norton.
_____ (1972), *The Child's Toys and the Old Man's Reasons.* Godkin Lectures. New York: Norton, forthcoming.

Erikson, J. (1966), Eye to Eye. In: *The Man-Made Object,* ed. G. Kepes. New York: Braziller, pp. 50-61.

Freud, S. (1910), The Antithetical Meaning of Primal Words. *Standard Edition,* 11:153-162. London: Hogarth Press, 1957.

Geertz, C. (1972), The Balinese Cockfight. *Daedalus,* 101(1):1-37.

Gill, M.M., & Brenman, M. (1959), *Hypnosis and Related States.* New York: International Universities Press.

Holton, G. (1952), Introduction to *Concepts and Theories in Physical Science.* Reading, Mass.: Addison Wesley.

———(1970), Roots of Complementarity. *Deadalus,* 99(4):1015-1055.

———(1971-1972), On Trying to Understand Genius. *Amer. Scholar,* 41:95-110.

———(1972), Mach, Einstein and the Search for Reality. In: *The 20th Century Sciences,* ed. G. Holton. New York: Norton.

Jeffers, R. (1941), The Excesses of God. In: *Selected Poems.* New York: Random House (Vintage), 1969, p. 72.

Kazin, A. (1965), *Starting Out in the Thirties.* New York: Atlantic-Little Brown.

Krips, J. (1954), Album Notes, Beethoven's Ninth Symphony. Angel Records.

Langer, W. L. (1958), The Next Assignment. *Amer. Historical Rev.,* 63:283-304.

Lifton, R. J. (1968), *Death in Life.* New York: Random House.

———(1973), The Struggle for Cultural Rebirth, *Harpers,* April, 1973, pp. 84-90.

Loevinger, J. (1963), Conflict of Commitment in Clinical Research. *Amer. Psychol.,* 18:241-251.

Maharishi Mahesh Yogi (1972), *Science of Creative Intelligence* (Videotape #7). Los Angeles: Maharishi International University.

Manuel, F., & Manuel, F. (1972), Sketch for a Natural History of Paradise. *Daedalus,* 101(1):83-128.

Odets, C. (1950?), Personal notes, unpublished, "Psychology."

———(1958), Diary, 12/14.

Ornstein, R. (1972), *The Psychology of Consciousness.* New York: Viking.

Poincaré, H. (1908), Science and Method. In: *The Foundations of Science.* Lancaster, Pa.: Science Press, 1946.

Polanyi, M. (1958), *Personal Knowledge: Towards a Post-Critical Philosophy.* Chicago: University of Chicago Press, 1964.

———(1966), *The Tacit Dimension.* New York: Doubleday.

Spitz, R. A. (1965), *The First Year of Life.* New York: International Universities Press.

Tucker, R. (1968), The Theory of Charismatic Leadership. *Daedalus,* 97(3):731-756.

Wallerstein, R. S., & Sampson, H. (1971), Issues in Research in the Psychoanalytic Process, *Internat. J. Psycho-Anal.,* 52:11-50.

12

CONFESSIONS OF A TURTLE

WILLIAM GIBSON

"He could not endure the sedentary toil of creative art, and so remained a man of action"; so William Butler Yeats described a colleague who preferred talking to writing. I choose the text for three reasons. First, it is a reminder that art is not fantasy, it is labor, of the most painstaking, disciplined, and responsible kind. Secondly, I personally enjoy the poet's implication that all men are men of action, it is the artist who is something more. Thirdly, the quotation implies much about our present topic, fertility and sterility in the artist.

To say that art is not fantasy is of course only a partial truth; its inversion is what is wholly true, fantasy is not art. We are all men of fantasy too, and not one of us lacks the talent to compensate in his dreams for what he cannot wrest from the world of fact. Yet in the non-artist such fantasy is mostly a dead end, a kind of mental onanism which procreates nothing. The mystery of art lies in why the public is willing to give the artist its respect and money for his dreams, and the answer to this question is not to be found solely in searching the deprivations of the artist as the source of his art. Such deprivations, and the fantasies they give birth to, are commonplace enough, and to each his own; they have no marketable value.

George Klein was a midwife to these paragraphs: as program chairman of the American Psychological Association panel in 1959, he arranged a symposium on "Fertility and Sterility in the Artist," and invited me to participate. Whatever their claim for inclusion in this volume, these pages are witness to George's avid interest in the artist. Recycled and extended, they appear in a recent book of mine, *A Season in Heaven* (New York: Atheneum, 1974).

Art is means. If we are to find any clue to the mystery of art — and I should say that I for one do not here propose or promise to — we must look not to the artist's individual neuroticism, but to those social terms wherein and whereby his work joins him to his fellowmen. These terms are designated as form. This word in the general means everything and nothing; I shall presently clarify, by specific examples, what it means to me.

Let me ease into my personal comments via some impersonal ones. Yeats notwithstanding, I think Turgenev came close to the truth when, of one of his characters who was a novelist, he said, "Like most writers, he was a cold man." The character of the artist no doubt permits of a multitude of variations; yet in my own observation most artists, however externally sociable, have something withheld, secretive, and wary in them, something which in some faraway corners of the world is called schizoid. At the same time, every successful writer has the knack of seducing the public into supporting him — if only posthumously — in exchange for sharing with that public certain of his experiences, peculiarly organized, so as to range from entertainment to revelation. This is the paradox of the artist: that he can be, and often is, so cold and unfeeling in his relations with his fellowmen, and simultaneously possesses, in a measure beyond anyone else, the social tact to move their hearts. I think it is only in the realm of form that this paradox is resolved.

Now what do we — I beg your pardon, what do I — mean by form, in literature? I begin with the material of the medium, language, and with its simplest unit, a word. We could pick any at random; I pick one I have used several times here, "art." I have only to speak this word, and a bridge, more or less adequate, is magically erected between the world of my private experience and that of each listener — more, between a certain fraction of my world and a corresponding fraction of his. The word does this work between us: it selects, and even arranges, this fraction out of the unorganized welter of the speaker's experience; and it directs the listener's understanding in selecting and arranging a similar fraction out of his.

Language is thus in its very nature a formal ordering of experience. Most of us use it semiliterately, that is, semi-responsibly: with it we manage to transact the business of the world, and confuse each other while doing so. It leaves much unsaid, and obviously is inexact, or I should not be defining form at such length.

Its nature as an instrument of formal order, while basic and prerequisite to aesthetic form. . .

Now let us leave that sentence hanging, and ponder the power of the word "while." It sets up in every ear a tension of anticipation, which demands fulfillment. It will not get it here, the example is meant only to show how the internal ordering of language itself, in sentence structure, permits the creation of a certain power relationship between speaker and listener. With this power relationship we stand on the thresh-hold of aesthetic form. When a literary man structures a sentence, everything in it, even the punctuation, is directed—knowingly and not—at controlling the response of the reader; the difference between this semicolon and a period, for instance, is in part a manipulation of tempo.

Look again now at the sentence by Yeats with which I opened: "He could not endure the sedentary toil of creative art, and so remained a man of action." How much Yeats accomplishes in it with two words, "so remained," is evident by the number I took to paraphrase it, "all men are men of action, it is the artist who is something more." Yeats's two words are more compelling than my fourteen in much the same way that Jack Dempsey's most convincing punches traveled only six inches; and this force of concentration is also part of what I mean by form.

I said earlier, "Art is means." There is a touch of aesthetic form in this sentence—it lies in the odd marriage between the singular verb "is" and plural predicate "means"; if I said instead, "Art is manner," a color would go out of the sentence. A better writer has done better with this same odd marriage. In *Othello,* when Desdemona disembarks, one of the charac-ters exclaims, "The riches of the ship is come on shore." Ignoring the variety of beauties in this sentence, and attending only to the tension between "riches" and "is," we see what a loss we suffer if we alter one word: "The riches of the ship have come on shore." It is the genius of the author that he knows what he can do to us with that word "is"; we spy in it his instinct for good form, however he treated his wife and children.

In another way, consider how Oscar Wilde outwits us, to our pleasure, when he writes, "Poor Lady So-and-So, since her husband's death her hair has turned quite golden with grief." By sheer structure he leads us towards the cemetery and we end up in the beauty parlor. This too is form.

The very sound of language is form. Take two lines from a Shakespearean sonnet, "O how shall summer's honey breath hold out / Against the wrackful siege of battering days." He is speaking here of the passing of youthful beauty, and he not only delivers this ideational content; he not only enlarges it by the reverberations of symbolic imagery, on another plane; in a third and most sensuous way, he puts it in our very ear in the texture of sounds, shifting it from the gentle music of "Oh how shall summer's honey breath hold out" to the shockful consonants of "Against the wrackful siege of battering days."

Here too we have another dimension of sound entirely, in the pattern of sonnet form. The music of each word takes its syncopated place within larger musics, the five-beat line, the rhyme scheme, the fourteen lines which are given as the external profile of sonnet form. I think by now it should be clear that when I say "form" I do not mean only that profile, which differentiates say sonnet form from limerick form. I mean everything in the piece, from the single unit of the word up to and including its external shape, the organization of sense, sound, image, punctuation, sentence structure, pattern in fine and in toto.

I have spoken only of the organization of language; this is but one dimension of such larger patterns as the novel and the drama, in which the writer must give formal ordering also to the events of his action and to the human substance of his people. Obviously all of this adds up to backside-breaking work, and every night when we put our boys to bed I tell them,

"Don't become writers! Become psychologists." The wonder is not that the artist has periods of sterility; it is that he manages any fertility at all.

The question arises, why go to so much trouble? I wish now to leave the level of abstraction to bolder minds, and come down to that of autobiography, where I am the only authority. Here however I must reverse my field, and tell the truth: writing, when it goes well, is no trouble at all, and hardly deserves the name of work. It is one of life's chief delights, enhances my capacity to take delight in the rest of life, however insipid, and is so indistinguishable from play that often, in the midst of it, I stop and wonder at how I was born so lucky that the citizenry supplies me with food, clothing, and shelter, simply for building with my colored blocks. For many years it did not; but this in no way robbed the play of its inherent pleasures or significance for me.

I said, when it goes well. When it goes badly, my experience is precisely the opposite: it is one of life's chief burdens, diminishes my capacity to enjoy anything, however delectable, and is so indistinguishable from cesspool cleaning that I often wish I had taken that up instead—at least the content is there, given, and in full view. I know of no artist who would not sell a lung to be always in the state of creative grace, and of none who does not cyclically go into that state of damnation, seemingly eternal, wherein he is as sterile as a stone.

This figure of speech is not arbitrary; I feel quite physiologically that some process of petrification has overtaken my brain, and some other elusive organ in the region of my heart, with the result that I live through each day on approximately twenty per cent of my metabolic vitality. No activity other than writing unlocks the remaining eighty per cent for my use. The terms of the contest seem hardly fair, my mouse of a twenty per cent must lash my mountain of an eighty per cent into getting up on its feet and walking. I think, if only I had the eighty per cent to assist me I could carry off any or all of the tasks that stare fishily up at me from my desk; but who in his right mind asks me to lift them and my own dead weight simultaneously? I: who am not in my right mind. I always know — seem to know — what it is I wish to work on; if I had to submit a synopsis of a project in application for a grant I could get up four any day of the week, and describe each eloquently and persuasively. The only thing I cannot do is write it. When I sit down to try, the living words in which it is to be clothed do not come; the idea is as speechless as a manikin, and the only sound to be heard is the snoring of my eighty per cent.

It can slumber on, my little gypsy sweetheart, for weeks and even months. During this period I become a very prompt correspondent; I occupy myself also with moving my growing collection of manikins around from shelf to shelf of my workroom. The one fatal tactic for me to adopt is to become a man of action and go to the movies during work hours, or turn in any other way consumer. My emotional tone ranges from ennui to despair. I think it is in this phase that many would-be writers escape into such lazy and cowardly professions as lion-taming, jet-piloting, and polar exploration. I myself have only one technique for ending the phase; it is to sit at my desk and survive it. I polish this manikin and I polish that manikin, and lo and behold, the day comes when one of them — one that I have had in stock perhaps for only twenty-four hours — opens its idiot's face and speaks. It speaks genuine words which, whatever their content, say one thing to my moribund self, "Lazarus, come forth!" and my eighty per cent opens one eye. Sometimes he closes it again. But if what is on the desk interests him enough to open the other, rise, and settle down to serious play, I am back in business.

I can only guess at what has happened in this moment. The sensation is one of things, internal and external, opening up; and I understand this too in terms of form. Parenthetically, I should add that that I never write first drafts. They may turn out to have been first drafts, but what my hand commits to paper has nothing tentative about it; I rewrite it phrase by phrase, often a dozen times in a sentence, but the completed paragraph, page, opus, is meant to stand as a final and total formulation; and most of the time it is. I have criteria which tell me when this finality in each unit is achieved. No doubt some of them are intuitive, and others deceptive; but I am aware in the moment of writing that I am gazing in two directions at once, in to myself and out to an audience, and what I put down on paper must satisfy standards in both directions or it will not put down.

The standards facing out are concerned entirely with those aspects of form I have in part enumerated—logical sense, sound, image, structure—as the means of making the unit not only intelligible to the mind of whatever audience I am aiming at, but impactful upon its physique; they are intended to insure, insofar as it lies within my powers, that the audience shall not only comprehend what I said, but feel what I felt. This emotional reverberation is the sine qua non of these standards.

The standards facing in partake in the same aspects of form, but their sine qua non is discovery. The moment of inspiration is a moment of discovering something new and unwritten in myself. I think this is a reason I often fail in writing the projects I know I want to write: in a sense, a condition of writing is not knowing. Such discoveries may range from a minute turn of phrase to the over-all concept of a large piece. It is not necessary that I understand what it is I am discovering about myself; my touchstone for the occurrence of discovery is my thoracic excitement, and the act of wording it on paper is accompanied by an elation and a sense of liberation. I think the liberation has to do with the freeing of something hitherto imprisoned, and the elation with—additionally—the sense of power over the anticipated audience.

But I wish to stress that this discovery inward, and formulation outward, happen simultaneously, or so close thereto that I often cannot say which has come first. My belief is, it can be either. As a corollary, it is a curious thought that the eighty per cent which must awaken to work the material is itself the material to be worked.

I have spoken of working badly, and of working well, but not of a third phase, which is working too well. I have had three experiences in my life, each lasting for a month or two, when the eighty per cent took over and ran me so mercilessly I thought its formal designs were mainly upon my life. Each of these was with a play. I have had this experience often enough with a poem for a day or three, but I am speaking now of one protracted flight in which my pencil could not keep up with the outpouring, three or four hours of sleep a night sufficed, a mouthful was a meal, and at the end of six weeks of twenty-hour workdays I had written one full-length play and half of another, and lost fifteen pounds. By this time, which began as a blessing and ended as a nightmare, I felt outrageously used, hag-ridden, and exploited. I also felt some fear that at any moment I might float away into heaven like a toy balloon, so tenuous grew my ties to this earth. If my description of my state of mind while working badly seems in any way analogous to the clinical state of depression, this of working too well will suggest its antithesis; and I will support it by revealing that, in two of these three experiences, my judgment of those objective attributes I have here called form proved to be sadly illusory. The puddings have yet to be eaten, which is a kind of proof too.

I wish now to bring these confessions into some recognizable configuration, if only that of a question mark. If most writers are cold men, is it not perhaps that they function somewhat as human iceboxes? — preserving certain of their experiences in themselves, frozen and unfelt, against that day when all the conditions for thaw luckily meet. I think the conditions are essentially those of mastery. Such experiences escape from the artist only when he has a net of form to waken and catch them in, and it is the very net with which he catches his public. Perhaps the public supports him to wake them too, and share in the mastery. Pending the miraculous convergence of these conditions, the artist is silent, and waits.

I should like to close with another text, a poem of great nobility, which might have been called — though it is not — "The Artist." It is by Ogden Nash:

> The turtle lives 'twixt plated decks
> Which practically conceal its sex.
> I think it clever of the turtle
> In such a fix to be so fertile. *

*Copyright 1940 by Ogden Nash. Quoted by permission of the Estate of Ogden Nash and J. M. Dent & Sons Ltd.

PUBLICATIONS OF GEORGE S. KLEIN

Klein, G. S., & Schoenfeld, N. (1941), The Influence of Ego-Involvement on Confidence. *Journal of Abnormal and Social Psychology*, 36:249-258. Also in: *Understanding Human Motivation*, ed. C. L. Stacey & M. F. Demartino. Cleveland: Howard Allen, 1958, pp. 211-222.

_____ (1942), The Relation between Motion and Form Acuity in Parafoveal and Peripheral Vision and Related Phenomena. *Archives of Psychology*, Monograph No. 275.

Warden, C. J., Ross, S., & Klein, G. S. (1942), *Laboratory Manual for Experimental Comparative Psychology*. New York: Edwards.

Klein, G. S. (1943), The Subjective Difficulty of Six Psychomotor Tests. *Research Bulletin*, Psychol. Res. Unit No. 1, Nashville, Tenn.

_____ (1944), The Reliability and Validity of a "Clinical"-Type Interview Record. Psychol. Res. Unit No. 1, Nashville, Tenn.

_____ with Clinical Project Staff (1944), Validation of Ratings Based on Nine Clinical Techniques. *Research Bulletin*, Psychol. Res. Unit No. 1, Maxwell Field, Ala.

_____ (1948), An Application of the Multiple Regression Principle to Clinical Prediction. *Journal of General Psychology*, 38:159-179.

_____ (1948), Self-Appraisal of Test Performance as a Vocational Selection Device. *Educational and Psychological Measurement*, 8:69-84.

_____ (1949), Adaptive Properties of Sensory Functioning: Some Postulates and Hypotheses. *Bulletin of the Menninger Clinic*, 13:16-23.

_____ (1949), The Circular Error in Radar Observer Training. In: *Psychological Research on Radar Observer Training*, ed. S. W. Cook. U. S. Government Printing Office.

_____ (1949), A Clinical Perspective for Personality Research. *Journal of Abnormal and Social Psychology*, 44:42-49. Also in: *Perception, Motives, and Personality*. New York: Knopf, 1970, pp. 117-128.

_____ & Schlesinger, H. J. (1949), Where Is the Perceiver in Perceptual Theory? *Journal of Personality*, 18:32-47.

_____ (1951), The Personal World through Perception. In: *Perception: An Approach to Personality*, ed. R. R. Blake & G. V. Ramsey. New York: Ronald Press, pp. 328-355. Also in: *Perception, Motives, and Personality*. New York: Knopf, 1970, pp. 129-161.

_____ & Krech, D. (1951), The Problem of Personality and Its Theory. *Journal of Personality*, 20:2-23.

_____ & Schlesinger, H. J. (1951), Perceptual Attitudes toward Instability: Prediction of Apparent Movement Experiences from Rorschach Responses. *Journal of Personality*, 19:289-302. Also in: *A Rorschach Reader*, ed. M. H. Sherman. New York: International Universities Press, 1960, pp. 288-301.

—— —— & Meister, D. E. (1951), The Effect of Personal Values on Perception: An Experimental Critique. *Psychological Review*, 58:96-112.

—— & Krech, D. (1952), Cortical Conductivity in the Brain-Injured. *Journal of Personality*, 21:118-148. Also in: *Psychopathology: A Source-Book*, ed. C. F. Reed, I. E. Alexander, & S. S. Tomkins. Cambridge: Harvard University Press, 1958, pp. 527-553.

Krech, D., & Klein, G. S., eds. (1952), *Theoretical Models and Personality Theory*. Durham: Duke University Press.

Klein, G. S. (1953), The Menninger Foundation Research on Perception and Personality, 1947-1952: A Review. *Bulletin of the Menninger Clinic*, 17:93-99. Also in: *Menninger Quarterly*, 8:11-15, 1954.

Smith, G. J. W., & Klein, G. S. (1953), Cognitive Controls in Serial Behavior Patterns. *Journal of Personality*, 22:188-213. Also in: *Percept-Genetic Analysis*, ed. U. Kragh & G. Smith. Lund, Sweden: Gleerups, 1970, pp. 238-256.

Klein, G. S. (1954), Need and Regulation. In: *Nebraska Symposium on Motivation*, ed. M. R. Jones. Lincoln: University of Nebraska Press, pp. 224-274. Also in: *Perception, Motives, and Personality*. New York: Knopf, 1970, pp. 162-200.

—— Holzman, P. S., & Laskin, D. (1954), The Perception Project: Progress Report for 1953-1954. *Bulletin of the Menninger Clinic*, 18:260-266.

Holzman, P. S., & Klein, G. S. (1954), Cognitive System-Principles of Leveling and Sharpening: Individual Differences in Assimilation Effects in Visual Time-Error. *Journal of Psychology*, 37:105-122.

Klein, G. S. (1956), Perception, Motives, and Personality: A Clinical Perspective. In: *Psychology of Personality*, ed. J. L. McCary. New York: Logos Press, pp. 122-199. Revised version, Motives and the Perception of Objects, in: *Perception, Motives, and Personality*. New York: Knopf, 1970, pp. 37-114.

Holzman, P. S., & Klein, G. S. (1956), Intersensory and Visual Field Forces in Size Estimation. *Perceptual and Motor Skills*, 6:37-41.

—— —— (1956), Motive and Style in Reality Contact. *Bulletin of the Menninger Clinic*, 20:181-191.

Klein, G. S. (1957), Discussion of A Study of the Preliminary Stages of the Construction of Dreams and Images, by Charles Fisher. *Psychoanalytic Quarterly*, 26:155-156.

—— (1958), Cognitive Control and Motivation. In: *Assessment of Human Motives*, ed. G. Lindzey. New York: Rinehart, pp. 87-118. Also in: *Perception, Motives, and Personality*. New York: Knopf, 1970, pp. 201-231.

—— Spence, D. P., Holt, R. R., & Gourevitch, S. (1958), Cognition without Awareness: Subliminal Influences upon Conscious Thought. *Journal of Abnormal and Social Psychology*, 57:255-266.

—— (1959), Consciousness in Psychoanalytic Theory: Some Implications for Current Research in Perception. *Journal of the American Psychoanalytic Association*, 7:5-34. Also in: *Perception, Motives, and Personality*. New York: Knopf, 1970, pp. 235-263.

—— (1959), Introduction to: On Perception, Event Structure, and the Psychological Environment: Selected Papers by Fritz Heider. *Psychological Issues*, Monograph No. 3:v-vii. New York: International Universities Press.

—— (1959), On Subliminal Activation. *Journal of Nervous and Mental Dis-*

ease, 128:293-301. Also in: *Perception, Motives, and Personality*. New York: Knopf, 1970, pp. 264-277.

Smith, G. J. W., Spence, D. P., & Klein, G. S. (1959), Subliminal Effects of Verbal Stimuli. *Journal of Abnormal and Social Psychology*, 59:167-176. Also in: *Percept-Genetic Analysis*, ed. U. Kragh & G. Smith. Lund, Sweden: Gleerups, 1970, pp. 77-92.

Klein, G. S., & Holt, R. R. (1960), Problems and Issues in Current Studies of Subliminal Activation. In: *Festschrift for Gardner Murphy*, ed. J. G. Peatman & E. L. Hartley. New York: Harper, pp. 75-93.

Bruner, J. S., & Klein, G. S. (1960), The Functions of Perceiving: New Look Retrospect. In: *Perspectives in Psychological Theory*, ed. S. Wapner & B. Kaplan. New York: International Universities Press, pp. 61-77.

Klein, G. S. (1961), On Inhibition, Disinhibition, and "Primary Process" in Thinking. In: *Proceedings of the XIV International Congress of Applied Psychology*, Vol. 4, *Clinical Psychology*, ed. G. Nielson. Copenhagen: Munksgaard, pp. 179-198. Also in: *Psychoanalysis in America: Historical Perspectives,* ed. M. Sherman. Springfield, Ill.: Charles C Thomas, 1966, pp. 456-473. Also in: *Perception, Motives, and Personality*. New York: Knopf, 1970, pp. 281-296.

———— (1962), Blindness and Isolation. *The Psychoanalytic Study of the Child*, 17:82-93. New York: International Universities Press. Also in: *Perception, Motives, and Personality*. New York: Knopf, 1970, pp. 310-321.

———— Gardner, R. W., & Schlesinger, H. J. (1962), Tolerance for Unrealistic Experiences: A Study of the Generality of a Cognitive Control. *British Journal of Psychology*, 53:41-55.

Eagle, M. N., & Klein, G. S. (1962), Fragmentation Phenomena with the Use of the Stabilized Retinal Image. *Perceptual and Motor Skills*, 15:579-582.

Klein, G. S. (1963), Credo for a "Clinical Psychologist": A Personal Reflection. *Bulletin of the Menninger Clinic*, 27:61-73. Also in: *Perception, Motives, and Personality*. New York: Knopf, 1970, pp. 415-426.

Fiss, H., Goldberg, F. H., & Klein, G. S. (1963), Effects of Subliminal Stimulation on Imagery and Discrimination. *Perceptual and Motor Skills*, 17: 31-44.

Klein, G. S. (1964), Semantic Power Measured through the Interference of Words with Color-Naming. *American Journal of Psychology*, 77:576-588.

Gill, M. M., & Klein, G. S. (1964), The Structuring of Drive and Reality: David Rapaport's Contributions to Psycho-Analysis and Psychology. *International Journal of Psycho-Analysis*, 45:483-498. Also in: *The Collected Papers of David Rapaport*, ed. M. M. Gill. New York: Basic Books, 1967, pp. 8-34.

Klein, G. S. (1965), On Hearing One's Own Voice: An Aspect of Cognitive Control in Spoken Thought. In: *Psychoanalysis and Current Biological Thought*, ed. N. Greenfield & W. Lewis. Madison: University of Wisconsin Press, pp. 245-273. Revised version in: *Drives, Affects, Behavior*, Vol. 2, ed. M. Schur. New York: International Universities Press, 1965, pp. 87-117. Also in: *Perception, Motives, and Personality*. New York: Knopf, 1970, pp. 322-353.

———— (1966), The Several Grades of Memory. In: *Psychoanalysis—A General Psychology: Essays in Honor of Heinz Hartmann*, ed. R. Loewenstein, L Newman, M Schur, & A. Solnit. New York: International Universities

Press, pp. 377-389. Also in: *Perception, Motives, and Personality*. New York: Knopf, 1970, pp. 297-309.

Eagle, M. N., Bowling, L., & Klein, G. S. (1966), Fragmentation Phenomena in Luminous Designs. *Perceptual and Motor Skills*, 23:143-152.

_____ Wolitzky, D. L., & Klein, G. S. (1966), Imagery: Effects of a Concealed Figure in a Stimulus. *Science*, 151:837-839.

Fiss, H., Bokert, E., & Klein, G. S. (1966), Waking Fantasies following Interruption of Two Types of Sleep. *Archives of General Psychiatry*, 14:543-551.

Klein, G. S. (1967), Peremptory Ideation: Structure and Force in Motivated Ideas. In: Motives and Thought: Psychoanalytic Essays in Honor of David Rapaport, ed. R. R. Holt. *Psychological Issues*, Monograph No. 18/19:78-128. Also in: *Cognition, Personality, and Clinical Psychology: A Symposium Held at the University of Colorado*, ed. R. Jessor & S. Feshbach. San Francisco: Jossey-Bass, pp. 1-61. Also in: *Perception, Motives, and Personality*. New York: Knopf, 1970, pp. 357-412.

_____ Barr, H. L., & Wolitzky, D. L. (1967), Personality. *Annual Review of Psychology*, 18:467-560. Palo Alto, Cal.: Annual Reviews.

_____ & Wolitzky, D. L. (1967), Vocal Isolation: The Effects of Occluding Audible Feedback from One's Own Voice. In: *The Organization of Human Information Processing*. Report of the Symposium of the XVIII International Congress of Psychology, Moscow, 1966, ed. F. Kliz. Berlin: Akademie-Verlag, pp. 157-174. Also in: *Journal of Abnormal Psychology*, 75:50-56, 1970.

_____ (1968), Psychoanalysis: Ego Psychology. *International Encyclopedia of the Social Sciences*, 13:11-31. New York: Macmillan & The Free Press.

Fiss, H., Klein, G. S., Shollar, E., & Levine, B. E. (1968), Changes in Dream Content as a Function of Prolonged REM Sleep Interruption. *Sleep Study Abstracts*, p. 217.

Gill, M. M., & Klein, G. S. (1968), Rapaport, David. *International Encyclopedia of the Social Sciences*, 13:325-327. New York: Macmillan & The Free Press.

Klein, G. S. (1969), Discussion comments in: Toward a Unity of Knowledge, ed. M. Grene. *Psychological Issues*, Monograph No. 22:237-239, 287-288. New York: International Universities Press.

_____ (1969), Freud's Two Theories of Sexuality. In: *Clinical-Cognitive Psychology: Models and Integrations*, ed. L. Breger. Englewood Cliffs, N. J.: Prentice-Hall, pp. 136-181. Also in: *Psychoanalytic Theory: An Exploration of Essentials*. New York: International Universities Press, 1975, pp. 72-120. Also in: Psychology versus Metapsychology: Psychoanalytic Essays in Honor of George S. Klein, ed. M. M. Gill & P. S. Holzman. *Psychological Issues*, Monograph No. 36:14-70. New York: International Universities Press, 1975.

Fiss, H., Ellman, S. J., & Klein, G. S. (1969), Waking Fantasies following interrupted and Completed REM Periods. *Archives of General Psychiatry*, 21:230-239.

Klein, G. S. (1970), The Ego in Psychoanalysis: A Concept in Search of Identity. *The Psychoanalytic Review*, 56:511-525. Revised version in: *Psychoanalytic Theory: An Exploration of Essentials*. New York: International Universities Press, 1975, pp. 121-160.

———— (1970), Orientations from Psychoanalysis. In: *Perception, Motives, and Personality.* New York: Knopf, pp. 14-36.

———— (1970), *Perception, Motives, and Personality.* New York: Knopf.

———— (1970), Two Theories or One? (Dos Teorias o Una?). *Revista de Psicoanalisis,* 27:553-594. English version in: *Bulletin of the Menninger Clinic,* 37:102-132, 1973. Also in: *Psychoanalytic Theory: An Exploration of Essentials.* New York: International Universities Press, 1975, pp. 41-71.

Wolitzky, D. L., Klein, G. S., & Dworkin, S. F. (1971), Repression: Effects on an Hypnotically Induced Fantasy. In: *Hypnose: Aktuelle Probleme in Theorie, Experiment und Klinik,* ed. A. Katzenstein. Berlin: Verlag Volk und Gesundheit, pp. 213-232. Also in: *Psychoanalysis and Contemporary Science,* 4. New York: International Universities Press, 1976.

Klein, G. S. (1972), The Vital Pleasures. *Psychoanalysis and Contemporary Science,* 1:181-205. New York: Macmillan. Also in: *Psychoanalytic Theory: An Exploration of Essentials.* New York: International Universities Press, 1975, pp. 210-238.

———— (1973), Is Psychoanalysis Relevant? *Psychoanalysis and Contemporary Science,* 2:3-21. New York: Macmillan. Also in: *Psychoanalytic Theory: An Exploration of Essentials.* New York: International Universities Press, 1975, pp. 17-40.

Fiss, H., Klein, G. S., & Shollar, E. (1974), "Dream Intensification" as a Function of Prolonged REM-Period Interruption. *Psychoanalysis and Contemporary Science,* 3:399-424. New York: International Universities Press.

Klein, G. S. (1975), *Psychoanalytic Theory: An Exploration of Essentials.* New York: International Universities Press.

INDEX

ABOUT THE AUTHORS

MARGARET BRENMAN-GIBSON received her Master's degree from Columbia University and her Ph.D. in psychology from the University of Kansas. She was on the staff of the Menninger Foundation in the 1940's and served there as director of the Department of Psychology. She was the first American nonmedical person both to obtain full clinical psychoanalytic training and to become a training and supervising psychoanalyst. She is the author of several books and numerous papers. Her research is in the nature of altered states of consciousness and the creative process, an area that encompasses phenomena as diverse as hypnosis and creativity in contemporary artists. She is now on the senior staff of the Austen Riggs Center.

WILLIAM GIBSON, the husband of Dr. Margaret Brenman-Gibson, is the author of a dozen books—poetry (*Winter Crook*), fiction (*The Cobweb*), autobiography (*A Mass for the Dead*), plays (*The Miracle Worker*)—and the co-author of two sons.

MERTON M. GILL received his M.D. from the University of Chicago in 1938, and is a graduate of the Topeka Institute for Psychoanalysis. He has been a staff member of the Menninger Foundation, the Austen Riggs Center, and Yale University Medical School. Since 1963, he has pursued a full-time academic career, consecutively at the Downstate Medical Center of the State University of New York, New York University, and since 1971 as a Research Scientist Awardee of NIMH at the Abraham Lincoln School of Medicine of the University of

Illinois. His books include *The Initial Interview in Psychiatric Practice,* with Newman, Redlich, and Sommers, *Hypnosis and Related States,* with Margaret Brenman, and *Topography and Systems in Psychoanalytic Theory.* He edited *The Collected Papers of David Rapaport.*

ROBERT R. HOLT received his Ph.D. from Harvard University in 1944. He was staff psychologist at the VA Hospital in Topeka, Kansas, from 1946 to 1949, and a member of the staff of the Menninger Foundation from 1947 to 1953, serving as Director of the Psychological Staff from 1950 to 1953. In 1953, he went to New York University (where he is now Professor of Psychology) to direct the Research Center for Mental Health; he was Co-Director of the Research Center with George Klein from 1963 to 1969. He holds a Research Career Award from NIMH.

PHILIP S. HOLZMAN received his Ph.D. from the University of Kansas in 1952. He was on the staff of the Menninger Foundation for over 20 years, and was Director of Research Training. He received full clinical psychoanalytic training at the Topeka Institute for Psychoanalysis. Since 1968, he has been Professor in the Departments of Psychiatry and Behavioral Sciences at the University of Chicago and a training and supervising analyst at the Chicago Institute for Psychoanalysis. He is the author of books and numerous papers on clinical and experimental topics. He holds a Research Scientist Award from NIMH.

JANE LOEVINGER has a Ph.D. in psychology from the University of California at Berkeley. She has taught at Berkeley as well as at Stanford and the University of Colorado. Currently she is Research Associate in the Social Science Institute and Professor of Psychology at Washington University in St. Louis. She holds a Research Scientist Award from NIMH. She is the author of many scientific papers. Her recent research has been in the measurement of ego development.

HANS W. LOEWALD received his M.D. from the University of Rome Medical School in 1934. He is a training and supervising analyst and a member of the faculty of The Western New England Institute for Psychoanalysis and the Yale University School of Medicine, where he is Clinical Professor of Psychiatry. He has written on clinical and theoretical aspects of psychoanalysis.

BENJAMIN B. RUBINSTEIN graduated from the Medical School of the University of Helsinki, Finland, in 1936. He was a specialist in psychiatry and neurology in Finland. Since 1947 he has resided in the United States. He received his psychoanalytic training in London from 1937 to 1939 and in Topeka, Kansas, from 1948 to 1952. He was on the staff of the Menninger Foundation from 1947 to 1953. Since 1953, he has been in psychoanalytic practice in New York City. Currently he is co-director of research at the New York Psychoanalytic Institute. His writings have probed aspects of psychoanalytic theory.

ROY SCHAFER is Clinical Professor of Psychology in Psychiatry in the Division of Mental Hygiene of the Yale University Health Services. He is also a training and supervising analyst at The Western New England Institute of Psychoanalysis and will be the first holder of the Sigmund Freud Memorial Professorship at University College, London, during the academic year 1975-1976. In addition to numerous articles, he has published *The Clinical Application of Psychological Tests, Psychoanalytic Interpretation in Rorschach Testing, Projective Tests and Psychoanalysis,* and *Aspects of Internalization.* A new work, provisionally entitled *A New Language for Psychoanalysis,* will be published soon.

ROBERT S. WALLERSTEIN received his M.D. from Columbia. He was trained in internal medicine, psychiatry, and psychoanalysis. He was with the Menninger Foundation from 1949 to 1966 and served as its Director of Research. He spent a year as a Fellow at the Center for Advanced Study in the Behavioral Sciences. From 1966 to 1975 he was Chief, Department of Psychiatry at Mount Zion Hospital, San Francisco, and is now Chairman, Department of Psychiatry, University of California, San Francisco and Director of the Langley-Porter Neuropsychiatric Institute. He is a training and supervising analyst at the San Francisco Psychoanalytic Institute and a past president of the American Psychoanalytic Association. In 1968 he received the Heinz Hartmann Award of the New York Psychoanalytic Institute.

PSYCHOLOGICAL ISSUES